LATIN FORMS OF ADDRESS

Latin Forms of Address
From Plautus to Apuleius

ELEANOR DICKEY

OXFORD
UNIVERSITY PRESS

OXFORD
UNIVERSITY PRESS

Great Clarendon Street, Oxford OX2 6DP

Oxford University Press is a department of the University of Oxford.
It furthers the University's objective of excellence in research, scholarship,
and education by publishing worldwide in

Oxford New York

Athens Auckland Bangkok Bogotá Buenos Aires Cape Town
Chennai Dar es Salaam Delhi Florence Hong Kong Istanbul Karachi
Kolkata Kuala Lumpur Madrid Melbourne Mexico City Mumbai Nairobi
Paris São Paulo Singapore Taipei Tokyo Toronto Warsaw

with associated companies in Berlin Ibadan

Oxford is a registered trade mark of Oxford University Press
in the UK and in certain other countries

Published in the United States
by Oxford University Press Inc., New York

© Eleanor Dickey 2002

British Library Cataloguing in Publication Data

Data available

Library of Congress Cataloging in Publication Data

Dickey, Eleanor.
Latin forms of address: from Plautus to Apuleius / Eleanor Dickey.
p. cm.
Includes bibliographical references (p.) and indexes.
1. Latin language—Address, Forms of. 2. Latin language—Social aspects—Rome.
3. Social interaction—Rome. 4. Forms of address—Rome. 5. Names, Personal—Rome.
6. Names, Latin. I. Title.
PA2343.D53 2002
478–dc21
ISBN 0-19-924287-9

1 3 5 7 9 10 8 6 4 2

Typeset by Joshua Associates Ltd., Oxford
Printed in Great Britain
on acid-free paper by
Biddles Ltd., Guildford & King's Lynn

Dedicated to my grandparents,
Samuel Dickey
and
Louise Atherton Dickey,
whose inspiration and example
made this book possible.
May it be worthy of their memory!

ACKNOWLEDGEMENTS

I N writing this book I have had the privilege of being aided and advised by scholars far greater than I, whose generosity in sharing their detailed knowledge of a wide variety of subjects has transformed this work into something that I could never have produced unaided. To these men and women I owe an enormous debt; the words I can find to thank them here are in no way capable of expressing the full extent of my heartfelt gratitude. At the same time, none of these people can be held responsible for any errors which remain in this work.

J. N. Adams of All Souls College Oxford generously laid aside his own research to read and provide detailed comments on the entire work, giving me the benefit of his superb knowledge of non-literary Latin and scholarship on that subject, as well as his impeccably high standards. He also advised me on data collection and provided me with many references which I could not otherwise have found; his advice and criticisms have saved me from many pitfalls and pointed the way to some significant insights.

Philomen Probert of Wolfson College Oxford took time away from finishing her own dissertation to read a draft of the entire book; she offered many valuable suggestions and criticisms. Her encouragement and willingness to discuss my ideas as I was collecting and analysing the data also improved the book greatly.

Richard Burgess of the University of Ottawa provided me with suggestions for the improvement of Chapter 2 and gave me much assistance with the complexities of imperial titulature, as well as checking all my translations with meticulous care. His encouragement and support were also invaluable, as was his patient, prompt, and knowledgeable assistance with the computer problems which plagued this project.

Nicholas Horsfall read drafts of most of this book and provided me with provocative comments and many references to bibliographical material which I would not otherwise have found; his generosity and kindness to a younger scholar whom he has never even met were remarkable.

Glen Bowersock of the Institute for Advanced Study was kind enough to read and comment on Chapter 1, as well as giving me extensive help with epigraphical sources. I am extremely grateful to him for taking the time to share with me his vast knowledge of Roman history and the Latin language, and for being an inspiration to work with.

Miriam Griffin of Somerville College Oxford kindly looked at part of Chapter 2 and made some invaluable corrections, for which I am extremely grateful. Jim McKeown of the University of Wisconsin read and commented on several chapters, generously sharing with me his detailed knowledge of Latin poetry, while Louise Stephens of the University of Ottawa found time in her hectic schedule to critique my translations (much to their benefit). Oxford University Press's anonymous second reader also made a number of valuable suggestions.

Anna Morpurgo Davies of Somerville College and Donald Russell of St John's College Oxford advised me on organization, data collection, and the use of individual texts, giving me the benefit of their wisdom and immense knowledge. Heinrich von Staden, Joachim Szidat, Julia Gaisser, and David Langslow took time to answer various questions, make suggestions, discuss problems, and give me the benefit of their expertise; they too have improved the final product, and I am very grateful to them.

The librarians of the Institute for Advanced Study, especially Marcia Tucker, gave me help far beyond the call of duty and made it possible for this book to draw on resources which I could never have obtained on my own. Often, when this work is more complete than others on a given point, much of the credit should go to them. The librarians of the Bodleian and Ashmolean libraries in Oxford were also extraordinarily helpful, especially Jacqueline Dean and Mary Sheldon-Williams; this book would be woefully incomplete were it not for their unusual competence and unfailing kindness.

Heather Watson copy-edited the text with a combination of intelligence and meticulous thoroughness that earned her my admiration as well as my gratitude, and Hilary O'Shea, Jenny

Wagstaffe, and Enid Barker all displayed remarkable kindness and efficiency during the publication process. David Yerkes generously provided much-needed help with proofreading.

Heartfelt thanks go also to the Institute for Advanced Study and the Andrew W. Mellon Foundation, which provided me with a year of incredibly productive research time and with much-needed encouragement to write the best book that I could. Additional funding was provided by the University of Ottawa and by the Province of Ontario through the medium of the John Charles Polanyi prizes. Stephen Colvin and the members of the Yale classics department deserve many thanks for making it possible for me to use the resources of Yale University while collecting data, and I am very grateful for having been allowed to use the facilities of Merton College and the Centre for Linguistics and Philology on my trips to Oxford.

Many of my former colleagues in the erstwhile Department of Classical Studies at the University of Ottawa offered me encouragement and support at a very difficult time in all of our lives and made it possible for me to continue with this book; I am grateful to them for their kindness.

Last but not least, my mother, Barbara Dickey, has been unwavering in her support in times of trial and deserves many thanks for her encouragement.

CONTENTS

LIST OF TABLES

Introduction

Mane salutavi vero te nomine casu
  nec dixi dominum, Caeciliane, meum.
Quanti libertas constat mihi tanta requiris?
  Centum quadrantes abstulit illa mihi.

(Mart. 6. 88)

This morning I happened to greet you by your real name,
Caecilianus, and didn't call you my master. Do you ask
what such a great liberty is costing me? It robbed me of a
hundred pennies.

WHENEVER two Romans met, they had to choose between
different available address forms to use in greeting, and if they
made the wrong choice, the consequences could be unpleasant,
as the poet Martial tells us in this epigram. Yet what, precisely,
can we learn about Latin addresses from Martial's complaint?
The poet says that he was punished for using the wrong
address form, but the punishment was apparently a minor
one. How rigidly enforced, then, were the address rules involved? Why should Martial have used the address *domine*
'master' to Caecilianus, and how different would the situation
have been with another addressee, or another speaker? Do
Martial's rules apply to the Latin of other centuries as well
as to his own? Do they even apply consistently to his own time,
or was Martial (or Caecilianus) idiosyncratic? How can we tell?

This epigram is not unique in raising so many questions
about forms of address; far from it. Consider, for example, the
letter in which the second-century emperor Marcus Aurelius
addresses a favoured courtier as *magister carissime et dulcissime,
quem ego, ausim dicere, magis quam ipsam Romam desidero*
'sweetest and dearest teacher, whom I, dare I say so, desire
more than Rome itself' (Fro. 62. 6–7). What exactly did the
emperor intend to convey with this address? To what extent

was it conventional courtly politeness, and to what extent did it express genuine affection? How was the recipient expected to respond?

Several centuries earlier, Cicero wrote a dialogue in which he portrayed himself addressing his brother Quintus as *Quinte frater* 'brother Quintus' (*Leg.* 3. 26). Is this a phrase that Cicero actually used in conversation with his brother? If not, what did he call Quintus, and how can we tell? If Cicero had more than one way of speaking to his brother, were there differences in meaning or usage among the various addresses?

Still earlier, Plautus portrays a maidservant addressing a man and woman with *mi homo et mea mulier* 'my human being and my woman' (*Cist.* 723). Does this division imply that in Latin address usage a woman was not a human being? What level of politeness or rudeness were these addresses expected to convey? And would a Roman speaker ever have used them off the stage, or are they translations of Greek terms Plautus found in his originals?

Forms of address played a large part in social interaction in Latin, as they do in most languages, and Romans often felt strongly about the differences between one address form and another. Martial's complaints suggest that Latin speakers were almost as sensitive about address usage as modern Germans, who twice in the last thirty years have inflicted court cases and substantial fines on citizens who used the familiar *du* to addressees entitled to the formal *Sie* (Kretzenbacher and Segebrecht 1991: 31).

A potential visitor to Germany, if prudent, will learn when to use *du* and when to use *Sie*, and a foreign student coming to England would be wise to know the difference between addressing a teacher as 'Jim' and calling him 'Professor Smith'. Not only does such preparation prevent embarrassing mistakes, but it enables one to understand the full implications of remarks made by others. In the same way, an understanding of Latin forms of address enables us to appreciate a dimension of Latin literature largely inaccessible without them. Addresses are common in Latin: the works of Cicero alone contain 2,531 instances of direct address in the vocative case, and many more of other types of address. Thus if we can answer some of the questions which impede our understanding of Latin address forms (of which those asked at the start of this chapter are only a few), the answers will make a substantial difference to our understanding of Latin literature.

The study of Latin forms of address requires the resources not only of previous research on Latin language and literature, but also of that branch of linguistics which covers address theory, sociolinguistics. As this field is unfamiliar to many classicists, a brief explanation of how it can assist the present work is provided here.[1]

THE SOCIOLINGUISTIC STUDY OF ADDRESS FORMS

Sociolinguistics is the study of the way that language is used in society. It includes the study of regional and class dialects and accents, bilingual speakers who use different languages in different situations, differences in language used by or to men and women, and a host of similar topics. The sociolinguistic study of forms of address is generally agreed to have begun in 1960, with an article by Roger Brown and Albert Gilman entitled 'The Pronouns of Power and Solidarity'. This piece discussed the use of *tu* and *vous* in French, *du* and *Sie* in German, and the equivalent familiar and formal second-person pronouns (called 'T pronouns' and 'V pronouns' from the Latin *tu* and *vos*) in other European languages. The authors observed that one form was used both to intimates and to inferiors, while another was used both to non-intimates and to superiors. Brown and Gilman maintained (1960: 254–61) that the choice of pronouns was determined by the dimensions of power and solidarity in the relationship between speaker and addressee.

These important observations were followed in 1961 by an article by Roger Brown and Marguerite Ford in which they showed that the distinction in English between address by first name ('John') or by title and last name ('Mr Smith') functioned in the same way as the distinction between T pronouns and V

---

[1] I apologize to readers of my book on Greek forms of address for the similarity between what follows and sections 1.1 and 1.2 of that volume; some duplication in the introduction was unavoidable, but it does not occur elsewhere.

pronouns (called a 'T/V distinction') in European languages. A number of other relatively early articles on addresses are usually considered to have been important in the development of address theory. These include a 1969 article by Susan Ervin-Tripp which explained American English addresses by means of flow charts, a 1975 study of pronominal address in Italian by Bates and Benigni, and a 1976 study of children's pronominal address systems in French and Spanish by Lambert and Tucker.

A number of more recent works have devoted immense amounts of time and energy to exhaustive surveys of addresses and are worth mentioning for their detail and length. These include books by Agnieszka Kiełkiewicz-Janowiak (1992) on Polish and English, Sylvia Başoğlu (1987) on Turkish, Dilworth Parkinson (1985) on Egyptian Arabic, and Susan Bean (1978) on Kannada, as well as a dissertation on Korean by Juck-Ryoon Hwang (1975). It is, however, important to note that not all of these books are consistently reliable. Perhaps the best work has come from a project at Kiel University which produced the most comprehensive bibliography on the subject (Braun, Kohz, and Schubert 1986) and the best overview of address theory (Braun 1988). The project has also produced numerous works on address in individual languages, most of which are clear and accurate.[2]

Especially important from the point of view of our study are those works which have concentrated on earlier forms of language and on the history of addresses. Of these the best known is Paul Friedrich's study (1966) of pronominal address in nineteenth-century Russian, but dozens of others exist as well, on Old English, Chaucer, Shakespeare, Old French, and many other languages and periods.[3] The vast majority of these studies, however, have concentrated on relatively recent historical periods, and except for this book's companion volume

[2] For complete bibliography see Braun (1988: 5–6).

[3] Bakos (1955), Breuer (1983), Brown and Gilman (1989), Drown (1979), Evans (1967), Finkenstaedt (1963), Grimaud (1989), Guðmundsson (1972), Joseph (1987), Kempf (1985), Kisbye (1965), Lyons (1980), P. Mason (1990), Morrison (1988), Nathan (1959), Phillipps (1984), Replogle (1973), Salmon (1967), Wales (1983), Waterhouse (1982), Whalen (1982), Wolff (1986), (1988).

on Greek (Dickey 1996), almost no serious sociolinguistic work has been published on addresses in Latin, Greek, or other comparatively ancient languages. This lack does not indicate that such study is impractical because of the lack of native speakers of Latin currently available for interview; sociolinguistic studies of ancient languages have now been shown to be just as possible as those of modern languages.[4]

CATEGORIES OF ADDRESS

This body of work has provided us with a set of tools which can be employed to analyse any language. In order to use them, however, it is necessary to understand the technical terminology on which they are based. In a linguistic sense, 'address' is 'a speaker's linguistic reference to his/her collocutor(s)'.[5] This definition includes not only nouns (*'Mary*, how are you?' 'Would *Your Majesty* care to read this letter?') but also pronouns ('Could *you* close the window?') and second-person verb endings in inflected languages. It does not include words used to get the addressee's attention but not actually referring to him or her, such as 'hey' or 'excuse me'. Speakers of English may not see the point of classifying pronouns and verbs as addresses, because in English the pronoun 'you' can be used to anyone, but nevertheless these forms are references to the addressee and as such can be exploited in many languages to carry social meaning. In German the highly significant difference between the pronouns *du* and *Sie* can be carried by the verbs alone, for the command *Gib es mir!* is just as clearly a use of the *du* form as if the pronoun had been expressed.

This term is clearly a very broad one and needs further division. An obvious classification is one by parts of speech, into nouns, pronouns, and verbs, but this division is usually rejected by linguists on the grounds that it obscures the most fundamental distinctions among addresses; instead, addresses are classified into syntactically 'bound' and 'free' forms.[6] Bound forms are those integrated into the syntax of a sentence,

---

[4] For a detailed presentation of the evidence on this point, see Dickey (1996: 30–42, 249–55).
[5] Braun (1988: 7); see also Kiełkiewicz-Janowiak (1992: 13).
[6] Braun (1988: 303, 11–12); Kiełkiewicz-Janowiak (1992: 18, 20).

and free forms are those not so integrated. Thus in the request
'Mary, could you please open the window?' 'Mary' is a free
form and 'you' a bound form.

In English, as in most European languages, free forms tend to
be nouns and bound forms are usually pronouns or verbs, but in
the sentence, 'You! Open the window!' the pronoun 'you' is a
free form of address. Conversely, in 'Would Your Highness care
to open the window?' a noun is used as a bound form of address.
Verbs, however, are always bound forms. In Latin, this distinction between free and bound forms corresponds fairly
closely to the distinction between vocatives and non-vocatives.
The only difference is that it is possible in Latin to have
'nominatives for vocatives' and 'vocatives for nominatives'.[7]
Yet the very existence of such terms shows that there are some
syntactic constructions which classical scholars agree ought to
be vocatives, even if they are not filled by vocatives, and others
which ought not to be vocatives, even if they are. This category
of 'things that ought to be vocatives' consists of addresses not
integrated into the syntax of the sentence and therefore corresponds exactly to the category of free forms of address.

Some of the advantages of the bound/free classification can
be seen from the English examples above. 'You' when used as a
bound form has very little social meaning in English, but when
used as a free form it strongly suggests a lack of respect for the
addressee. Such a difference between bound and free meaning
is also found in pronouns in other languages and can occur with
nouns as well (Braun 1988: 11–12).

A less vital distinction, but one that is very useful in
explaining some of the peculiarities of Latin addresses, is the
distinction between addresses used to get someone's attention
and those used once contact has already been established.
There is no generally accepted terminology for expressing
this division, although it is often made[8] and can account for

---

[7] 'Nominative for vocative' is a construction in which a word that has a
distinct vocative form is found in the nominative as a free form of address, as
animus for *anime*. 'Vocative for nominative' is the use of the vocative case
when the word concerned ought, from the syntax of the sentence, to be in the
nominative. For a detailed examination of these phenomena, see Svennung
(1958: esp. 246–88 and 394–411).

[8] e.g. Fasold (1990: 3); Zwicky (1974: 790–1); Kiełkiewicz-Janowiak (1992:
20).

significant differences in usage; thus, for example, 'sir' can be used in American English to get the attention of virtually any unknown man, but it is rarely used in conversation once the addressee's attention is secured. Some types of address can only be used to attract someone's attention, as 'gentleman in the green shirt', spoken for example by a photographer arranging a group photograph (cf. Zwicky 1974: 791).

RULES OF ADDRESS

One of the most important conclusions reached by socio-linguists about address usage is that it is governed by rules stating which forms are used in which circumstances.[9] The rules of address usage are far from inviolable; indeed they can be broken to produce powerful effects, but the very fact that their violation is meaningful shows that they exist and that speakers are using them.[10] Indeed, one recent study has concluded that, 'Knowledge of the proper use of terms of address is . . . as important to the overall success of communication as knowledge of the conjugation of verbs would be' (Parkinson 1985: 225). The rules governing address usage in various cultures are often complicated, and it is frequently difficult to work out which factors do or do not influence the choice of addresses.[11] None the less, two elements will almost always play a part: the relationship of speaker and addressee and the social context of the utterance.

The relationship of speaker and addressee is made up not only of the identity of the addressee, but also of that of the speaker: age, sex, status, familiarity, kinship, and membership of a group all play a part. In studying forms of address one is often tempted to look for a simple correlation between the identity of the addressee and the address used, but such procedures are very risky. Although one person's position may sometimes be so unusual that he or she receives the same address from all possible speakers, it is usually the case that address usage 'is not predictable from properties of the addressee alone and not predictable from properties of the

---

[9] Brown and Ford (1961: 234); Philipsen and Huspek (1985: 94).
[10] Cf. Mühlhäusler and Harré (1990: 161-2); Braun (1988: 49-50).
[11] Cf. Mehrotra (1981: 135); Coulmas (1979: 242-3).

speaker alone but only from properties of the dyad'[12] (Brown and Ford 1961: 234). In English it is not only acceptable but even normal for one person to receive many different addresses from different speakers: a teacher could be addressed as 'Mrs Dillon' by her pupils, as 'Sarah' by her colleagues, as 'Sal' by her family, and as 'Mom' by her children.

The importance of context (setting, audience, and topic of discourse) in determining address usage is less universally recognized by linguists than that of speaker–addressee relationship, partly because surveys conducted by means of questionnaires or interviews often overlook this factor. Nevertheless, a number of recent studies have shown that although in certain dyads contextual factors may never be strong enough to outweigh speaker–addressee relationship in determining address usage, in many cases their influence can be crucial.[13] Some settings require certain forms of address: 'If he [your brother] is acting as the judge in a law court then calling him *Tom* will be considered disrespectful, while at the dinner table calling him *Your honour* will be perceived as equally rude' (Holmes 1992: 297).

The factor of audience is often difficult to separate from that of setting, but when this can be done audience is shown to be a significant influence on address usage. Mühlhäusler and Harré (1990: 145) report the case of a woman who addressed her mother-in-law with a familiar pronoun only when two other daughters-in-law, who used a formal address form, were not present. In a study of address between members of the US Marine Corps, it was found that 'perhaps the most influential single factor in determining the form of address employed is the audience . . . most of the time, address forms are drastically (but predictably) affected by the presence of others' (Jonz 1975: 70–1).

The effect on address usage of the topic of discourse is much less clear than that of the other factors mentioned, but it too has been found to be important in some languages, including Indonesian (Kridalaksana 1974: 20) and nineteenth-century Russian (Friedrich 1966: 229). Humorous purpose can also

---

[12] 'Dyad' is a linguistic term for two people talking to each other.
[13] Kridalaksana (1974: 19, 20); Friedrich (1966: 229); R. W. Howell (1968: 554); Southworth (1974: 183); Jaworski (1982: 262); J. Holmes (1992: 297).

affect the addresses used, for example by inflating the number and variety of terms.

At this point it might be objected that a crucial factor has been omitted, namely the feelings of the speaker towards the addressee and the general emotional level of the interaction. Of course this element does affect address usage, but it is not part of a fixed rule like the other factors mentioned. Addresses which follow the rules of the address system are known as 'unmarked' forms; they are the terms the addressee expects to hear and therefore cause no special reaction. Expression of emotion occurs when the rules determined by these other factors are broken; that is, when 'marked' addresses are used. A number of interesting studies have shown that even the choice of T or V pronouns can be caused by emotional factors (e.g. Friedrich 1966: 229), but every English speaker knows that whether a girl calls her brother 'David' or 'you pig' depends on what she is trying to express. One of the main purposes of our study is to identify the effects of the other factors so that we can tell when an address is being used to express a particular feeling.

This discussion of the factors affecting address choice has been simplified by assuming that both members of a dyad have the same set of sociolinguistic rules. This assumption was made by the early researchers of address theory, but it is now thought to be a rash one. Speakers of the same language are divided into a multitude of subgroups by regional dialects, age differences, social class, rural or urban origin, ideological or religious principles, etc., and these subgroups may have different norms of address usage. Many address studies have used only the upper-middle-class, adult, educated informants who are conveniently available in a university setting, and within this group there is relatively little variation in most modern European languages, owing to a long process of standardization (Braun 1988: 23–4).

Elsewhere, however, far greater differences are observable, so that often one cannot really speak of a single standard set of rules governing address behaviour in a given language (Braun 1988: 23). Some spectacular examples of this phenomenon can be observed even in earlier versions of European languages. Thus in medieval English '. . . in the 14th century, the lowest

classes would say *thou* to everybody, even to kings and queens
. . . because the honorific pronoun [*you*] was still outside their
repertoire of address pronouns' (Kiełkiewicz-Janowiak 1992:
79). A similar situation exists in Tolstoy's Russian, where 'a
bilingual, blue-blooded aristocrat became so inured to *vy* [the
Russian V pronoun] that he used it even to peasant children,
while receiving *ty* [the Russian T pronoun] from their parents'
(Friedrich 1966: 231).

We should certainly expect to find this variation in Latin as
well. Latin appears to have contained considerable internal
diversity, which could be visible to us both in differences
between one character's speech and another's within a given
work (as in Tolstoy), and in differences among the various
texts. The first type of difference is most likely to appear in
texts depicting the speech of slaves, women, and other distinct
social groups, while the second could appear anywhere. The
Latin examined for this study covers a chronological range of
over 400 years and comes from almost every genre; the authors
belong to different social groups and were trying to produce
different effects by their choice of language.

LEXICAL VERSUS ADDRESS MEANING

One of the most important discoveries that linguists have made
about address usage is that the meaning of a word when used as
an address may differ considerably from its 'lexical' or 'referential' usage. Thus in American English 'lady' as an address
implies scorn or ill-will on the part of the speaker, but in
referential use it has no such connotations (cf. Zwicky 1974:
790). A similar discrepancy occurs in British English with the
words 'love' and 'darling', which when applied referentially
imply strong affection but as addresses are used freely to total
strangers by train conductors, clearly without any implications
of strong affection (cf. J. Holmes 1992: 300). Indeed foreigners
who take the word in its lexical meaning and react with alarm
are met with total bafflement on the part of native speakers.
Another example is 'madam', which in reference is applied to
brothel-keepers but as an address is a polite way of speaking to
superiors or strangers and contains no suggestion that the

addressee is associated with a house of ill repute (*OED*: s.v. 'madam').

This distinction between lexical or referential and address meaning functions in a number of ways. As we have seen, some words have different lexical and address meanings. A word may also be used only referentially and not as an address, as 'physician' and 'great-aunt' in English (compare 'doctor' and 'grandmother', which have similar lexical meanings but are usable in address).[14] The reverse is also possible, for Greek ὦ τᾶν occurs only as a vocative. It is, however, important to realize that the examples commonly cited to illustrate a difference between lexical and address meaning, words like French *Monsieur* and German *Herr* which originally meant 'my lord' but no longer have that force when used in address, really reflect diachronic rather than synchronic variation, for they no longer mean 'my lord' in referential usage either.

Problems arise because, although lexical and address meaning are separate, they are not unrelated. Indeed the difference between the two arises only gradually:

When words start to be used as forms of address, it is mostly because of their lexical meaning, which qualifies them for certain situations and certain types of addressees . . . But once a word has entered the system of address, its development is less and less affected by its literal meaning; the former connection of lexical and social content is loosened, and the social meaning comes to be entirely determined by the interplay and interdependency of variants . . . There is no necessary correlation of social and lexical component, even less may social meaning be equated with the lexical one. (Braun 1988: 260–1)

In other words, there may be a stage in the development of an address form when it is not appropriate to distinguish the lexical and social meanings, but at other stages they must be kept apart. Braun concludes (1988: 264–5) that:

it is not a reasonable procedure to go by the lexical meanings of variants when analysing address systems in different languages. If a certain nominal variant indicates superiority or seniority in its lexical meaning, this does not justify the conclusion that it expresses superiority or seniority when used as a form of address as well . . . Under

[14] Zwicky (1974: 790–1); the examples are his, and the point about 'great-aunt' may be debatable, but this does not affect the argument as a whole.

favourable circumstances, lexical meaning may thus be a hint for
evaluating the position of an address variant, but no more than that.
As long as one does not know which is the stage of development of the
form in question, one has to be very careful about the lexical meaning.

Nevertheless the influence does not go in only one direction,
a fact which few linguists have noticed. As we have observed,
the original lexical meaning of *Monsieur* was 'my lord', but
Monsieur can now be used referentially in sentences like *Je ne
connais pas ce monsieur*.[15] In this case it seems likely that the
modern referential meaning, which is certainly not 'my lord',
has come from the address usage of *Monsieur* for any unfamiliar adult male, not directly from the original lexical meaning.
A further complication is that the way that one person refers
to another is related to the way that they address each other.
Thus if three Englishwomen are friends and address each other
by first names, they will also use first names when one is talking
to another about the third: 'Jane, you'll never guess what Mrs
Jones said to me yesterday!' is highly unlikely if both Jane and
the speaker normally address Mrs Jones as 'Sarah'. Because of
this similarity between the way that person A refers to person B
and the way that A addresses B, some scholars have failed to
distinguish between address and referential usage of words,
particularly of variants like 'Mr' and 'Mrs' versus first names.[16]
Yet such lack of distinction leads to erroneous conclusions, for
the way a person is referred to in conversation depends not
only on the way that A the speaker addresses B the person
referred to, but also on the way that B is addressed by the
person that A is currently talking to. The sentence given above,
which was so improbable if Jane was a woman who normally
addressed B as Sarah, is perfectly normal if Jane is the
speaker's 8-year-old daughter who normally addresses B as
Mrs Jones.
In English it is possible to predict with some accuracy the
circumstances in which the term used in reference will be the
same as that used in address, and there is evidence that other
modern European languages follow the same rules as English
in this respect (Dickey 1997*b*: 272). In a language like Latin

---

[15] Information from native speakers.
[16] e.g. Mühlhäusler and Harré (1990: 142); cf. Conant (1961: 19–21).

where adequate evidence of address forms may be lacking, it is very tempting to equate referential and address usage, but we shall avoid doing so whenever possible; if the use of referential evidence is unavoidable, we shall take our data only from those situations in which research on modern languages suggests that it should be the same as the address usage.

Still another complication is the fact that whenever a single word is used in two different senses under different circumstances, such as address and reference, speakers of the language may notice the discrepancy and react to it. The dual meaning may be exploited for humorous purposes, or one of the meanings may be avoided because the other one is seen as primary. Thus some people react to the generalized English addresses 'love' and 'darling' with objections such as 'I'm not your darling!' which indicate that they see more of a connection between the address and referential meanings than do the speakers of those terms.

The difference between address and referential usage, it must be noted, applies only to those words which have become an accepted part of a language's address system. The first time a term is used, neither speaker nor addressee can have an idea of its social meaning without reference to its lexical meaning. Thus for unique addresses, as well as for words which have only just begun to be used as addresses but will later become common, lexical meaning does provide a good guide to social meaning.

REGISTER

Another important contribution of the linguists to our study is their work on register. Register can be defined in a number of different ways (cf. Biber 1994: 32, 51–3), but essentially it refers to the use of different types of language in different situations: a student may not employ the same vocabulary and syntax in talking to her friends in her room as she does when talking to her professor in his office, and the language she uses to write an essay will be still another variety. This type of variation can also be called 'style' or 'genre', provided one remembers that it applies to non-literary forms of language just as much as to literary forms.

Linguists hold that all forms of a language are equal; none can be considered 'higher' or 'better' than another. Speakers of a language, however, very often do make such value judgements about registers, and an understanding of these judgements is essential to comprehension of how particular registers work in their social contexts. We know that the Romans considered some forms of language more elevated than others, and thus I shall refer to particular vocatives as belonging to 'higher' and 'lower' registers whenever the evidence suggests that the Romans themselves would have made such a classification.

Registers appear to work according to a rule called the 'style axiom': 'variation on the style dimension within the speech of a single speaker derives from and echoes the variation which exists between speakers on the "social" dimension'.[17] In other words, certain linguistic characteristics belong to a high register because they are associated with people who occupy a high status in the community; others belong to a low register because they are associated with speakers of lower status. But in fact each individual speaker is capable of producing more than one register (although not necessarily all of the registers used in the community) and will use the forms associated with high-status people when he/she is aiming at a high style, and the forms associated with lower-status people when aiming at a lower style.

The assumption is sometimes made that there is only one register which each speaker can use without a conscious effort and that only this one counts as that person's natural language. This assumption, if it is valid at all, holds true only for a very crude division of registers. Studies have shown that the speech of completely illiterate people can display measurable variation in register within the genre of casual conversation and without any conscious effort, according to the topic of conversation, the setting, and the identity of the addressee.[18] These variations in register often consist of smaller differences than those requiring conscious effort, but such is not always the case. An extreme version of register variation is bilingualism, and just as people exist who can shift without effort between two

[17] Bell (1984: 151); cf. Rickford and McNair-Knox (1994: 241).
[18] Dorian (1994); Rickford and McNair-Knox (1994).

languages, so there are people who have had sufficient experience of two radically different registers of the same language to enable them to shift without conscious application. The prevalence of such people in a community depends on the extent to which they are required to use different registers and the age at which these registers are learned.

It is sometimes thought that a person's 'real' language can be equated with the lowest of the registers he/she controls, but this assumption is seriously flawed. Most, if not all, people have more than one register which they use without conscious effort, and all of these must be accepted as their 'natural' language. Moreover, it is by no means certain that those registers which do require effort will always be 'higher' than those which do not. They will usually be higher, because in most societies it is more advantageous to imitate people of higher status than those of lower status. The reverse, however, does occur; in fact it has been particularly notable among younger, educated people in the late twentieth century. The trend in the use of forms of address in some parts of Italy has been for certain higher-status members of society to use the forms they associate with lower-status speakers, while the latter adopt the forms previously associated with the higher-status speakers. This results in an inversion of address usage, apparently without either party noticing that the other does not in fact use the forms being imitated (Bates and Benigni 1975: 276–9). A similar phenomenon can be observed with 'can' and 'may' and with the use of the subjunctive in British English. The use of 'may' and of the subjunctive is natural to certain people of educated backgrounds and is considered correct; precisely for this reason, several students of my acquaintance have with considerable effort trained themselves not to use 'may' or subjunctives in order to avoid the stigma of sounding pretentious.

An individual word may belong only to a specific register or registers, as English 'peruse' or 'spud', or may be common to many, as English 'the'. A word may also belong to different registers when used in different senses; thus, for example, English 'bitch' belongs to a much higher register in reference to a dog than when used of a human. As a result, the address and non-address meanings of a word may also belong to different registers. English 'sir' as an address to an unknown male ('Are these your gloves, sir?') belongs to fairly normal conversational language, while the referential use of 'sir', to which a name must be attached, belongs to a more formal register ('May I introduce Sir Kenneth Dover?').

An additional complication is that the distinction between high and low registers is not always identical to that between literary and non-literary registers. Forms used by people of high status in situations other than literary works are not 'literary' in the sense of being confined to literary contexts, though they may be literary in the sense of being usable in such contexts. It is also possible (see pp. 77–99 for an example) for a term which is regularly used by people of high status to be generally excluded from literary texts; in that case the form is both high-register and non-literary. Moreover, a term which is invented by the author of a literary work, if it contains low-register words or syntax or is assigned to a low-status character in a context which requires low-register language, can be presented as a low-register term (cf. p. 172); as a result some of the absurd, elaborate, and humorous insults and endearments in the comedies of Plautus and Aristophanes are both literary and low-register. In the majority of cases the Latin literary language is in fact drawn from the higher registers, but, as we shall see, the distinction between elevation and literary nature is an important one: high-register, non-literary addresses tend to have the features characteristic of high-register terms but not those characteristic of literary terms, while low-register, literary addresses show the opposite pattern.

Words belonging to a given register are normally used in a context requiring that register, but it is also possible for an author to switch registers for effect, as for example when Aristophanes includes a paratragic passage in a comedy, or when an English speaker becomes so angry that he descends to a lower register for purposes of invective. Such register shifts reveal a partial correlation between register and politeness or rudeness. If a register lower than appropriate is used in an interaction, this can signal a lack of respect for the addressee and hence be rude. If the register used is higher than expected, it can indicate special respect and hence politeness. The expression of emotion does not, however, necessarily require a shift of register; it is also possible to be rude in high registers and polite in low ones (see pp. 167–8). Great care must thus be exercised when determining the register of an address.

OTHER LINGUISTIC CONTRIBUTIONS

Some other distinctions among addresses are relevant as well. As set out by Brown and Gilman, the difference between a 'T pronoun' and a 'V pronoun' is that the former is used to intimates and inferiors and the latter is used to non-intimates and superiors. A language which has only one second-person pronoun, such as English, can still have a T/V distinction in nominal address forms (address by first name in English being equivalent to T, and title and last name to V). Closely connected to the idea of T and V is that of reciprocity or symmetry. Reciprocal address is a situation in which both speakers in a dyad use the same addresses or the same type of address to one another (Braun 1988: 13). Thus if speaker A uses *du* and speaker B uses *du*, or if A uses 'Mr Smith' and B uses 'Mrs Jones', or if A uses 'Jane' and B uses 'Lisa', the addresses are reciprocal, but if A uses *du* and B uses *Sie*, or if A uses 'Mr Smith' and B uses 'Lisa', or if A uses 'Jane' and B uses 'Mother', the addresses are non-reciprocal. In a non-reciprocal situation at least one speaker does not have the option of using the type of address that the other uses. If a T pronoun is used reciprocally, it may indicate intimacy, but if it is used non-reciprocally, it usually shows the addressee's inferiority. Reciprocity is thus an important concept to keep in mind, for the meaning of a term of address in a given context can depend on the way that the recipient of that term addresses the speaker.

Another area of sociolinguistics, the study of politeness phenomena, is closely related to address studies and has much to contribute to it. In particular it is useful to know that there are two types of strategy which can be called 'politeness'. One, known as 'negative politeness' and employed primarily to social superiors, consists of efforts to avoid hindering the addressee in any way or annoying him/her by undue familiarity; the other, 'positive politeness', is a strategy in which the speaker tries to gratify the addressee in some way (Brown and Levinson 1987: 101, 129). One of the commoner forms of positive politeness is the use of 'in-group identity markers', such as address forms which remind the addressee that he or she has a connection to the speaker (Brown and Levinson 1987: 107–9).

In address systems, as in other aspects of language, changes may occur over time; the question then arises whether there are detectable regularities in the way address systems change. Until recently very little work had been done on the diachrony of address systems (even works on historical forms of address tended to confine themselves to relatively short periods of time), although Brown and Gilman did discuss this issue in their article. In 1992, however, a book appeared which was devoted to historical address change. The author, Agnieszka Kiełkiewicz-Janowiak, concluded (1992: 48) that address change was brought about by 'the universal human trait to honour—and to reach for—power', which led people to try continually to address their superiors with more and more deference. Thus address change was initiated by the inferior in a given dyad and took the form of new terms being introduced as polite, being used more and more and losing their connotations of politeness, until a new and more deferent form was introduced and the old one was relegated to the status of a less polite address such as a T pronoun (1992: 48, 87, 117–18). This view is supported by her study of the history of address systems in Polish and English and by statements made by Braun (1988: 57), Keller (1990: 103–4), and Head (1978: 194). For the addresses she is discussing, Kiełkiewicz-Janowiak's explanation seems to be the only sensible one.

Other evidence, however, has led to opposite conclusions. Also in 1992 another sociolinguist, Wardhaugh, asserted (1992: 271) that in a hierarchy

those at the bottom seek to minimize their difference in status from those at the top and those at the top seek to maximize that difference. In trying to do this, members of each group use address terms as a resource in the resulting 'power' struggle, with those at the bottom using the most familiar terms they can manage to use and those at the top the most formal ones.

This statement is supported by far less documentation than the one above, but it too seems intuitively obvious, so it would be

well for us to keep an open mind when investigating Latin
addresses.

A belief long held by linguists is that 'there is a correlation
between the form and content of a language and the beliefs,
values, and needs present in the culture of its speakers'
(Saville-Troike 1989: 32). This theory is established beyond
any serious doubt, and it ought to apply to addresses as well as
to other elements of language. A recent book states that, 'The
claim that address usage reflects a part of social reality—the
relationships between the speaker and the addressee—is hardly
questionable.'[19] Indeed, it has been argued that there are
instances in which address usage provides a more accurate
guide to social reality than does referential usage. Thus Jarawa
referential usage does not provide different words for older and
younger siblings, but address usage does make such a distinction, and the distinction can be seen from extralinguistic
evidence to be important in the society (Conant 1961: 29).
Certainly address usage does provide clues about social
relations which could not be gathered from referential usage.
In Chinese, for example, the absence of any vocative for address
by a woman to her husband's elder brother or elder male cousin
reflected the fact that, traditionally, a woman was not supposed
to meet these relatives at all (Chao 1956: 230). Nevertheless, the
information encoded in address usage is not straightforward and
needs to be handled with caution. Perret's blithe assertion
(1968: 9) that 'un usage réciproque des termes d'adresse est le
signe d'une égalité entre les deux personnes'[20] has been refuted
by those who point out that two Germans who use *Sie* to one
another may have a very unequal status, and that children who
use *du* to their parents are not equal to them (Başoğlu 1987: 50).
The moral we ought to draw from these cases is that, while
address usage does reflect social reality in the culture concerned, it may not provide a complete view of that reality.[21] In

[19] Kiełkiewicz-Janowiak (1992: 8); see also Hwang (1975: 16), Başoğlu
(1987: 299), and Braun, Kohz, and Schubert (1986: xvii).
[20] 'A reciprocal usage of address terms is a sign of equality between the two
members of a dyad.'
[21] See Gates (1971: 36, 42–3) for some salutary warnings against overdoing
extrapolation from linguistic to social structure.

our study of Latin, then, we can be encouraged by the knowledge that we may be able to shed new light on Roman society and values, but we must beware of assuming that we hold the universal key to social relationships; other evidence about Roman culture cannot be disregarded.

PREVIOUS WORK ON LATIN FORMS OF ADDRESS

Although the Latin address system has never been studied as a whole, much important work has been done on various parts of it. The most comprehensive treatment is probably afforded by the entries in the *Thesaurus Linguae Latinae* for specific words; in many cases these entries represent the only study of a word's address usage, and in other cases they represent the best one. The usefulness of the *Thesaurus* as a tool for understanding the Latin address system is limited, however, by the fact that its entries are only on individual words and provide no information on larger patterns of usage, as well as by the exclusion of personal names.

Two studies involving Latin are devoted to address usage per se: J. Svennung's 1958 monograph *Anredeformen*, while exhaustive, covers a wide variety of languages and so cannot examine Latin in great detail, while Mary O'Brien's dissertation (1930) on the use of titles in Christian epistolography is concerned with one specific aspect of a late period of the language. As a result, while both can be useful on occasion, neither provides detailed information on the Latin address system in the classical period.

Other studies concentrating on the usage of a word or group of words in Latin give some attention to address usage. The most important of these are J. N. Adams's article (1978) on Cicero's use of personal names, Martin Bang's discussion (1921) of the titles *domine* and *domina*, studies of Latin insults by Ilona Opelt (1965) and Saara Lilja (1965*b*), Olli Salomies's book (1987) on Latin praenomina, and Donald McFayden's examination (1920) of the title *imperator*. Work on gender differences in Latin often has a bearing on the address system, especially Adams's article on terms used by women in comedy (1984) and Alan Sommerstein's discussion of names used for women (1980). Likewise, works on vulgar Latin, such as those of J. B. Hofmann (1951, 1985), often include information on the use of addresses. Commentaries on individual texts frequently discuss addresses as well and occasionally go beyond explanation of a particular passage to consider more general principles; the most useful from this perspective are those of A. N. Sherwin-White on Pliny (1966), Shackleton Bailey on Cicero (1965–70, 1977), J. E. B. Mayor on Juvenal (1888–9), and F. Bömer on Ovid (1957–8, 1969–86). Many other works also provide useful information on address usage; these are too numerous to list here but will be mentioned in the appropriate places. Issues related to but not included in this study, such as the positioning of vocatives in a sentence, the repetition of vocatives, the effect of the tone of voice, and the use of pronouns of address, have been treated in detail elsewhere, notably by G. Ferger (1889), A. Nehring (1933), G. Garitte (1942), E. Fraenkel (1965), K. Vretska (1976: ii. 512), J. Wills (1996: 50–8), F. Biville (1996a, 1996b, 1996c), and D. Shalev (1998). In general, information on the address usage of specific words is normally available for Latin, although it is scattered widely and in many cases hard to find. Treatments of larger questions, however, are rare and often inadequate.

THE SCOPE OF THIS STUDY

The present study aims to remedy this lack by considering the entire Latin address system over a period of four centuries. Nevertheless, some limitations have had to be imposed. The most important such restriction is chronological; in principle, this study stops at the end of the second century AD, though it is sometimes necessary to allude to later usage when this has a bearing on the period under consideration. The richness of address forms available in later Latin is extraordinary and in some ways more conducive to study than anything found in the classical period; it is to be hoped that someone else will eventually provide us with a full study of this period. The great difference between late Latin addresses and those of the classical period, however, means that they are normally of little use to us in our present attempt to clarify usage in classical literature.

The second main restriction concerns the nature of the interactions examined. Latin literature abounds in prayers and other addresses to deities; in some authors (e.g. Cato) such addresses account for the majority of all vocatives preserved. Yet these religious addresses do not follow the same address system as those between humans; they are often formulaic, sometimes archaic, and frequently use terms which could not be employed if the addressee were human. In order to avoid having our picture of Latin address usage among humans distorted by a large number of addresses from prayers, it is necessary to omit from consideration most addresses to deities. Addresses to gods and goddesses are included, however, when the addressee is physically present and visible to the speaker, as in conversations between two deities; these addresses, for the most part, do follow the same patterns as those to humans. The excluded addresses have not been completely ignored, though they are omitted from all statistics; they will be mentioned when the fact that a given address can be used to deities has a bearing on its use to humans.

The last major restriction on this study concerns the type of addresses included. Ideally it would be interesting to study all Latin forms of address, whether nominal, pronominal, or verbal, bound or free. Such a study would, however, generate so much data as to necessitate a much smaller corpus of texts, and much of the work spent on it would be wasted, since during our period pronominal and verbal addresses rarely carried more social force than the modern English 'you'. In the present study, therefore, only free forms of address (i.e. vocatives and nominatives clearly acting as vocatives) are included.[22] Again, however, the excluded addresses in cases other than the vocative have not been entirely ignored, but are used when possible to shed light on the vocative usage.

Within these restrictions an attempt has been made to cover as much literature as possible, but no claim is made for

---

[22] There is room for doubt on the status of *tu*, which is normally nominative but sometimes looks very like a vocative. It has, however, been omitted from this study because Vairel, after an exhaustive study of the apparent vocative uses, has decided that *tu* is 'toujours et exclusivement un nominatif' (1986: 56). On the use of *tu* in address see Ferger (1889: 37–40).

absolute completeness. Unlike its companion volume on Greek, this work is not a corpus-based study; I decided that the effort devoted to it would be best employed in trying to collect addresses from as large a body of text as possible, rather than in endlessly double-checking a smaller body of text to make sure that no addresses had been overlooked. Most of the data come from literary texts; these were collected by reading through the texts of all major authors within our period and noting the addresses found. A few texts belonging to the period have not been searched in this manner, either because they are too fragmentary or because they contain too few vocatives (e.g. Pliny's *Naturalis Historia* and Vitruvius' *De Architectura*). In addition, whenever practical (i.e. for addresses having a distinct vocative form and/or occurring relatively infrequently) an electronic search for each vocative was then conducted on the most complete corpus of Latin literature available electronically.[23] The combined results of the two searching methods (each of which provides a check on the accuracy of the other) suggest that the final set of data contains about 96% of the addresses from literature that could in theory be included; as there are 14,621 items of data from literature, around 600 addresses are probably missing.[24] Thus, although the literary data are not complete, they represent the vast majority of available addresses.

Non-literary texts are more problematic, as many are fragmentary and/or undatable. At the same time they provide invaluable evidence for the non-literary registers of Latin and so cannot be ignored. The richest source of addresses in the non-literary material is the corpus of over 10,000 Pompeian graffiti, all of which come from our period. Other good sources include funerary inscriptions and the Vindolanda tablets; official inscriptions contain very few vocatives. In collecting addresses for this study, I have tried to use clearly

---

[23] Packard Humanities Institute CD-ROM, 1991, searched using the Pandora program.

[24] The missing addresses are not distributed equally, owing to the search methods; most are to be found in fragments or in authors with very few addresses, and most are terms like *optime* or *mater* which are too common in non-vocative uses to be searchable electronically.

datable texts as much as possible in order to minimize distortion from addresses coming from after our period; some use of undated inscriptions is, however, unavoidable.

I have searched by hand[25] all of the Pompeian material (*CIL* iv), the Vindolanda material (*Tab. Vindol. II*), the main corpus of Latin letters (*CEL*), the Mons Claudianus ostraca (Bingen 1992, 1997), all inscriptions from the Republican period (*ILLRP*), and Dessau's standard selection of almost 10,000 inscriptions from a variety of periods (*ILS*). I have also conducted a series of electronic searches of the *Epigraphische Datenbank Heidelberg* (*EDH*), which contains over 30,000 inscriptions, largely those published in *L'Année Épigraphique* over the past century, with recent revisions of earlier readings. The search for non-literary evidence has thus been extensive, but the resulting corpus is still much less complete than that of the literary material. In particular, no attempt has been made at a systematic search of the main corpus of Latin inscriptions (*CIL*), because most of the inscriptions in that corpus are undated, and many were probably written after AD 200.

Table 1 gives more complete information on the distribution of the addresses found by author, date, genre, and register. There are a total of 820 non-literary addresses, bringing the final number included in this study to 15,441. This figure refers to complete addresses, not to individual words: when Cicero calls his brother *mi carissime frater* 'my dearest brother' (*Q. fr.* 3. 6. 6), this single address provides information on three separate vocatives. Most addresses, in fact, consist of only one word, but often they involve two or three, and sometimes (particularly in invective) a long string of words is produced. On average, the data contain almost one and a half times as many individual vocatives as there are complete addresses,[26] with the result that this study is based on examination of over 20,000 vocatives. This makes it, to my knowledge, the largest body of data ever gathered on address forms in a single language, ancient or modern (cf. Dickey 1996: 25–6).

The size of the corpus, however, does necessitate some

---

[25] Both by reading through the complete texts and by extensive use of indices.

[26] This figure cannot be exact, for sometimes the decision as to how to divide up a string of vocatives must be subjective.

Table 1. *Main texts included*

Author	Century	Total addresses	Principal genre(s) (for addresses)	Principal register(s) used
Plautus	III–II BC	1,669	comedy	low–middle
Ennius	III–II BC	48	various poetic	high
Terence	II BC	770	comedy	low–middle
Lucilius	II BC	23	satire	low–middle
Accius	II–I BC	22	tragedy	high
Varro	II–I BC	39	literary prose, satire	various
Cicero*	I BC	2,531	letters	low–middle
			literary prose	high–middle
Caesar	I BC	19	literary prose (history)	middle
Lucretius	I BC	20	didactic epic	high
Catullus	I BC	188	various poetic	high & various
Sallust	I BC	49	literary prose (history)	middle
Vergil	I BC	606	various poetic	high
Horace	I BC	259	various poetic	high & various
Propertius	I BC	261	elegy	high
Tibullus	I BC	72	elegy	high
Livy	I BC–I AD	425	literary prose (history)	middle & high
Ovid	I BC–I AD	1,168	various poetic	high
Seneca (elder)	I BC–I AD	309	literary prose (declamations)	middle
Phaedrus	I BC–I AD	43	verse fables	middle

Table 1 (*cont.*):

Author	Century	Total addresses	Principal genre(s) (for addresses)	Principal register(s) used
Valerius Maximus	I AD	62	literary prose	middle
Calpurnius Siculus	I AD	65	pastoral poetry	high
Seneca (younger)	I AD	198	literary prose	middle
		540	tragedy	high
Lucan	I AD	299	epic	high
Silius Italicus	I AD	369	epic	high
Petronius	I AD	90	novel	low & various
Columella	I AD	27	literary prose	middle
Curtius Rufus	I AD	52	literary prose (history)	middle
Persius	I AD	38	satire	various
Quintilian	I AD	237	literary prose (declamations)	middle
Valerius Flaccus	I AD	206	epic	high
Statius	I AD	503	epic	high
Martial	I AD	1,329	epigram	various
Tacitus	I–II AD	65	literary prose	middle & high
Juvenal	I–II AD	70	satire	various
Pliny (younger)*	I–II AD	181	letters	low–middle
			literary prose (oratory)	high–middle
Suetonius	I–II AD	43	literary prose (biography)	middle

Fronto*	II AD	242	letters	middle
Apuleius	II AD	294	literary prose	high–middle & various
Gellius	II AD	68	literary prose	middle
Calpurnius Flaccus	II AD	51	literary prose (declamations)	middle
pseudo–Quintilian	II? AD	666	literary prose (declamations)	middle
Other	various	405	various	various
Total literary		14,621		
Pompeii	I AD and earlier	471	graffiti	low & various
Vindolanda	I–II AD	67	private letters	low–middle
Other letters	various	46	private letters	low–middle
Inscriptions	various	236	epitaphs, etc.	various
Total non-literary		820		
TOTAL		15,441		

* indicates that the total for an author includes some addresses from letters written not by him, but by others to him.

Note: Addresses in spurious works traditionally attributed to an extant author are included in the figures for that author, except in the case of Quintilian. Addresses in his *Declamationes Minores*, which may well be spurious but are probably roughly contemporary with Quintilian or slightly later (Winterbottom 1984: xiv–xv), are listed under his name, while the *Declamationes Maiores*, which are certainly spurious and were composed much later, are listed as pseudo–Quintilian. The purpose of this division (which is followed throughout this work) is to allow a clear distinction between two very different collections of declamations. The *Institutio Oratoria*, which is certainly genuine, contains only 22 vocatives (apart from those in quotations of Cicero's works, which were not counted because they are already included in the totals for Cicero).

The works of Tacitus are different from one another in character and do not all use the same registers, but because of the small number of addresses in each (no work except the *Annales* has more than 20) distinctions of address usage cannot safely be made.

limitations on the type of analysis and discussion that can be
undertaken within the compass of a single volume. A thorough
discussion of the peculiarities of each individual term, let alone
of each passage containing a vocative, would soon start to
resemble a large dictionary. While in some senses that might
be desirable, it would have the disadvantage of obscuring some
larger, fundamental rules which explain many of the more
specific points and which are often more revealing than lists
of details. This work thus concentrates on the use of individual
passages to illustrate more important principles, rather than on
those passages for their own sake. Regrettably, owing to
limitations on space even discussion of the fundamental rules
has to be selective; for example, the Latin address system
contains not only rules relating to the choice of specific
terms, but also rules relating to the position of vocatives in
the sentence. The latter set of rules, while important, seems to
be less closely connected to the former set of rules than those
rules are to one another, and it has already been the subject of
some excellent research (see p. 21); I have therefore decided to
concentrate on the choice of words instead. Similarly, there is
only minimal discussion (see pp. 250–3) of the rules determining when addresses are used at all and when they are omitted,
although this topic could form a book in itself. Thus this work
omits much that is interesting and worthy of inclusion; it is to
be hoped that other scholars will choose to fill some of the gaps
that it leaves.

In the companion volume on Greek, an appendix was
provided listing references to all addresses in the corpus,
with the exception of proper names. This appendix was
needed because of the extent to which that work relied on
statistics, and it was possible to provide it not only because the
corpus of data used in that study was smaller than our present
collection, but also because the personal names, which in Greek
are unproblematic as addresses, could be omitted. These
factors reduced to 6,432 the number of references which had
to be listed in the appendix. In Latin such a listing is less
necessary because, since the lack of a uniform body of literature
makes statistical methods largely unsatisfactory for dealing
with the address system, the present work relies on statistical
comparisons less than did the work on Greek. A complete list

of references is also less practical for Latin because names could not reasonably be omitted from such a listing; the use of Roman nomenclature is one of the more difficult issues of the address system. A Latin list would thus be two and a half times as long as the Greek one and would take up one third of this book. In this work, therefore, a complete list of references is not provided, and references are given in the text and footnotes to the extent practical. Because of the large volume of data, these references are normally examples, not a complete set; the reader should not assume that no other occurrences of a word or usage have been found unless this is specifically stated.

In order to compensate somewhat for the lack of an overall listing, a representative sample of references for the 505 most significant addresses is provided in the Glossary. The Glossary is designed to be consulted either in conjunction with or separately from the text and has several functions. First and foremost, it provides some of the detailed information on individual words which is necessarily omitted from the text (number of occurrences, authors in which the word appears, etc.); in addition, it contains a selection of references and summarizes the relevant arguments presented in the text, so that a reader wishing only for a simple statement of a given word's address usage and some examples in Latin authors can easily find this information in the Glossary. It is hoped that this glossary will be of use not only to those reading ancient literature, but also to those wishing to include addresses in their own written or spoken Latin. Also intended as an aid to active users of Latin are the usage charts which summarize the main rules of the address system discussed in Part II. Like the Glossary, these charts can be used independently of the text by those looking for a simple summary of the rules of the address system.

The editions cited are listed on pp. 370–3; abbreviations and numerical references follow the system of the *Oxford Latin Dictionary* whenever possible (see pp. 370–3 for exceptions). Adherence to the chosen text has not been completely rigid; in general I have tried to avoid basing arguments on conjectures or corrupt passages, and so some vocatives have been omitted from consideration even when they appear in the text chosen.

Latin words are quoted in the vocative when their address

usage is under discussion, which is most of the time. When referential usage is the point at issue, however, they are quoted in the nominative. In discussions of individual words, spelling has normally been standardized to the form used in the *Oxford Latin Dictionary*, but when an entire passage is quoted, the spelling used in the preferred text is followed for the sake of internal consistency. Addresses discussed in the abstract are usually quoted in the masculine singular; if an address does not occur in that form, it is quoted in the feminine or plural form that does occur. The Glossary lists all the different forms in which each address has been found.

Translations of vocatives are always translations of the lexical meaning, not a socially equivalent English address (which, if it exists, has in most cases a very different lexical meaning). They are intended only as a rough guide for non-classicists, and they are not provided for words and passages quoted only in footnotes. All translations are my own, but they do not differ significantly from other scholars' interpretations except where such discrepancies are noted. In particular, to avoid bias in doubtful cases, I have never interpreted passages as discussions of what someone is or should be called unless I could find precedent for such interpretation.

Familiarity with the major Latin authors is assumed in the text, but for reference purposes a brief summary of the dates, genres, and registers associated with those who provide the most addresses is given in Table 1. It must be remembered both that the Latin register system was far more finely gradated than the rough division given in this table, and that no author remains consistently in one register. In addition, the distinction between literary or non-literary language and high or low register (p. 16) should be kept in mind.

LATIN LITERATURE AND ITS PRESENTATION OF THE ADDRESS SYSTEM

Certain facts about Latin literature must be taken into account when using it as a source for information on the Latin language. The most important of these is probably the issue of style or register. The literary texts included in this study reflect a wide variety of registers, and in consequence a variety of address patterns. In this sense the Latin address system is far more difficult to recover than the address system of ancient Greek, for while in Greek one can rely on a large corpus of Athenian literature from the fifth and fourth centuries, in which across several prose genres and one poetic genre (New Comedy) a very consistent address system can be identified (Dickey 1995: 269), in Latin no such uniformity exists.

I have argued elsewhere that the identification of a consistent address system is an indication of success in recovering the conversational register of the language concerned. Does the lack of consistency in Latin mean that we cannot recover the conversational register? Fortunately not. Our Latin data provide us not with one internally inconsistent system (the sign of a literary register like that of Greek tragedy, which has a highly varied address system), but with a number of different yet internally consistent systems. Thus one can reconstruct with a fair degree of confidence the address system of comedy, that of Cicero, or that of the writers of the Vindolanda tablets. The difficulty is that there are too many different systems, and not enough data on each. Each genre tends to provide ample information on some types of interaction but far too little on others, meaning that our overall picture has many gaps. We know, for example, how lovers addressed each other in classical poetry, but there are very few such addresses in classical prose. Interactions among slaves are very common in comedy but virtually absent in classical poetry.

These gaps are more serious in some cases than in others. Each genre belongs to a register or registers, and while in theory we would want to have data on all types of interaction in each register, in practice some interactions were confined to certain registers in life as well as in literature. Classical poetry, for example, normally represents a high register of literary Latin, and slaves probably did not often use this type of language to one another in any case; the lack of slave interactions in classical poetry is thus not a serious problem for us. On the other hand, Roman lovers probably did use registers other than the high one, and thus the scarcity of interactions between lovers in classical prose is unfortunate.

The Latin language was far from fixed during the period under consideration. While post-classical writing has a tendency to imitate classical style, that tendency is not normally strong enough to extend to the use of the classical address system (in Greek, by contrast, the address system of Lucian is largely identical to that used by Plato more than five centuries earlier). The result is that different address systems existed at different periods, and each of those systems involved a full set of registers. Thus the Latin address system can be thought of as a three-dimensional grid, with the first dimension being the different types of interaction, the second the register, and the third the date. We cannot come close to filling in all the points on the grid, even allowing for the fact that some will never have been filled in real life. We shall simply have to concentrate on those sections which can be reconstructed, and note what is missing.

In some ways, however, the variety available in Latin gives us opportunities; we shall be able to observe the differences between periods and registers, and so to recognize passages in which the address used belongs to a register other than that of the surrounding text. Such register shifts (as, for example, when a character who normally uses a fairly high register becomes angry and uses a low register for invective) were immediately obvious to the Romans, but they can be more difficult for us to spot. Once one knows the register of particular Latin addresses, register shifts can often be detected, but in many cases we need to know more about the registers of specific passages in order to determine the registers of the individual vocatives used.

It is thus fortunate that there are certain register-dependent stylistic traits of Latin addresses which seem to function independently (for the most part) of the particular words used. The simplest such distinction is that complex addresses (those made up of two or more words, not counting the particle *o*) are more likely to be found in texts exhibiting a more literary style, while those registers closer to conversational language have a stronger preference for one-word addresses. Thus in the tragedies of Seneca, which contain perhaps the most literary language of any text considered for this study, 29% of addresses consist of more than one word, while in the plays of Terence and the prose passages of Petronius, which are probably as close to conversational language as our literary evidence gets,[27] 13% (Terence) to 17% (Petronius) of addresses consist of more than one word; likewise 17% of the addresses in graffiti are complex.[28]

When this general tendency is further explored, it turns out to result from a number of more specific address rules, which divide the literary and non-literary texts more sharply. Addresses in the more literary texts frequently include words not in the vocative case (adverbs, dependent gentives, etc.), as *o lux immensi publica mundi, Phoebe pater* (spoken by Phaethon to his father the sun, Ov. *Met.* 2. 35–6), while the more conversational registers very rarely allow such words to form part of an address. For example, 18% of the addresses in Seneca's tragedies include at least one word not in the vocative case, while such words are found in only 1% of the addresses in Terence, 2% of those in the graffiti, and 3% of those in Petronius. Addresses consisting of more than three words, likewise, are strongly characteristic of literary texts; such addresses account for 14% of the addresses in Seneca's tragedies but only 1% of those in Terence, Petronius, and the graffiti.

At the same time, certain types of complex address occur freely in the less literary registers and may even be characteristic of them. Notable among these is the use of a single word (usually a name) modified by *mi* or some other form of *meus*, a formula which accounts for 20% of the complex addresses in Petronius, 69% of those in Terence, and 5% of those in the graffiti, but which does not occur at all in Seneca's tragedies (see Ch. 7). Another is the use of several names (e.g. gentilicium and cognomen) when more than one is needed to identify the addressee. Thus 40% of the complex addresses at Pompeii and Herculaneum consist of names alone; it is easy to see why multiple names are more necessary in graffiti than in words spoken in the presence of the addressee. Another, rarer type of complex address admissible in the more conversational registers is that in which a single word (or a word

---

[27] Cf. Boyce (1991: 73); Hofmann (1951: 2).

[28] All statistics relating to the graffiti are tentative, because of the fragmentary nature of the remains and the difficulty of interpreting them; in this case the figure might be as low as 15% if different judgements were made about individual graffiti, but it could not be significantly higher than 17%.

modified by a form of *meus*) is repeated, as *o Thais, Thais* (Ter. *Eu.* 91).[29]

Since most authors show at least some variety in register, we would expect the extent to which literary and conversational addresses are found in the various types of complex address to be more polarized than the figures for more and less literary texts. Often this is in fact the case, although frequently the distinctions are obscured because the more common addresses tend to belong to more than one register. Thus, for example, the address *coniunx* 'spouse' seems to be a literary form, since it is confined almost exclusively to poetry and never found in a text associated with the conversational register. *Coniunx* is used in complex addresses in 54% of its occurrences; the addresses in which it appears involve words not in the vocative case 15% of the time and consist of more than three words 17% of the time, but only 1% of the time do they involve one of the specific types of complex address mentioned above as being acceptable in the conversational register. On the other hand, the address *ere* 'master' seems to be less literary and more conversational, since it is used exclusively by slaves and occurs primarily in comedy. *Ere* is used in complex addresses 12% of the time; only 2% of the time does it occur in an address consisting of more than three words or containing words not in the vocative case, but 4% of the time it occurs in one of the 'conversational' types of complex address.

These differences suggest that the extent to which a word is used in complex addresses, and the type of complex addresses in which it occurs, can be used as criteria to help us determine the word's register. Other clues to register are the normal register of the work in which a word is found, the social level of the speaker, the nature of the interaction, and the use (if any) of register-specific language in the speech which contains the address. In this work, when addresses are stated to belong to a specific register or registers and no specific explanation of the grounds for this judgement is given, a combination of these criteria has been used.

---

[29] For such repetitions see Wills (1996: 50–8) and Hofmann (1985: 179).

One hazard faced by students of Latin literature is that addresses may reflect the needs of the audience rather than being dependent solely on interaction between speaker and addressee. Such addresses occur in oratory, where absent persons may be apostrophized not with the address the speaker would actually use to them, but with one that will enable the audience to understand who is being addressed. Thus Sallust has an envoy apostrophize his father with *Micipsa pater* (*Jug.* 14. 9), although fathers were not normally addressed by name in Latin. These addresses also occur in poetry, where one type of them developed a life of its own. This type is the 'variational' address, a vocative from a poet to a character in his poem, or an object or place mentioned in it, which is used for poetic variation or metrical reasons in place of a reference in another case.[30] Such vocatives are often found at the end of a list of people or things, as

> tum primum radiis gelidi caluere Triones
> et vetito frustra temptarunt aequore tingi,
> quaeque polo posita est glaciali proxima Serpens,
> frigore pigra prius nec formidabilis ulli,
> incaluit sumpsitque novas fervoribus iras.
> te quoque turbatum memorant fugisse, Boote,
> quamvis tardus eras et te tua plaustra tenebant.
>   (Ov. *Met.* 2. 171–7)

Then for the first time the icy Bears [constellations] grew hot from the sun's rays, and tried in vain to plunge themselves in the forbidden sea. The Serpent, who lies closest to the frigid pole, till then sluggish and a threat to no one because of the cold, grew hot and derived new anger from the heat. They say that you too fled in confusion, Boötes, although you were slow and your wagons held you back.

They do not, however, always occur as parts of lists. Although normally spoken by the poet in his own voice, they can also be put into the mouth of another character who is acting as narrator for part of the story or who is alluding to some earlier incident, as when Hercules says

---

[30] Cf. Bömer (1969–86: i. 286); H. Fränkel (1945: 214).

> ergo ego foedantem peregrino templa cruore
> Busirin domui saevoque alimenta parentis
> Antaeo eripui nec me pastoris Hiberi
> forma triplex nec forma triplex tua, Cerbere, movit.
>
> (Ov. *Met.* 9. 182–5)

For this did I subdue Busiris, who defiled temples with the blood of strangers, and snatch his mother's nourishment from savage Antaeus, and remain unmoved by the threefold form of the Spanish shepherd, and by your threefold form, Cerberus?

Variational addresses are really references that happen to be in the vocative case,[31] identifying for the reader the person or object concerned, and as a result they often fail to follow the rules obeyed by other addresses.

Not all addresses from an author to his characters, however, are variational. When Lucan addresses his character Caesar as *perfide* 'treacherous', saying

> quam magna remisit
> crimina Romano tristis fortuna pudori,
> quod te non passa est misereri, perfide, Magni
> viventis!
>
> (9. 1059–62)

How great a crime grim fortune spared Roman decency, since she did not allow you, treacherous one, to take pity on Pompey the Great while he was alive!

this is not a variational address, for *perfide* is not an identification of the addressee for the reader. This type of address by an author to his characters normally does follow the rules of the address system.

Latin literature contains some contexts in which a word in another case can act almost, but not quite, like a vocative. The assumption is sometimes made that in these, if not elsewhere, address and referential usage must be equivalent, but this is not the case. One such situation is the headings or salutations of letters, which refer to the addressee in the dative, as *Marcus Quinto fratri salutem* 'Marcus to his brother Quintus, greeting'. This dative refers to Quintus and is addressed by Cicero to his

---

[31] They may go back to Homer's addresses to characters such as Eumaeus, e.g. τὸν δ' ἀπαμειβόμενος προσέφης, Εὔμαιε συβῶτα (*Od.* 14. 55).

brother, just like the vocatives within the letter, so how can there be any difference between them?

Yet there is a difference. Cicero's letters to his brother Quintus always have the salutation *Marcus Quinto fratri salutem* (preserved 19 times). The addresses within these letters are frequent and varied, but they never employ the collocation *Quinte frater* 'brother Quintus' and only once the name *Quinte* (*Q. fr.* 2. 15. 2). In fact there is reason to believe that Cicero never addressed his brother as *Quinte frater* when actually speaking or writing directly to him (cf. p. 261), yet *Quinto fratri* was his standard salutation in the dative.[32] It is thus unsafe to use letter headings as evidence of address usage.

With these cautions, then, we shall turn to the Latin address system and see to what extent it can provide answers to the questions posed at the start of this work.

---

[32] An analogous situation exists with Cicero's letters to Atticus: 213 of these letters have the salutation preserved, and in 212 cases this salutation is *Cicero Attico salutem* 'Cicero to Atticus, greeting'. Within these letters, however, the vocative *Attice* does not appear until 18 years into the collection, in 50 BC (*Att.* 6. 1. 20); until that point the only vocative names used for Atticus are his original gentilicium, *Pomponi*, and his praenomen, *Tite* (*Att.* 2. 16. 3, 3. 4, 3. 9. 2, 3. 15. 7, 3. 19. 3, etc.). The letter headings in this collection are often thought to be spurious (Constans 1940: 46–8; Shackleton Bailey 1965–70: i. 277), but a major reason cited for rejecting them is the discrepancy between the headings and the vocatives. The assumption that the two should match is unwarranted, since no such agreement is found in the letters to Quintus.

PART I

Addresses

Names

DEMEAS. o qui vocare?
GETA.   Geta.
DEMEAS.   Geta, hominem maxumi
   preti te esse hodie iudicavi animo meo.[1]

DEMEAS. O—how are you called?
GETA.   Geta.
DEMEAS.   Geta, I have
   today decided that you are a man of great worth.

NAMES are of central importance to the Latin address system, so much so that in some situations, despite all the other types of address available, a speaker prefers to ask an interlocutor's name before addressing him or her. Our data contain 5,948 addresses consisting only of names[2] and an additional 532 combining names with other words, together representing 42% of the total data and making address by name by far the most common type of address in Latin. Yet as the figure of 42% shows, names were not always used in address. How did a Roman decide when to use names and when to avoid them? If an addressee could not be addressed by name, what options were available to a Roman speaker? And when a character had more than one name, how did Romans determine which to use in address?

None of these questions is easy to answer, but one can point to factors which are clearly relevant. In some situations, such as address to a large group or to a nameless object, the use of names is impossible, while in others, such as address to a total stranger, it poses difficulty and so will not be attempted without a good reason. In addition, linguistic evidence from other cultures suggests that in some types of interaction, such

---

[1] Ter. *Ad.* 891–2; cf. Donatus ad loc. and Martin (1976: 226).
[2] Including names modified by *mi/mea* and/or preceded by the particle *o*.

as addresses from children to their parents, the use of names may violate social convention, and that some emotions, such as anger, may be communicated partly by switching from the use of names to another type of address. In addition, address by name can be characteristic of a specific register or registers rather than of the language as a whole.

The first of these factors, the number and species of the addressees, has nothing to teach us about Latin and so will be excluded by restricting the scope of this chapter to addresses directed to individual humans.[3] This restriction reduces our pool of data to 11,066 addresses, of which unmodified names make up 53% and modified names another 4%. Yet these overall percentages conceal considerable differences among individual authors: Cicero uses unmodified names 89% of the time when addressing individual humans, Tacitus does so 92% of the time, and Columella and Varro both use names 100% of the time, but Vergil and Ovid use such vocatives only 35% and 38% of the time respectively. This distinction is probably due to genre differences between prose and poetry, for the younger Seneca uses unmodified names 85% of the time in his prose works, but only 18% of the time in his tragedies.

It is no accident that the percentage of name addresses in Seneca's tragedies is so much lower than that in Ovid, for considerable differences are also found among different types of poetry. Vergil uses address by name alone only 24% of the time in the *Aeneid* but 66% of the time in the *Eclogues*. Catullus uses such address 33% of the time in poem 64, but 50% of the time in his other poetry. Terence and Martial use names alone as often as many prose writers, 74% and 86% respectively, but

---

[3] The following statistics thus omit not only plural addresses, but also all those to gods (whose complex variety of names and epithets poses difficulties beyond the scope of this study), animals, places, objects, etc. Data in this chapter are also restricted to the use of the addressee's own name, a name the speaker believes to be the addressee's own name, or a pseudonym; some other addresses apply the name of a divinity or famous human to an addressee having a different name (as *mea Iuno* from a man to his wife, Pl. *Cas.* 230), but these represent a completely different phenomenon from that of address by the addressee's own name and will be discussed later (p. 212). Addresses to groups are discussed in Ch. 12 and those to non-humans, including the names sometimes used in such addresses, in Ch. 13.

Statius and Silius do so only 25% of the time and 30% of the time respectively.

In Latin, then, the use of unmodified names in address is partly register-dependent: while acceptable in all literary registers, it is standard in some genres and rare in others. The genres using more addresses by name are, on the whole, those which seem for other reasons to be less obviously elevated in style and closer to conversational Latin, which suggests that the frequent use of such addresses was characteristic of conversational Latin as well. In classical Greek, unmodified names were by far the most common form of address in conversational language of the educated classes, but in many literary genres, particularly elevated ones such as tragedy and epic, address by name alone was very often replaced by other types of address (Dickey 1995, 1996: 47–8, 250–5). It is likely that in Latin as well, authors of highly literary works consciously reduced the frequency of addresses by name alone for the sake of elegance; unmodified names are a rather uninteresting and repetitive form of address, and the Latin poets, like the Greek ones, probably preferred to replace names that would be used in ordinary conversation with more exotic and varied addresses.

Some variations among different authors, however, seem to result from factors other than style. Names are very rare in the declamations, for example, and this is clearly due to the fact that since most cases in the declamations are hypothetical, none of the characters have names. Terence uses address by name alone 75% of the time, somewhat less often than Cicero; the reason is that Terence more often portrays conversations between close relatives, who in both authors often use kinship terms, and addresses from slaves, who often use titles to their masters.[4] Plautus' even lower figure of 42% is due partly to the same factors, partly to long scenes of invective containing large numbers of vocative insults, but probably also to stylistic differences, as it has been noted with regard to completely different areas of the address system that 'Terence contents himself with conventional terms . . . which were in common

---

[4] Terence's address system is unlikely to be simply borrowed from Greek New Comedy, for Menander uses unmodified names for only 40% of his addresses.

use in his time, whereas Plautus takes a special delight in coining new and picturesque expressions of his own' (Lilja 1965b: 82). Livy uses names 69% of the time, owing to numerous addresses to nameless characters.

A variety of factors thus affects the use of names in Latin. The underlying system in most of our texts seems to be one in which names are widely employed as a standard form of address: names are used unless the relationship between speaker and addressee is one which specifically calls for other terms such as titles or kinship terms, or unless insults or other marked addresses are warranted by the context. Terence and the prose authors followed this system to a large extent, while most of the poets embellished it to produce a more varied effect. The precise rules determining which relationships require avoidance of names vary from one author to the next, but on the whole there is more agreement than disagreement on this point: Terence's system does not seem to be very different from Cicero's.

The use of names as a standard form of address, however, means that in any given case where a name is not used, the rule producing that omission is not primarily a rule about the use of names, but a rule about the other form of address which replaces it. Precise rules for the use of names versus other addresses thus cannot be given until these other address forms have been examined; from one point of view, most of this book is an answer to the question 'When were names used in address in Latin?' All we can say at this point is that once an addressee's name was known,[5] it was apparently used in every interaction where not specifically prohibited by another address rule; names were thus the default address in the classical Latin system, as in ancient Greek and indeed in English.

The principle of names as default addresses is clearly observed in classical and pre-classical Latin, and in those periods most authors seem to share a common set of rules for determining when the default system is used (allowing for stylistic differences). Towards the later part of our period, however, the situation changes, especially in the less literary texts. Gellius uses address by name alone only 30% of the time,

[5] The problem of unknown and nameless addressees is discussed in Ch. 9.

Pliny and his correspondents 32% of the time, and in Fronto's letters the figure is only 11%. Petronius uses address by name alone 44% of the time. Such address never occurs on the Vindolanda tablets (*c.* AD 100) at all, though it is common in the Pompeian graffiti (before AD 79).

From this evidence it seems likely that during the first century AD names ceased to be the primary form of address between unrelated adults. Their place was apparently taken by polite terms such as *domine* 'master', *frater* 'brother', *carissime* 'dearest', and *magister* 'teacher'. The letters preserved at Vindolanda and elsewhere make it clear that by the end of the first century the vocatives in letters were very rarely by name alone and normally did not include names at all; the contrast with Cicero's epistolary style is striking. By Fronto's time this change had penetrated to the highest levels of the intelligentsia, at least as regards personal letters. In literary works, one can first see a decline in the use of names in Petronius, whose usage imitates non-literary language much more than other authors of his era; not until the second century did more elevated works show evidence of the change that had already taken place in conversational language. Some authors of this period, such as Tacitus, ignored the non-literary developments altogether and retained the classical system in this respect.

This interpretation of the data is strengthened by the evidence of Apuleius. While most prose authors are consistent in their use of names from one work to another, he is not. In the *Apology*, an oratorical work heavily influenced by Cicero's speeches, Apuleius uses address by name alone 91% of the time. In the *Metamorphoses*, which belongs to a genre that did not exist in the classical period and hence is less tied to classical models, he uses address by name alone only 23% of the time.[6] This difference suggests that, for Apuleius, the use of names as a default form of address went along with the use of a classicizing style and genre.

When address by name alone ceases to be a default, it does not seem to become a marked address form. In some types of language it disappears altogether, and in those where it

---

[6] Other works of Apuleius contain too few addresses to humans to make their evidence meaningful.

remains it seems to continue to be used as a default, just one less often employed. It is possible that in conversational language of the second century AD nominal addresses sounded impolite and/or archaic, but no solid evidence on this point is available.

The rule that names are a default makes the problem of nominal address in classical Latin appear simpler than it actually is, for Roman men possessed several names and could thus be addressed by name in a variety of different ways.[7] Yet not every character in Latin literature is a Roman man; approximately 2,500 names,[8] or 40% of all names in our data, are addressed to characters who bore only one name: mythological figures, Greeks, Carthaginians, slaves, etc. For such people a default address by name did indeed produce a simple system, and so there is no more to be said about this class of names. Names for women pose special problems, as Roman women often, but not always, bore only a single name; they will be discussed at the end of this chapter. The question of which name to use in address is thus one which we shall at present confine to the names of free male Romans.

Originally Romans, like other Indo-European peoples, had only a single name.[9] Traces of this single-name system remain in Latin, but by the time of our earliest inscriptional evidence

[7] There does not seem to be a significant distinction between the way in which different names are chosen when an address is by name alone and when it includes other words in addition to the name, so both modified and unmodified names are discussed together in the following sections; as we have seen, however, most nominal addresses do not include modifiers.

[8] This figure cannot be exact, because sometimes, especially when pseudonyms are used, it is unclear how many names an addressee is supposed to have had.

[9] What follows is an overview of the highly complex issue of Roman nomenclature, on which much good work has appeared in recent years. The facts given here are generally accepted, but their interpretation, and the causes of the changes in nomenclature clearly visible in inscriptions, are often disputed. It is not possible to list here all works on the subject, but the most important and most useful for our purposes here are Bonfante (1948); Doer (1937); E. Fraenkel (1935: 1648–70); Gallivan (1992); Kajanto (1965, 1977a); Morris (1963); Nicolet (1977); Salomies (1987); Salway (1994); Schulze (1904); Shackleton Bailey (1965–70: i. 402–3, 1992, 1995, 1996); Syme (1958); Wiseman (1970).

the evolution to a system of two names was nearly complete.[10]
The first of these two was a praenomen or given name (e.g.
Publius), and the second a nomen gentilicium or inherited
name, often formed with an *-ius* suffix (e.g. *Cornelius*); of
these it was the praenomen that continued the original single
name. While there were many different gentilicia, praenomina
were normally chosen from a very small pool of names; not
only was the general pool restricted, but in many families
only an even more limited subset of the available praenomina
was normally used, resulting in frequent homonymity.

In the early Republic[11] a third name, the cognomen, made its
appearance. Cognomina were in origin unofficial nicknames,
but they rapidly became heritable along with gentilicia,
although it was also possible for a new cognomen to be added
during a man's lifetime. There was no limit on the number of
names a Roman could have; if a man already bearing a cognomen acquired another one, it was simply appended to his
existing names and formed an additional cognomen, sometimes
called an agnomen. There were in the Republican period three
main types of cognomen for freeborn Romans: most common
was the inherited type (e.g. *Scipio*), but there were also numerous instances of the honorific type, commemorating a victory or
other important fact about the man in question (e.g. *Africanus*),
and the adoption type, in which a man who changed his name
upon being adopted added the suffix *-anus* to his original
gentilicium and made it into a cognomen (e.g. *Aemilianus*
from *Aemilius*). In keeping with their origin as nicknames,
cognomina did not become part of official nomenclature for
several centuries and were still omitted in official state documents as late as the second century BC, though they appear
much earlier in private inscriptions (Kajanto 1977*a*: 66–7).

The use of cognomina began among the aristocracy and did
not extend to plebeians until the late second century. At this
point, however, cognomina appeared not only among freeborn
plebeians but also among freedmen and enfranchised foreigners. Most slaves and foreigners had only one name, and that

[10] It is thought that the two-name system was in place by at least the 7th
cent. BC (Salway 1994: 125).
[11] Perhaps as early as the 5th cent., and certainly by the mid-4th cent.
(Kajanto 1977*a*: 64–5).

name normally did not belong to the small group of Roman
praenomina, nor did it have the *-ius* suffix characteristic of the
gentilicium. When a slave was freed or a foreigner was granted
citizenship, however, he took a new praenomen and gentilicium
(normally from the family of the person responsible for his
freedom or citizenship) and retained his old individual name as
a cognomen. This usage spread rapidly, so that from the
beginning of the first century BC nearly all freedmen and
enfranchised foreigners used cognomina. Freeborn native
Romans of the plebeian class, on the other hand, normally
did not do so until the beginning of the empire (Kajanto 1977*a*:
67–9). Thus for most of the Republic possession of a cognomen
was characteristic of nobles, while lack of one was characteristic
of lower orders (except, of course, at the very lowest level of
freedmen and new citizens). This tendency was not universal,
for noble families which lacked cognomina (e.g. the Antonii)
and non-noble ones which possessed them are both attested,
but it was strong nevertheless.

At the end of the Republic, however, there was a dramatic
increase in the use of cognomina by non-nobles,[12] so that in the
first century AD nearly every Roman citizen possessed the three
names that came to be known as the *tria nomina* and seen as the
distinctive mark of the free Roman (Juv. 5. 127; Quint. *Inst.* 7.
3. 27). This increase in the use of the cognomen went along
with a change in the nature of cognomina, for while aristocratic
cognomina were normally inherited, passed on to all the sons of
a family, the new plebeian cognomina resembled those used by
freedmen and foreigners in being individual names (Salomies
1987: 305). Thus each son of a non-aristocratic family received
a cognomen different from that of his brothers.

When all males in a family shared the same nomen and the
same (if any) cognomen, the praenomen was important as the
only way that brothers could be distinguished from one
another, but the development of individual cognomina made
the praenomen partly redundant. Often it then became fossilized and heritable, resulting in brothers sharing both praenomen and gentilicium but being distinguished by their
cognomina. Eventually, in the late empire, the praenomen
disappeared altogether. Meanwhile the simplicity of the *tria*

[12] Salomies (1987: 280–2) gives some revealing figures.

nomina had been further eroded by the second-century practice of giving not only multiple cognomina, but also multiple gentilicia, resulting in very long, cumbersome names of which only a few elements could actually be used in any normal setting. In the later empire, however, this trend reversed itself and names became fewer; finally, at the very end of the empire, gentilicia disappeared altogether and the former Romans were left with a single name as at the beginning of their history, though this single name was in fact descended not from the original praenomen but from the cognomen.[13]

The significant variations within the Roman system of nomenclature and the complexity of its evolution make the address usage complicated as well. In English, most people can be addressed either by their first names (e.g. 'Samuel') or by last name (normally with a title, e.g. 'Mr Smith'), and some have nicknames (e.g. 'Sam') as alternatives to the first name;[14] address by first name and last name (e.g. 'Samuel Smith') is also possible, though it is a recent development and largely confined to the genre of the letter. The average English speaker is thus likely to be addressed by name in two or at most four different ways. A Roman man possessing the *tria nomina*, however, could be addressed by name in eight different ways. The speaker could use all three names (or more if the addressee had more), two names, or one. If two names were used, they could be praenomen + gentilicium, praenomen + cognomen, gentilicium + cognomen, or cognomen + gentilicium. If one name was used, it could be any one of the three.

---

[13] Other late phenomena important for the history of the naming system are the use of praenomina as gentilicia and the creation of the *signum*, an additional name which was not integrated into the *tria nomina* but could be attached to them by terms such as *qui et* 'who [is] also [called]'. The *signum* could be used in address like a cognomen (e.g. *ILS* 8380), but it is extremely rare during our period.

[14] Those people who always use their nicknames instead of the full first name, of course, provide no more address options than those who never use a nickname at all. The same is true of people who use their middle names as first names; apart from such people, English speakers are not normally addressed by a middle name, so middle names do not provide an additional address option.

The number of names used is apparently determined by factors different from those influencing the choice of one name over another, so the question of number can be examined first. In our data addresses using one name are by far the commonest, representing 90% of the approximately 3,700 Roman male names. Virtually all the remaining addresses use two names, so that address by three names occurs less than 1% of the time. Single-name address can be found at all periods and in all genres, from Ennius (*Sat.* 6) to Gellius (2. 26. 16); it is the most common type of name address to Roman men in all authors examined except Livy and Columella. Address by multiple names, on the other hand, is extremely rare in poetry. It is never used by Lucan or Silius, who between them produce 156 addresses by name to Roman men, and accounts for only 2% of such addresses in Martial, 3% each in Catullus and Ovid, and 5% in Horace; other poets as well rarely or never use double names, but as they less often produce addresses by name to male Romans the avoidance is less striking. I have found no examples of triple-name vocatives in poetry.

In prose authors the percentage of double names varies widely. Cicero uses them in 16% of his addresses by name to Roman men, and similar figures can be found for Gellius and Valerius Maximus, while Apuleius does so 9% of the time, the elder Seneca 7% of the time, and the younger Seneca only 1% of the time. Columella, however, uses double names 56% of the time, and Livy does so 84% of the time. Triple names occur only three times in literature, in Cicero (*Q. Rosc.* 3), Valerius Maximus (6. 2. 11), and Scribonius Largus (*pr.*).

Inscriptions and graffiti contain a higher proportion of multiple names than most literary texts; 19% of addresses by name use more than one name, and 4% use three or more names. Although epigraphical evidence accounts for less than 10% of our total evidence for the address usage of Roman names, it supplies 82% of the examples of address by three or more names. In most cases the prevalence of multiple names in inscriptions seems to be due to a need for identification.[15] In a letter or a literary work, one name is normally sufficient to indicate who the addressee is, since there are a limited number

[15] The use of *Ti. Caesar Germanice* in Claudius' oration (*ILS* 212. ii. 20) is a notable exception.

of possibilities, while on a gravestone (which may identify a deceased man only by addressing him), more complete information is frequently necessary. Most multiple names in epigraphic texts, therefore, tell us little about the normal use of nominal address.

The largest body of nominal addresses to Roman men, 1,024 vocatives, comes from the works of Cicero. Cicero's use of names has been meticulously analysed by Adams, who concludes after an examination of data from both referential and address usage that the number of names used is determined by the formality of the context: the more formality, the more names.[16] Thus three names are reserved for highly formal settings, two for formal settings, and one for informal situations, though even in formal speeches a single name is often used of one's opponent, and a greater number of names can indicate greater respect (1978: 145–7). Our data from Cicero largely support Adams's conclusions; in both the letters and the philosophical dialogues, which are supposed to sound like informal conversations, almost all the addresses use single names, so that multiple-name addresses are restricted almost entirely to the speeches, which are more formal.

Even in speeches, however, double names are used only 34% of the time in address. Men attached to the opposing side, whether the actual opponent under attack or his advocates and supporters, receive double names only 18% of the time. Men not belonging to the opposition, however, are double-named 64% of the time in address. The distinction of respect is far from absolute, for single names are not infrequently used even to address judges, as Piso (*Q. Rosc.* 37, 38, 45) or Caesar (*Lig.* 6, 7, 10, etc.), and the only triple-name vocative in Cicero is addressed to an opponent (*Q. Rosc.* 3).

Several factors seem to affect the use of multiple names as addresses in Cicero's speeches. The tendency for opponents to receive single names is important, but almost as important is the tendency for several names to be used the first time a man is addressed in a given speech, or the first few times, and for

---

[16] Adams (1978); important qualifications of the points made in this article can be found in Shackleton Bailey (1992: 3–8, 1995: 1–10, 1996: 1–12). A number of earlier studies on Cicero's name usage exist (e.g. Axtell 1915, Thylander 1954) but are superseded by Adams's work.

single names to be used thereafter. Thus Gaius Fannius
Chaerea is addressed first as *C. Fanni Chaerea* (*Q. Rosc.* 3)
and then always as *Fanni* (8, 16, 24, 37 (*bis*), 50, 55), while
Gaius Erucius is first addressed as *C. Eruci* (*S. Rosc.* 38) but
then normally as *Eruci* (43, 44, 45, etc.). The same pattern can
be seen with ten other frequently addressed men,[17] and traces
of it are often visible for men less commonly addressed; it is
probably connected to the formality factor, since the initial
address could well be considered a more formal moment than
subsequent ones. There is also a tendency for double names to
appear the last time a man is addressed, if this is near the end of
the speech. This habit is much less strong than that of using
multiple names initially, but it still appears in eight different
speeches.[18] It may be connected to a tendency for double
names to be used (to a person normally addressed with a
single name) to emphasize a particular point connected with
the addressee. Identification of such passages is of course
subjective, but they must include *Mil.* 100, *Lig.* 16, and
Deiot. 34. This phenomenon reminds one of the custom in
some American families whereby parents address their children by their full names only when reprimanding them for
serious misdeeds.

Some speeches contain a large number of double-name
vocatives to a person who is never single-named; this often
seems to correlate to greater formality and deference on the
part of the speaker. Thus in the *Pro Marcello*, Cicero's speech

---

[17] T. Attius is first addressed as *T. Atti* (*Clu.* 62, 65), but afterwards often
as *Atti* (84, 86, etc.); M. Porcius Cato is first *M. Cato* (*Mur.* 3, 13) but then
Cato (34, 60, 63, etc.); Ser. Sulpicius Rufus is first *Ser. Sulpici* (*Mur.* 7), then
often *Servi* (9, 10, 21, etc.) or *Sulpici* (25, 30); Caesar is first *C. Caesar* (*Lig.* 1,
4; *Deiot.* 1, 4), then often *Caesar* (*Lig.* 6, 7, 10, etc.; *Deiot.* 4, 7, 8, etc.);
Q. Caecilius Niger is first *Q. Caecili* (*Div. Caec.* 12, 20), then only *Caecili* (22,
27, 30, etc.); Sex. Naevius is first *Sex. Naevi* (*Quinct.* 36), then normally
Naevi (37, 79, 84) or *Sexte* (38, 40); C. Calpurnius Piso is first *C. Piso* (*Q.
Rosc.* 7, 21, 22; *Caec.* 34), then normally *Piso* (*Q. Rosc.* 37, 38, 45; *Caec.* 36, 64,
81, etc.); Titus Labienus is first *T. Labiene* (*Rab. Perd.* 6), then only *Labiene*
(11, 17, 19, etc.); Decimus Laelius is first *D. Laeli* (*Flac.* frag. Med.), then
only *Laeli* (frag. Med., 6, 23, etc.); L. Manlius Torquatus is first *L. Torquate*
(*Sul.* 3), then only *Torquate* (5, 8, 11, etc.).

[18] *M. Cato* (*Mur.* 83), *C. Caesar* (*Lig.* 37; *Deiot.* 43), *P. Dolabella* (*Phil.* 1.
31), *M. Antoni* (*Phil.* 2. 118), *Q. Hortensi* (*Ver.* 1. 153), *Sex. Naevi* (*Quinct.*
93), *C. Piso* (*Q. Rosc.* 51).

of gratitude to Caesar delivered in the Senate, Caesar is addressed as *C. Caesar* ten times[19] but never with one name;[20] in contrast, the *Pro Ligario*, which was delivered in the forum, and the *Pro Rege Deiotaro*, which was delivered in private in Caesar's house, are also addressed to Caesar but often use the vocative *Caesar*.[21] The *Pro Quinctio* contains repeated addresses to the judge C. Aquilius Gallus, who is always addressed as *C. Aquili* (1, 4, 5, etc.); at the time of this speech Cicero was only 26 years old and not yet established as an orator. It is thus not surprising that he is here more formal and respectful of the judge than in later speeches.

Thus the most important factor in Cicero's choice of one or two names is, as Adams stated, formality: in informal settings single names are virtually always used in address, while in more formal ones multiple names are also an option. When multiple names are possible, however, a variety of factors influences the extent to which that option is used. A higher level of formality, greater deference to the addressee, the introduction of a new addressee, and the need to emphasize specific points will all result in a higher incidence of multiple names, while unemphatic addresses to a man who has previously been addressed will normally employ single names unless unusual formality and/or deference is called for.

We have so far looked only at Cicero's usage, which formed the basis of Adams's study and for which there is more evidence than for the usage of other authors. To what extent did other authors follow the same pattern? Several studies (Vidman 1981; Jones 1991, 1996) have found patterns of double-name usage in Pliny's letters that differ to some extent from those described by Adams. The differences do not, however, concern this aspect of address usage, for all nominal vocatives in Pliny's letters employ only single names. As Pliny never addresses the emperor Trajan by name in a letter, all the contexts are informal enough to call for single names in Cicero as well. The letters of Fronto and

---

[19] 2, 4, 7, 9, 16, 23, 26, 32, 33, 34.

[20] Gotoff (1993: 20, 181) implies that there are three instances of single-name address in this speech, but I cannot find them in any version of the text, including Gotoff's own.

[21] *Lig.* 6, 7, 10, etc.; *Deiot.* 4, 7, 8, etc.; cf. Gotoff (1993: 20, 181).

Seneca, likewise, almost always[22] use single names in address
and contain addresses by name only in contexts informal
enough for this usage to match Cicero's. Petronius, whose
works contain nominal addresses only in contexts where we
would expect Cicero to use a single name, uses only single
names.

Livy is the author one would expect to differ from Cicero if
any author does, for Livy uses multiple names in address far
more often than does Cicero. Yet in fact Livy's rules of usage
seem to be the same as Cicero's on this point: his single names
normally occur in informal settings,[23] while double names are
usually found in public assemblies, Senate speeches, and other
formal contexts.[24] Livy shares Cicero's tendency to use double
names at the beginning, and sometimes at the end, of a series of
vocatives in a formal speech, while using single names in the
middle;[25] since most of the speeches recorded by Livy are
comparatively short and contain only one or two addresses to a
given individual, however, this tendency is less visible here
than in Cicero's speeches.

The clearest indications of the meaning Livy saw in address
by single and double names come from passages containing
both types of name to the same addressee. The consul Paulus is
twice quoted addressing the young Publius Scipio Nasica; on
the first occasion he uses *Nasica* in an informal rebuke (44. 36.
12), and on the second he uses *P. Nasica* in a formal speech to
his council (44. 38. 3). Likewise Lucius Tarquinius Collatinus
is addressed as *Collatine* by his wife Lucretia in front of a few
close friends (1. 58. 7) but as *L. Tarquini* by the consul Brutus
in a speech before the Roman people (2. 2. 7).[26] Appius
Claudius the decemvir is repeatedly addressed as *Appi* by the
father and fiancé of the girl he attempts to seize, in emotional
(and usually defiant) reactions to his cruelty (3. 45. 6, 10, 3. 47.

---

[22] Exceptions only at Sen. *Ep.* 14. 13 (for identification) and Fro. 105. 21.

[23] e.g. 1. 41. 3, 1. 58. 7, 25. 18. 6, 44. 36. 12.

[24] e.g. 1. 26. 7, 2. 2. 7, 2. 45. 12, 3. 21. 7.

[25] Double: 9. 34. 6, 9. 34. 23, 30. 30. 22, 39. 37. 9; Single: 9. 34. 8, 9. 34. 21,
30. 30. 28, 39. 37. 14.

[26] This example is complex, because the particular names chosen are also
important: Collatinus helped overthrow his kinsman Tarquinius Superbus,
and so address by cognomen serves to distance him from the tyrant, but the
use of the gentilicium is intended to emphasize the connection.

7, 3. 48. 5), but once he has been deposed, the girl's father addresses him as *Appi Claudi* in the calm formality of a legal trial (3. 56. 4).

It thus looks as though Livy had the same rules as Cicero for determining how many names to use in address; the high frequency of double names in Livy's works is merely due to his tendency to record formal much more than informal speech. Other prose authors seem to follow these rules as well. Most addresses in Apuleius' *Apology* use only one name, but the initial address to the judge uses two (1), as do the first two addresses to one of Apuleius' opponents (30, 46) and several others to the judge (28, 35, 91, 99). The declamations attributed to Quintilian include address by name only in the hypothetical case of a soldier tried before Gaius Marius, in which the general is addressed as *C. Mari* at the beginning and end ([Quint.] *Decl.* 3. 2, 16), but as both *Mari* (3. 7, 14) and *C. Mari* (3. 4, 6, 10) in the middle. The two orations in the *Appendix Sallustiana* both feature double names for the initial addresses, followed by single names.[27]

Gellius and the elder Seneca normally use single names but also occasionally double names;[28] their practice seems to match that of Cicero, though it is difficult to be sure because many of the addresses are quoted with insufficient context. Valerius Maximus tends to use variational addresses in his own voice (see p. 35), and these sometimes need to violate Ciceronian rules in order to identify the character concerned adequately, but he appears to follow Ciceronian rules when identification is not an issue, though perhaps with a tendency to employ double names less often than Cicero would. Particularly notable is his use of the triple-name address *C. Iuli Caesar* from a man making a formal claim on Caesar in the forum (6. 2. 11). Tacitus, Columella, Quintilian, and Varro have a tendency to use double names in addressing the dedicatee of a work;[29]

[27] Double: [Sal.] *Cic.* 1, 2; [Cic.] *Sal.* 1. Single: [Sal.] *Cic.* 5, 6; [Cic.] *Sal.* 4, 13, 15. One oration also has a double name as the final address and one in the middle: [Cic.] *Sal.* 10, 21.

[28] Double only at Gel. 5. 13. 6, 20. 6. 11; Sen. *Suas.* 7. 9, *Con.* 2. 4. 13.

[29] Tac. *Dial.* 1. 1; Col. 1 *pr.* 2, 1. 1. 15, 2. 1. 1, 3. 1. 1, etc.; Quint. *Inst.* 1 *pr.* 6, 4 *pr.* 1, 6 *pr.* 1; Var. *R.* 2 *pr.* 6, 2. 11. 12. Cf. also [Cic.] *Rhet. Her.* 1. 1 and SL *pr.*

Cicero almost always uses single names to dedicatees[30] but can also employ double ones (*Top.* 1). It is likely that dedications can be viewed as more or less formal, and it is also probable that the need to identify a dedicatee clearly would lead to the use of multiple names for reasons separate from those governing other addresses.

Other prose authors give inconclusive results, largely because of their small numbers of nominal addresses to Roman men. The poets, as we have seen, very rarely use multiple names in address; we can now explain this tendency as the natural result of the lack of formal oratorical settings in poetry. Those double names that do occur seem to be provided largely for identification of a dedicatee or other contemporary figure.[31]

The rules governing the use of single versus multiple names are thus probably the same in all texts examined: single names are the rule in informal settings, while in formal ones multiple names are often used, though single names are common there as well when the speaker is indicating a lack of deference for the addressee and in the midst of speeches which have already used one or more double-name addresses to the same character. As triple names are so rare in address, it is not really possible to determine from our data whether they are in fact more formal than double names in address usage, but since address usage of multiple names seems on the whole to follow Adams's rules of referential usage on other points, it is most likely that triple names were more formal than double ones in address as well as referential use.

There remains the issue of which name or names is chosen. When one name is used, it is normally the cognomen in our data: cognomina account for 78% of single-name addresses, gentilicia represent another 16%, and praenomina only 6%. The predominance of cognomina is especially striking when one considers that some of the characters addressed do not have a cognomen at all. Adams has studied Cicero's usage on this point and concludes that because of the aristocratic origins of the cognomen, reference to a man of high status[32] is normally

---

[30] e.g. *ND* 1. 1, *Tusc.* 1. 1, *Fin.* 1. 1, *Orat.* 1, *Sen.* 1, *Amic.* 2, *Parad.* 1.

[31] e.g. Hor. *Carm.* 2. 11. 2, *Ep.* 1. 2. 1; Ov. *Pont.* 2. 8. 2; Juv. 15. 1.

[32] Exactly how high is a difficult issue. Some discussions of nomenclature

by cognomen when one name is used. Those of lower status, on the other hand, are often referred to by gentilicium even if they possess a cognomen, though the use of cognomina to express solidarity with a man of lower rank is not uncommon (1978: 154, 165). In private, a speaker could upgrade a man of lower status by using his cognomen, and men who rose in status would be referred to by cognomen or gentilicium according to the extent to which the speaker accepted their rise (1978: 150–1).

The division between the relative status of those addressed by cognomen and gentilicium seems to be the same in our Ciceronian address data as in Adams's mostly referential sample, except that the cognomen appears to be more common in our data: men possessing a cognomen are given this name 87% of the time in single-name address (excluding instances of the praenomen). This difference between address and reference is not surprising, since addresses are normally used in the presence of the addressee and thus do not lend themselves to the kind of downgrading behind the referent's back that Adams found in referential usage. Many of the addressees who receive gentilicia rather than cognomina are nobles whose cognomina were not in general use.[33] Others are men of lesser rank.[34] Atticus, who rose in rank, is addressed at first as *Pomponi* (*Att.* 3. 4, 3. 9. 2, 3. 22. 3, etc.) and later as *Attice* (*Att.* 6. 1. 20, 6. 2. 9, 6. 6. 4, etc.).

An additional complication not discussed by Adams, however, is that men with more than one cognomen can be

---

draw the line between nobles and non-nobles (for the Roman definition of 'noble' see Shackleton Bailey 1986), others between senators and non-senators.

[33] P. Clodius Pulcher, *Clodi* at *Att.* 1. 16. 9, *frag. orat.* 15. 32b; Q. Hortensius Hortalus, *Hortensi* at *Ver.* 1. 27, 36, 99, etc.; Ser. Sulpicius Rufus, *Sulpici* at *Mur.* 25; C. Cassius Longinus, *Cassi* at *Fam.* 12. 1. 1; C. Laelius Sapiens, *Laeli* at *Rep.* 1. 20, 31, 33, etc. See Adams (1978: 152–3). P. Sulpicius Rufus in the *De Oratore*, who is addressed only as *Sulpici* (1. 99, 104, 132, etc.), may fall in this category as well; Cicero never uses his cognomen in either address or reference, and there was another Sulpicius Rufus who did not make use of his cognomen (Adams 1978: 153).

[34] C. Fannius Chaerea, *Fanni* at *Q. Rosc.* 8, 16, 24, etc.; A. Cluentius Habitus, *Cluenti* at *Clu.* 149; C. Fannius Strabo, *Fanni* at *Amic.* 9, 25. See Adams (1978: 154–5).

addressed or referred to by cognomen in more than one way, and such a choice may be significant as well. In the *De Re Publica*, for example, one of the characters is Publius Cornelius Scipio Aemilianus Africanus, who could theoretically be addressed by name in more than 20 different ways. His nephew Q. Aelius Tubero always uses the address *Africane*, which is clearly flattering because the name commemorates a military victory (1. 15, 16, 26, 2. 64), but C. Laelius Sapiens, an older man whom Aemilianus respected like a father (1. 18), normally uses the more neutral *Scipio* (1. 30, 54, 59, 71, 3. 45, 4. 4) and only once *Africane* (1. 46). In single-name reference to Aemilianus, Cicero normally uses *Scipio* (1. 14, 15, 16, etc.) but sometimes *Africanus* (1. 17, 18, 38, etc.). The name *Aemilianus*, frequently used by modern writers because it is the only one by which this Publius Cornelius Scipio Africanus could be distinguished from his adoptive grandfather of the same name (who also appears in the *Republic* and is there known as *Africanus*),[35] is never used in this dialogue in either address or reference. This omission is presumably because *Aemilianus*, recalling as it does the fact that its referent was originally born into the family of the Aemilii, is out of place in a work which emphasizes his family heritage as a Scipio.

Cicero exploits Aemilianus' variety of names when depicting a conversation among members of his family in the *Somnium Scipionis* (*Rep.* 6). The elder Africanus appears in a dream to his adopted grandson Aemilianus, who finds him alarming, and with the address *Scipio* urges him not to fear the apparition but to heed its words (6. 11). He foretells the young man's future successes, including the destruction of Carthage which will entitle him to the cognomen *Africanus*,[36] and then twice

---

[35] *Rep.* 1. 27, 6. 10, 15, 17, 20, 26.

[36] It is unclear whether Scipio Aemilianus could be called *Africanus* before the destruction of Carthage in 146 BC. His grandfather says of that event *hanc [Karthaginem] hoc biennio consul evertes, eritque cognomen id tibi per te partum, quod habes adhuc hereditarium a nobis* (Cic. *Rep.* 6. 11) ('This city you will within the next two years overthrow as consul, and you will acquire by your own merits the cognomen which until now you have had as an inheritance from us'); this suggests that in Cicero's view *Africanus* was in some sense part of Scipio Aemilianus' name before 146, but in that case it must also have belonged to his adoptive father (as indeed the grandfather's *nobis* suggests), of whom it does not seem to be used in extant sources. My suspicion is that the

addresses him as *Africane* (12, 13). The ghost of Aemilianus' real father, L. Aemilius Paulus, then appears and is greeted with hugs and tears rather than fear; he addresses his son affectionately with his praenomen, *Publi* (15), and then calls him by his adoptive cognomen, *Scipio*, when exhorting him to imitate the elder Africanus (16). Aemilianus does not address his father by name, but he does so address his adoptive grandfather, calling him respectfully *Africane* (26).

A very different use of multiple cognomina can be seen in the *Pro Cluentio*. There Cicero attacks C. Aelius Paetus Staienus, whom he consistently refers to as *Staienus*[37] and never addresses. He does, however, quote an ingratiating address from another man to Staienus, and this uses the other cognomen, *Paetus*. Cicero describes the incident as follows:

Tum appellat hilari voltu hominem Bulbus ut blandissime potest: 'Quid tu' inquit 'Paete?'—hoc enim sibi Staienus cognomen ex imaginibus Aeliorum delegerat ne, si se Ligurem fecisset, nationis magis suae quam generis uti cognomine videretur—'qua de re mecum locutus es, quaerunt a me ubi sit pecunia.' (72)

Then Bulbus, with a smiling face, addressed the man as flatteringly as he could: 'Paetus', he said—for Staienus had picked out for himself this cognomen from the ancestors of the Aelii lest, if he had called himself *Ligur*, he should be thought to take his name from his nationality [i.e. to be a Ligurian] rather than from his family— 'Guess what? On the subject you spoke to me about, they are asking me where the money is.'

Clearly Cicero's normal use of *Staienus* is as conscious, and as significant, a choice as this use of *Paetus*.

Other authors do not appear to follow Cicero's status distinction between cognomen and gentilicium, whether in address or in reference. Salomies argues that in Cicero's day the normal form of single-name reference was by cognomen for all men who had one, regardless of rank, unless that cognomen

cognomen *Africanus* was not part of Aemilianus' name before 146. Cf. Büchner (1984: 451).

[37] This name was in origin Staienus' gentilicium, but by the time of the speech it had become his adoptive cognomen, as Cicero acknowledges when he refers to the man as C. *Aelius Staienus* (65); cf. Shackleton Bailey (1992: 10).

was not in general use, in which case a gentilicium would be
used (1987: 253–4); at a later period the cognomen seems to
have been used referentially for almost everyone (Vidman
1981: 593; Jones 1991: 158).

In address, while authors other than Cicero do not make
distinctions of status, they sometimes employ the gentilicium,
even to men possessing a cognomen. A number of different
factors appear to lead occasionally to the use of the gentilicium,
though it is clear that address by cognomen is the norm in
prose, and though a number of authors (including Livy,
Petronius, Tacitus, and Fronto) never use lone gentilicia.[38]
Thus opponents use a gentilicium to Pompey (V. Max. 6. 2.
8), whose self-selected and highly flattering cognomen,
Magnus, was difficult even for his supporters to use (Adams
1978: 160–1). A gentilicium can also be used to distinguish the
addressee from another man bearing the same cognomen but a
different gentilicium (Apul. *Apol.* 46). There are a few
examples of gentilicia to famous deceased poets: Lucretius at
Sen. *Ep.* 110. 7, Horace at Suet. *Poet.* 40 (p. 45 Re.). These
addresses seem to belong to a category of literary figures,
especially poets, who can easily be referred to, as well as
addressed, with one name on account of their fame; in such
cases the name used must be the one that is standard for that
individual in such reference, not the one that ordinary address
rules would dictate.[39] The use of gentilicia to deified rulers in
the formulaic *dive Iuli* and *dive Claudi*[40] is similarly uncon-
nected to address rules.

Like prose writers, most poets[41] prefer cognomina for single-
name address, but their preference is less strong, so they
provide us with many more examples of address by gentilicium. They too seem to ignore Cicero's status distinctions

[38] In epigraphical texts, as well, most single-name addresses are by cognomen, but gentilicia occasionally occur (e.g. *ILS* 7534; *O. Claud.* 367. 9).
Notable is the alternation, apparently without a significant difference in
meaning, between *Trebi* and *Valens* in addresses to Trebius Valens at Pompeii
(e.g. *CIL* iv. 7618, 7619; cf. 7614).

[39] Cf. Jones (1996: 91) and the oft-quoted question *Tacitus es an Plinius?*
'Are you Tacitus [cognomen] or Pliny [gentilicium]?' (Plin. *Ep.* 9. 23. 3).

[40] V. Max. 1. 6. 13, 6. 8. 4; Sen. *Apoc.* 10. 4.

[41] Catullus, who uses gentilicia 76% of the time, is a notable exception; cf.
Fordyce (1961: 342).

between the two types of nomenclature. Thus Horace politely addresses Lollius Maximus, who may have been the son of a consul (E. Fraenkel 1957: 315), as *Lolli* (*Ep.* 1. 18. 1), and he calls the future emperor Tiberius *Claudi* in a highly deferential context (*Ep.* 1. 9. 1). Whereas in prose address by gentilicium is rarely used without an identifiable reason, however, in poetry it sometimes seems to occur randomly.

Metrical convenience probably contributed to the poets' more frequent and apparently unmotivated use of gentilicia. Ovid discusses the problem of unmetrical names explicitly, saying (*Pont.* 4. 12. 1–16):

> Quo minus in nostris ponaris, amice, libellis
>   nominis efficitur condicione tui,
> aut ego non alium prius hoc dignarer honore,
>   est aliquis nostrum si modo carmen honor.
> lex pedis officio fortunaque nominis obstat,
>   quaque meos adeas est via nulla modos.
> nam pudet in geminos ita nomen scindere versus,
>   desinat ut prior hoc incipiatque minor,
> et pudeat, si te, qua syllaba parte moratur,
>   artius appellem Tuticanumque vocem.
> et potes in versum Tuticani more venire,
>   fiat ut e longa syllaba prima brevis,
> aut ut ducatur, quae nunc correptius exit,
>   et sit porrecta longa secunda mora:
> his ego si vitiis ausim corrumpere nomen,
>   ridear, et merito pectus habere neger.

The shape of your name, friend, prevents your entry into my poems. I would consider no other more worthy of the honour (if our poem conveys any honour), but metrical rules and the chance form of your name prevent the exercise of my duty; there is no way in which you could enter my verse. For I am ashamed to divide your name between two lines, so that it would both end one and begin the next, and would be ashamed to shorten the long syllable and call you Tuticănus. You can also come into the verse as Tŭticanus, with the first long syllable shortened, or with the second syllable, which is now short, lengthened. If I should dare to mar your name with such flaws, I would be laughed at and be rightly said to have no understanding.

The name *Tuticanus* is a gentilicium; although some members of this family bore the cognomen *Gallus*,[42] this man cannot

---

[42] Cf. Cichorius (1922: 80–1, 324–5), but note that his identification of

have had a cognomen, or Ovid's excuse would be ludicrous. Tuticanus must have had a praenomen, but praenomina, in addition to being stylistically inappropriate, are useless in dedications because of the large number of men possessing each one. In such a situation Ovid found himself in serious trouble when the addressee's one usable name was metrically awkward; we can assume from his difficulty here that similar difficulties with other names sometimes led poets to use a gentilicium instead of the cognomen which they would ideally have preferred.

Clarity, as well as metre, probably affects the use of gentilicia. Ovid twice addresses his son-in-law P. Suillius Rufus by gentilicium (*Pont.* 4. 8. 1, 89), although the man's cognomen is metrically unproblematic. *Rufus* is a very common cognomen and thus of limited use in identification; Vidman (1981: 593) has observed that Pliny, despite his normal preference for cognomina over gentilicia in single-name reference, tends to use gentilicia for clarity when the cognomen is *Rufus*. Cicero, similarly, avoids references of the form praenomen + cognomen when the cognomen is *Rufus* or another very common name (Shackleton Bailey 1992: 6, 1995: 6, 1996: 2). Although the address *Rufe* does occur in both prose and poetry (including at Ov. *Pont.* 2. 11. 1, 28, 4. 16. 28), it is not common, and a number of the men addressed by gentilicium alone in our sample bear this cognomen; Pliny, for example, uses address by lone gentilicia only twice, and on both occasions the addressee has the cognomen *Rufus*.[43] One cannot say for certain that avoidance of a common cognomen is the main reason for Ovid's use of a gentilicium to Suillius,[44] but it was probably a factor in his decision.

Some general conclusions may be drawn about the use of

Ovid's Tuticanus with the poet (Cornelius) Gallus is incorrect; there is therefore no evidence that this member of the family shared the cognomen.

[43] *Ep.* 9. 19. 5; other men named Rufus addressed by gentilicium include Nasidienus (Hor. *S.* 2. 8. 84), Minucius (Sil. 7. 386, 9. 564), Canius (Mart. 7. 69. 1, 10. 48. 5), possibly Caelius (Catul. 58. 1, 100. 5, 8), Ser. Sulpicius (Cic. *Mur.* 25), P. Sulpicius (Cic. *De Orat.* 1. 99 etc.).

[44] It is possible that Suillius did not use his cognomen, for Tacitus refers to him repeatedly (*Ann.* 4. 31, 11. 1 ff., 13. 42, 13. 43) but never mentions the cognomen.

cognomen and gentilicium in address. While Cicero appears to make a distinction in status between the two names, no other author can be shown to do so, and thus it seems that the status distinction was not a generally accepted address rule in Latin. In prose writers the number of gentilicia declines dramatically over time, from Varro (who uses them for 61% of the single-name addresses in the *Res Rusticae*, though never to men known to possess cognomina) to the second-century authors, who virtually never use them. In poets gentilicia are often more frequent than in contemporary prose writers, and there is considerable fluctuation in usage from one poet to the next, but a sharp decline is still visible over the period from Catullus to Martial. Petronius' complete avoidance of address by gentilicium is striking. It is likely that the use of gentilicia as single-name addresses disappeared or virtually disappeared from ordinary speech during the late Republic and beginning of the empire, when address by cognomen became possible for most men and thus could be normalized as a standard form. This change must have been taking place during Cicero's lifetime, and it is possible that it was a contributing factor in his shift from use of the gentilicium to the cognomen in addresses to Atticus.

It was also possible for a man to be addressed by his praenomen, though this occurred much less frequently than address by cognomen or gentilicium. The use of praenomina has been explored not only by Adams, but also by Syme (1958), Powell (1984, cf. also 1988: 95–6), and Salomies (1987).[45] In the case of the praenomen there do not appear to be major differences between Ciceronian and non-Ciceronian usage, nor between address and referential use (cf. Salomies 1987: 252–3).

The normal use of the praenomen, in both address and reference, is for the speaker's close relatives; this usage is far

---

[45] There is also an early article on the use of the praenomen (Paoli 1925), but it is largely useless, being based on random observations rather than any systematic study of the available evidence. Later work shows that most of the author's conclusions are simply incorrect (cf. Salomies 1987: 252 n. 265); note in particular that the fiction of a 'formal' use of the praenomen can be traced to Paoli and has no basis in reality.

more common than any of the others.[46] The rare aristocratic praenomina *Appius*, *Kaeso*, and *Servius* can, however, be used freely by anyone and appear to function like cognomina;[47] this usage is perhaps most striking in Horace's address to two men as *Bibule et Servi*, which gives the first a cognomen and the second one of the special praenomina with no difference in sense (*S.* 1. 10. 86). This phenomenon could be related to the tendency for common cognomina such as *Rufus* to be replaced by gentilicia in single-naming. Perhaps an underlying factor in the choice of names was the ability of the name used to distinguish its addressee from other men, so that names which served as good distinguishing features were normally used among outsiders, while those which were less good were used (possibly as in-group identity markers, cf. p. 18) among people who would in any case know who was meant.

There are also a number of circumstances in which ordinary praenomina can be used as addresses outside the family. Sometimes they occur as expressions of contempt,[48] and they are occasionally employed by Romans in imitation of Greek usage (since Greeks, having themselves only one name, at first had a tendency to use praenomina alone of Romans).[49] In addition, praenomina can be used neutrally for fictitious characters, especially in drama; thus some of Martial's addresses by pseudonym employ praenomina,[50] though most use cognomina. On rare occasions praenomina also seem to be

---

[46] e.g. Cic. *Off.* 1. 1 (son), *De Orat.* 1. 1 (brother), *Rep.* 6. 15 (son), *De Orat.* 2. 249 (son); Luc. 9. 85 (son); Hor. *S.* 2. 3. 171, 173 (sons); Gel. 15. 7. 3 (grandson); Suet. *Aug.* 51. 3, 71. 2, etc. (stepson); Sen. *Con.* 1 *pr.* 9 (son). See Salomies (1987: 255–60); Adams (1978: 161–2); Shackleton Bailey (1996: 11). On the rarity of the praenomen elsewhere see Fordyce (1961: 342).

[47] e.g. Cic. *Fam.* 4. 1. 1, *Mur.* 9; Sil. 17. 300; Luc. 5. 188, 225; Liv. 3. 45. 6, 9. 34. 8, 10. 8. 4, 39. 37. 14, etc. See Salomies (1987: 260–3); Adams (1978: 153); Syme (1958: 173).

[48] e.g. Cic. *De Orat.* 2. 286, *Caec.* 102, *Quinct.* 38, 40, *Dom.* 47, *Mil.* 33 (though with Sextus Clodius the praenomen also serves to distinguish the addressee from Publius Clodius); Mart. 1. 5. 2, 3. 62. 8; Juv. 2. 21; Gel. 11. 8. 4. See Salomies (1987: 263–6); Adams (1978: 162); Wilkins (1892: 376); Leeman *et al.* (1981–96: iii. 329); Shackleton Bailey (1992: 6, 1996: 11).

[49] e.g. Lucil. 93–4; perhaps Enn. *Ann.* 336, 337. Cf. Powell (1984); Salomies (1987: 270–3); Baslez (1996).

[50] e.g. 2. 30. 6, 3. 11. 1, 4. 72. 1, 5. 75. 1, 10. 98. 11. See Salomies (1987: 273–5).

utilized to avoid ambiguity with other potential addressees sharing the same name except for the praenomen (Cic. *Fin.* 5. 6, 71, 86).

Address by praenomen could also have a flattering sense, for Horace advises using it in legacy-hunting:

> 'Quinte', puta, aut 'Publi' (gaudent praenomine molles auriculae), 'tibi me virtus tua fecit amicum.'
>
> *(S.* 2. 5. 32–3)

Say 'Quintus', for instance, or 'Publius' (impressionable ears love a praenomen), 'your virtue has made me your friend.'

Horace also quotes another man making a request to him with his praenomen *Quinte* (*S.* 2. 6. 37); this flattering usage is found in other authors as well, but it is not common.[51] The author who uses it the most is Petronius, in whose work the only character addressed by praenomen is the rich freedman Trimalchio. Trimalchio in fact is never addressed by any other name, and since the main difference between him and the other characters is that he is much richer and more powerful, this difference in nomenclature is likely to be connected with his status. Trimalchio is called *Gai* by one of his guests (67. 1), by his slaves (74. 7), and in an appeal (75. 2): *idem et Scintilla flens dixit ac per genium eius Gaium appellando rogare coepit ut se frangeret* 'Scintilla, weeping, said the same and, calling him *Gaius*, began to beg him by his guardian spirit to soften his stance.' The fact that the narrator specifically mentions the use of the praenomen as one of the elements of Scintilla's plea shows that it had a flattering and appeasing tone.

Persius also illustrates the flattering nature of the praenomen when he describes the obsequious use of *Marce* to address a man who used to be a slave called *Dama* but is now a freedman and consequently named *Marcus Dama* (5. 81). In this passage the flattery may come from the fact that *Marcus* is a new name and thus a symbol of the freedman's new status. That the praenomen was specially indicative of freedom is explicitly stated by the grammarian Pompeius (*GLK* v. 141. 11–13): *Sic definierunt maiores nostri, habes in antiquis artibus: praenomen est quod ad dignitatem pertinet. nullus enim servus habet*

---

[51] Aside from the passages mentioned in the text, only at Ov. *Pont.* 4. 1. 35, 4. 15. 18; Mart. 4. 55. 1, 10. 73. 8.

praenomen; non licet, non potest fieri. 'Thus our ancestors explained it, and you have it in the ancient grammatical treatises: the praenomen is what relates to rank. For no slave has a praenomen; it is not allowed, and it cannot be done.'

Yet a freed slave received not only a new praenomen, but also a new gentilicium. Address by gentilicium would have indicated a freedman's change of status just as clearly as address by praenomen, but Persius does not mention Dama's gentilicium at all, nor does Petronius mention Trimalchio's. There must be some additional reason why the praenomen was chosen for flattery in these two cases, not to mention in the situations mentioned by Horace, one of which does not involve freedmen at all.

Salomies (1987: 267–9) argues that in the first century AD and earlier slaves regularly addressed their masters by praenomen, and that the flattering use of the praenomen arose as an extension of this servile usage. There is in fact very little evidence to show which name slaves used to their masters, since in our data slaves frequently use *ere* 'master' rather than a name to address their masters and since much of the information on servile speech comes from comedy, in which the characters do not bear the *tria nomina*. As far as I know, the only preserved example of address by name from a slave to a master bearing the *tria nomina* is the address to Trimalchio in Petronius; this does indeed use the praenomen, but as the free characters also address Trimalchio as *Gai*, it is hardly a specifically servile usage.

Salomies does present evidence that slaves sometimes referred to their masters by praenomen, but this is a far cry from evidence that *address* by praenomen was so standard among slaves as to sound characteristically servile when spoken by a free man. Free men, of course, used address by praenomen frequently, to their sons, brothers, and other close male relatives. In these circumstances, even if slaves did have a tendency to use praenomina, a praenomen in the mouth of a free man is more likely to have sounded familial than servile (cf. Kiessling and Heinze 1961: 285).

That the flattery sometimes attached to the praenomen originally had a familial rather than a servile tone is also suggested by the use in Horace. Horace gives, in different passages, three addresses for flattering rich men whose money the speaker wants. Two of these are kinship terms, *frater* 'brother' and *pater* 'father' (*Ep.* 1. 6. 54), and the third is the praenomen. The utility of familial addresses in legacy-hunting is obvious: a legacy-hunter wants to get the rich man to treat him like a close relative, since it is to such relatives that Romans traditionally left their money. Addressing him as a father, brother, or other close relative is a step in the desired direction, while addressing him as a master is not.

The situation is somewhat different when an address involves two names rather than one. In such cases, Adams observes that Cicero addresses and refers to contemporary nobles with praenomen + cognomen, but to non-nobles normally with praenomen + gentilicium, even if Cicero respects them enough to use cognomina for informal, single-name reference.[52] Address between a noble and a man of lower rank could be non-reciprocal in formal situations, with the noble being addressed with praenomen + cognomen while his inferior received praenomen + gentilicium; in more informal interaction, however, the same two men might use reciprocal address by cognomen alone (Adams 1978: 150, 154). Our data from Cicero agree with Adams's findings; in this case Adams has already discussed all the address data, so the agreement needs no comment.

In reference Cicero also has two additional possibilities for double-naming, gentilicium + cognomen and cognomen + gentilicium. He seems to have considered these options rather inelegant, since he uses them primarily in letters, but they become very common in imperial literature. Cicero very rarely uses these combinations for nobles, though other authors, even those contemporary with Cicero, do so freely (Shackleton Bailey 1965–70: i. 402–3, 1995: 7–9). Adams suggests that

[52] Adams makes the distinction sound fairly clear-cut, but Shackleton Bailey notes a substantial number of exceptions (without invalidating Adams's general principle). Non-nobles, especially ones with unusual cognomina, are not infrequently referred to with praenomen + cognomen (Shackleton Bailey 1992: 5–6, 1995: 3–6, 1996: 6; but cf. Solin 1992: 499–500). Nobles not contemporary with Cicero may be named with praenomen + gentilicium and are normally so named if they lived before the 3rd cent. BC, even if they possessed cognomina (Shackleton Bailey 1996: 1–5).

both combinations of gentilicium and cognomen developed in
the late Republic in response to the existence of men of
ambiguous status, who were not entirely entitled to be named
with praenomen + cognomen but would be offended to receive
praenomen + gentilicium. The usefulness of this intermediate
system in an age of increased social mobility guaranteed its
swift acceptance (Adams 1978: 165–6). It is generally believed
that the inverted order, cognomen + gentilicium, came about
through a partial equation between praenomen and cognomen
in speakers' minds when cognomina started to replace praenomina as the names chiefly used to identify individuals within a
family, so that the cognomen was used in the position formerly
occupied by the praenomen.[53]

Almost all Cicero's double-name addresses use one of the
two older forms of naming, and the one example of a newer
type of name address in his work is a complicated insult:
L. Calpurnius Piso Caesoninus, whose mother came from an
obscure family with the gentilicium Calventius, is addressed as
Caesonine Calventi (*Prov.* 7). All that can be concluded from
this is that Cicero normally avoids the newer forms in address,
though he uses them in reference.

As in the case of the use of cognomen and gentilicium
individually, other authors do not always adhere to Cicero's
status distinctions for double-name usage in address or reference. Livy, who provides by far the most data on this point,
uses praenomen + gentilicium for 89% of his double-name
addresses and praenomen + cognomen for all the others. In
his works praenomen + cognomen is reserved for nobles as in
Cicero,[54] and non-nobles always receive praenomen + gentilicium, but nobles as well frequently receive praenomen + gentilicium like non-nobles.[55] Especially notable is L. Aemilius

[53] Adams (1978: 165); Wiseman (1970: 211–13); Syme (1958: 174); see also
Shackleton Bailey (1992: 7–8). Gudeman (1914: 185) incorrectly equates this
type of inversion with other, rarer types but provides some interesting further
information.

[54] Used only for M. (Claudius) Marcellus (25. 6. 1, 5), Ser. (Sulpicius)
Galba (45. 37. 9), L. (Aemilius) Paulus (22. 39. 4, 17), P. (Cornelius Scipio)
Nasica (44. 38. 3), P. (Cornelius) Scipio (38. 48. 7), L. (Cornelius) Scipio (37.
7. 8, 38. 48. 7).

[55] Ap. Claudius (Pulcher) at 39. 36. 6, P. Cornelius (Scipio) at 28. 41. 1,
Q. Fabius (Maximus) at 28. 43. 7, etc.

Paulus, who while consul is addressed by the same speaker, in the same speech, both as *L. Aemili* (22. 39. 1) and *L. Paule* (22. 39. 4, 17), without any significant difference in tone.

For Livy, as for Cicero, there are only two possible forms of double-name address but four options for double-name reference.[56] Some other authors also restrict themselves to these two address possibilities, though because of their less frequent use of double names the restriction is less significant. The writer of the pseudo-Caesarian *De Bello Africo* uses double names for Caesar's addresses to a group of officers he is dismissing for misconduct (54. 4, 5); most receive praenomen + cognomen, but one receives praenomen + gentilicium. None of these men is known from other sources, so we cannot be sure of their status, though the fact that they are unknown, and that their names are not recognizably noble, may suggest that their status was not of the highest. It is, however, notable that the one addressed with praenomen + gentilicium is a Fonteius, and none of the known holders of that gentilicium had cognomina. It is thus likely that Caesar is depicted as using praenomen + cognomen to his officers, even when displeased with them, whenever they had cognomina, and that the only time the gentilicium is used is when the addressee has no cognomen. Columella repeatedly addresses the dedicatee of his work, Publius Silvinus, with praenomen + cognomen (1 *pr.* 2 etc.); the man is otherwise unknown. The author of the *Ad Herennium* uses both praenomen + gentilicium (1. 1, 4. 18, 4. 47) and praenomen + cognomen (2. 17, 4. 38); many of his addressees are difficult to identify, but at least one of the men addressed with praenomen + cognomen was an aristocrat. Pliny the elder addresses Cicero with praenomen + gentilicium (*Nat.* 7. 116). Fronto uses praenomen + gentilicium, though his addressee is of the highest rank possible (*M. Aureli*, 105. 21).

Other authors, however, prefer the newer address forms. Valerius Maximus uses praenomen + gentilicium only to characters without a generally accepted cognomen (2. 2. 3, 2. 6. 8), while those with cognomina receive either gentilicium + cognomen (2. 7. 6) or cognomen + gentilicium (5. 3. 5), never

---

[56] Livy uses both gentilicium + cognomen and cognomen + gentilicium in reference, e.g. 4. 14. 6, 4. 23. 1. Cf. Ogilvie (1965: 570).

praenomen + cognomen. Suetonius uses gentilicium + cognomen (*Aug.* 23. 2). Apuleius addresses the judge before whom he delivers his *Apology* both with cognomen + gentilicium (1) and with gentilicium + cognomen (28, 35, 91, 99), while one of his opponents receives gentilicium + cognomen as well (30, 46). Tacitus uses only the form cognomen + gentilicium for double-name address (*Dial.* 1. 1), and the same is true of Varro, despite his early date.[57]

Some authors use both earlier and later types of address but make a distinction in their use. Quintilian consistently uses cognomen + gentilicium for his own double-name addresses (*Inst.* 1 *pr.* 6, 4 *pr.* 1, 6 *pr.* 1) but quotes earlier orators using the earlier forms (e.g. 6. 3. 86). In the same way the younger Seneca addresses a contemporary with gentilicium + cognomen (*Ben.* 3. 1. 1, 4. 1. 1, 5. 1. 3) but uses praenomen + cognomen for the historical figure M. (Porcius) Cato (Uticensis).[58]

The poets are divided in their practice. Horace uses both gentilicium + cognomen (*Ep.* 1. 3. 1) and cognomen + gentilicium (*Ep.* 1. 2. 1, *Carm.* 2. 2. 3). Juvenal uses gentilicium + cognomen (8. 39–40, 15. 1). Martial occasionally uses praenomen + gentilicium[59] or cognomen + gentilicium (6. 85. 1), but most frequently gentilicium + cognomen.[60] Catullus addresses Cicero with praenomen + gentilicium.[61] Ennius and Lucilius use only praenomen + gentilicium,[62] but Valerius Soranus (early first century BC) uses praenomen + cognomen (frag. 7).[63]

Other combinations of names occasionally appear as well.

[57] *R.* 2 *pr.* 6, 2. 11. 12, both addressed to the otherwise unknown dedicatee Turranius Niger.

[58] *Ep.* 14. 13; Cato was noble enough to be called *M. Cato* in the heading of Cicero's letters to him (*Fam.* 15. 3, 15. 6).

[59] 1. 107. 1, 10. 44. 1; the first of these addressees had a cognomen which Martial uses elsewhere.

[60] 4. 71. 1, 7. 41. 1, 7. 47. 1, 7. 68. 1, 10. 33. 1, 11. 52. 1, 11. 106. 1, 12. 95. 4.

[61] 49. 2; it has been argued that the flattery in this poem is insincere, and an address to Cicero as a man of less than noble status would fit this interpretation well. Since the *Marrucine* of 12. 1 is probably not a cognomen (Nisbet and Hubbard 1978: 167), this is Catullus' only double-name address.

[62] Enn. *Ann.* 104; Lucil. 1238. Probably neither addressee possessed a cognomen.

[63] The only other possible example of this combination in poetry, to my knowledge, is *Sexte . . . Sabine* at [Verg.] *Cat.* 5. 6, but the names are there so separated that they should probably be considered two distinct addresses.

9.52.1-2⟨

The elder Seneca quotes an address by cognomen + praenomen
(*Con.* 2. 4. 13), and Ovid perhaps one by gentilicium + praenomen (*Pont.* 4. 1. 1–2; see Helzle 1989: 44). Ovid also uses
address by cognomen + cognomen (*Pont.* 2. 8. 2, 3. 5. 6), a
combination which becomes common in referential use during
the empire (Vidman 1981: 588).

Inscriptions and graffiti show a variety of forms for multiple-
name address. There are some examples of praenomen + gentilicium, most of them early,[64] and many, mostly later, of
gentilicium + cognomen, cognomen + gentilicium, and cognomen + cognomen.[65] Longer nominal addresses on inscriptions
are not restricted to the *tria nomina*; in keeping with their
purpose of identification, they can include additional cognomina and even filiation.[66]

We can thus see a certain progression in all genres from the
use of the Ciceronian address forms at an early date to the use
of gentilicium and cognomen, in either order, at a later date.
This progression, however, does not take place at the same rate
in all authors; Varro and Horace use only the newer address
forms and Livy only the older ones, although Livy wrote at a
later date. When the newer forms are used, they tend to be
given to all addressees regardless of status, but the use of the
older forms is problematic. For Cicero praenomen + gentilicium may have been an address form that indicated non-noble
status when employed to a man with a cognomen, but other
authors use it freely to men of even the highest rank, without
any derogatory implications. It has been suggested that for
Pliny reference by praenomen + gentilicium sounded formal
and archaic in contrast to the more usual gentilicium + cognomen (Sherwin-White 1966: 113; Vidman 1981: 594), and this
seems to be true of such addresses in many imperial authors.

Evidence for the use of praenomen + cognomen is divided for
both address and reference. Some non-Ciceronian sources
appear to use this type of reference as a noble form of
nomenclature (Syme 1958: 172), but Pliny apparently uses it

---

[64] e.g. *ILLRP* 962, 1111; *CIL* iv. 10643.

[65] e.g. *ILLRP* 1109; *CIL* iv. 343, 2098, 2312, 4338, 5140, 5349, 5574, 7247,
7429; *ILS* 1967.

[66] e.g. *ILLRP* 692a, 961, 1141; *CIL* iv. 1901, 2413d (cf. *CIL* iv, p. 743),
8040; *ILS* 8123, 8125, 8139.

primarily to refer to historical characters (Sherwin-White 1966: 113; Vidman 1981: 593–4). In address, the evidence of the *De Bello Africo*, and probably that of Columella, suggests that some authors would use praenomen + cognomen to anyone possessing a cognomen, regardless of his status, while Livy and perhaps Seneca, like Cicero, restrict praenomen + cognomen to nobles. This conflicting evidence cannot be resolved; all one can say is that some authors followed the Ciceronian usage while others apparently did not. The status distinction in the use of this form of the name thus clearly did exist in the Latin language as a whole, not just in Cicero's mind, but at the same time it was not so strong that it could not be ignored.

The fact that the association of praenomen + cognomen with nobility is the only one of Cicero's status distinctions for which there is evidence in other authors may be connected with the fact that this is the only one of these distinctions for which the Latin language provides a logical motivation. To the extent that the use of praenomen + cognomen was confined to the Republican aristocracy, it was restricted to the group of men most likely to possess inherited rather than individual cognomina (see above, p. 48). Since an inherited cognomen was passed down within a specific family, it always went with the same gentilicium (or, in the case of cognomina used by several families, with the same few gentilicia): when a Roman heard *Scipio*, he could automatically supply *Cornelius*, because every Scipio was also a Cornelius. In terms of the information it conveyed about its bearer's position in society, the gentilicium was a Roman's most important name throughout the period of this study; it was so central that it was often called simply the *nomen* 'name', and to this day ancient Romans are arranged in alphabetical order by gentilicium in reference works, just as modern Europeans are listed under their last names. It was thus normally important to include the gentilicium in referring to an unfamiliar Roman, unless he possessed a cognomen from which his gentilicium could be understood. The naming system praenomen + cognomen may well have evolved as an aristocratic system because reference to a noble as *P. Scipio* carried more information than reference to him as *P. Cornelius*, while in reference to a man with a non-inherited cognomen, praenomen + gentilicium carried more important information than praenomen + cognomen. The breakdown of the predictable Republican system of aristocratic nomenclature, however, made omission of the gentilicium increasingly impractical and thus led to the abandonment of the form praenomen + cognomen in the imperial period.

Addresses to Roman women are inevitably different from those to men, for they are based on a different system of nomenclature. Before the development of the gentilicium, Roman women possessed praenomina like those of men (*Gaia*, *Marca*, *Publia*, etc.), and although women belonging to other Italian tribes retained their praenomina into the historical period and bore two names like men, the feminine praenomen was abandoned at Rome by the third century BC (Kajanto 1972: 13, 14, 17, 19). In most cases the hereditary cognomina of the nobility were not given to girls either, so that a daughter of P. Cornelius Scipio would be simply *Cornelia* (Kajanto 1977b: 150). Thus from the third century BC (or earlier) until the beginning of the empire, most Roman women had only one official name, the gentilicium (though the use of praenomina seems to have survived in some rural areas as an archaic feature: Kajanto 1972: 26).

Naturally this nomenclature posed problems of clarity in families of several daughters, all of whom had identical names, and this difficulty was solved by the creation of a series of unofficial nicknames for daughters, usually based on their order of birth: *Maior*, *Minor*, *Maxima*, *Prima*, *Secunda*, *Tertia*, *Quarta*, etc. (Kajanto 1972: 28–9). The situation changed with the rise of individual cognomina at the beginning of the empire, for that shift was accompanied by an extension of these cognomina to women, and this in turn led to the disuse of the nicknames (Kajanto 1972: 30; cf. Gallivan 1992: 58–60).

In studying nominal addresses to women we face several difficulties. Referential use of women's names has not been studied in the way that Adams studied male names, so we are tackling a relatively small body of vocatives in ignorance of the conventions governing the use of the same names in other cases. If in the case of men referential and address uses of names are closely related, which they seem to be, the lack of such background is serious in the case of women. In addition,

Cicero very rarely addresses women, making our body of
nominal addresses to women not only smaller but much less
cohesive and more difficult to handle than the equivalent
corpus of male addresses, of which the most useful part is
the Ciceronian material. Moreover, as less is known about
individual Roman women than about men, it is often more
difficult to identify a female addressee and find out whether she
had any names in addition to the one by which she is addressed.
Despite these difficulties, however, some observations can be
made.

In our literary data, women are never addressed by more
than one name, even when they certainly possessed two. This
is not surprising, since women are rarely addressed in the type
of formal situation that would trigger double-naming for men.
Two women are addressed by name in orations: Clodia in
Cicero's *Pro Caelio* (50) and Apuleius' wife Pudentilla (*Apol.*
85). As Clodia probably had only one name, it would be rash
to conclude on the basis of Pudentilla alone that women with
two names could not be addressed by both in a formal
situation.

In epigraphical texts women, like men, can be addressed
freely by two names and even by filiation.[67] That these
addresses were not entirely natural and occurred only for the
sake of clarity is suggested by one inscription which opens by
addressing the deceased woman as *Herennia Crocine* to identify
her and then asks the reader to say to her *Crocine, sit tibi terra
levis* 'Crocine, may the earth over you be light' (*ILS* 8130; cf.
EDH 002876).

Republican women are virtually always addressed by gentilicium when names are used, though some of them must have
had nicknames as well. Thus Cicero calls his wife *Terentia*
(*Fam.* 14. 1. 5, 14. 2. 2, 14. 3. 1, etc.), his brother Quintus
addresses his as *Pomponia* (*Att.* 5. 1. 3), Varro addresses his as
Fundania (*R.* 1 *pr.* 1), etc.[68] The love poets of the first century
BC bypass the Roman name system and normally use pseudonyms to women, typically Greek names and ethnics.[69]

---

[67] e.g. *ILLRP* 934; *CIL* iv. 9223; *ILS* 8125, 8139, 8190.

[68] Also *Porcia*, V. Max. 4. 6. 5; *Iulia*, Luc. 10. 77; *Cornelia*, Luc. 5. 726, 8.
42; *Scribonia*, Prop. 4. 11. 55; *Cornelia*, Juv. 6. 167.

[69] e.g. *Lesbia* (Catul. 5. 1), *Delia* (Tib. 1. 1. 57), *Lydia* (Hor. *Carm.* 1. 8. 1),

I have found only one example of address by feminine
nickname, and it is undoubtedly significant that this is addressed to a little girl by her father (*mea Tertia*, Cic. *Div.* 1.
103). It is likely that such addresses were common to girls in
families with more than one daughter, but once the girl
married and left home she seems to have been addressed by
her real name; that is, her gentilicium.

As women acquired cognomina, however, the address situation altered dramatically. Augustus' wife, who did not have a
cognomen,[70] is addressed as *Livia* both by the emperor and by
others,[71] but his granddaughter is addressed as *Agrippina*
(Suet. *Cal.* 8. 4). Petronius quotes a number of addresses to
women, and those names which are not Greek appear to be
cognomina: *Fortunata* (47. 5), *Scintilla* (69. 2). Apuleius addresses his wife with her cognomen *Pudentilla* (*Apol.* 85).
Martial, when addressing real contemporary women, normally
uses the cognomen: *Flacilla* (5. 34. 1), *Polla* (7. 21. 2, 7. 23. 3,
10. 64. 1), *Marcella* (12. 21. 1), *Nigrina* (4. 75. 1), but *Iulia* (6.
13. 1) and *Sempronia* (12. 52. 3), both to women who probably
did not have cognomina. When inventing pseudonyms for
women, however, Martial uses address by cognomen and
gentilicium with about equal frequency.[72] This difference
could be due to the force of earlier tradition in favour of
female address by gentilicia, for Martial's pseudonyms for
males are much more often cognomina than gentilicia. I have
found no other addresses by gentilicium to women of the
imperial period.[73]

Cynthia (Prop. 1. 3. 22), *Phylli* (Hor. *Carm.* 4. 11. 3), *Lyde* (Hor. *Carm.* 3. 28.
3), *Lyce* (Hor. *Carm.* 3. 10. 1). The probability that *Lesbius* (Catul. 79. 1; cf.
Syndikus 1984–90: iii. 37) is intended to suggest Clodius indicates that some
of these names could be treated as gentilicia on occasion.

[70] Unless one counts *Augusta*, by which she does not seem to be addressed
in extant sources.
[71] Suet. *Aug.* 99. 1, *Cl.* 4. 1 etc.; Ov. *Pont.* 3. 4. 96, 4. 13. 29; *Epic. Drusi* 3
etc. Seneca also quotes an address to her by her adoptive gentilicium, *Iulia*
(*Dial.* 6. 4. 3).
[72] Cognomina: e.g. *Paula* 9. 10. 1, *Catulla* 8. 54. 3, *Maximina* 2. 41. 6;
gentilicia: e.g. *Claudia* 8. 60. 2, *Laelia* 10. 68. 2, *Caelia* 7. 30. 1.
[73] The woman whom Seneca frequently addresses as *Marcia* in *Dial.* 6 was
the daughter of A. Cremutius Cordus, and thus *Marcia* is probably her
cognomen rather than her gentilicium; even if it is a second gentilicium, such
second gentilicia seem to have functioned as cognomina when borne by

In the case of women, then, the nominal address system does not appear to display any of the complexity we have seen in the case of men. We can tentatively conclude that when women did not have cognomina, they were addressed by gentilicium unless they had sisters and were still living with them, in which case they could be addressed by a nickname. When women did have cognomina, however, they were apparently always addressed by cognomen.

women (Kajanto 1977*b*: 156), and thus the address is for all practical purposes an address by cognomen.

2

Titles

Cum voco te dominum, noli tibi, Cinna, placere:
saepe etiam servum sic resaluto tuum.

(Mart. 5. 57)

Don't get too self-satisfied, Cinna, when I call you
'master': I often greet your slave that way too.

TITLES are expressions of respect. The Latin title *dominus*
'master' expressed so much respect that the early emperors did
not presume to demand it, and its assumption by later emperors was considered proof that the Romans had been reduced
to slavery. How then could Martial use it to a slave? And if the
principal meaning of *dominus* is a master, often of slaves, why
are there no attested uses of *domine* addressed by a slave to his
master? If the feminine *domina* was a term of affection for a
mistress, why are women never addressed as *domina* in classical
love poetry? And if the emperor Trajan made a point of
refusing the title *dominus*, why did Pliny consistently address
him as *domine*? The problems surrounding the use of *domine*
and *domina* are complex and cannot be properly answered
without a unified study of Latin titles.

Latin titles, and particularly *dominus/a*, have been studied in
great detail over a period of several centuries. Unfortunately,
despite the effort expended, scholars have failed to reach a full
understanding of this term, especially in its address usage.[1]

---

[1] Discussion of *dominus/a* can be found in numerous notes and commentaries; more lengthy treatments include those of Lipsius (1607: 509–10),
Spanheim (1671: 729–33), Eckhel (1798: viii. 364–6), Schoener (1881: 26–
33), Mommsen (1887–8: ii. 760–3), Hardy (1889: 78), Neumann *et al.* (1903),
Bang (1921: 82–8; often cited in English translation as Friedlaender (1913),
but note that Friedlaender's appendix is really by Bang and that the translation, based on an earlier edition, is somewhat inaccurate), Kapp (1930),
Svennung (1958: 25, 338–46), Sherwin-White (1966: 557), Adams (1995: 118–
19).

This failure results from three causes: consideration of one or
two meanings of this multifaceted term in isolation from other
contemporary uses,[2] confusion of the referential and vocative
meanings, which are different,[3] and confusion of Latin *dom-
inus/a* with the equivalent Greek terms δεσπότης/δέσποινα and
κύριος/κυρία.[4] The present discussion will thus attempt to study
the address usage of *domine* and *domina* as a whole and as
distinct from (though not, as it turns out, completely independent of) both referential usage and Greek usage.

The basic lexical meaning of *dominus* is an owner, etymo-
logically the owner of a house but by extension also the owner
of anything capable of being possessed, such as land, slaves,
animals, and material goods. One would thus expect the
vocative *domine* to be used primarily by slaves to their masters,
while *domina* should be used by slaves to their mistresses.
There is, however, startlingly little evidence of such a usage.
The masculine *domine*, as far as I can tell, never occurs in Latin
literature as an address from a slave to his master, while
domina, though it does occur, is very rare in this sense and
comparatively late. Moreover, the only such examples of
domina I have found (Petr. 105. 8, Apul. *Met.* 5. 2) are in
texts where this address is used generally by people other than
slaves, and these passages seem more likely to be examples of
that general usage than sole proof of a specifically servile use.[5]

This omission is not due to a lack of addresses by slaves to

[2] Virtually all discussions of the term have this flaw, which largely results
from the fact that the word is part of the imperial titulature, amatory
language, and several other categories of speech which do not normally
overlap.

[3] Mommsen (1887–8: ii. 762 n. 3) did notice this distinction but failed to
appreciate its full extent, and later scholars often failed to heed his observa-
tion.

[4] The identification between *dominus/a* and κύριος/a is complete for some
scholars, e.g. Bang (1921: 83); in earlier writers there is sometimes a tendency
to equate *dominus* more with δεσπότης, e.g. Eckhel (1798: viii. 366). These
identifications are partly based on equivalences assumed by ancient writers;
such ancient assumptions could illuminate the meaning of the Latin words
and will be discussed below. Nevertheless, evidence for the use of κύριος or
δεσπότης (the two terms are in fact far from identical) in Greek is not in itself
evidence for the use of *dominus* in Latin, except in cases where the Greek
author was clearly thinking of the Latin word rather than the Greek one.

[5] Cf. their classification by Kapp (1930: 1938. 55–6).

their masters in Latin literature, for such do occur not infrequently, especially in comedy. Slaves in such situations are not obliged to use a title (cf. p. 234), but when a title is used, it is *ere/a* rather than *domine/a*.[6] *Erus* and *era* also mean 'master' and 'mistress', but there is an important distinction between these words and *dominus/a* in referential usage. When the latter term is applied to a master of slaves in early Latin, it is used primarily by free men and women, while slaves themselves normally (though not always) refer to their owners as *erus/a*.[7] No reason for this distinction has ever been proposed, but it seems to me that slaves might have objected to a word meaning 'owner' because it put them in the same class as inanimate objects; perhaps they preferred *erus* (which is more often translatable as 'master' than as 'owner') because it referred less harshly to their own status. The theory that slaves used *erus* as something of a euphemism could also explain why this word does not seem to belong exclusively to low-register language: it is used by slaves notably more often than by free men, but the latter do not treat the word as belonging to an unacceptable register.

Thus *dominus/a* was much less a part of the speech of slaves than was *erus/a*. This distinction in referential usage indicates that the lack of evidence for the use of *domine/a* as an address from slaves to their masters and mistresses is not an accident of survival, but a reflection of actual practice: when slaves used a title to address their masters or mistresses, they used the title that they preferred in referential usage as well, *erus/a*. They did not use *domine/a*, because the titles *dominus* and *domina* were not a normal part of their language.

There is, however, one potential problem with this explanation: most of the evidence for *erus/a* comes from comedy, and the word is rare in later Latin; at some point it must have disappeared from use, as it has no descendants in the Romance languages (Ernout and Meillet 1979: 202). Could *domine/a* have

---

[6] *Ere*: Pl. *Cas.* 632, etc.; Ter. *Eu.* 57, etc.; Hor. *S.* 2. 3. 265; *era*: Pl. *Cist.* 544, etc.; Ter. *Ad.* 295, etc.; Sen. *Med.* 426, etc.

[7] Köhm (1905: 167): '*erus* ist das der Sklavensprache angehörige Wort, während *dominus* mehr den Herrn als Besitzer des Sklaven bezeichnet und in der Mehrzahl der Fälle von Nichtsklaven gebraucht wird.' Cf. Ernout and Meillet (1979: 201).

replaced *ere/a* as a normal address from slave to master sometime after the death of Terence, and if so, when? The rarity of
erus/a outside comedy tells us little by itself, for a term used
primarily by slaves is bound to be relatively scarce in genres
other than comedy, even if its actual popularity does not
decline over time. Yet the lack of attestation in Romance
makes it certain that *erus/a* did in fact disappear—the difficulty
lies in establishing the date of that disappearance. Seneca
depicts nurses using only *era* to their mistresses, never
domina (*Phaed.* 267, *Med.* 426), but given the elevated language
of Senecan tragedy these attestations could be archaisms.
Horace in his *Satires* has a slave use *ere* rather than *domine* to
his master (2. 3. 265), and this is a context in which we would
expect verisimilitude more than archaism. In referential usage
erus/a is attested in Cicero (*Rep.* 1. 64), the elder Seneca (*Con.*
3. 9), and possibly Petronius,[8] as well as in a number of texts
which have little bearing on conversational usage.[9] It thus
seems that *ere/a* probably went out of use sometime after
Horace; at that point slaves might have started using *domine/a*
to their masters and mistresses, though there is little evidence
that they actually did.

It thus seems that for Latin at least until the time of
Horace, we can believe the evidence of our data that *domine*
and *domina* were not used as addresses from slaves to their
masters and mistresses. Such a result has important consequences for our understanding of the function of these
addresses. Most previous explanations of the attested uses of
domine assume that they grew out of the use from a slave to

[8] 74. 15, 105. 6. There are textual problems in both places; see W.-F.
Friedrich (1936: 850).

[9] Cf. W.-F. Friedrich (1936). One passage in particular, while highly
atypical (but cf. Ennius *incerta* 46), may provide additional evidence of a
classical distinction between *era* and *domina*: *dea, magna dea, Cybebe, dea
domina Dindymi, procul a mea tuos sit furor omnis, era, domo* (Catul. 63. 91–3).
Here the author is acting so servilely and abjectly as to use the address *era*,
otherwise attested only in the mouths of actual slaves. *Era* stands alone, as is
virtually always the case elsewhere; we have seen (pp. 32–3) that such
isolation is often the sign of an address in common use, while purely literary
terms are more likely to be part of a larger phrase including words not in the
vocative case, as is *domina* here. This typological argument suggests that, for
Catullus, *era* in the mouth of a servant was a non-literary address and *domina*
a literary one.

his master;[10] since this usage now seems not to have existed, new explanations are needed for all the other uses. All but one (imperial titulature) of these uses are senses in which the referential usage is comparatively rare, and it is thought that the referential usage in these cases is derivative from the address usage, rather than the other way around.[11]

The earliest evidence for the use of *domine* or *domina* as an address is a fragment of Lucilius (second century BC): *cum mei me adeunt servuli, non dominam ego appellem meam?* (730) 'When my servants are in attendance, should I not address my beloved as "mistress"?'[12] The usage in question here is that of *dominus/a* for a lover, one which is well attested in referential usage in love poetry.[13]

English 'mistress' is an obvious but misleading parallel for *domina* in this sense. In current English, 'mistress' is used only of a woman who is involved with a man to whom she is not married, while Latin *domina* is a much broader term, covering 'mistresses', wives, and women who are desired from afar but remain as uninterested in their admirers as Galatea was in Polyphemus.[14] In addition, 'mistress' exists only in the feminine, while in Latin a male lover or object of desire can just as easily be termed *dominus* (e.g. Ov. *Ars* 1. 314) as a female *domina*. And the Latin terms, as Lucilius shows, were used as addresses, whereas in current English 'mistress' is not a plausible address from a lover to the object of his affections.

Although the classical poets use both *dominus* and *domina* of lovers in referential usage, it is striking that no Latin poet ever addresses his beloved as *domina* in extant literature.[15] The

[10] e.g. Mommsen (1887–8: ii. 761 n. 1).

[11] Kapp (1930: 1924. 30–2, 1937. 83).

[12] Although it is certainly open to dispute, the interpretation of the passage expressed in my translation is the traditional one (cf. Charpin 1978–9: ii. 161; Marx 1904–5: ii. 261; Warmington 1938: iii. 239), though Krenkel (1970: ii. 403) translates *Wenn meine eigenen jungen Sklaven sich fragend an mich wenden, soll ich nicht freundlich erwidern: 'An meine Herrin ⟨wendet euch!⟩'* (On Krenkel's unreliability see Gratwick 1973.) The fragment is quoted by Nonius (238. 21) with the comment *appellare est familiariter respondere*; aside from that, it has no context.

[13] e.g. Prop. 1. 1. 21; Tib. 2. 3. 5; for a longer list of references, see Kapp (1930: 1938).

[14] e.g. Ov. *Tr.* 4. 3. 9, *Ep.* 13. 143, *Met.* 13. 837.

[15] A possible exception to this statement is Ov. *Am.* 2. 15. 11, where

address usage of *domine* is well known to Ovid, however, since
he mentions it on two occasions. He describes the unfortunate
maiden Byblis, who succumbed to an incestuous passion for
her brother, as progressing gradually from sisterly affection to
incest. At the point where her love is no longer innocent, *iam
dominum appellat* 'now she calls him "master"' (*Met.* 9. 466).
Elsewhere, Ovid describes the attempts made by a woman to
arouse him once they were in bed together. These include *et
mihi blanditias dixit dominumque vocavit et quae praeterea
publica verba iuvant* 'and she spoke blandishments to me and
called me "master", and in addition obscene terms that
titillate'.[16] Propertius seems to have known of the address
usage of *domina*, for he says of his rivals for Cynthia's affection

> pulsabant alii frustra dominamque vocabant:
> mecum habuit positum lenta puella caput.
>
> (2. 14. 21–2)

Others knocked in vain and called her 'mistress': my girl, uncon-
cerned, kept her head alongside me.

From these passages we can gather that *domine* and *domina*
were addresses with specifically sexual connotations which
could be used like terms of endearment to flatter, win over,
and arouse a lover. The fact that Ovid describes *domine* being
used in bed suggests that the addresses might have been a part
of private amatory language; if so, this could explain why they
were not used directly in love poetry. It is difficult to draw too
many conclusions from Lucilius' comment, since we do not

Madvig has suggested an emendation which would produce the vocative
domina. The vocative is in none of the manuscripts, however, and Madvig's
emendation is rejected by most modern editors; see especially McKeown
(1987– : iii. 321).

[16] *Am.* 3. 7. 11–12. It is sometimes thought that Ovid is here calling *domine*
a *verbum publicum* and that this passage can thus be connected to Seneca's
characterization of the generalized *domine* as a *verbum publicum* (*Ep.* 3. 1).
Such a relationship is unlikely, however, for the use of *praeterea* here suggests
that *domine* is not one of the *verba publica*; in addition, Seneca seems to be
using *verbum publicum* to mean 'word used in its non-philosophical sense', and
that meaning cannot be applied to this passage. If one wishes to reinterpret
this passage and call *domine* a *verbum publicum*, it is best to follow Lilja (1965a:
87), who suggests that such a designation of *domine* would mean that it was in
common use as an endearment.

have its context, but apparently the speaker is suggesting that *domina* should not be used to address a lover in front of the servants. If so, that would fit with an address from private amatory language, which would indeed be avoided in front of servants. That such language existed and could be mentioned (though not used directly) by the poets is clear, for Martial explicitly labels some other addresses as suitable only for the bedroom (10. 68).

Against this interpretation it could be argued that the language of the Roman love poets was so literary, so removed from ordinary speech, that no inferences about usage outside literature can be drawn from it. The poets played with and developed certain themes without regard for external realities, and one of these motifs was the *servitium amoris* 'servitude of love', with which the use of *domina* in love poetry is intimately connected.[17] Does the fact that *servitium* was a literary theme mean that the use of *domine* and *domina* to lovers was a poetic fiction? Several factors suggest that it does not. The amatory use of *domina* is first attested in Lucilius and cannot therefore have been invented by the classical poets. Moreover, while the theme of *servitium amoris* consistently reflects the subjugation of a man to a woman, not that of a woman to a man,[18] there does not seem to be a corresponding difference between *domine* and *domina* in poetry. Finally, the literary theme must have had a starting point, and part of that starting point could well have been the use of *domine/a* for lovers in ordinary speech (cf. Lilja 1965a: 87). The fact that the poets built up a literary topos involving extensive referential use of the term *domina* thus does not mean that we should not believe them when they refer to the addresses *domine* and *domina* as being part of private amatory language.

The earliest direct attestations of *domine/a* as amatory vocatives come from the first century AD. *Domina* occurs in Pompeian graffiti[19] and is also attested in Petronius in a letter

---

[17] See e.g. Copley (1947); Lilja (1965a: 76–89); Nisbet and Hubbard (1970: 374–5); Lyne (1979); McKeown (1987– : ii. 64–5); Murgatroyd (1981); Veyne (1983: 9–23, 147–65); R. D. Brown (1987: 252); Wyke (1989: 36).

[18] Copley (1947: 289, 295); Murgatroyd (1981: 604).

[19] *CIL* iv. 8364, perhaps 1991, 6865; possibly *domine* at 1871; *domina* in referential usage, probably of lovers, *CIL* iv. 1736, 8824, 9246; *dominus*

from a lover to his beloved (Petr. 130. 1). Both graffiti and love
letters are likely contexts for private amatory language and thus
tend to confirm the theory that the vocative was excluded from
the poets because of its subliterary register.

At some point, however, the public use of *domine/a* in this
sense may have become more acceptable. A fragment attributed to Seneca says that one of the courtesies a husband would
be wise to pay his wife, like celebrating her birthday, is calling
her *domina*.[20] Somewhat later Scaevola (second century AD) and
Paulus (second to third centuries AD) quote the vocatives
domine carissime and *domina uxor* without embarrassment as
addresses between husband and wife (*Dig.* 24. 1. 57, 32. 41. 0),
and such husband–wife interchanges are more common in the
later empire.[21] It is not, however, clear that these examples
between a married couple should be taken as cases of amatory
language rather than as examples of the use of *domine/a* to
family members (discussed below). I am inclined to suspect the
latter, in which case there is little evidence that *domine/a*
between lovers ever moved from amatory to public language.
Indeed, if one discounts the married couples, there is little
evidence of any sort for the amatory usage after the first
century AD, and it may be that it died out when the generalized
use came into fashion and diluted its force.

How did this amatory usage originate? It seems probable (cf.
Kapp 1930: 1937. 83) that the address usage came first, being
developed by the second century BC, and the referential usage
grew out of it by the late first century BC. The referential
meaning would thus have originally been 'he/she whom I
address as *domine/a*'. The address usage cannot, as we have
seen, have developed out of an address used by slaves to their
masters; if it had, lovers would have been called *ere/a*.[22] Nor is

probably of a husband, *CIL* iv. 1665. *Domina* without context, *CIL* iv. 2634,
4187.

[20] Frag. 13. 51, from *De Matrimonio*; cf. Bickel (1915: 16).

[21] Cf. Treggiari (1991: 414). There is also inscriptional evidence (often
undated, but none of it early) for the address use of *domina* to wives (*CIL* vi.
15106, 29026; *EDH* 002460, 006845, 006848) and *domine* to husbands (*CIL* vi.
11252; probably *EDH* 000443), as well as for the referential use of *domina* for
wives (*CIL* v. 6039, vi. 11458, 14351, 20116, xii. 682a).

[22] Neither of these addresses is ever used to lovers in surviving texts, but
era is very occasionally applied referentially to a lover (Catul. 68. 136; perhaps

it likely to have developed out of any of the other address uses of *domine/a*, for all are first attested much later than the amatory use. The amatory address is thus probably the original vocative usage of *domine/a* and developed from the referential usage of *dominus/a* as an owner or master. The speaker was thus characterizing himself or herself as the possession of the addressee, though since he or she was refraining from using servile language this was probably not the same as calling himself a slave—'you are so exalted as to own me, a free man/woman' rather than 'I am so humble as to be your slave' may have been the original implication, though we cannot be certain.

The original vocative usage of *domine/a*, then, was probably its use to lovers, though this is poorly attested because it belonged to a subliterary register. The next development seems to have been the use of *domine* to members of the speaker's family.[23] The earliest reference to the custom of addressing one's father as *domine* is often[24] thought to be a comment in a letter by Marcus Brutus, the tyrannicide, that *dominum ne parentem quidem maiores nostri voluerunt esse* 'our ancestors did not want even fathers to be masters' (Cic. *Ad Brut.* 1. 17. 6). If one takes this as a reference to linguistic usage, it shows that by the second half of the first century BC the use of *domine* to address one's father, or of *dominus* to refer to him, was well established. This passage need not, however, be referring to language, for Brutus could simply be saying that previous generations abhorred tyranny even in parents.

A more certain reference to the practice is Suetonius' comment that Augustus *dominumque se posthac appellari ne a liberis quidem aut nepotibus suis vel serio vel ioco passus est atque eius modi blanditias etiam inter ipsos prohibuit* 'and after that Augustus did not allow anyone to call him "master" seriously or in jest, not even his children and grandchildren, and he

also Ov. *Ep.* 9. 78, but note that according to tradition Hercules was in fact Omphale's slave).

[23] The feminine *domina* may not be attested in this sense within our period (depending on the view one takes of addresses to wives), but later evidence suggests that it was probably used like *domine*.

[24] Schoener (1881: 27); Citroni (1975: 258); P. Howell (1980: 285).

forbade them to use such blandishments even among themselves' (*Aug.* 53. 1). The *ne . . . quidem* 'not even' suggests
that his younger relatives would naturally have addressed
Augustus as *domine*, while the usage was less natural from
other people. Since in Suetonius' day *domine* was as common
in address to unrelated men as to relatives, perhaps even more
common (see below), it is unlikely that Suetonius invented
this qualification of Augustus' orders. The remark can thus be
attributed to Augustus himself and suggests that by the end
of the first century BC the use of *domine* to fathers and
grandfathers was already normal, and that it was considered
flattering.

A third piece of evidence comes from Livy, who includes in a
speech (in theory delivered in 195 BC but in practice obviously
composed by Livy himself, at least as regards details of this
type) the statement *et vos in manu et tutela, non in servitio debetis
habere eas* [*uxores et filias*] *et malle patres vos aut viros quam
dominos dici* 'and you should hold them [your wives and
daughters] in guardianship, not in slavery, and should prefer
to be called fathers or husbands rather than masters' (34. 7.
13).[25] This passage implies that for Livy addresses of *domine* to
husbands and fathers were, if not standard, at least usable.

The combined evidence of these passages suggests that
domine was probably established as an address for fathers in
the late first century BC. It is not clear, however, to what extent
the address was originally limited to fathers. Ovid, as we have
seen, describes Byblis' calling her brother *domine* as a sign of
the sexual rather than sororal nature of her affection, though it
is also notable that neither Byblis nor her brother realizes this
clearly. Perhaps the fact that this address did not make Byblis'
feelings obvious shows that *domine* was also usable to brothers
in this period?

In the first century AD the use of *domine* for fathers seems to
have been well established. Martial sneers at an acquaintance
with

---

[25] Livy seems to connect the use of *domine* with slaves here, but the
connection is probably an example of a speaker's linking two otherwise
separate meanings of a word (probably for rhetorical effect in this case); cf.
pp. 13, 92–3.

> A servo scis te genitum blandeque fateris,
>   cum dicis dominum, Sosibiane, patrem.   (1. 81)

You know that you are the son of a slave and you fawningly admit it, Sosibianus, when you call your father 'master'.

This is normally taken to mean that Sosibianus was the off-spring of an illicit union between his mother and one of his father's slaves, and that Martial was playing on the lexical meaning of *dominus* in order to make a joke using what was otherwise an unremarkable address form.[26]

Later in the imperial period *domine* is attested between relatives enough to make it clear that the usage continued for centuries and that this term was usable to members of all generations, not just fathers.[27] Examples are rare, however, and it could be that the familial usage, like the amatory one, waned once the generalized usage became common. Certainly it is notable that the papyrus letters of the 'Tiberianus archive' make a sharp distinction between the address *domine*, used only to unrelated addressees, and *pater* 'father', which is consist-ently used to the writer's father;[28] this address distinction is the more notable since in reference the dative *domino* is used in the headings of both types of letter (*P. Mich.* viii. 467. 1, 468. 2, 472. 1).

Domine to relatives probably began as an address from younger to older relatives and then was extended to kin of the same and younger generations. It seems to have been a flattering address, for Martial uses *blande* 'flatteringly' to describe it and Suetonius speaks of *blanditiae*, but it is not clear exactly what type of flattery was originally involved. It could be that the use of *domine/a* to lovers continued into a use to spouses, and that this use was then picked up by children in addressing their parents, whom they heard being so addressed by the other parent; eventually this practice then spread to other relatives. The historical connection with amatory lan-guage could then explain why the address belonged to a subliterary register.

[26] P. Howell (1980: 285); see also Citroni (1975: 258).
[27] Son to father at *ILS* 8377; father-in-law to son-in-law at Fro. 176. 10; cf. in dative from aunt to nephew at *CIL* v. 1706.
[28] *Domine*: *P. Mich.* viii. 472. 8, 11, 20–1, 24; *pater*: *P. Mich.* viii. 467. 4, 18, 468. 4, 8, 20, 23, 31, 41 (all early 2nd cent. AD).

Yet I know of no parallels for the spreading of an amatory term in this fashion, and it is perhaps more likely that the familial usage of *domine* arose directly from referential use. The paterfamilias was the *dominus* of the household, and so he could have been addressed as *domine* in simple recognition of that fact. Such an origin looks as though it would produce a meaning very similar to the servility traditionally attached to *domine* by scholars, but in fact no such subservience is required. The use by children of an address borrowed from their father's slaves would have implied that they too had the position of slaves, but an address that simply acknowledges the position of the father as master of the house and slaves need carry no such implications, especially when it is not used by the slaves themselves. Romans could address a king as *rex* 'king' without implying that they were his subjects (p. 106, cf. also p. 238), and so they could have addressed the master of a household full of slaves as *domine* without implying that they shared the position of those slaves.

This explanation fits well with what little can be observed of the tone of the familial *domine*, which seems to convey generalized politeness rather than servility or sexual affection. It would not conflict with the later use of the term to younger family members, for there is a parallel for such a development in the use of 'master' with a name to boys by their elders in English. The subliterary register of familial *domine*, however, is difficult to account for, since *dominus* in other cases is a perfectly acceptable word in literature.

There is also a third use of *domine/a*, as a general address for people who are neither relatives nor lovers of the speaker. This usage appears in Petronius, who provides several examples (20. 1, 24. 1, 86. 7) of *domine* and *domina* used to acquaintances; the contexts are polite but not subservient. At the same period the younger Seneca comments that *obvios, si nomen non succurrit, 'dominos' salutamus* 'when we run into people whose names we don't remember, we address them as "master"' (*Ep*. 3. 1). This too suggests a polite usage but one without extreme deference. Seneca's casual reference to the practice, as an illustration of something else, shows that it was common and well known in his day; the fact that it is so rarely directly attested in literature suggests that this usage, like the two already discussed, belonged to a subliterary register.

Another piece of first-century evidence comes via Suetonius, who reports that the emperor Claudius used to call the spectators at the games *domini* (*Cl.* 21. 5); this occurs in the context of the emperor's making jokes, encouraging the audience to laugh, and generally behaving in an undignified manner. Quintilian also mentions an instance of an orator addressing a legatee as *domine* while making a witty retort (*Inst.* 6. 3. 100). The address also appears in a few relatively early documents, where it again seems to be polite but not servile.[29]

In the second century we have much more direct evidence for the generalized use of *domine/a*; even more can be found in later centuries, when the term was highly popular and eventually developed into Mr/Mrs equivalents in some Romance languages.[30] In the Vindolanda tablets, which begin shortly before the start of the century, *domine* is very common and the address *domina* probably occurs as well.[31] Other preserved documents from the second century use this address frequently; it tends to be addressed to superiors and is polite, but it is certainly not servile.[32] Adams (1995: 118–19) has shown that in some types of document, such as letters of recommendation, the use of *domine* seems to be required by the formula of the letter, irrespective of the relative status of speaker and addressee.

[29] *P. Ryl.* iv. 608. 6; *CEL* 82. 7; *CIL* iv. 1991, 6865 could be examples of generalized *domina* and 1871 of generalized *domine*, but they could also be amatory terms (cf. n. 19 above). A different usage of *domine* is reflected in *scaenae domine* (*CIL* iv. 3877) and *dominus scaenicorum* (*CIL* iv. 5399). The address is probably used for Jupiter at *CIL* iv. 6864.

[30] For some of the later Latin evidence, see *CEL* 187. 2. 4, 191. 1. 8, 191. 38b. 4, 191. 39. 9, 199. 1. 5, etc.; Bang (1921: 82–8); Kapp (1930: 1925–6 and 1938–9); O'Brien (1930: 82–3); Engelbrecht (1893: 12, 32, 51–2). For the Romance developments see Svennung (1958: 358–66).

[31] *Domine*: 37 examples out of 67 addresses: *Tab. Vindol. II* 166. 2, 167. 1, 168. 2, 169. 2, 170. 1, 171. 2, 172. 2, 173. 1, 175. 4, 176. 2, 225. 5, 234. i. 3, 238. 3, 239. 3, 248. 14, 250. 4, 250. 5, 252. 5, 255. 15, etc. *Domi[na]* at 294. 3. Cf. Adams (1995: 118–19).

[32] *P. Mich.* viii. 472. 8, 11, 20–1, 24; *P. Oxy.* i. 32. 7, 21; *CEL* 149. 3, 158. 6, 169. 32, 174. 3, 177. 3; *ILS* 5795, 7259, 8380; *O. Claud.* 367. 3; *Pap. Soc. Ital.* 1026 C 6; *EDH* 000724, 008693, 018450.

The term is also found in literature of this period. Juvenal, though he does not use the address directly, mentions it as an address used by legacy-hunters to rich men and as a flattering greeting for good customers (5. 137, 8. 161). Apuleius' *Metamorphoses* contain a number of actual examples of both *domine* and *domina*, usually in situations where some politeness is required but servile deference would be out of place.[33] In his *Apology* Apuleius mentions being called *parens* 'parent', *dominus*, and *magister* 'teacher' by Pontianus (97). Apart from that, Apuleius' own speech, which begins *Maxime Claudi quique in consilio estis* 'Claudius Maximus and you who are in council' (1), is notably free of the address *domine*, though his opponent begins with *domine Maxime* (102). This shows that *domine* in Apuleius' day cannot have been obligatory when addressing superiors. Bang (1921: 85) suggests that it also shows Apuleius' lack of servility as contrasted with his opponent, but it is likely that Apuleius was trying to display elegance and erudition rather than freedom of spirit. *Domine* in classical Latin had not been acceptable in literature in any sense, and even in the first century AD it seems to have belonged to a subliterary register. Since Apuleius throughout his speech emphasizes his cultural superiority, he probably avoided *domine* as belonging historically to the wrong register. At the same time, the fact that his opponent did begin with *domine* suggests that the term was by that period generally acceptable in formal settings.

Gellius, another lover of erudition, never uses *domine/a*. It has been plausibly suggested that some of the addresses he quotes are deliberate substitutions for an avoided *domine/a* (Bang 1921: 85), a practice which could again be due to a feeling that *domine* was inappropriate for literature. Fronto, whose literary elegance is unimpeachable but who was not above the use of informal language in his letters, several times uses *domine* to address friends. Thus M. Gavius Squilla Gallicanus is *domine frater* 'master brother' (185. 14), while C. Arrius Antoninus is *domine fili carissime* 'my master, dearest son' (189. 10). The emperor Marcus Aurelius also once addresses Fronto as *domine magister* (105. 10). This combination of *domine* with other words, and in particular with *frater*

[33] 2. 14, 2. 20, 2. 24, 2. 26, 3. 11, 4. 17, 5. 31, 6. 22 (*domine fili*; cf. Kenney 1990: 220).

and other kinship terms, is typical of documentary texts; it first appears *c.* AD 100 and becomes very common later.[34] Its use has been immortalized by Pallades' late Greek epigram (*Greek Anthology* 10. 44):

> Ἢν ὁ φίλος τι λάβῃ, "Δόμινε φράτερ" εὐθὺς ἔγραψεν·
> ἢν δ' αὖ μή τι λάβῃ, τὸ "Φράτερ" εἶπε μόνον·
> ὤνια γὰρ καὶ ταῦτα τὰ ῥήματα. αὐτὰρ ἔγωγε
> οὐκ ἐθέλω "Δόμινε", οὐ γὰρ ἔχω δόμεναι.

If a friend gets a gift, he at once writes back saying 'master brother', but if he doesn't get anything, he just says 'brother'. For even these words are for sale. But I don't want to be called 'master', because I have nothing to give.[35]

All of this evidence consistently points to an interpretation of *domine* and *domina* as polite but subliterary, conveying courtesy but little or no deference. Martial, however, seems to have a slightly different view of the address, one involving more subservience. He reports that he had to call his patron *domine*, and that an accidental use of the name instead lost him his daily dole.[36] He debates the issue of using the address to a prospective patron (10. 10. 5) and comments with relief that he can address an ex-patron by name instead of with *domine* (2. 68). A man of whose bounty Martial initially had high hopes received *domine* until Martial got to know him better, gave up hope, and addressed him by name instead (1. 112). And when others use the address to Martial himself, he enjoys the flattery (4. 83). Martial seems to read more deference into this address than do other authors, a fact which cannot be explained by weakening over time, for Seneca, who gives the term very little force, wrote considerably earlier than Martial.

Yet there are also other passages which suggest that Martial,

---

[34] e.g. with names: *Tab. Vindol. II* 166, 167, 170, 171, 172; with *fili*: *CEL* 199. 1. 5, 199. 2. 4, 9; with *frater*: *Tab. Vindol. II* 247, 252, 255. 15, 260. 4, 295. 9, 345. ii. 5; *CEL* 177. 3, 187. 2. 4, 191. 6. 8, 191. 38b. 4; *EDH* 018450. See Cugusi (1992: i. 43) for further references.

[35] There is a pun here on Latin *domine* and the Greek word for 'to give', which at this period would have been homophonous.

[36] 6. 88; see p. 1. Martial is here complaining that his patron is so stingy that he does not have much to lose by using the wrong form of address (cf. Shackleton Bailey 1993: ii. 69).

despite his comments about addresses to patrons, also recognized the type of use envisioned by Seneca and practised by other authors. He describes a magpie addressing people as *domine* (14. 76), which may be equivalent to the 'hello' often uttered by a modern parrot; if this was a word the magpie picked up on its own, it must have been very common, though the bird could also have been taught a rarer address. The other pertinent passage, the comment to Cinna quoted at the start of this chapter, is disputed in both text and interpretation. It is normally taken to be a direct reference to Seneca's usage to unknown addressees: Martial calls Cinna's slaves *domine* when he cannot remember their names.[37] Supporters of this interpretation conclude that Martial did not really consider the address *domine* to be subservient, since he was prepared to use it to inferiors as low as slaves, and that he is not to be taken seriously when he complains about its subservient sense elsewhere.

It has, however, also been suggested that this reference could be to the amatory use of *domine* rather than the generalized one;[38] if Cinna's slave is an attractive boy, then Martial, who is certainly aware of the referential use of *dominus* for attractive boys (cf. 11. 70. 2, 12. 66. 8), may mean that he uses the amatory *domine* to the slave. In general, the second interpretation, with its play upon two very different uses of *domine*, seems more in keeping with Martial's style; the difficulty with it is that the amatory *domine* may have died out by this period. Whichever explanation one chooses, the joke suggests that Martial did not always attach as much deference to the use of *domine* as some of his other remarks suggest.

Why then does Martial talk elsewhere as if he finds the enforced use of *domine* an imposition of slavery? Perhaps because he is making a connection between reference and address usage which most Romans ignored. The referential use of *dominus* in its sense of 'owner', 'master of slaves' did not die out; it existed side by side with the address usage, just as the English word 'master' still exists alongside derivatives like 'Mr Smith' and German *Herr* exists alongside *Herr Schmidt*,

---

[37] White (1978: 81 n. 25); Svennung (1958: 342); Bang (1921: 86).
[38] Shackleton Bailey (1993: i. 405); counter-arguments in P. Howell (1995: 140–1).

and just as English 'love' and 'darling' exist as genuinely affectionate terms alongside the generalized addresses used to strangers. While most native speakers do not think about such anomalies, there are some who object to generalized 'darling' and others who object to generalized 'Mr', in both cases because they see a connection which other speakers ignore.[39] Martial probably spotted the inconsistency between the literal meaning of *domine* and its address usage and exploited it for his own purposes; his statements therefore tell us very little about the normal address meaning of *domine*, so we can take the evidence of the other sources at face value.

How and when did the generalized usage of *domine* and *domina* develop? It seems to have been fairly common in speech by the mid-first century AD, to judge from the evidence of Seneca and Petronius, but there is no trace of it in the classical period. This lack of classical evidence is unlikely to be accidental, since quite apart from Cicero's silence, Horace discusses at some length terms which could be used in flattery of patrons and rich men[40] without ever mentioning the one which Juvenal and Martial found most appropriate for such a context. It is thus most probable that this use of *domine* began at the very end of the first century BC or the beginning of the first century AD.

The generalized use thus seems to be slightly later than the familial use; this fits with the evidence that in the time of Augustus *domine* was more normal within the family than between unrelated men (cf. pp. 85–6). The simplest explanation for its origin is that it grew out of the familial usage as soon as the latter had become established. Latin speakers had long had a tendency to use kinship terms outside the family in polite address; such use can be found as early as Plautus and is well attested in Horace and other writers who discuss flattering addresses (see pp. 120–2). It is likely that address by praenomen spread from a familial to a flattering usage in the same way (p. 66), and *carissime* 'dearest', another common element in flattery, probably also started as an address for relatives and

---

[39] Cf. p. 13. The first group is composed of certain types of feminists, and the second of certain types of Pennsylvania Quakers. For a Greek parallel, see Dickey (1996: 179–80).

[40] *S.* 2. 5. 23–38, *Ep.* 1. 6. 54–5, 1. 7. 37–8.

other people very close to the speaker (p. 138). These parallels
suggest that as soon as *domine* became accepted as a familial
address, it would have been usable in flattery.

This explanation has a number of advantages over the
traditional view that *domine* spread from servile address to
general use. Even aside from the fact that slaves did not use this
address, the traditional explanation conflicts with actual evidence for usage, which is not at all servile, even in the earliest
attestations. In order to explain this conflict while keeping the
traditional explanation, one must assume a long process of
weakening between the initial spreading of the term to free
speakers and the time of Seneca; this long process is difficult to
reconcile with the complete lack of classical attestation and
with the fact that the term does not seem to weaken significantly during our period. Moreover, the frequent pairing of
domine with *frater* and other kinship terms is hard to reconcile
with a fundamentally servile meaning, but easy to understand if
the term is a familial one.

If our reinterpretation of generalized *domine* is correct, it
means that Roman flattery has been fundamentally misunder-
stood in modern times. Imperial Romans were not, after all, a
servile lot who addressed their social superiors with the
grovelling deference due to absolute masters; instead they
tried to express affection for their superiors, addressing them
like close relatives. In other words, Roman flattery exemplifies
positive rather than negative politeness.

There is also a fourth usage of *domine/a*, as an address to
emperors (and, occasionally, their wives). This usage cannot be
earlier than the Augustan age, and most of our evidence for it is
indirect; historians frequently comment on emperors who
refused the title *dominus* and those who welcomed it. Essentially the title, in its referential usage, became more and more
widespread over time, until by the end of the empire it was
completely obligatory. Certain emperors, notably Augustus,
Tiberius, and Trajan, made a point of refusing the title, while
others, such as Domitian, insisted upon it; ancient writers,
including contemporaries of the emperors concerned, make it
clear that this difference was seen as a key sign of whether an

emperor was a good one treating his subjects as free men, or a tyrant treating them as slaves.[41]

The way the preferences of the emperors are described gives the impression that the objection was to both address and referential usage of *dominus*. Suetonius says that Augustus

domini appellationem ut maledictum et obprobrium semper exhorruit. Cum spectante eo ludos pronuntiatum esset in mimo: 'O dominum aequum et bonum!' et universi quasi de ipso dictum exultantes comprobassent, et statim manu vultuque indecoras adulationes repressit et insequenti die gravissimo corripuit edicto; dominumque se posthac appellari ne a liberis quidem aut nepotibus suis vel serio vel ioco passus est atque eius modi blanditias etiam inter ipsos prohibuit. (*Aug.* 53. 1)

always loathed the appellation of 'master', as being an insult and a reproach. Once he was watching the games when the line 'O just and good master!' was spoken in a mime, and everyone approved it with great joy as if it had been spoken of him. He at once suppressed the unseemly adulation with both expression and gesture, and on the following day he reproached them with a most severe edict. After that he did not allow anyone to call him 'master' seriously or in jest, not even his children and grandchildren, and he forbade them to use such blandishments even among themselves.

Here the initial utterance was not an address, but Augustus' reaction to it suggests that he banned address as well as referential usage. On the other hand, Suetonius' wording indicates that until the incident described here, Augustus did allow his children, and perhaps other people as well, to address him as *domine*. Perhaps until this incident Augustus had not minded receiving *domine*, since the address was not very subservient; a term generally used for parents was not unsuited to the *pater patriae*. Being referred to as a *dominus*, however, was distinctly different and not in keeping with the image Augustus wanted to project, for the referential usage suggested slavery in a way that the address did not. He therefore reacted strongly against it, so strongly that he banned the use of the word to him altogether, even in its more innocuous address usage.

[41] e.g. Mart. 10. 72; Plin. *Pan.* 2. 3; for more information on the usage of individual emperors, see Kapp (1930: 1927–8); Mommsen (1887–8: ii. 760–3); Bömer (1957–8: ii. 91–2).

The other references to emperors' refusals to accept the title
are ambiguous as to which usage is meant. Tiberius, says
Suetonius, *dominus appellatus a quodam denuntiavit, ne se
amplius contumeliae causa nominaret* 'when a certain man
called him "master", warned him not to insult him any
more' (*Tib.* 27). Tacitus says of the same emperor that
*acerbeque increpuit eos qui divinas occupationes ipsumque dom-
inum dixerant* 'he bitterly rebuked those who called his business
"divine" and himself "master"' (*Ann.* 2. 87). On the subject of
Domitian's eagerness to accept the title, however, Suetonius is
clearly thinking of referential rather than address usage:

adclamari etiam in amphitheatro epuli die libenter audiit: domino et
dominae feliciter! . . . pari arrogantia, cum procuratorum suorum
nomine formalem dictaret epistulam, sic coepit: dominus et deus
noster hoc fieri iubet. unde institutum posthac, ut ne scripto
quidem ac sermone cuiusquam appellaretur aliter. (*Dom.* 13. 1–2)

On his feast day he liked to hear the crowd in the amphitheatre shout
'Good fortune to our master and mistress!' . . . with equal arrogance,
when he dictated a letter for circulation in the name of his procura-
tors, he began thus: 'Our master and god orders this to be done.'
From this the custom afterwards arose that not even in speaking or
writing did anyone call him anything else.

In the case of Trajan a difference can be seen between
address and referential usage. Trajan, in contrast to his pre-
decessor Domitian, did not accept the title *dominus* and was not
referred to as such.[42] Pliny, who was overjoyed at this development, never refers to Trajan as *dominus* in his extant
writings, while he does so refer to Domitian;[43] he makes it
clear (*Pan.* 2. 3) that to refer to an emperor as *dominus* is to call
him a tyrant. Yet in address, Pliny's standard vocative to
Trajan in his letters is *domine*.[44] The tacit acceptance (on
both sides) of this distinction between address and referential
use indicates that by the time of Trajan the generalized address
usage of *domine* had become more stabilized, and its separation
from referential usage could be taken for granted.

Pliny's choice of addresses was influenced by the genres in

[42] Mart. 10. 72; Mommsen (1887–8: ii. 762).
[43] *Ep.* 4. 11. 6, *Pan.* 2. 3, 45. 4, 52. 7, 63. 6.
[44] 82 examples, e.g. *Ep. Tra.* 10. 2. 1, 10. 3a. 1, 10. 4. 6; cf. Sherwin-White
(1966: 557).

which he wrote. In the letters *domine* is his normal address to
Trajan, but in the *Panegyric* (containing 41 addresses to the
same emperor) it never appears. This further evidence that the
domine used to emperors was the subliterary, generalized one is
corroborated by other literary texts; literature of course
abounds in dedicatory and laudatory addresses to emperors,
but in such contexts *domine* is strikingly rare. I have found only
two examples: one is *domine frater*, addressed probably to
Trajan, in the *De Munitionibus Castrorum* (45) formerly attributed to Hyginus. The writer of this technical treatise had no
literary pretensions, and the language is far from elevated, so
domine frater is at home here, like *domine* in Pliny's letters. The
other passage is an address from Martial to Domitian (8 *pr.* 1);
Martial's style is in general elegant, and he does not use this
address anywhere else (despite the number of occasions on
which he refers to it), so the subliterary, generalized *domine* is
out of place here. It therefore seems likely that Martial used
domine because of Domitian's specific fondness for the title
dominus. This passage, I think, is the only case in extant Latin
literature of a genuine 'imperial' *domine*; all other examples I
have found of the address to an emperor are in fact the
generalized *domine*.

  Fronto's letters to various Antonine emperors contain almost
as many examples of *domine* as Pliny's. In contrast to Pliny,
who always uses *domine* alone, Fronto often adds modifiers like
dulcissime, *optime*, and *desiderantissime*;[45] at first glance these
are startlingly affectionate, and one can see why their presence
led Schoener to describe Fronto's *domine* as a *Liebkosungswort*
(1881: 29). However, in Fronto's day these superlative adjectives had lost most of their force (see Chapter 4), so their
presence need not imply that *domine* conveyed strong affection.
Most of Fronto's literary works are lost, so one cannot be
certain whether he followed Pliny's practice of avoiding *domine*
in such contexts, but it is notable that all the addresses in those
literary fragments that do survive use terms other than
domine.[46]

---

[45] e.g. 37. 21, 43. 25, 72. 12, 73. 9, 74. 3, 81. 7, 82. 24, 109. 9.
[46] Addresses to the emperor in the literary fragments normally employ
Marce (224. 17, 228. 17, 233. 16).

The Latin use of *domine* is often connected with the contemporary usage of Greek terms meaning 'master'; such
comparisons are unhelpful when Greek is simply equated
with Latin, but if the necessary distinctions are made the
Greek evidence can be enlightening. I have treated these
Greek addresses at length elsewhere (Dickey 2001) and shall
give here only a summary of the results. Greek writers in the
imperial period had two equivalents of *dominus/a*: δεσπότης/
δέσποινα and κύριος/κυρία. Δεσπότης was the stronger of these
terms, corresponding closely to the referential meaning of
dominus as an owner or absolute master, while κύριος could
also refer to a guardian or head of household. In the vocative,
δέσποτα was a deferential and highly respectful term; it is only
occasionally found in a weakened sense. Its feminine δέσποινα
had a similar meaning but was also applicable to lovers
(Dickey 1996: 99). Κύριε/α, by contrast, was a much more
generalized address usable to equals, though still capable of
expressing deference on occasion; it was often used within the
family like *domine/a*.

Most of the time these Greek terms are used in texts originally written in Greek, not in translations of Latin; in such
situations they give us no information on Latin usage. This is
true even in examples of imperial titulature, whenever it is
unclear exactly which Latin term is intended by the Greek.
Reference to emperors as κύριος in Greek becomes common
earlier than the use of *dominus* in Latin inscriptions,[47] and
κύριος seems to be as much or more the equivalent of *princeps* as
of *dominus* in imperial contexts (H. Mason 1974: 64); thus one
cannot assume that any Greek titulature containing κύριος is
necessarily a translation of *dominus*.

In some texts, however, it is clear that a Greek author was in
fact translating *dominus*. Sometimes this occurs in papyrus
documents, when a letter is given first in Latin and then in
Greek; in such situations the vocative *domine* seems always to
be translated with κύριε, though the evidence is not extensive.[48]

---

[47] Mommsen (1887–8: ii. 762); H. Mason (1974: 64). On the use of κύριος
and δεσπότης for the emperor see also Hagedorn and Worp (1980) and Bréhier
(1906: 163–4, 168).

[48] *P. Oxy.* ix. 1202. 15, xii. 1466. 4; probably originally *Pap. Soc. Ital.* x.
1101. 6.

Translation also occurs in discussions of imperial titulature, and in such cases referential *dominus* becomes δεσπότης.[49] This pattern suggests that the ancients had a tendency to equate the address *domine* with κύριε and referential *dominus* with δεσπότης; in fact it is likely that the vocative κύριε (which essentially did not exist before the first century AD) was created in order to provide an equivalent for *domine*, since δέσποτα was too subservient to be used in this way (Dickey 2001). The Greek perception of such a distinction between *domine* and *dominus* thus provides additional evidence that the Latin address was not servile in character, even at an early period.

In conclusion, the Latin address *domine/a* was not normally used by slaves, as is generally supposed, but had three main functions, all of which belonged to a subliterary register. First to emerge was the amatory usage, followed by a familial usage which in turn probably gave rise to the generalized usage. The first of these expressed erotic affection, the second familial affection or respect, and the third a mild politeness. Most examples of the address *domine* used to emperors are not directly related to the use of *dominus* as an imperial title, but are part of the generalized use. Although in most cases the address meaning of *domine/a* was thoroughly separate from the referential meaning, on a few occasions some Romans seem to have connected the two uses, resulting in objections to the address usage.

If emperors were not addressed as *domine* in literature, how were they addressed? A wide variety of terms was available, but the most common were *Caesar*, *Auguste*, *princeps*, and

---

[49] Dio Cassius 55. 12. 2, 57. 8. 1–2, 67. 4. 7 (Zonaras 11. 19). It is perhaps also relevant that Servius (on *Aeneid* 6. 397) assumes that Vergil could have equated referential *domina* and δέσποινα. Other passages are often cited in this context, but most (such as Dio Chrysostom 1. 22; Dio Cassius 51. 12. 2; Philo, *Legatio ad Gaium* 208) provide no guarantee that the author was thinking of the Latin rather than the Greek word; as such they are no help to us. One passage which could be helpful is Philo, *Legatio* 154, where Mommsen (1887–8: ii. 756 n. 2) and some others read τὸ μὴ δεσπότην μήτε θεὸν ἑαυτὸν ἐθελῆσαι προσειπεῖν, ἀλλὰ καὶ ἂν λέγοιτό τις, δυσχεραίνειν (about Augustus). The text of this passage is, however, doubtful, and most editors now prefer to read τὸ μηδέποτε θεὸν ἑαυτὸν ἐθελῆσαι προσειπεῖν, ἀλλὰ κἂν εἰ λέγοι τις δυσχεραίνειν, so it can no longer be taken as evidence.

imperator.[50] Pliny's writings provide a good sense of the
relative force of these addresses. While in his later letters he
uses only *domine* to Trajan, in earlier ones Pliny goes back
and forth[51] between *domine* (always used alone) and *imperator*
(always modified).[52] This usage suggests that *imperator* was
informal enough to occur in a letter, but more formal than
domine, and that it was abandoned as Pliny became more
comfortable in his relationship with the emperor. The *Panegyric*, on the other hand, represents a much more formal
register, since it is a speech before the Senate. Here *domine*
never appears, and *imperator* is rare. The usual address is
Caesar alone, which occurs 34 times. The fuller address
Caesar Auguste is used at the beginning, and *Auguste* is also
twice paired with *imperator* but does not occur alone. *Princeps*
does not appear as a self-standing address but is implied by
optime principum, fortissime imperatorum 'best of chiefs, stron-
gest of commanders' (91. 1).[53]

A hierarchy of register can thus be created for Pliny's works,
with *Caesar Auguste* as the most formal term, followed by
Caesar, then *imperator*, with *domine* also available at a subliterary level. Evidence for other periods suggests that this
hierarchy is generally applicable to imperial addresses in the
first two centuries. *Caesar Auguste* occurs elsewhere only in
formal speeches,[54] while *Caesar*, alone or with an appropriate
adjective, is the preferred address to emperors in literature,

[50] For the referential usage of these terms, see Mommsen (1887–8: ii. 763–
86); Syme (1958); McFayden (1920); Schoener (1881).

[51] This progression from variable address patterns in the earlier letters to a
consistent one in the later letters suggests that whatever editing the letters
received before publication did not seriously affect address usage.

[52] The first letter contains only the vocatives *imperator sanctissime* and
imperator optime (1. 1, 1. 2), the second and third use *domine*, the fourth uses
both *imperator optime* (4. 1) and *domine* (4. 6), and then *domine* takes over,
imperator resurfacing briefly for *indulgentissime imperator* (10. 2) and *optime
imperator* (14. 1) before being abandoned for the following hundred or so
letters. Sherwin-White (1966: 556) suggests that in some of these cases there
are specific reasons for the use of *imperator*.

[53] *Imperator*: 38. 5; *Caesar*: 9. 3, 14. 1, etc.; *Caesar Auguste*: 4. 3, 5. 2;
imperator Auguste: 16. 2, 56. 1. The only other address to the emperor in this
speech is *pater Traiane* (89. 2).

[54] Suet. *Aug.* 58. 2; Val. Mes. *orat.* 20. On the origins of this combination
see Syme (1958: 183).

especially poetry; it occurs in Vergil, Horace, Ovid, Calpurnius Siculus, Lucan, Martial, and Juvenal, as well as prose writers such as Vitruvius, both Senecas, Valerius Maximus, Tacitus, and Suetonius.[55] Fronto uses it in his letters to all three emperors, but not as often as he uses *domine*.[56] A few specific passages shed more light on the use of *Caesar* to emperors.[57] Maecenas is described in the *Appendix Vergiliana* (*Eleg. Maec.* 155) as addressing the absent emperor with *Caesar* on his deathbed in a last expression of affection (he also uses the address *mi care*, 'dear to me' or 'my dear', 171). Suetonius describes a young speaker beginning a Senate speech with *patres conscripti et tu Caesar* 'enrolled fathers and you, Caesar' (*De Oratoribus* 71 (p. 88 Re.)) and comments that *propter quod simulata oratione plenissime a Tiberio conlaudatus (est)* 'on account of which he was abundantly praised by Tiberius with an insincere speech'.[58] All of this suggests that *Caesar* was flattering and that it was the standard address for an emperor in formal and poetic registers, though *Auguste* could be added to *Caesar* for what was probably a higher level of official formality. The address was also usable to men who while not emperors had a right to the title or name *Caesar*; thus Tacitus quotes Senate speeches containing *Caesar* to Tiberius before he officially became emperor (*Ann.* 1. 12, 1. 13).

---

[55] Hor. *Carm.* 1. 2. 52, 4. 15. 4, *Ep.* 2. 1. 4; Verg. *G.* 1. 25, 1. 503, 2. 170; Calp. *Ecl.* 4. 94, 4. 143; Ov. 12 times, e.g. *Tr.* 2. 27; Juv. 4. 135, 8. 171; Luc. 1. 41; Mart. 53 times, e.g. 1. 4. 1; Vitr. e.g. 4 *pr.* 1; Sen. *Con.* 6. 8; Sen. *Cl.* 1. 1. 1, 1. 1. 5, 1. 11. 2, 2. 1. 1, 2. 2. 1; Tac. e.g. *Ann.* 2. 37; V. Max. 1 *pr.*; Suet. e.g. *Tib.* 59. 1. For the use of this address in the later empire (which is complicated by the new hierarchical distinction between *Augusti* and *Caesares*) see Schoener (1881: 19–21).

[56] Fifteen times, e.g. 1. 7.

[57] The address is of course also used to Julius Caesar, but there it functions strictly as a name.

[58] It is difficult to know quite what to make of this, especially as the text of *simulata oratione* is doubtful, but the most likely explanation is that Senate speeches at this period normally opened with an address only to the senators (even Pliny's *Panegyric*, which is primarily addressed to the emperor, opens with the address *patres conscripti* alone (1. 1, 3. 4) and does not address the emperor until 4. 3), so adding *Caesar* at that stage constituted flattery of Tiberius. By the later 2nd cent., however, Senate speeches routinely began with an address to the emperor, even when he was not present (see Van den Hout 1999: 30).

Imperator, by contrast, is not used as an address to the emperor in poetry (though the poets do use this address in other senses) and is much less common than *Caesar* in formal prose.[59] It appears occasionally in Vitruvius (e.g. 2 *pr.* 4), who also combines it with *Caesar* at the beginning of his work (*imperator Caesar*, 1 *pr.* 1), and in works of the elder Pliny (*iucundissime imperator*, *Nat. pr.* 1) but is found most often in Fronto's and Pliny's letters; in Fronto, as in Pliny, *imperator* is much less common than *domine*.[60] It is also notable that Fronto uses this address primarily to Antoninus Pius, with whom he had a more distant relationship than with Marcus Aurelius or Lucius Verus; the only time he uses it to Marcus, to whom Fronto was especially close, it appears not in his own voice but in the mouth of another subject (10. 16). The only time this address occurs in Suetonius, it is as a formal salute from gladiators (*Cl.* 21. 6). *Imperator* is also found as an address in inscriptions (e.g. *ILS* 5865a, 6870).

Imperator was of course primarily a military term, and the earlier emperors apparently felt a certain discomfort about allowing the term to be used by people other than soldiers (see Dio Cassius 57. 8. 1–2). The address was, however, quickly extended to use by non-soldiers in non-military contexts (e.g. Vitruvius). It is nevertheless possible that soldiers continued to use this address more than other ones (as a US Navy officer of my acquaintance had a tendency to refer to her President as 'the Commander-in-Chief'), thus reinforcing its military register. This is suggested by Dio's remarks, and also by the fact that Suetonius quotes this vocative only as an address from gladiators. Such usage would explain the low register of the term: it was not terribly subservient (soldiers were, after all, no more in the power of the emperor than other men, and at some periods arguably much less) but did belong to the language of the military camp. In terms of imperial nomenclature *imperator* can also be regarded as the praenomen of Augustus and some later

---

[59] In addresses to 3rd- and 4th-cent. emperors *imperator* is more common than in our data (Schoener 1881: 8–10), suggesting that its usage evolved over time; perhaps the increased role of the military in creating emperors influenced this change.

[60] Six times, e.g. 162. 7.

emperors,[61] but there is no evidence that when used alone in address it could convey any of the nuances of the praenomen (cf. pp. 63–7).[62]

Auguste alone, though it does not appear in Pliny's writings, is also an imperial address. The term is, by the nature of the title (or cognomen) *Augustus*, restricted to actual emperors. It seems to belong to a high literary register, since it occurs primarily in the poets, who use it as a less frequent alternative to *Caesar*.[63] The passages in which *Auguste* appears are perhaps on average somewhat more laudatory than those using *Caesar*, but it is difficult to be certain, since most addresses to emperors are laudatory to some extent. The term is rare in prose except in the collocation *Caesar Auguste*, but it does appear once in Suetonius (*Nero* 46. 3) and once in Tacitus (*Ann.* 1. 43), both in quotations; it does not seem to be used for prose dedications as is *Caesar*. This suggests that *Auguste* may be somewhat more elevated than *Caesar*.

Princeps, though a standard term of reference for the emperor, is relatively rare in address.[64] In neither address nor referential use is it restricted to emperors, even after the founding of the principate; thus Statius calls Amphiaraus *princeps tripodum* 'prince of the tripods' (*Theb.* 8. 367), and both Cicero (*Phil.* 8. 28) and Livy (32. 21. 1; cf. Briscoe 1973: 204–5) use *principes* as an address for dignitaries. When used to the emperor as an address, *princeps* is elevated and poetic and never occurs alone; thus Ovid uses *mitissime princeps* 'very mild chief' (*Tr.* 2. 147) and Martial *pudice princeps* 'pure chief' (9. 5. 2). This fact, and the comparative rarity of the term, suggest that *princeps* was not a part of the Latin address system except in very poetic language; *principes*, however, probably was.

Another title (or cognomen) sometimes used to address emperors is *Germanice* 'conqueror of Germany'. *Germanicus* was not part of the standard imperial titulature but rather

[61] Syme (1958: 176–9, 184–5); McFayden (1920); Augustus' official *tria nomina* were *Imperator Caesar Augustus*.

[62] For the later use of this address, see Schoener (1881: 14–16).

[63] Hor. *Carm.* 4. 14. 13; Prop. 2. 10. 15, 4. 6. 38; Ov. *Met.* 1. 204, *Tr.* 2. 509; Mart. 11 times, e.g. 4. 27. 1. For the Christian use of *Augustus* see O'Brien (1930: 128–9).

[64] For the use of this address in the later empire, when it was more common, see Schoener (1881: 25–6).

belonged to certain individuals, some emperors and some not; the address seems to have been usable exactly like the referential use. Thus Ovid uses *Germanice* to address Caesar Germanicus, son of Drusus Claudius Nero; this address functions like the cognomen it is, with *Caesar Germanice* used for the formal dedication at the beginning of the *Fasti* (1. 3) and both *Caesar* and *Germanice* used alone in the rest of the work.[65] At a later period, Martial, Statius, and Silius all use *Germanice* as an address to the emperor Domitian, who had assumed the title *Germanicus*.[66] Here *Germanice* seems to hold much the same position as *Auguste* in the imperial address system: it occurs only in poetry and tends to be laudatory in tone.

While these titles are the only ones that appear to have been in common use to emperors, most Latin titles (except *ere*) were addressed to emperors occasionally. The imperial titles, in contrast, were rarely used to Roman citizens of lower rank, except for *domine* and *imperator*. Like *domine*, *imperator* is used to non-emperors in the majority of examples preserved in literature. The basic address meaning that one would expect from this word, that of a soldier addressing his commander, was certainly a part of the military address system and is attested in Caesar as well as in declamations of various periods and in more historical contexts in Livy and Valerius Maximus.[67] Equally authentic seems to be the use by others to a Roman general, as from Catullus to Caesar, enemy soldiers to Caesar, or envoys to a general.[68] Occasionally the term is used sarcastically or as a joke (Pl. *Mil.* 1160, Cic. *Pis.* 91). Although some of the non-imperial examples come from authors writing after the establishment of the empire, all are addressed to men who lived before it. There is thus no evidence that after the establishment of the empire the address *imperator* remained in military use to commanders other than emperors.

A variety of other titles was also in use for people other than

[65] e.g. 1. 31, 1. 63; the *Caesar* addresses may well be left over from the original dedication of the *Fasti* to Augustus (see Bömer 1957–8: i. 17–18).
[66] Mart. 5. 3. 1, etc.; Stat. *Silv.* 1. 1. 5, etc.; Sil. 3. 607.
[67] Caes. *Civ.* 3. 91. 3; Calp. *Decl.* 3; [Quint.] *Decl.* 3. 1, 3. 5, etc.; Liv. 7. 10. 2, etc.; V. Max. 9. 9. 2, etc.; Sen. *Ben.* 5. 24.
[68] Catul. 29. 11; [Caes.] *Afr.* 35. 4; Sal. *Cat.* 33. 1.

emperors. We have already noted *ere* 'master' and *era* 'mistress' from slaves to their masters and mistresses (pp. 79–80); this term's restriction to one setting makes it the simplest of Latin titles. It does, however, have a late derivative *mi erilis*, which occurs twice in Apuleius, both times in conversations between two free women (Apul. *Met.* 4. 27, 9. 16). This seems to be an ingratiating, low-register term which is not really subservient, very much like *domina*. I have found no evidence for it in other authors and suspect it of being Apuleius' invention.

Apart from *ere* and *era*, the title best attested as an address in early Latin is *patrone* 'patron'. The word *patronus* could be applied to any citizen who acted as the protector of a less well-off friend, and *patrone* as an address takes the perspective of that friend. Thus Cicero is so addressed in a grateful letter from M. Curius (*Fam.* 7. 29. 2), Horace quotes the term in an angry address to a Roman noble from his client (*Ep.* 1. 7. 92), and Catullus calls the Muse *patrona virgo* 'patron virgin' (1. 9).[69]

Plautus provides the largest body of information on the use of *patrone*, but his evidence must be treated with care. The expected sense of the term occurs in the *Menaechmi*, where a slave, thinking that he has just been freed, immediately addresses his former master with *salve, mi patrone* 'greetings, my patron'.[70] In other passages, *patrone* is used in a more extended sense by slaves and prostitutes to free men who have been helpful to them (e.g. *Mos.* 746, *Mil.* 915). In the largest body of Plautine examples, however, *patrone* is used as a form of gross flattery by a master to his slave. Thus one master makes a request of his slave Olympio with *Olympisce mi, mi pater, mi patrone* 'my little Olympio, my father, my patron' (*Cas.* 739), and another expresses gratitude to his slave with *mi anime, mi Trachalio, mi liberte, mi patrone potius, immo mi pater* 'my soul, my Trachalio, my freedman, rather my patron, indeed my father' (*Rud.* 1265–6). That slaves enjoyed this kind of flattery is shown by *As.* 651–3, where a slave says *sed*

[69] This reading of the text has been doubted but is now generally accepted; see Thomson (1997: 198–200); Ellis (1889: 7); Fordyce (1961: 86–7). For the later usage of *patronus*, see O'Brien (1930: 85–6).

[70] 1031, cf. also 1032; one of the ways in which patron–client relationships developed was that a former master became the *patronus* of his freedmen.

tibi si viginti minae argenti proferentur, quo nos vocabis nomine?
'But if twenty silver minae of silver are offered to you, by what
name will you call us?' Receiving the answer *libertos* 'freedmen', he asks *non patronos?* 'not patrons?', to which his
desperate master hastily replies *id potius* 'yes, rather that'
(and does in fact use this address shortly afterwards, at 689).
It is very unlikely that *patrone* was ever used to flatter slaves
except in comedy,[71] but the deferential tone of the address in
these examples was probably applicable in real life as well.

Another term for patrons is *rex*. The basic referential meaning of *rex* is 'king', and in address it is frequently used as a
compliment to a king or god, whether real (Ov. *Pont.* 1. 8. 21)
or mythological (Verg. *A.* 11. 344). It seems also to be used
once to the emperor[72] and is applied to figures who are virtually
functioning as kings even if they do not technically hold that
title, as Hannibal (Sil. 8. 211). Cicero also once uses it to a
Roman priest bearing the ritual title *rex* (*Dom.* 127). The
speaker is normally a subject of the king addressed, but the
term can also be used by others without any connotations of
subservience, as for example when Roman envoys are engaging
in negotiations with an enemy king (Sal. *Jug.* 102. 5). It belongs
to a higher register than *domine* and is much more common in
literature; in everyday life, however, *rex* in this sense was
probably rare except at the courts of kings.

From a very early period, however, *rex* could also be used to
refer to patrons; this usage does not seem to have been affected
by the Romans' well-known loathing of the use of *rex* for an
actual Roman monarch.[73] Address usage in this sense may be

[71] For the difference in the master–slave relationship between comedy and
real life, see Segal (1987, esp. chs. 4–5).

[72] Stat. *Silv.* 4. 1. 46. It is often argued that the text is corrupt because of
the impossibility of this vocative at this period (e.g. Mommsen 1887–8: ii. 764
n. 4; Håkanson 1969: 111–12), but there are no other signs of corruption, and
the manuscript reading is defended by a number of scholars (e.g. Coleman
1988: 81–2; Bishop 1954: 96–7). I would retain the reading *rex* (and its
interpretation as a vocative, which can only be avoided by a very unnatural
reading of the Latin), on the grounds that if this address could be used in
flattery to a patron (see below), it should not be too pejorative to use to an
emperor—especially not one who liked to be called *dominus et deus*.

[73] Cf. E. Fraenkel (1960: 182–3); White (1978: 81). For the referential use
of *rex* in private letters, see e.g. Bowman and Thomas (1996: 324); Cugusi
(1992: ii. 177); *P. Mich.* viii. 472. 2.

early as well, but the first evidence for it is in Horace, where the poet says to Maecenas *rexque paterque audisti coram, nec verbo parcius absens* 'you have heard me call you "king" and "father" to your face; I use no less generous language behind your back' (*Ep.* 1. 7. 37–8). It is notable that when Horace actually quotes an address to a patron, however, the term used is *patrone* (*Ep.* 1. 7. 92). This difference suggests both that *patrone* was not as deferential as the address *rex* (i.e. it was not worth reminding one's patron that one had used it), and that it belonged to a higher register and so was more admissible in literature. In later literature *rex* is frequently coupled with *domine* (as with *pater* here) in discussions of address to patrons and prospective patrons.[74] The frequency of these references and the absence of any direct attestation in literature show that *rex* in this sense probably was, like *domine*, common but subliterary as an address. It seems, however, to have remained restricted to the patron/client relationship and never developed the generalized usage of *domine*.

The feminine *regina* 'queen' is used primarily to queens or goddesses, very often by people who are not actually their subjects; as such it is, like *rex* to kings, complimentary rather than subservient. In a few passages *regina* is used to a woman who is not a queen, in an extended use more general than that of *rex* and belonging to a higher register than *domina*. Two such passages come from poetry: Martial addresses Lucan's widow Polla Argentaria as *regina . . . Polla* (10. 64. 1), and Jason addresses the unknown Medea as *regina* (V. Fl. 5. 385). One could classify the extended usage as strictly poetic were it not for a case in Petronius (128. 2), where a lover addresses a rich woman as *regina* in a mortified plea, and an example at Pompeii (*CIL* iv. 2413h). It thus looks as though *regina* had an extended sense in non-literary usage, though it is likely to have been much less common than generalized *domina*. The tone is clearly highly respectful; in all three cases the speaker is making an important request of the addressee.

Other titles belonged to the Republican system of offices. Here it is sometimes difficult to distinguish between titles and occupational terms; in this section I have included only titles of offices important enough to have honoured any holder thereof.

[74] Mart. 10. 10. 5, 1. 112. 1, 2. 68. 2, 4. 83. 5; Juv. 8. 161.

Evidence is not plentiful, but it looks as though titles of high
office like *dictator* and *consul* could be used instead of names in
address to holders of those offices.[75] Such usage is attested for
both titles in historical texts; *consul* is also attested in writings
contemporary with the consul concerned and was certainly a
part of non-literary as well as literary language, though it
belongs to a fairly formal register.

Most of the preceding titles are deferential to some degree,
and intended to be used for superiors. There is also a group of
primarily literary titles which are complimentary without being
deferential: *dux* 'leader', *ductor* 'leader', *rector* 'ruler, guide,
helmsman', *regnator* 'ruler', *moderator* 'director', *domitor* 'conqueror', *dominator* 'ruler', and *dominatrix* 'ruler'. These addresses recognize someone's status as a leader, ruler, or guide
and praise him or her for that rank, but they do not imply any
subordination of the speaker. Thus Augustus in a letter addresses Tiberius as *iucundissime . . . vir fortissime et dux*
νομιμώτατε 'most delightful, bravest man, and most law-
abiding leader' (Suet. *Tib.* 21. 4), and Statius addresses a
parrot as *psittace dux volucrum* 'parrot, leader of birds' (*Silv.*
2. 4. 1), while Evander calls Aeneas *o Teucrum atque Italum
fortissime ductor* 'O bravest leader of Trojans and Italians'
(Verg. *A.* 8. 513), and *ductor* is even once used in an order
from a commander to a military officer under him (Sil. 7. 329).
Rector can be more complimentary, since *regere* 'rule' implies
more power than *ducere* 'lead', and is often used to gods as well
as humans (e.g. Verg. *A.* 8. 572). It does not imply subordination either, however, as it is used by Mercury in a rebuke to
Hannibal (Sil. 3. 173) and by Jason to the helmsman of his ship
(V. Fl. 8. 197). The other addresses in this group are rare, but
they seem to follow the same principle; thus Ovid has a rich
man address a strange fisherman as *o qui pendentia parvo aera
cibo celas, moderator harundinis* 'O controller of the fishing rod,
you who hide the hanging fishhook with a little bait' (*Met.* 8.
855–6).

The Latin language thus contained a wide range of titles,[76]

---

[75] *Dictator*: Liv. 7. 13. 3, 22. 30. 3; Sil. 8. 269; *consul*: Luc. 6. 791; Sil. 5. 83;
Cic. *Phil.* 2. 30; Fro. 27. 22, 29. 7, etc. (for Fronto, always in the form *consul
amplissime*).

[76] This range becomes even greater in the late empire, when abstractions

from the subliterary register to the formal and poetic ones. Some titles expressed great deference, while others seem to have conveyed none at all and could be used by superiors. Some were restricted to holders of a particular office, and others were usable to virtually anyone. Some could be used only by speakers in a certain relationship to the addressee, and others were more general. The rank of the addressee was only one element among many determining which title was used; context, setting, and the speaker's identity also played a role.

such as *iustitia* 'justice', *clementia* 'clemency', and *beatitudo* 'blessedness' are also used as titles; see O'Brien (1930: 1–71).

3

Kinship Terms

HIPPOLYTUS. Committe curas auribus, mater, meis.
PHAEDRA. Matris superbum est nomen et nimium
  potens:
  nostros humilius nomen affectus decet;
  me vel sororem, Hippolyte, vel famulam voca,
  famulamque potius: omne servitium feram.

(Sen. Phaed. 608–12)

HIPPOLYTUS. Entrust your cares to my ears, mother.
PHAEDRA. The name of 'mother' is proud and too
  powerful; a more humble name is more appropriate
  to our feelings. Call me 'sister', Hippolytus, or 'maidservant', preferably 'maidservant': I would bear any
  slavery.

IN Seneca's *Phaedra*, Hippolytus sees *mater* 'mother' as a
soothing address for his distressed stepmother, while she,
burdened by her incestuous love for him, recoils from the
address and suggests a different kinship term before deciding to
abandon kinship metaphors entirely (cf. Boyle 1985: 1330–1).
Addresses using kinship terms are not infrequently attempts to
define the nature of a relationship in which no blood ties exist,
and their use may be contested by an addressee who refuses
that definition of the relationship, as does Phaedra and as do
the women in the following passage of Plautus,[1] where a young
man is trying to retrieve his beloved *meretrix* from her mother's
house:

ALCESIMARCHUS. Meae issula sua aedes egent. ad me sine ducam.
SELENIUM.   Aufer manum.
AL. Germana mea sororcula.
SE.   Repudio te fraterculum.

---

[1] The text of much of this passage is doubtful; I follow Lindsay's edition
(Oxford, 1904).

AL. Tum tu igitur, mea matercula.
MELAENIS.   Repudio te puerculum.
                                                (Pl. *Cist.* 450–2)

ALCESIMARCHUS. My house needs its little dear. Let me take her.
SELENIUM.   Hands off!
AL. My own true little sister . . .
SE.   I reject you as my little brother.
AL. Then you in that case, my little mother . . .
MELAENIS.   I reject you as my little boy.

Of course, the most common use of kinship terms is as addresses to relatives (henceforth the 'literal' use). As such they are largely unproblematic: *mater* as an address to the speaker's biological mother is simply standard in Latin. Many relatives, such as sons and wives, can be addressed not only with kinship terms but also by name or with other words, but the question of which type of address is used when belongs to an examination of interactions among relatives and so will be postponed until Chapter 10; this chapter concentrates on the non-literal use of kinship terms. An overview of the Latin kinship terms most often used in address, and the relatives they nominally designate, is given in Table 2.[2]

In many passages the addressee of a kinship term does not have the genetic relationship to the speaker that the lexical meaning of the word would suggest. These uses require more investigation, particularly as for some terms they are actually more common than the literal sense. One such alternative use is that of kinship terms found in a grammatical construction indicating that the kinship is not to the speaker but to someone else. The most common such construction is a vocative with possessive genitive: thus *gnate Tonantis* 'son of the Thunderer' ([Sen.] *Her. O.* 1151) relates the addressee to Jupiter, whereas *gnate* alone would relate him to the speaker. *Nate* and *nata*, since they often function as participles meaning 'born (from)' rather than as nouns meaning 'son' and 'daughter', frequently use an ablative instead of the genitive, as *Iove nate* 'born from Jove' (Liv. 1. 7. 10). *Coniunx* and some other nouns can also take an adjective defining the object of the relationship, as

---

[2] For more information on Latin kinship terms, see Harrod (1909—cf. p. 130 for caveats), Moreau (1978), Saller (1997), and sources cited therein.

Table 2. *Kinship terms most often used in address*

Addressees	Male	Female	Gender-neutral
Parents	*pater* 'father'	*mater* 'mother'	*parens* 'parent'
	genitor 'father'	*genetrix* 'mother'	
Children	*fili* 'son'	*filia* 'daughter'	*liberi* 'children'
	(g)nate 'son'	*filiola* 'little daughter'	*progenies* 'progeny'
	sate 'offspring'	*(g)nata* 'daughter'	*proles* 'progeny'
		sata 'offspring'	*propago* 'progeny'
			suboles 'offspring'
Siblings	*frater* 'brother'	*soror* 'sister'	
	germane 'brother'	*germana* 'sister'	
Spouses	*vir* 'husband'	*uxor* 'wife'	*coniunx* 'spouse'
	marite 'husband'		
Other	*socer* 'father-in-law'	*noverca* 'stepmother'	*nepos* 'grandchild'
	gener 'son-in-law'	*nurus* 'daughter-in-law'	
	patrue 'uncle'		
	sator 'progenitor'		

Thesea coniunx 'Thesean spouse' for Phaedra (Sen. *Phaed.* 129).

Such constructions can be used in a variety of ways. Most often they are employed with *(g)nate*, for in so doing they form a patronymic. As we shall see (pp. 210–12), Latin poets can use a single-word patronymic (e.g. *Aesonide* for Jason, son of Aeson) as an elegant and polite way of addressing heroes in literary works. The same is largely true of periphrastic patronymics or metronymics formed with *nate*: *nate dea* 'goddess-born' is a standard polite address, not only for Aeneas in Vergil, where it is common,[3] but also for Aeneas in other poets and for other appropriate mythological heroes such as Phocus and Achilles.[4] As the form *nate dea* illustrates, the periphrastic patronymic is more flexible than the single-word kind because it can be used with words other than names. It is thus usable for less complimentary addresses as well, as *Arcades, o saxis nimirum et robore nati* 'Arcadians, O certainly born from stones and oak' (Stat. *Theb.* 4. 340); basically the form itself has little

[3] 11 times, e.g. *A.* 1. 582, 615, 2. 289, 3. 311; on Vergil's use of this term as following Homeric tradition, see Moseley (1926: 88).

[4] Aeneas: Ov. *Met.* 14. 246, 15. 439; Sil. 8. 81; others: Ov. *Met.* 7. 690, 12. 86, 13. 168; Hor. *Epod.* 13. 12.

meaning but will be as complimentary or uncomplimentary as the other words involved make it.

In theory any other word meaning 'son', 'daughter', etc. should be able to form periphrastic patronymics as easily as (g)nate, but in practice such addresses are less common. It is particularly notable that fili, which has the same lexical meaning as (g)nate and is common in the literal address use, very rarely appears as part of a patronymic address.[5] The reason for this difference could be that (g)nate, with its obvious etymological connection to nascor 'to be born', was more suitable to such constructions than fili, but I doubt that this is the correct explanation. In Greek, where τέκνον 'child' has the same obvious connection to the verb τίκτω 'to be born' and παῖ 'boy', the main alternative, has much less of a kinship meaning than fili, it is nevertheless παῖ rather than τέκνον which is normally used to form periphrastic patronymics in address (Dickey 1996: 52). In the case of (g)nate and fili, I think the real reason for the difference is that fili as a vocative is primarily a prose word and (g)nate a poetic one, and patronymics in Latin are a poetic form of address.

Likewise (g)nata is used in this construction much more than filia, as Pandione nata 'born from Pandion' (Procne, Ov. Met. 6. 634) or o magni gnata Tonantis, incluta Pallas 'daughter of the great Thunderer, renowned Pallas' (Sen. Ag. 356–7). A number of other kinship terms are highly poetic and always or almost always appear as part of such constructions: propago, as Troiana propago 'Trojan progeny' (Ov. Am. 3. 6. 65), progenies, as o bona matrum progenies 'O good progeny of mothers' (Catul. 64. 23), proles, as deum certissima proles 'most certain progeny of the gods' (Verg. A. 6. 322) or Poeantia proles 'progeny of Poeas' (Ov. Met. 13. 45), and sate and sata, which are necessarily used with ablatives, as virgo sata Nocte 'virgin sprung from Night' (Verg. A. 7. 331).

The mythological tradition, with its emphasis on ancestry, favoured identifying people by their parents over identification via other relatives, and thus such periphrastic constructions are more common with words for offspring than with words for parents. Nevertheless 'parent' words are also so used on occasion, resulting in periphrastic teknonyms like Aeneadum

[5] Exceptions include Andr. frag. 2; Catul. 37. 18; ILLRP 961.

genetrix 'mother of the Aeneadae' (Lucr. 1. 1) or *alma parens Idaea deum* 'nurturing Idaean mother of the gods' (Verg. *A.* 10. 252); such addresses are normally highly poetic and very often used to gods and goddesses. Perhaps for this reason they more frequently involve the poetic terms *genitor*, *genetrix*, *sator*, and *parens* than the more prosaic *pater* and *mater*. When the addressee of a teknonym is human, he is often an emperor, in which case the address tends to be very complimentary and not literally true, as *parens orbis* 'parent of the world' (Mart. 9. 5. 1), *magnorum proles genitorque deorum* 'progeny and father of great gods' (Stat. *Silv.* 1. 1. 74), or *pater patriae* 'father of the country' (Ov. *Tr.* 2. 181). Teknonymic addresses to emperors, in fact, appear to be developed from those to gods. Like the periphrastic patronymics, however, periphrastic teknonyms are not inherently polite, only usually so; it depends on the genitive used. Thus when addressed to people other than gods or emperors these vocatives can carry a variety of meanings: *tot natorum memoranda parens* 'notable parent of so many children' ([Sen.] *Oct.* 932–3) is polite, but *fraudum genitor* 'father of deceits' (Sil. 13. 738) is not.

Whereas patronymics normally identify the addressee as the offspring of a specific individual and praise him or her by asserting the connection to that person, teknonyms convey a different kind of praise, that of parenthood in general. It is not a connection to the world that is creditable in an emperor, but his status as parent of it. For this reason patronymics normally contain a name or a word referring to a specific individual, as *dea* 'goddess', while teknonyms are much more likely to use generalities not referring to individuals, like *deorum* 'the gods' or *mundi* 'the world'. I have found very few examples of teknonymic addresses containing the actual name of a specific individual, and those which do refer to individual offspring in one way or another are apparently restricted to female addressees: thus *mater Alcidae incluti* 'mother of renowned Alcides' for Alcmena ([Sen.] *Her. O.* 1832), *mater Amoris* 'mother of Cupid' for Venus (Ov. *Ars* 1. 30), *P. Cordi mater* 'mother of Publius Cordius' (*ILLRP* 853), and *Cornelia, mater Gracchorum* 'Cornelia, mother of the Gracchi' (Juv. 6. 167–8).

There is also an overall gender difference in the extent to which different terms are used in such periphrastic constructions: terms for mothers are so used 10% of the time, but those for fathers only 5% of the time. This difference is also visible in addresses for siblings, which are used periphrastically 2% of the time for males but 4% for females, and in those for spouses, which are so used 3% of the time to men but 15% of the time to women. In Greek, women's names were often avoided in public, and females were identified by their male relatives (Schaps 1977); while the Romans used names freely to address and refer to women (cf. pp. 240–1), this gender discrepancy in the use of kinship terms suggests that Latin speakers nevertheless had a certain tendency to use identification by means of relatives more often for females than for males.

Kinship terms for siblings are rare and poetic in periphrastic constructions, but there are enough examples to make it clear that they belong with the patronymics rather than the teknonyms in the sense that they connect the addressee to a specific individual rather than glorifying siblinghood in general. They are most often used to addressees with important siblings, as *impiger Aenea, volitantis frater Amoris* 'energetic Aeneas, brother of winged Cupid' (Tib. 2. 5. 39), or *Turni soror* 'sister of Turnus' (Juturna, Ov. *Fast.* 1. 463); as a result, they are normally complimentary.

The addition of a genitive or adjective to a word meaning 'wife' is not uncommon in poetry and is occasionally found in prose. Such addresses can be complimentary (e.g. *laudati iuvenis rarissima coniunx* 'exceptional spouse of a lauded young man', Stat. *Silv.* 5. 1. 11), uncomplimentary (e.g. *uxor pauperis Ibyci* 'wife of poor Ibycus', Hor. *Carm.* 3. 15. 1), or neutral (e.g. *Xenophontis uxor* 'Xenophon's wife', Cic. *Inv.* 1. 51) depending on the spouse concerned. They may be used of divinities, as *nympha, Numae coniunx* 'nymph, spouse of Numa' (Ov. *Fast.* 3. 262), as well as of humans.

Husbands, on the other hand, are rarely identified via their wives. The exceptions are the consorts of important goddesses (e.g. *Persephonae coniunx*, Prop. 2. 28. 48), who can be complimented by a reference to their wives as ordinary mortals cannot. Tibullus also addresses his beloved's husband as *fallacis coniunx incaute puellae* 'careless husband of a deceitful girl' (1. 6. 15), but this address is a special case, because in an illicit affair the husband cannot be named.

A few periphrastic kinship terms stand apart from the above description of usage. These are addressed to relatives for whom there exists no standard vocative kinship term in Latin. Such vocatives relate the addressee primarily to the speaker via the person named in the genitive; as such they function like literal kinship terms, but like other periphrastic uses they are poetic. Thus Ilia addresses her grandmother with *Venus . . . genetrix patris nostri* 'Venus . . . mother of our father' (Enn. *Ann.* 58), Oedipus calls Creon *germane nostrae coniugis* 'brother of our wife' (Sen. *Oed.* 210), and Plautus has an uncle address his nephew[6] with *fratris mei gnate* 'son of my brother' (*Poen.* 1196).

The periphrastic use of kinship terms, while not identical to the literal use, is easily derivable from it and can be understood without difficulty as a poetic variation in the address system. Less closely connected are two other uses, the transferred and the extended, in which a kinship term occurs without a genitive or other modifier but still is applied to an addressee who does not stand in the relationship to the speaker suggested by the lexical meaning of the term. In extended usage, the address relates the addressee to the speaker; both the quotations at the start of this chapter are of this type. In transferred usage, as in the periphrastic uses already examined, the vocative relates the addressee to a third party rather than to the speaker; the difference between periphrastic and transferred usage is that in the latter no grammatical indication of non-literal usage is given.

The most common type of transferred usage is the use of the address expected from a third person who is the topic of conversation or whom the speaker wishes to bring to mind, rather than that expected from the speaker. Thus Latinus' wife Amata calls her husband *genitor* when discussing their daughter Lavinia (Verg. *A.* 7. 360; cf. Horsfall 2000: 250), and Medea is addressed as *mater* in condemnation of her treatment of her children (Verg. *Ecl.* 8. 48). Proteus likewise apostrophizes the absent Eurydice with *dulcis coniunx* 'sweet spouse' when taking Orpheus' point of view (Verg. *G.* 4. 465), while Martial uses *marite* to a man whose wife's lover is the topic of discussion

[6] Strictly speaking, his first cousin once removed, but this comes to the same thing in Latin; see p. 274.

(2. 83. 1), and Silius has a warrior address as *socer* the father-in-law of an enemy he has just killed (5. 318). Seneca even has Atreus address his brother Thyestes as *pater* when talking about the children he has just made Thyestes eat (*Thy.* 1004).[7]

Essentially the use of transferred kinship terms is a poetic phenomenon, but it is also fairly common in the declamations, where the lack of names or real identities for the imaginary characters frequently makes it impossible to use the normal Latin address system. Thus when a case involves the addressee's treatment of one of his or her close relatives, it is not uncommon for transferred kinship terms to be used, relating the addressee to the person under discussion. Calpurnius Flaccus has a speaker address an unrelated man as *pater* because he is the father of the dead boy at issue (*Decl.* 35), and Seneca describes a man calling his wife *noverca* because she is his dead son's stepmother (*Con.* 9. 6. 1). Orators in the declamations can also use transferred kinship terms in relation to their clients; thus the client's father may be addressed as *pater* (Sen. *Con.* 7. 8. 2), his mother as *mater* (Quint. *Decl.* 388. 10), and his stepmother as *noverca* (Sen. *Con.* 7. 1. 20).[8]

Especially interesting is the frequent use, in declamations, of *marite* from an orator to his client's husband (e.g. [Quint.] *Decl.* 10. 5) and the complete absence of transferred kinship terms for wives in the orators (despite repeated addresses to married women). How could Roman orators be able to identify a nameless man by his relationship to his wife but unable to address a woman by her relationship to her husband? The explanation seems to be that speakers in the declamations are always male; if a woman's part is taken, the speech is written from the point of view of an advocate rather than that of the woman concerned (cf. Quint. *Decl.* 260. 1; Bonner 1949: 52). If

---

[7] For other examples of transferred kinship terms in poetry, see Mart. 2. 34. 6, 3. 85. 2; Catul. 61. 135, 184, 189; Verg. *Ecl.* 8. 30, 50; [Verg.] *Aetna* 587, *Ciris* 191; Luc. 7. 675; Sen. *Thy.* 429, 442, *Med.* 1024, *Tro.* 785, *Phaed.* 1191, 1256; Stat. *Theb.* 7. 342; [Ov.] *Epic. Drusi* 22, 341. Cf. also *ILS* 5219, 6728.

[8] Other examples of transferred kinship terms in the declamations include Sen. *Con.* 7. 8. 2, 9. 5. 16, 9. 6. 3, 9. 6. 19; Quint. *Decl.* 259. 16; [Quint.] *Decl.* 2. 13, 6. 7, 8. 15, 8. 18, 10. 4, 10. 5 (*bis*), 10. 10 (*bis*), 10. 11, 10. 13, 10. 14, 10. 16, 10. 18, 10. 19, 18. 10, 18. 15, 19. 4, 19. 9, 19. 10 (*bis*), 19. 11, 19. 16. *Frater* to a client's brother at Quint. *Inst.* 9. 2. 20 may be evidence that this practice also occurred in actual orations.

a male speaker were to address a woman with a transferred
kinship term meaning 'wife', he would be using an address
indistinguishable from that used to his own wife, and apparently the exclusive and proprietary nature of the marriage bond
made such addresses unacceptable in Latin in a way that
transferred terms for other relatives were not. I have found
no examples of either transferred or extended use of terms for
'wife' by males (nor of such use of terms for 'husband' by
women) in Latin prose, and very few in poetry (Luc. 7. 675;
Verg. *G*. 4. 465).

It is also possible, though only in poetry, to use transferred
kinship terms to relate several people to each other rather than
to another person. Thus we find *socer, beate nec tibi nec alteri,
generque Noctuine, putidum caput* 'father-in-law, a blessing
neither to yourself nor to another, and son-in-law Noctuinus,
rotten head' ([Verg.] *Cat*. 6. 1–2; cf. also Catul. 29. 24) and *boni
coniuges* 'good spouses' (Catul. 61. 225–6). In this class also
belong the frequent invocation of groups of goddesses as
sorores, whether they are the Fates (Luc. 6. 703), the Furies
(Sen. *Her. F*. 110), or the ubiquitous Muses (Mart. 2. 22. 1,
etc.).[9]

Still another use of transferred kinship terms is in address to
a group of people, all of whom presumably stand in the
relationship expressed with regard to someone, though not to
the same individual nor to each other. In these passages kinship
terms are used in an almost absolute sense. Thus Vergil has an
old Trojan woman address the other Trojan women as *matres*
(*A*. 5. 646), and Seneca's Alcmena apostrophizes mothers with
matres.[10] The most common use of such terms, however, is not
in poetry but in the declamations, where they are used to elicit
sympathy in appeals to the audience. Thus we find addresses
such as *omnes liberi, omnes parentes* 'all children, all parents'
([Quint.] *Decl*. 4. 12) or *patres . . . fratres . . . mariti*.[11]

Transferred kinship terms are not by nature a polite or

[9] Other passages in which such usage occurs include Catul. 33. 1–2, 8;
[Verg.] *Culex* 18; Stat. *Silv*. 1. 4. 123, *Theb*. 7. 628.

[10] *Her. O*. 1854. See also 1894; Verg. *A*. 7. 400 (cf. Horsfall 2000: 271, 275–
6); Luc. 2. 38.

[11] Sen. *Con*. 1. 5. 1. See also 3. 1; Quint. *Decl*. 246. 9; [Quint.] *Decl*. 5. 12,
7. 12.

impolite form of address; their meaning depends on the context
and the identity of the person to whom the addressee is related.
They are found with most types of kinship term, but (g)nate
and (g)nata, which are so common in periphrastic usage,
conspicuously lack a transferred sense.

Extended kinship terms relate the addressee to the speaker like
literal ones but are used to a person who does not stand to the
speaker in the relationship indicated by the lexical meaning of
the term. Of course, kinship terms are sometimes used by a
speaker who erroneously thinks he is related to the addressee or
who is pretending to be related, but in most cases the speaker of
an extended kinship term does not intend to imply an actual
genetic connection. Extended kinship terms can be used to
relatives for whom the address system does not provide literal
kinship terms. Thus Medea addresses her aunt Circe as *mater*
(V. Fl. 7. 242, 248) and is addressed by her as *nata* (7. 229),
while she calls her grandfather *genitor* (Sen. *Med.* 33). More
common is the use of extended kinship terms to address in-
laws, although the vocatives *socer*, *gener*, and *nurus* occur as
well. Thus a father-in-law (or the father of one's fiancée) can be
called *pater*, and a mother-in-law *mater* or *genetrix*.[12] Ovid also
has Dido address Cupid as *frater Amor* when thinking of him
as her brother-in-law (*Ep.* 7. 32), and Suetonius quotes
Tiberius addressing his daughter-in-law Agrippina with *filiola*
'little daughter' (*Tib.* 53. 1).

Extended kinship terms are also used to people who are
completely unrelated to the speaker but share some characteristic of the relative whose kinship term they receive. Women
addressed as *mater*, for example, are old (at least in comparison
with the speaker) and are often being treated with affection
and/or respect. Thus Medea uses *mater* affectionately to her
nurse (V. Fl. 5. 353), but Turnus uses *mater* in a rebuke to an
elderly priestess.[13] On occasion *mater* is used as a polite address

[12] Verg. *A.* 11. 410, 12. 13, 50, 74; V. Fl. 8. 350; Ov. *Met.* 9. 326.
[13] Verg. *A.* 7. 441; cf. Horsfall 2000: 299. Alexander the Great uses *mater* to
Darius' captive mother Sisigambis in Curtius (3. 12. 17, 25, 5. 2. 20), but note
that Alexander's habits probably exemplify Greek rather than Latin usage,
since this address is found in Greek sources earlier than Curtius (Diodorus 17.
37. 6).

for complete strangers who happen to be older women. Such usage goes back to Plautus, who has a shipwrecked girl address a strange priestess as *mater* (*Rud*. 263, 289) and is also found in Petronius, where a student uses *mater* to an elderly vegetable-seller in a polite request for directions (7. 1; the woman views the address as *urbanitas* and is delighted), and in Ovid, where a little girl greets an unknown old woman with *mater* (*Fast*. 4. 513). Apuleius uses both *mater* and *parens* in this fashion.[14] This evidence suggests that the extended use of *mater*, in contrast to the periphrastic and transferred uses, may have been a part of conversational as well as literary language.

Pater is likewise used as a polite or affectionate address to older men, whether or not the speaker knows them. Thus Horace calls his friend Trebatius *pater optime* (*S*. 2. 1. 12), and Vergil has Aeneas use the address to Acestes (*A*. 5. 533); at the other end of the literary spectrum, Petronius several times uses the address in requests to older men (98. 8, 100. 5), while Plautus has a youth politely greet an unknown older man with *pater*.[15] Several comments by ancient authors suggest that using the address *pater* was a common way to be polite or affectionate to older men in the classical period. Horace concludes a discussion of how to be a successful flatterer with *frater, pater adde; ut cuique est aetas, ita quemque facetus adopta* 'add "brother" or "father": adopt each person politely according to his age' (*Ep*. 1. 6. 54–5) and tells his patron Maecenas *rexque paterque audisti coram, nec verbo parcius absens* 'you have heard me call you "patron" and "father" to your face; I use no less generous language behind your back' (*Ep*. 1. 7. 37–8; cf. Horsfall 1993: 59). Ovid, discussing the disguised Myrrha's affair with her unsuspecting father, remarks of their night together *forsitan aetatis quoque nomine 'filia' dixit: dixit et illa 'pater', sceleri ne nomina desint* 'perhaps, using a name that suited her age, he called her "daughter", and she called him "father", so that their crime might not lack its names' (*Met*. 10. 467–8). Marcus Brutus, in a letter to Atticus, remarks that *licet ergo patrem appellet Octavius Ciceronem, referat omnia, laudet,*

---

[14] *Met*. 1. 21, 2. 3, 3. 12 (cf. Van der Paardt 1971: 94–6), 4. 26, 9. 17.

[15] *Rud*. 103; other examples of extended *pater* include Ov. *Ars* 1. 548; Stat. *Theb*. 7. 248; V. Fl. 4. 25.

gratias agat, tamen illud apparebit, verba rebus esse contraria
'even though Octavius may call Cicero "father", report everything to him, praise him, and thank him, nevertheless it will be
apparent that his words are opposed to his deeds' (Cic. *Ad
Brut.* 1. 17. 5).

Despite the explicit connection between *pater* and age drawn
by both Horace and Ovid, the term is also used to addressees
not significantly older than the speaker. Maecenas was probably not much older than Horace, and Plautus has an old man
use *mi pater* to a slave who is probably his junior.[16] Curtius
depicts Alexander's soldiers as addressing him with *pater* (9. 3.
16); the soldiers may have been recruited at a fairly tender age
but have since been with Alexander for a long time, which
means that given Alexander's own youth they cannot be much
younger than he.

In all three of these cases the subjection of speaker to
addressee is stressed more than usual, and it is likely that on
occasion the element of respect and affection in the address
pater outweighed the age factor. Likewise the reverse can
occur; Plautus provides several examples of *pater* being used
patronizingly to unknown old men by people behaving far from
respectfully (e.g. *Mos.* 952, *Trin.* 878). But both these and the
use to youthful addressees are rare; the addressee of *pater*, like
that of *mater*, is normally both old and receiving respect and/or
affection. In Plautus' *Rudens*, a youth who is extremely grateful
to his slave thanks him with a string of vocatives: *mi anime, mi
Trachalio, mi liberte, mi patrone potius, immo mi pater* 'my soul,
my Trachalio, my freedman, rather my patron, indeed my
father' (1265–6). This seems to be a string of compliments in
increasing order of hyperbole, and it is significant that *mi pater*
is the most complimentary of them all.

Pater is also very common as an address to gods, most often
Jupiter[17] but also virtually any other male deity.[18] Such

---

[16] *Cas.* 739; the slave's youth is suggested by the facts that he is about to be
married (the old man is depicted as well past the age appropriate for love) and
that he has been the speaker's ἐρώμενος, a role normally reserved for the
younger partner.

[17] The name *Juppiter* in fact contains the address *pater* already, since it is an
archaic vocative equivalent to Ζεῦ πάτερ. This fusion, and the Greek parallel,
suggest that the habit of addressing the sky-god as 'father' is a very ancient
one; the fact that the word *pater* fused only with the vocative (which came to

[See p. 122 for n. 17 cont. and n. 18]

terminology is common in referential usage as well (see e.g. the discussion by Gellius at 5. 12). *Pater* can also be used to emperors, in which case it is highly deferential,[19] and *patres conscripti* is the standard address for senators (cf. pp. 284–5).[20]

Other words for 'father' seem to carry the same range of meanings as *pater*, but in the classical period these terms are apparently poetic as extended addresses. *Genitor* and *parens* can be used for gods (e.g. Verg. *A.* 4. 208; Stat. *Theb.* 1. 696) or to respected men, as *invicte parens* 'invincible parent' in praise to Scipio (Sil. 17. 651) and *sancte . . . o genitor* 'O holy father' to Fabius Maximus from Minucius in thanks for saving his life and army (Sil. 7. 737). The latter episode is also reported by Livy using *pater* (22. 30. 2) and by Greek authors with πάτερ (Plutarch, *Fab. Max.* 13. 8), which suggests that the incident has a historical basis but that the address *genitor* has been supplied for poetic elegance.

In the later empire, however, *parens* came to be used just as *pater* had been employed in the classical period. Apuleius says in his *Apology*,

Audistine vocabula, quae mihi Pontianus frater tuus tribuerat me parentem suum, me dominum, me magistrum cum saepe alias, tum in extremo tempore vitae vocans . . . (97).

Did you hear the titles which your brother Pontianus had conferred upon me, calling me his parent, his master, and his teacher, not only on many other occasions, but even in the last moments of his life . . .

Apuleius' style is far from conversational, but the reference here to the subliterary address *domine* suggests that *parens* is not simply a product of his literary flair. Somewhat later, the *Historia Augusta* describes a new emperor greeting the senators and equestrians cordially with *unumquemque, ut erat aetas, vel*

be used as a nominative), and not with the other cases, indicates that it was used more in address to Jupiter than in reference to him.

[18] e.g. Bacchus, Ov. *Met.* 11. 132; Ammon, Sil. 14. 440; Apollo, Verg. *A.* 3. 89; Mars, Stat. *Theb.* 3. 11; Hercules, Prop. 4. 9. 71; Janus, Mart. 10. 28. 7. *Mater* is also used for goddesses, as Catul. 63. 9.

[19] e.g. Ov. *Tr.* 2. 574; Calp. *Ecl.* 4. 146; Stat. *Silv.* 5. 1. 167; V. Fl. 1. 11; Plin. *Pan.* 89. 2.

[20] For the use of *pater* in the late empire, see O'Brien (1930: 85).

fratrem vel filium vel parentem adfatus blandissime est[21] 'He
addressed each one in a very flattering manner, as brother or
son or parent, according to his age'.[22] *Pater* could still be used
in an extended sense, however, at least in referential usage, for
in discussing Marcus Aurelius the *Historia Augusta* comments
*cum . . . ab aliis modo frater, modo pater, modo filius, ut cuiusque
aetas sinebat, et diceretur et amaretur* 'since he was called
brother, father, or son by different people, as each one's age
allowed, and loved accordingly' (4. 18. 1).

Terms for parents are not the only type of kinship term which
can appear in an extended usage. Horace and the *Historia
Augusta*, as we have seen, consider *frater* a term of flattery
for men younger than those who would receive *pater* or *parens*,
and Juvenal agrees, quoting a host flattering a rich guest with
vis, frater, ab ipsis ilibus? 'brother, would you like a piece of the
flank, no less?' and commenting *o nummi, vobis hunc praestat
honorem; vos estis frater* 'O money, you are the one he honours,
you are the "brother"!' (5. 135–7; see Mayor 1888–9: i. 265).
Quintilian also mentions the practice: *Certe quotiens blandiri
volumus iis qui esse amici videntur, nulla adulatio procedere ultra
hoc nomen potest, quam ut fratres vocemus* 'indeed whenever we
want to flatter those who seem to be our friends, no servile
flattery can surpass this one, that we call them "brothers"'
(*Decl.* 321. 4).

The extended use of *frater* is clearly friendly, but it need
convey neither deference nor sincere affection; in most cases it
seems to be no more than mildly polite. Its first attestation
comes from Cicero, who quotes a letter from one of Verres'
henchmen (the freedman Timarchides) to another
(Q. Apronius) containing the line *volo, mi frater, fraterculo
tuo credas* 'my brother, I wish you would trust your little
brother!' (*Ver.* 3. 155). This address does not appear to
convey particular flattery, though it is clearly cajoling. A
letter of *c*.23 BC uses *mi frater* in giving concerned advice to a
friend in difficulty (*CEL* 8. 7). A similar meaning is found in
Petronius, who repeatedly uses *frater* between friends and

---

[21] 9. 4. 1. *Fratrem* is an emendation for the *patrem* of the MSS.

[22] For the use of *parens* as a title in late Latin, see Friedlaender (1921–3: i.
77); O'Brien (1930: 85).

homosexual lovers of equal rank (11. 3, 13. 2, 91. 2, 129. 1),
Apuleius,[23] and Martial, who in a prose dedication addresses a
friend as *frater carissime* (9 *pr.* 1).

Frater is common in documents of the first two centuries AD,
especially letters, as an address for unrelated men.[24] In such
works *frater* seems to be a polite address for men of status
approximately equal to the speaker; it is friendly but does not
indicate any real intimacy. Fronto uses the term not infrequently in letters to his friends, but never to members of the
imperial family, however close his relationship to them.[25] Two
passages suggest that addressees could sometimes be insulted
by the extended use of *frater*: Martial complains about someone who calls him *frater* when there is no similarity between
them, and invites him to desist or risk being called *soror* in
return (10. 65), and when an ass greets a boar with *frater* in
Phaedrus (1. 29. 5), the boar is insulted by the implication of
similarity he sees in the address.

Although some of these passages call *frater* a flattering
address and others use it as an insult, there is no real conflict
among the different authors. *Frater* implies that the addressee
is close to the speaker and that the speaker is fond of him; its
use is a positive politeness strategy (cf. p. 17). Such a strategy
can backfire if used to someone who thinks of himself as the
speaker's superior and would prefer to keep his distance, and
clearly the use of *frater* did on occasion have this unintended
result. This risk is probably behind the normal restriction of
frater to addressees who are the speaker's equals or only
slightly superior to him socially (cf. Adams 1995: 119).

[23] *Met.* 2. 13, 9. 7. In view of the widespread nature of the extended usage,
Venus' address to Mercury as *frater Arcadi* (Apul. *Met.* 6. 7) is likely to be
another example of it, and one should not assume (as e.g. Kenney 1990: 198)
that this address makes Venus, in Apuleius' pantheon, Mercury's actual
brother and therefore Zeus' daughter.

[24] e.g. *Tab. Vindol. II* 210, 233. b. 3, 247, 248, 250. 17, 252, 255. 15, 259,
260, 265, 295, 300. 10, 301. 4, 309. 15, 310; *P. Oxy.* vii. 1022. 10; *CEL* 177. 3
(and often in later letters); *O. Claud.* 2. 3, 2. 9; *ILS* 8380; *EDH* 018450; Wâdi
Fawâkhir ostraca (Guéraud 1942) 1. 10, 2. 19, 4. 2; NB esp. 2. 6–9. On the use
of *frater* in such texts see Kepartová (1986); Adams (1995: 119); Bowman,
Thomas, and Adams (1990: 40); Cugusi (1973: 656–7, 660); Friedlaender
(1921–3: i. 77). For Christian usage see O'Brien (1930: 84); Engelbrecht
(1893: 10–12, 23). For the (in my view non-existent) 'military' use of *frater* see
p. 219.   [25] 176. 21, 177. 8, 185. 14, 188. 7.

Frater and generalized *domine* (pp. 88–94) have much in common as addresses, but their usage is not identical. *Domine* can be used freely to superiors, perhaps because it suggests the superiority of the father rather than the equality of the brother, and I know of no instances in which it is perceived as an insult. A hierarchy of flattery in which *domine* comes above *frater* is suggested not only by Fronto's use of *domine* to members of the imperial family and of both terms elsewhere, but also by Juvenal's discussion of legacy-hunting, in which he indicates that in order to be addressed as *frater* by an important Roman, one must be rich, while in order to be addressed as *domine* one must be not only rich but also childless (5. 132–9). At the same time there was a large overlap between the two terms, resulting in the occasional use of both *frater* and *domine* from the same speaker to the same addressee (*Tab. Vindol. II* 248, 250) and in the frequent combination of the two in *domine frater* (cf. p. 91). Another respect in which *frater* resembles *domine* is in its similarity to Greek usage, for Greek ἄδελφε 'brother' was also used to unrelated men at this period (Dickey 1996: 88).

Soror appears to function like *frater*.[26] Unrelated female friends address each other as *soror* in literature from the first century BC: Vergil's dying Camilla bids farewell to her friend Acca with *Acca soror* (*A.* 11. 823), Valerius Flaccus' Lemnian women exhort each other to crime with *soror* (2. 143), and witches in Apuleius also use the address to each other (*Met.* 1. 12, 1. 13). The address is the main one used between two unrelated women at Vindolanda.[27]

In addition, both *soror* and *frater* seem to have had a sexual meaning under certain circumstances. Plautus, as we have seen, has a young man address his beloved as *sororcula* (on the diminutive cf. Fruyt 1989) and depicts her refusing him with *repudio te fraterculum* (*Cist.* 451). Martial airs the issue more fully, saying

> O quam blandus es, Ammiane, matri!
> quam blanda est tibi mater, Ammiane!
> fratrem te vocat et soror vocatur.
> cur vos nomina nequiora tangunt?

---

[26] For the Christian usage of *soror*, see O'Brien (1930: 87).
[27] *Tab. Vindol. II* 291. 3, 11, 12, 292. i. 2, 292. b back, 293.

> quare non iuvat hoc quod estis esse?
> lusum creditis hoc iocumque? non est:
> matrem, quae cupit esse se sororem,
> nec matrem iuvat esse nec sororem.   (2. 4)

O how nice you are to your mother, Ammianus! How nice your
mother is to you, Ammianus! She calls you 'brother', and you call her
'sister'. Why do such decadent names attract you both? Why are you
not content to be what you are? Do you think this is a funny game? It
is not: a mother who wants to be a sister enjoys being neither mother
nor sister.

One can hardly help thinking here of Phaedra asking Hippolytus to call her *soror* (p. 110); clearly the address could convey
a double meaning on occasion.[28]

Kinship terms for children are less often used in an extended
sense than those for parents and siblings, perhaps because there
are so many other terms in Latin for addressing young people.
Ovid, as we have seen, suggests that an older lover could call a
girl *filia* (*Met.* 10. 467), and Fronto uses *fili* like *frater* in letters
to non-imperial friends.[29] The writer(s) of the *Historia Augusta*
considers *filius* to be the equivalent of *pater* or *parens* for
flattering younger men (pp. 122–3). Apuleius uses *fili* as an
address from older men and women to younger men (*Met.* 4.
12, 9. 27) and from himself to an invented dedicatee (*Mun.* 1,
Pl. 2. 1), while Gellius has Apollinaris Sulpicius use it to a
young man (13. 20. 5); the term seems to be basically affectionate but can be used ironically, as in Gellius.[30] Terms for
spouses are never, as far as I can tell, used in an extended sense;
this is probably due to the same factors that restricted their use
in a transferred sense (pp. 117–18).

No matter how common the extended usage of kinship terms
became, however, this use never supplanted the literal one;
Latin in the period under discussion had no kinship terms like
the Egyptian Arabic word for 'uncle', which can be used in

---

[28] For such double meanings in referential use, see Petr. 127. 1–2; [Tib.] 3.
1. 26.

[29] 187. 14, 189. 10, 190. 14; cf., at a later date, *CEL* 199. 1. 5, 199. 2. 4, 199.
2. 9. For Christian usage see O'Brien (1930: 83–4); Engelbrecht (1893: 10–12,
23–4).

[30] Cf. also probably *filius salax*, *CIL* iv. 5213, and *filia*, *CIL* iv. 10149.

address only to men who are not the speaker's uncle (Parkinson 1985: 98). The two possibilities were always present, and this double potential meaning could be used for effect. Plautus exploits this in the *Rudens*, where the youth Plesidippus greets an unknown old man, Daemones, and is teased by Daemones' slave Sceparnio, who intentionally misinterprets the address:

P L. Pater salveto, amboque adeo.
D A.   Salvo' sis.
S C. Sed utrum tu masne an femina es, qui illum patrem
    voces?
P L.   Vir sum equidem.
S C.   Quaere vir porro patrem.
D A. filiolam ego unam habui, eam unam perdidi:
    virile sexus numquam ullum habui.   (103–7)

P L. Greetings to you, father, indeed to both of you.
D A.   Hello.
S C. But are you a man or a woman, you who call him
    father?
P L.   I'm a man, of course.
S C.   Then look for your father somewhere else, man.
D A. I had one little daughter, and I lost her, my only child.
    I never had any male children.

The opposite joke occurs in the *Captivi*, where an old man discovers that a certain slave is in fact his son and addresses him with *exoptate gnate mi* 'my longed-for son'. The slave, knowing nothing of the discovery of his parentage, takes the address as an extended kinship term:

                        hem, quid 'gnate mi'?
    attat, scio qur te patrem adsimules esse et me filium:
    quia mi item ut parentes lucis das tuendi copiam.
                              (1006–8)

Hey, what's this 'my son'? Oh, I know why you are pretending that you are my father and I your son: because you give me the chance to see light [i.e. to live], just as parents do.

These jokes suggest that the extended use of kinship terms was widespread in ordinary speech even at an early period. Both passages could in theory have been borrowed from Greek models, since Greek kinship terms are also used in an extended sense in Menander (e.g. *Dyskolos* 492–5), but it is unlikely that

Plautus would have done so once, let alone twice, if the jokes had not made sense in Latin. We can thus conclude that although the periphrastic and transferred uses of kinship terms probably belonged only to literature, the extended use was common to literary and non-literary Latin throughout the period under discussion.

4

Terms of Endearment, Affection, and Esteem

AGORASTOCLES. exora, blandire, expalpa.

MILPHIO.   faciam sedulo.

. . . .

MI. mea voluptas, mea delicia, mea vita, mea amoenitas,
   meus ocellus, meum labellum, mea salus, meum
      savium,
   meum mel, meum cor, mea colustra, meu' molliculus
      caseus—

. . . .

AG. sicine ego te orares iussi?

MI.   quo modo ergo orem?

AG.   rogas?
   sic enim diceres, sceleste: huiius voluptas, te opsecro,
   huius mel, huius cor, huius labellum, huiius lingua,
      huiius savium,
   huius delicia, huiius salus amoena, huiius festivitas:
   huiiu' colustra, huiius dulciculus caseus, mastigia,
   huiius cor, huiius studium, huiius savium, mastigia;
   omnia illa, quae dicebas tua esse, ea memorares mea.
MI. opsecro hercle te, voluptas huiius atque odium meum,
   huiius amica mammeata, mea inimica et malevola,
   oculus huiius, lippitudo mea, mel huiius, fel meum,
   ut tu huic irata ne sis . . .

                              (Pl. *Poen.* 357–95)

AGORASTOCLES. Win her over by entreaty, flatter her,
   coax her!

MILPHIO.   I'll do my best.

. . . .

MI. My pleasure, my delight, my life, my pleasantness,
   my little eye, my lip, my salvation, my kiss, my
   honey, my heart, my colostrum, my soft little
   cheese—

. . . .

A G. Is that the way I told you to plead with her?

M I.   So how should I plead with her?

A G.   You ask?

You should be speaking like this, you villain: *his* pleasure, I beg you, *his* honey, *his* heart, *his* lip, *his* tongue,
his kiss, *his* delight, *his* sweet salvation, *his* delightfulness, *his* colostrum, *his* sweet little cheese, you
whipping-stock; *his* heart, *his* ardour, *his* kiss, you
whipping-stock; all those things which you were
saying as yours, you should be saying as mine.

M I. By Hercules, I beg you, his pleasure (and my hatred),
his buxom friend (and my spiteful enemy), his eye
(my conjunctivitis), his honey (my gall), do not be
angry at him . . .

T H E Latin address system contains a large number of different
ways of expressing affection, respect, admiration, and similar
emotions. Often such feelings are expressed using a kinship
term, a title, or the praenomen, as we have already seen. In this
chapter we shall examine the Latin address system's other ways
of showing affection and esteem.

One very common method of expressing such emotions is
by means of an affectionate or respectful adjective such as
carissime 'dearest', which can be used alone or added to a
name, kinship term, or other type of address. Thus one finds
not only the simple *carissima* (Ov. *Tr.* 3. 3. 27), but also *mi
carissime frater* 'my dearest brother' (Cic. *Q. fr.* 3. 6. 6), *Lucili
carissime* 'dearest Lucilius' (Sen. *Ep.* 23. 6), *mi magister
carissime* 'my dearest teacher' (Fro. 109. 11), etc. There are
many such adjectives in Latin; Table 3 lists those which are
used often enough to be considered a part of the address
system, and further information on individual words is given
in the glossary.[1]

---

[1] Harrod (1909) and Nielsen (1997) discuss the (mainly referential) usage of
many of these adjectives in sepulchral inscriptions, based on data from
undated inscriptions ranging from the 2nd cent. BC to the 6th cent. AD. As
they make no attempt at any chronological divisions, and as the bulk of the
epigraphic material appears to be later than the evidence used for this study,
differences between their findings and mine do not necessarily represent a
synchronic difference between the use of terms of affection in address and in
inscriptions. It is nevertheless worth noting that Harrod's and Nielsen's
findings are strikingly different from those presented in this chapter, both
as regards the use of individual words and as regards larger patterns; for

[*See p. 133 for n. 1 cont.*]

Table 3. *Some adjectives expressing affection and/or respect*

	Latin	Translation	Number of occurrences
Positives	*Alme*	nurturing	6 +
	Amate	beloved	4
	Amoena	pleasant	2
	Beate	happy	6
	Belle	pretty, nice	2
	Bone	good	49
	Callide	clever, skilled	2 +
	Candide	kind	9 +
	Care	dear	52
	Caste	pure	4 +
	Clare	famous	8 +
	Culte	refined	3
	Die	divine	2
	Digne	worthy	13
	Dilecte	beloved	8
	Diserte	eloquent	2
	Divine	divine	5
	Docte	learned	13 +
	Dulcis	sweet	27 +
	Egregie	excellent	3
	Exoptate	longed-for	2
	Exspectate	eagerly awaited	5
	Facunde	eloquent	7
	Felix	happy	22
	Fida	loyal	12
	Fidelis	loyal	2
	Formose	good-looking	15
	Fortis	strong, brave	3
	Fortunate	fortunate	7
	Generose	noble	4
	Grata	pleasant, welcome	6
	Impiger	energetic	2
	Inclite	famous	22 +
	Insperate	unexpected	3
	Invicte	invincible	15 +
	Iocose	full of fun	2
	Iucunde	delightful	4
	Iuste	just	3

Table 3 (*cont.*):

	Latin	Translation	Number of occurrences
	Laudande	to be praised	2
	Lecte	chosen	5
	Lepide	charming	3
	Macte	honoured, blessed	20 +
	Magnanime	great-souled	7
	Magne	great	31 +
	Mellite	honey-sweet	2
	Memorande	to be spoken of	7
	Mitis	mild	3
	Mulsa	honeyed	2
	Pia	holy	4
	Potens	powerful	5
	Praeclare	brilliant	2
	Pudice	pure	4
	Pulcher	beautiful	3
	Sacer	sacred	4
	Sancte	holy	11 +
	Sperate	longed-for	3
	Suavis	pleasant	3
	Venerande	venerable	11 +
	Venuste	attractive	3
	Verende	to be revered	2
	Vetule	elderly	2
Comparatives	*Carior*	dearer	3
	Dulcior	sweeter	2
	Maior	greater	6
	Melior	better	3
Superlatives	*Amicissime*	very friendly	7
	Amplissime	very great	7
	Carissime	very dear	122
	Clarissime	very famous	6
	Desiderantissime	greatly desired	4
	Dignissime	very worthy	8
	Disertissime	very eloquent	6
	Doctissime	very learned	6
	Dulcissime	very sweet	59
	Fidelissime	very loyal	4
	Fidissime	very loyal	15 +

Latin	Translation	Number of occurrences
Fortissime	very strong	38
Gratissime	pleasantest	7
Honestissime	very honourable	2
Indulgentissime	very kind	3
Iucundissime	very delightful	33
Iustissime	very just	6
Lepidissime	very charming	6
Maxime	very great	36 +
Mitissime	very mild	12 +
Optatissime	very desired	3
Optime	best	122 +
Piissime	very dutiful	2
Placidissime	very tranquil	6 +
Pulcherrime	very beautiful	17
Rarissime	very rare	4
Sanctissime	very holy	23
Suavissime	very pleasant	12
Summe	highest, supreme	12 +

In referential usage, adjectives normally have three degrees: positive, comparative, and superlative. For most words the positive degree simply attributes a quality to the referent, as

example, Harrod finds little distinction (except in frequency) between *bonus* and *optimus* (1909: 36), *dulcis* and *dulcissimus* (1909: 37), or *sanctus* and *sanctissimus* (1909: 39), while the adjectives *bene merens/meritus*, *pientissimus*, and *piissimus*, all rare or unattested in our data, are among the most common terms in Harrod's (1909: 1, 10, 13) and Nielsen's (1997: 179, 185). If these discrepancies do have a synchronic component, it could be a result of the highly formulaic nature of most sepulchral inscriptions (Nielsen 1997: 175–6); that it is not simply a difference between address and referential usage is suggested by Nielsen's observations on the general rarity of *bene merens*, *piissimus*, and *pientissimus* in classical literature (1997: 181, 193).

O'Brien (1930: 88–160) discusses the use of flattering adjectives by Christian writers. Her evidence appears to be more similar to mine than is the inscriptional material, especially as regards the use of the positive and superlative (e.g. she lists *carissimus* as common (1930: 94–6) but records no instances of *carus*, and many other positive/superlative pairs show similar results), but there are still a number of differences. Further information on flattering terms can be found in Zilliacus (1949: 51–3), Bang (1921: 77–81), and Hirschfeld (1901).

carus 'dear'. The comparative measures the referent against something else and declares it to have a quality to a greater extent, as *carior* 'dearer', or sometimes simply indicates that the quality is present to a certain extent, without a specific comparison, as *carior* 'rather dear'. The superlative either measures the referent against all members of a group, as *carissimus* 'dearest', or indicates in absolute terms that a quality is present to a high degree, as *carissimus* 'very dear'. There is no stylistic or register difference among the degrees, but there is a clear difference in meaning which normally results in the superlative's being a stronger term than the positive.

The address usage of degrees of comparison, however, seems to be very different from the referential use. The *carus* family, for example, shows sharp stylistic differences among the different degrees when used in address. The superlative *carissime* is the most common form, occurring 122 times, and is well represented in both poetry (20% of its occurrences) and prose (80%). The positive *care*, on the other hand, is found in prose only twice out of 52 examples, while the comparative *carior* occurs only three times and is exclusively poetic. These figures do not arise from some peculiarity of the word *carus*, for similar figures can be found for the whole corpus of affectionate adjectives. Our data contain a total of 1,172 such adjectival addresses, of which 45% are positive, 53% superlative, and only 2% comparative. All of the comparatives and 94% of the positives are found in poetry, as against only 45% of the superlatives.

The restriction of comparative adjectives to poetry is not difficult to understand. Comparatives normally require an ablative of comparison to complete their sense and thus are used as addresses only as part of larger vocative phrases; they do not have a meaning as addresses without some indication of what the addressee is compared to. Since such larger phrases are largely confined to poetry (cf. pp. 32–3), comparatives are also poetic.

The restriction of the positives, however, is more perplexing. One might expect poetic texts to use fewer superlatives than prose ones because of the metrical difficulties posed by the long and unwieldy superlative ending, but in fact superlatives are common in poetry; there are 262 examples. What is rare is the use of positives in prose: there are only 31 examples of such positives,[2] and more than half of these could not have been replaced by a superlative because they are from stems which rarely or never form a superlative, as *macte* 'honoured', *bone* 'good',[3] and *vetule* 'elderly' (i.e. 'old chap'). For some reason, the use as addresses of affectionate adjectives in the positive degree was avoided in Latin prose, though the words involved (see Table 3) may be very common and not at all poetic in cases other than the vocative.

This restriction is also surprising because the division we find is one between prose, in which positives very rarely occur as addresses, and all types of poetry, in which positives are common. Normally when there are stylistic differences in the use of addresses, the usage of Plautus and Terence coincides with that of prose rather than poetry, or provides a third option; it is most unusual for comedy and classical poetry to agree where prose usage differs. Yet in this case we seem to find precisely such agreement: when employing affectionate adjectives, Plautus and Terence use positives 68% of the time, while other poets do so on average 61% of the time and prose writers only 9% of the time.

There is a third unexpected element to the use of degrees of comparison. Given the referential usage of the positive and superlative, one would expect the superlative to be stronger than the positive in address; if *care* 'dear' is an affectionate address, *carissime* 'very dear, dearest' should be an even more affectionate one. Yet when one reads passages of Latin literature in which these addresses occur, such a difference is not apparent; indeed if anything the reverse appears to be true. In the *Metamorphoses* Ovid puts the address *care* in the mouth of a loving wife pleading with her husband not to undertake a voyage without her (11. 440), while he gives *carissima* to a girl asking a friend to tell her a story (13. 747). Statius uses *care*

[2] For this and the preceding figure occurrences in epigraphical texts are not included, since many inscriptions form partial lines of poetry and so cannot easily be divided into poetic and prosaic texts.

[3] *Optimus* functions as the superlative for *bonus*, but it belongs to a different stem, and there is a sharp difference between the address meaning of *bone* and *optime* (see below and Glossary) which makes it impossible to substitute one for the other.

to lament his beloved dead son (*Silv.* 5. 5. 79) but addresses the dedicatees of his poems, men who appear to have been at some distance from him, with *carissime* (*Silv.* 1 *pr.*, 2 *pr.*).

Such comparisons contain a measure of subjectivity, which is very difficult to avoid when trying to evaluate the amount of affection conveyed by an address and which makes statistical data on such matters less than fully reliable. Some objectivity can, however, be provided by basing statistics not on the tone of the interaction but on the relationship between speakers and addressees, which can be classified more objectively. Addresses normally used between lovers or close relatives are likely to be, on average, more affectionate than those normally used between casual acquaintances, so relationship is an indirect guide to the strength of an affectionate address.

If one classifies the occurrences of *care* and *carissime* in this way, one finds that the positive is used 63% of the time to relatives, spouses, and lovers and only 37% of the time to friends and more distant acquaintances; the superlative, on the other hand, is used 21% of the time to relatives, spouses, and lovers and 79% of the time to friends and acquaintances. This difference is so pronounced that, even though the superlative of this word is more than twice as common as the positive in our data, addresses to relatives, spouses, and lovers use *care* more often than they use *carissime*.

Many of the adjectives with which we are concerned cannot be tested in this way. *Magne* 'great', for example, is not used to relatives etc. significantly more often than is its superlative *maxime* 'greatest', but since *magne* and *maxime* express respect more than affection, their relative strength could not in any case be measured by the closeness of the relationship between speaker and addressee. The only other word in our data which clearly indicates affection and which occurs with enough frequency in both positive and superlative to give meaningful statistics is *dulcis* 'sweet', and with this word as well the postive appears to have more force than the superlative. *Dulcis* is used 60% of the time to relatives, spouses, and lovers,[4] while *dulcissime* 'sweetest' is so used only 18% of the time.

---

[4] In this total are included addresses to someone else's wife etc. by a speaker who is taking the viewpoint of the addressee's husband etc. (e.g. *dulcis*

Some of the adjectives which cannot be tested by counting relationships also seem to be stronger in the positive than in the superlative. This is not true of the two most frequent such adjectives, *bone* and *magne*, probably because *bone* and *optime* have completely separate address meanings and are not related to one another on any kind of continuum (see Glossary), while both *magne* and *maxime* carry so much respect that no significant difference can be discerned between them. Some less common adjectives, however, display a clear distinction between positive and superlative. *Sancte* 'holy' is normally used to gods, and human addressees rarely receive it unless they are emperors or otherwise of very exalted rank; *sanctissime* 'holiest', on the other hand, is often used as a general polite term for people of ordinary status, especially jurors.[5] Likewise, *docte* 'learned' tends to be addressed to famous poets or great mythological figures connected with song, while *doctissime* 'most learned' is more often used simply to the speaker's friends. This repeated pattern suggests that the subjective impression one gets from reading Latin literature, that adjectives conveying various types of praise are often weaker rather than stronger in the superlative when used as addresses, is in fact accurate in a more objective sense as well.

There are thus three peculiarities in the address usage of affectionate adjectives: the positive is poetic, the superlative is weaker than the positive, and the stylistic division involved does not follow the normal genre divisions of the address system. All three of these anomalies can be explained by the hypothesis that affectionate adjectives, as addresses, underwent a severe process of weakening in pre-classical Latin. Originally the superlative was indeed stronger than the positive, but it was gradually used more and more, so that eventually it replaced the positive altogether. The poets then reintroduced the positive as a stronger form of address to contrast with the now weakened superlative.

coniunx, Verg. *G*. 4. 465) and addresses to objects connected with or standing for a lover (*dulces exuviae*, Verg. *A*. 4. 651).

[5] Cf. Sherwin-White (1966: 556). Christian writers, despite their normal preference for superlatives, use the appellation *sanctus* much more often than *sanctissimus* (O'Brien 1930: 116–19), perhaps because the superlative was so weakened that it no longer suggested any significant degree of holiness.

Such a process of weakening and replacement may sound implausible at first glance, but from a linguistic point of view it is a normal development. The spreading and weakening of polite forms of address, sometimes leading to the total elimination of the less polite alternative, is common in modern languages and forms a pattern well known to sociolinguists (Braun 1988: 59–64). In English, for example, the address 'mister' has been weakened from its original meaning of 'master', and 'you' has been weakened from a polite pronoun to a universally applicable one, resulting in the elimination of the less polite 'thou'. A more dramatic example can be found in Romanian, where the form *dumneata*, originally a very polite address meaning 'your lordship', has been weakened to the point where it is usable to inferiors and contrasts with a more polite variant, *dumneavoastră* (Braun 1988: 43, 60). There is even a parallel for the reintroduction, as a more polite form, of an address which had formerly been the less polite variant and then been eliminated altogether. This parallel is found in some varieties of American Spanish, where the polite second-person pronoun, *vos*, in most registers completely displaced the less polite one, *tu*, and *tu* was then reintroduced as a more polite variant (Weber 1941: 107; Braun 1988: 58–9).

How exactly might the Latin weakening we propose have taken place? Perhaps in early Latin positives were normally used to express affection and respect, and superlatives to express particularly strong affection and respect. This usage would explain the presence of positives as well as superlatives in comedy; in the time of Plautus superlatives had not yet replaced positives in non-literary language. Then, like English 'you', the forms expressing a higher degree of praise were gradually extended to more and more interactions, until eventually they displaced the less favourable variants altogether. This process would have been complete by the time of Cicero, who virtually always uses these adjectives in the superlative as addresses, and would explain the extreme rarity of positives in prose. But just as the elimination of 'thou' made English 'you' cease to be a polite pronoun, because it no longer contrasted with a less polite alternative (cf. Braun 1988: 59), so the elimination of the positive caused superlative addresses to lose much of their force. Latin authors of the classical period would thus have resorted to various devices to strengthen these adjectives when they wanted to convey more force than the weakened superlative allowed. One such device, widely employed by the poets, was the reintroduction of positive forms of adjectival addresses, which despite having gone out of use in everyday speech would still have been available in archaic poetry as models of polite address. These positives, once they had been absent from conversational language for a generation, would have sounded not weak, but archaic and poetic, qualities that made them perfect candidates for reintroduction into poetry as stronger variants of the superlatives. This solution would have been in effect by the late first century BC, as the classical poets use positives freely.

If the above scenario in fact reflects a historical process in Latin, we ought to be able to observe some traces of it in extant literature. And indeed, such are observable. One piece of evidence is the frequency of positives in various early Latin poets. The earliest author in our corpus to use these adjectives as addresses is Plautus, who does so on 52 occasions. He uses them in the positive 71% of the time, or 57% if one excludes words with no attested superlative form, which could not easily be replaced by superlatives. Ennius, next in chronological order and with 12 examples, uses positives 58% of the time, or 50% excluding words without superlatives. Terence, with 11 examples, uses positives 55% of the time, or 17% if one excludes words without superlatives. Other early poets produce too few such adjectival addresses to make their evidence useful. These three, however, do provide evidence that the positive was gradually replaced by the superlative in addresses in early Latin, and indeed that the positive was declining fast enough to have virtually disappeared before the birth of classical poets such as Vergil.

Another piece of evidence concerns the reinforcement of superlatives in non-poetic genres. If the poets reintroduced the positive to give a stronger alternative to the weakened superlative, what did prose writers do, or people in ordinary conversation? Any need the poets felt for a more forceful form should have been felt by others as well, even if they did not adopt the same solution. And indeed such a need is apparent elsewhere. The non-poetic way of dealing with it seems to have been to use two or more superlatives together to express particular affection. Thus Cicero in addressing his brother uses two superlatives, as *mi carissime et suavissime frater* 'my dearest and most pleasant brother' (*Q. fr.* 2. 6. 4) or *mi optime et optatissime frater* 'my best and most desired brother' (2. 7. 2), 80% of the time when he uses affectionate adjectives at all.[6] In addresses to non-relatives, on the other hand, his affectionate superlatives are double only 33% of the time and single 67% of the time.[7] In addresses to relatives other than his brother, or in depictions of addresses from other men to their relatives, Cicero's superlatives are double only 50% of the time,[8] but when a single superlative is used, it is often in close proximity with another endearment, as *meae carissimae animae* 'my dearest souls' (*Fam.* 14. 14. 2), where the use of *animae* replaces the second superlative. If Cicero's system of double superlatives was the standard solution to the problem of their weakened force, it is not surprising that the poets felt the need for a different and specifically poetic solution, for multiple superlatives are highly cumbersome and suited neither to the metrical exigencies nor to the linguistic concision of classical poetry.

It is notable that, like the single superlatives before them, Cicero's double superlatives seem to have been weakened over time. In the time of Fronto two superlatives were apparently no longer sufficient to convey special force, for three or more (in one case, Fro 13. 11–13, as many as six) could be used even in the relatively distanced situation of an emperor writing to a favoured courtier.[9]

Another piece of evidence in favour of the weakening theory would be proof that superlative addresses were in fact stronger than positives in early Latin. That proof, unfortunately, cannot

[6] Two superlatives: *Q. fr.* 2. 6. 4, 2. 7. 2, 2. 15. 2, 3. 4. 6, 3. 5. 9, 3. 7. 9, *De Orat.* 2. 10, *Leg.* 3. 25. One superlative: *Q. fr.* 3. 5. 4, 3. 6. 6.

[7] Two superlatives: *Fam.* 11. 21. 3, *Rep.* 1. 70. One superlative: *Fam.* 7. 33. 1, *Att.* 6. 2. 9, *Sen.* 39, *Leg.* 2. 52. These figures include Cicero's depiction of addresses by other men to their friends, as well as his own addresses to his friends.

[8] Double: *Fam.* 14. 5. 2, 14. 4. 6, *Rep.* 6. 15. Single: *Fam.* 14. 4. 6, 14. 14. 2, *Sen.* 79.

[9] For further multiplication of superlatives in Christian writers, see the examples given by O'Brien (1930: 88–160).

be provided, since it would have to be based on repeated use of the same word in both degrees, and the address data involved are too thinly scattered to provide such information. It is, however, notable that superlatives at this period do not show the obvious signs of weakening detectable in classical Latin. They are never used in pairs as in later Latin, one superlative clearly being sufficient in itself. They usually occur in moments of great emotion or when gross flattery is required, as *exoptatissime* 'most longed-for' from a slave to his long-lost master in joyful recognition (Pl. *Trin.* 1072), *optime* and *festivissime* 'most delightful' from a slave and a youth in happy gratitude to the youth's father (Ter. *Ad.* 983), or *lepidissime* 'most charming' in exaggerated flattery (Pl. *Men.* 148, *Mil.* 1382). Conspicuously absent is the unemotional and rather formulaic superlative seen in Trajan's repeated use of (*mi*) *Secunde carissime* to Pliny,[10] and it is difficult to find early Latin equivalents even of the less formulaic but still casual and not overtly emotional or flattering type of superlative seen in Cicero's *mi suavissime Volumni* (*Fam.* 7. 33. 1) or *dulcissime Attice* (*Att.* 6. 2. 9).

Thus, although it cannot at present be shown that the superlatives of affectionate and respectful adjectives carried more force than the positives when used as addresses in early Latin, there is evidence that these superlatives were stronger then than in later Latin, and evidence that the use of positives in address was declining steadily in pre-classical Latin. These findings support the theory that the positive of affectionate adjectives was replaced by the superlative in the address system of early Latin, that the superlative was severely weakened by the classical period, and that the classical poets then reintroduced the positive as a stronger type of address.

A different kind of weakening appears with the terms *candide* 'kind, white, clear',[11] *mitis* 'mild', *mitissime* 'mildest', and

[10] Plin. *Ep. Tra.* 10. 16. 1, 10. 18. 2, 10. 20. 1, etc.

[11] Although this term has a variety of possible meanings, the fact that in address usage it functions like *mitis* etc. rather than like words praising physical beauty (which are not used deferentially to superiors) suggests that its address meaning when applied to humans is consistently 'kind'.

placidissime 'kindest, most tranquil'.[12] These four terms, or
these three stems (since *candidus* does not form a vocative
superlative, nor *placidus* a vocative positive) are used as addresses only in classical and post-classical poetry, and a shift in
usage is visible between the two periods. In classical poetry
(principally Ovid), there is a difference between the way these
terms are used in the poet's own voice and the way they are
used in the mouths of characters. Characters use them exclusively in address to divinities,[13] while the author himself uses
them only 35% of the time to divinities, and the rest of the time
to humans (or occasionally places).[14] When the addressee is
human, the address often expresses great deference for a
distant superior, as *mitissime princeps* 'mildest chief' for the
emperor (Ov. *Tr.* 2. 147), but it can also be less distanced, as
mitissima coniunx 'mildest wife' for the author's wife (Ov. *Tr.* 4.
3. 35).

In post-classical poetry (principally Statius) the terms
remain deferential, and the range of possible addressees is
not extended, but the restrictions on speakers disappear.
Characters use such addresses 57% of the time to humans
and only 43% of the time to divinities,[15] while authors in
their own voice use them to humans (or places) 89% of the
time.[16] Thus the shift that has taken place involves not whether
the terms can be used to mortals, but how often, and by whom,
they are so used.

The only explanation I can envision for such a shift is that
the addresses involved were weakened shortly before or during
the classical period. If at an earlier period these addresses were

[12] Statistics and references provided in support of this point include the
addresses in prayers which are normally excluded from this book, since the
issue cannot be discussed without them.

[13] Ov. *Met.* 1. 380, 5. 497, 11. 623, *Ep.* 18. 61.

[14] Divinities: Hor. *Carm.* 1. 18. 11; Prop 2. 15. 1 (to *nox*, which is more an
abstraction than a divinity here); [Tib.] 3. 6. 1; Ov. *Fast.* 1. 637, 3. 772, *Pont.*
2. 8. 51; Germ. *Arat.* 104. Humans etc.: Hor. *Epod.* 14. 5, *S.* 1. 10. 86, *Ep.* 1.
4. 1; Ov. *Tr.* 1. 11. 35, 2. 1. 27, 147, 4. 3. 35, 4. 10. 132, *Pont.* 2. 2. 39, 2. 9. 5,
4. 15. 32, *Am.* 3. 6. 105.

[15] Divinities: Sen. *Ag.* 818; Stat. *Silv.* 3. 4. 100, *Theb.* 10. 126. Humans:
Stat. *Theb.* 1. 448, 7. 355, 547, *Ach.* 1. 729.

[16] Divinities: Stat. *Silv.* 5. 4. 1. Humans etc.: *Laus Pis.* 258; Stat. *Theb.* 2.
382, *Silv.* 1. 2. 201, 2. 1. 167, 3. 3. 43, 3. 3. 167, 3. 3. 208; Mart. 12. 9. 1.

used only for gods, but then they were weakened enough to be usable to humans as well, there would have been a period at which the usage to humans was seen as an innovation with no parallel in previous literature. If that period coincided with Ovid's lifetime, it is easy to see why Ovid might have hesitated to put such addresses into the mouths of his characters, who are often mythological heroes from whose lips such flattering neologisms would be particularly inappropriate. In Ovid's own world, however, the use of these addresses for humans was probably proliferating, and Ovid joined in that movement when speaking in his own voice. There was nothing inappropriate in his use of these addresses to mortals, merely in his characters' use of them. Somewhat later, however, these addresses would have lost their connotations of being the latest in innovative flattery; indeed Ovid's employment of them probably helped them become part of standard literary language. For Statius, the use of such terms for humans was by no means unprecedented, and hence he could put this type of address even into the mouths of mythological heroes.

Weakening is not the only phenomenon affecting respectful and affectionate adjectives. While in general issues involving particular words cannot be discussed here but are summarized in the Glossary, there are a few points which need to be considered in more detail. One is the question of gender differences in the use of addresses. *Formose* 'good-looking', *pulcher* 'beautiful', and *pulcherrime* 'most beautiful' are used both by lovers and by people expressing more general admiration. When these terms are used by a lover or would-be lover to the object of his or her affection, there seems to be a distinction between them: *pulcher* and *pulcherrime* are used only by women,[17] while *formose* is used exclusively by men (both to women and to boys).[18]

The one apparent exception I have found to this rule is *formose* from Sappho to Phaon in [Ovid]'s *Heroides* (15. 95), and this passage appears on closer examination to be more a confirmation of the gender distinction than anything else.

[17] Pl. *Mil.* 1037; Verg. *A.* 10. 611; Ov. *Met.* 8. 49, 9. 492, 14. 373, *Ep.* 4. 125.

[18] Verg. *Ecl.* 2. 17, 2. 45, 7. 67; Ov. *Ep.* 16. 271.

Sappho is portrayed as having a very masculine desire for a youth substantially younger than herself, commenting *quid mirum si me primae lanuginis aetas abstulit, atque anni quos vir amare potest* 'what wonder if the age of first down, and the years which a man could love, carried me away?' (15. 85–6). It is therefore likely that Ovid deliberately assigned her the address a man would use to a boy, rather than the one a woman would normally use to a man.

Certain other affectionate adjectives seem at first glance to have gender restrictions as well, but these restrictions are probably illusory. Both *dulcissime* 'sweetest' and *suavissime* 'most pleasant' are used exclusively by men in all contexts. Their positives *dulcis* and *suavis*, however, are used freely by women as well as by men, and an alternative explanation for the apparent restriction of the superlative to men can be found. These superlatives are used as addresses primarily in prose, and it is a fact of Latin literature that affectionate addresses from women, like most types of address from women, are rare in extant prose. Thus *carissime*, the most common affectionate adjective, is used by men 96% of the time in prose; one would not, however, want to say that it had actual gender restrictions, since it is used by women 33% of the time in poetry. As a result, if an affectionate adjective which occurs primarily in prose is not attested in the mouths of women, one cannot conclude from such a distribution that it was actually a characteristically male address.

The address *macte* 'honoured, blessed' poses special problems. *Macte* is in form a fossilized vocative of the almost entirely obsolete *mactus*, but in early Latin it is not normally used as an address. Rather it tends to be coupled with an ablative and a form of the verb 'to be' in phrases such as *macte esto virtute* 'be honoured for thy virtue' (Pac. *trag.* 146) and thus to act as a nominative. In silver Latin *macte* is more likely to be used as a genuine address, though in many cases it is difficult to determine whether it is an address or an exclamation. *Macte* was probably obsolete (except in ritual and highly literary language) from a very early period, and few principles can be observed to govern its usage.[19]

[19] For further information, see Servius on *Aen.* 9. 641; Conington (1883: 230–2); Neue and Wagener (1892–1905: ii. 178–81); Wünsch (1914: 127–30);

Most of the time, the adjectives in Table 3 are used in expressions of genuine praise or affection. In some passages, however, their meaning is more complex. Horace, for example, has the philosopher Damasippus say *o bone, ne te frustrere, insanis et tu stultique prope omnes* 'O good man, do not deceive yourself, you too are insane, and so are almost all stupid people' (*S. 2. 3. 31–2*). Gellius quotes the learned Fronto refuting a grammarian who had asserted that *praeterpropter* 'more or less' was not a part of cultivated speech with *'audistine,' inquit 'magister optime, Ennium tuum dixisse "praeterpropter" . . . ?'* 'have you heard, best teacher, that your Ennius said *praeter-propter . . . ?'* (19. 10. 13). Gellius gives some insight into this type of use when he quotes his own reply to an ignorant and offensive grammarian and explains his linguistic goals as follows: *tum vero ego permotus agendum iam oblique ut cum homine stulto existimavi et 'cetera,' inquam 'vir doctissime, remotiora gravioraque si discere et scire debuero, quando mihi usus venerit, tum quaeram ex te atque discam . . .'* 'then I was really upset, but I thought it best to handle the matter indirectly as one does when dealing with a stupid man, and I said "Very learned man, if I ought to learn and to know other things that are more abstruse and more important, when the need arises, then I shall inquire of you and learn them . . ."' (6. 17. 4).

What these passages and others like them have in common is that the speaker is normally a philosopher or other learned man, speaking to someone of lesser knowledge and intellectual ability. Such a 'philosophical' use of apparently polite addresses also occurs in Greek, where it is especially character-istic of Socrates' language in Plato and Xenophon but also appears in later literary works, particularly those with some connection to Plato (Dickey 1996: 107–44). The Greek words used in this way include (among many others) ἄριστε 'best', βέλτιστε 'best', ἀγαθέ 'good', and σοφώτατε 'very wise', which are in lexical meaning largely equivalent to the Latin addresses we have seen in a philosophical usage. It seems very likely that

Birt (1928); Palmer (1938); Skutsch and Rose (1938); Walde and Hofmann (1938–54: ii. 4–5); Gonda (1959); Ogilivie (1965: 265); Fordyce (1977: 77); Hardie (1994: 205–6); Oakley (1997–: ii. 133–4); and further bibliography given in these works.

this particular type of irony in Latin is borrowed directly from the Greek, for it is largely confined to learned speakers in learned contexts. Moreover this usage, explicitly characterized by Plato as the proper way for an educated man to correct someone (*Phaedrus* 268 d–e), is precisely the type that one would expect to be borrowed by Romans wanting to show their cultivated background.

The address *bone* 'good', however, is particularly common in derogatory contexts and is not restricted to learned speakers. *Bone* can be perfectly polite,[20] but it is also frequently used in negative contexts at the same periods and even by some of the same authors as the polite examples.[21] In comedy the term is normally used to address slaves, sometimes in a friendly tone but more often in rebukes or expressions of criticism.[22] Occasionally comic characters employ it to free men or women, but then either the addressee is of very low status or the address is impolite.[23] In later Latin it apparently was possible to use *bone* as a genuinely polite address to important people, but the term was always readily usable in less positive contexts. A general sense of weak politeness is suggested by Seneca's comment that *omnes candidatos 'bonos viros' dicimus* 'we call all candidates for election "good man"' (*Ep.* 3. 1), though one cannot be certain that this passage refers to address rather than referential use.

The derogatory use of *bone*, especially in comedy, seems to go beyond the philosophical irony we have seen, to biting sarcasm without even a veneer of politeness. Such sarcasm is common only with *bone*, though it is not impossible with other adjectives: Cicero at one point says to Verres *sed tamen tu, sancte homo ac religiose, cur Tauromenitanis item foederatis navem imperasti?* 'But why did you, holy and devout man, nevertheless requisition a ship from the people of Tauromenium, who are also [i.e. like the people of Messana, from

[20] e.g. Verg. *A.* 11. 344; Catul. 61. 225; Hor. *Carm.* 4. 5. 5. See also O'Brien (1930: 94).

[21] e.g. Catul. 39. 9; Cic. *S. Rosc.* 58; Sil. 8. 269.

[22] Friendly: e.g. Pl. *Cas.* 724, *Per.* 788; Ter. *An.* 846, *Ad.* 556. Unfriendly: e.g. Pl. *Bac.* 775, *Capt.* 954; Ter. *An.* 616, *Ph.* 287. Cf. Martin (1976: 185); Hofmann (1951: 150).

[23] Low status: Pl. *Per.* 789 (new freedwoman), *Cur.* 610 (parasite); impolite: Pl. *Ps.* 1145.

whom he did not requisition one, allegedly because their treaty status protected them] allies by treaty?' (*Ver.* 5. 49).

The syntactic constructions in which polite adjectives are found vary somewhat between the genres. In prose such addresses are normally adjectival; that is, they modify a noun in the vocative case, as *clarissimi viri* (Cic. *Agr.* 2. 50) or *dulcissime Attice* (Cic. *Att.* 6. 2. 9), and are very rarely used alone as addresses. Poets, while using the adjectival construction frequently, also use these adjectives alone, i.e. substantivally (20% of the time in classical poetry). Syntactic peculiarities restricted to certain types of word include the frequent use of a dative (usually *mihi* 'to me') with adjectives expressing the speaker's feelings, as *o cara mihi* 'O dear to me' (Prop. 3. 10. 11), *frater animo meo carissume* 'brother dearest to my soul' (Sal. *Jug.* 14. 22), *o frustra miserae sperate sorori* 'O object of vain longing for your miserable sister' (Ov. *Ep.* 11. 123), and the occasional use of a partitive genitive with most types of superlative (but not *carissime*), as *fidelissime servulorum* 'most faithful of slaves' (Sen. *Con.* 6. 2), *optime regum* 'best of kings' (Verg. *A.* 11. 353), *pulcherrime rerum* 'most beautiful of things' (Ov. *Ep.* 4. 125). Comparatives, as noted above, normally take an ablative of comparison, as *o mihi me coniunx carior* 'O wife dearer to me than myself' (Ov. *Tr.* 5. 14. 2), *o matre pulchra filia pulchrior* 'O daughter more beautiful than her beautiful mother' (Hor. *Carm.* 1. 16. 1), *gnate mihi longa iucundior unice vita* 'only son, far more delightful than life to me' (Catul. 64. 215).

Not all affectionate and respectful addresses are adjectives; nouns can be used as well, though less frequently than adjectives. Such nouns may be of two types: those which have a lexical meaning denoting a human being and are thus used as addresses in a more or less literal sense, and those which have another lexical meaning and so are more figurative when employed as addresses. The first of these categories contains relatively few words, some of which are used very frequently, while the second contains a large variety of rarer terms.

The most common noun in the literal group is perhaps so common partly because it can also function as an adjective.

This term is *amice* 'friend', which is normally a noun in address (as in phrases like *amice carissime* 'dearest friend', Petr. 71. 5), but sometimes behaves as an adjective (as in *lector amice* 'friendly reader', Ov. *Tr.* 3. 1. 2). *Amice* is also the most positive of these nouns; it is followed in that respect by *hospes* 'guest, host, foreigner', and then by *comes* 'companion' and *socia* 'partner'. The differences between these terms, however, involve more than a simple hierarchy of intensity. *Amice* is a term which can be used reciprocally (e.g. Verg. *A.* 6. 507, 509) and which can convey simple affection[24] or remind the addressee of his status as a friend and the obligations attendant thereon;[25] it is very occasionally used in other senses as well.[26] *Amice* is also used instead of a name on occasion, as when Ovid says:[27]

> O mihi post nullos umquam memorande sodales,
>> et cui praecipue sors mea visa sua est,
> attonitum qui me, memini, carissime, primus
>> ausus es adloquio sustinuisse tuo,
> qui mihi consilium vivendi mite dedisti,
>> cum foret in misero pectore mortis amor,
> scis bene, quem dicam, positis pro nomine signis,
>> officium nec te fallit, amice, meum.
>>> (*Tr.* 1. 5a. 1–8)

O you whom I must always mention first among my comrades, you to whom my fate seemed particularly your own, you who I remember, dearest one, first dared to sustain me with your encouragement when I was overwhelmed, and who gave me gentle advice to live when the love of death filled my miserable heart, you know well whom I mean when these indications are given instead of your name, nor, friend, do you fail to recognize my obligation.

Hospes, on the other hand, is in literature normally restricted to addressees who do not have the same homeland as the speaker, whether they are friends or strangers. It does not,

---

[24] e.g. *dulcis amice*, Horace to Maecenas, Hor. *Ep.* 1. 7. 12; *amice optime*, Marcus Aurelius to Fronto, Fro. 50. 25.

[25] e.g. *mitis amice*, Ovid to Sextus Pompey, Ov. *Pont.* 4. 15. 32; *Rufe mihi frustra ac nequiquam credite amice*, Catul. 77. 1.

[26] e.g. Mart. 4. 80. 2 (patronizing); Hor. *Ep.* 2. 2. 1 (with dative relating the friendship to someone else). For the Christian usage see O'Brien (1930: 79).

[27] Cf. also Ov. *Pont.* 4. 12. 1–2, quoted on p. 61.

however, have the limitations of Greek ξένε 'stranger, guest', which is used by natives to foreign visitors but not vice versa (Dickey 1996: 146). Latin *hospes* can be fully reciprocal, as between Aeneas and Evander in Vergil (*A.* 8. 188, 364, 532) or Hermes and an old peasant in Ovid (*Met.* 2. 692, 695). Like Greek ξένε (Dickey 1996: 149), *hospes* is occasionally used between two compatriots who meet abroad, even when it could not be used between the same two in their own land (Pl. *Poen.* 1050). The 'foreigner' element in the address meaning is so strong that the use of the term by a native shows that the addressee is known to be a foreigner, as an anecdote related by Cicero reveals:[28]

ut ego iam non mirer illud Theophrasto accidisse, quod dicitur, cum percontaretur ex anicula quadam quanti aliquid venderet et respondisset illa atque addidisset 'hospes, non pote minoris,' tulisse eum moleste se non effugere hospitis speciem, cum aetatem ageret Athenis optimeque loqueretur omnium.   (*Brut.* 172)

So I'm not now surprised at what is said to have happened to Theophrastus. He had asked a certain little old lady how much something cost. When she added to her reply, 'It can't be any less, stranger', he was upset that he was still taken for a foreigner, when he had long lived at Athens and spoke Attic better than anyone.

In inscriptions, *hospes* is sometimes used as an address to future readers of the inscription; the readers' nationality cannot of course be specified.[29] Like *amice*, *hospes* is an unambiguously friendly term; indeed it can even be too friendly on occasion. Plautus portrays a man who requests help using *hospes* receiving a rejection with *non sum hospes, repudio hospitium tuom* 'I am not your guest, I reject your hospitality' (*Rud.* 883; cf. also *Poen.* 685).

While *amice* and *hospes* are normally used to the speaker's own friends or guests, *comes* 'companion' and *socia* 'partner',

---

[28] Cf. Quint. *Inst.* 8. 1. 2. This anecdote may have been translated from the Greek, but the presence of an original ξένε should not affect its relevance for the meaning of Latin *hospes*. Ancient translations were by no means literal, and if *hospes* had not carried the meaning of 'foreigner' which is required to make sense of this passage, Cicero would have substituted a different address such as *advena* 'visitor'.

[29] e.g. *ILLRP* 797, 808, 819, 971, 972, 973; *CIL* iv. 8899, 9158; *ILS* 6037, 6038, 7734, 8168, 8190, 8204.

which are much rarer, tend to be used of someone else's associates. The person involved is normally indicated by a genitive.

Although gender distinctions in usage are rare among the adjectives in this chapter, they are common with these nouns. *Amice* is used as we have described only when addressed to men, and in such circumstances the speaker is nearly always male as well. The feminine address *amica*, which is much rarer,[30] really means 'girlfriend' and is used only by men to women they love. *Hospes*, like *amice*, has only male addressees, but unlike *amice* its speaker is frequently female. Sometimes no love interest is involved, as in the anecdote about Theophrastus, but often there is an unfulfilled romantic element. Thus Vergil's Dido addresses Aeneas as *nate dea* 'born from a goddess' when she first meets him (*A.* 1. 615), but as *hospes* once she becomes attracted to him (1. 753), and then as *hospes* again when he deserts her, commenting bitterly *hoc solum nomen quoniam de coniuge restat* 'since this name alone is left from that of husband'.[31] Such a comment implies that she would not have called him *hospes* during the intervening period, though Vergil does not provide any addresses which allow us to test this implication. Similarly Medea calls Jason *hospes* before eloping with him, but not afterwards (V. Fl. 7. 454, 8. 53), and Tarpeia uses this address to her beloved but unattainable Tatius (Prop. 4. 4. 55), while various Ovidian women do likewise (*Met.* 4. 338, 10. 620). It thus appears likely that *hospes* when used by a woman is a term which stresses the fact that the addressee is not at present her lover, though it is friendly enough to suggest some willingness on her part for matters to progress further.

In the singular, *comes* is used exclusively to men, while *socia* is used exclusively to women; the two seem to be roughly

---

[30] Probably confined to Plautus, though sometimes suggested as an emendation at Tibullus 3. 6. 55. The referential meaning of *amica* changed between the time of Plautus and that of Cicero, so that by the classical period it meant 'prostitute', and this change eliminated the word from the address system; a parallel can be found in the Greek ἑταίρα, which means 'prostitute' and is not used in address, while the masculine ἑταῖρε, which simply means 'companion', is frequently so used. See Adams (1983: 348–50); Knoche (1956: 180); Dickey (1996: 138–9).

[31] 4. 323–4; on Dido's use of *hospes* see further Gibson (1999).

equivalent in meaning. The difference in stem is probably due to a reluctance on the part of classical Romans to form masculine singular vocatives of words with nominatives in *-ius*; *comes* was thus used to replace the missing masculine vocative of *socius* (cf. Dickey 2000). Thus when Seneca's Hercules addresses Lichas, he says *comes laboris Herculei, Licha* 'Lichas, comrade of the labour of Hercules' (*Her. O.* 99), but when he addresses Athena in a similar vein, he calls her *laborum socia et adiutrix* 'partner and helper of my labours' (*Her. F.* 900). In the plural, on the other hand, *comites* is used freely to both males and females, while *socii* is addressed only to men (normally warriors). The plural is more common than the singular for both of these words (the reverse of the usual pattern), and in both cases seems to belong to a less elevated register of language; indeed there seems to be a total separation of singular and plural address meaning.

Nouns used figuratively in address are much more numerous than those used literally. Table 4 lists the members of this group which are common enough to appear in the Glossary.[32] A look at this table shows us that Latin is very different in this respect from English, in which many of these categories would not normally provide terms of endearment. Of particular interest is the large number of animal names used as endearments. Terms referring to animals also produce insults in Latin (see Chapter 5), and indeed on occasion the same animal can be used both as an insult and as a term of endearment (*asine* 'ass' is an insult at Cic. *Pis.* 73, while *asellus* 'little ass' is an endearment at Gel. 15. 7. 3).[33] There is reason to believe that the use of animal names as vocative endearments was more common in conversational Latin than these figures would suggest, for such addresses are frequently referred to by Latin authors, compared to the number of times that they are actually used;

[32] Fridberg's 1912 dissertation discusses many of these words and provides more information on their referential usage and on Greek parallels (or the lack thereof). Her treatment is valuable in many respects and provides a useful collection of data, but it is based (both in the case of Greek and in the case of Latin) on a somewhat limited selection of texts, and her statements about the non-occurrence of words are not always correct.

[33] On the relationship of these words to each other see Housman (1930).

Table 4. *Nouns used figuratively as affectionate addresses*

	Latin	Translation	Number of occurrences
Words meaning 'life' and/or 'soul'	*Anima, -ae*	soul, life	21
	Anime	mind, soul	13
	Animule	little soul	2
	Vita	life	26
Words designating parts of the body	*Cor*	heart	3
	Lingua	tongue	1
	Ocelle	little eye	6
	Ocule	eye	7
Words for emotions	*Amor*	love	3
	Cura	care	9
	Delicia, -ae	delight	9
	Desiderium, -a	desire	3
	Gaudium, -a	joy	7
	Spes	hope	18
	Voluptas	pleasure	37 +
Words for help the addressee gives the speaker	*Levamen*	solace	2
	Opportunitas	opportunity	2
	Praesidium, -a	protection	4
	Regimen	guidance	2
	Salus	safety, salvation	11
	Solamen	solace	2
Words for animals	*Catelle*	puppy	1
	Columba	dove	1
	Lepus	hare	1
	Passer	sparrow	2
	Pullus	chick	1
Words for other elements of the natural world	*Lumen, -a*	light	3
	Lux	light	23
	Mel	honey	12
	Mellilla	little honey	1
	Sidus	star	2
Words for positive qualities	*Amoenitas*	pleasantness	2
	Festivitas	delightfulness	4
	Lepos, -es	charm	3
	Pietas	piety, sense of duty	2
	Suavitudo	pleasantness	2

	Latin	Translation	Number of occurrences
Words for reputation	Decus, -a	honour	47 +
	Gloria	glory	12
Other	Pax	peace	3
	Savium	kiss	3

Note: Numbers given are the occurrences of the address as an endearment, not total occurrences of the address.

probably they belonged to a lower register of language than is normally directly reflected in literary texts.[34]

Thus Horace remarks *strabonem appellat paetum pater, et pullum, male parvus si cui filius est* 'a father calls a child with a squint "Winky", and if someone has a son who is too small, he calls him "Chick"' (*S.* 1. 3. 44–6). Martial remarks of a woman's affection *cum me murem, cum me tua lumina dicis* 'when you call me your mouse or your eyes' (11. 29. 3). Plautus provides a number of such passages, including one in which a slave teasing a courtesan orders her to use endearments to him as follows: *dic igitur med aneticulam, columbam vel catellum, hirundinem, monerulam, passerculum putillum* 'so call me duckling, dove or puppy, swallow, jackdaw, tiny little sparrow'.[35] Suetonius relates that the populace fondly called the young Caligula *sidus* 'star'[36] and *pullus* 'chick' (*Cal.* 13), and the scholiast to Persius 3. 16 gives *columbus* 'dove', *pullus*, and *passer* 'sparrow' as endearments used to boys by their nurses (Iahn 1843: 296). Festus (245 = p. 284 Lindsay) reports that the ancients referred to ἐρώμενοι as *pulli*; this usage is probably related to the homosexual sense of *passer* found in Juvenal.[37]

In early Latin, there appears to be a difference of usage

[34] Cf. Adams's discussion of words characteristic of homosexuals (1984: 53).

[35] *As.* 693–4; some of these terms should perhaps not be taken too seriously (see pp. 156–7).

[36] A parallel for this word can be found in Horace, *S.* 1. 7. 24–5: *solem Asiae Brutum appellat, stellasque salubris appellat comites.*

[37] 9. 54; cf. also Apul. *Met.* 8. 26, 10. 22.

between these figurative addresses and the others we have
seen, as illustrated by the following two passages from
Plautus:

> mi animule, mi Olympio,
> mea vita, mea mellilla, mea festivitas,
> sine tuos ocellos deosculer, voluptas mea,
> sine amabo ted amari, meu' festus dies,
> meu' pullus passer, mea columba, mi lepus
>
> (*Cas.* 134–8)

My little soul, my Olympio, my life, my little honey, my delightfulness, let me passionately kiss your eyes, my pleasure, please let me
love you, my holiday, my sparrow chick, my dove, my hare.

> salve, insperate nobis
> pater, te complecti nos sine. cupite atque exspectate
> pater, salve.
>
> (*Poen.* 1259–61)

Greetings, father for whom we did not even hope, let us embrace you.
Desired and eagerly awaited father, greetings.

The first of these passages is spoken by the slave Olympio,
quoting the endearments he expects his new bride to say to him
at night, while the second is spoken by a daughter to her long-
lost father. The striking difference between them is that while
the daughter's endearments consist entirely of adjectives, the
bride uses almost exclusively figurative nouns (the one adjective she uses, *festus*, modifies one of these nouns rather than a
word more literally related to the addressee). These passages
are part of a larger tendency, in Plautus and in early Latin in
general, for endearments composed of figurative nouns to
express romantic affection, while adjectives (including sub-
stantivized adjectives) and nouns denoting people are more
often used for other types of affection.

In early Latin as a whole, I have found 244 endearments (i.e.
terms included in this chapter, not titles, kinship terms, or
praenomina). Of these, 121 are spoken in situations clearly
involving romantic affection and 123 in situations which
probably do not involve such affection.[38] The romantic endear-

[38] It is often difficult to be certain precisely what the tone of a passage is
intended to be, especially in the case of fragments; all fragments of uncertain
context have been assigned to this group.

ments employ figurative nouns 84% of the time, while the probably non-romantic ones use such nouns only 25% of the time. The difference between these figures would become even more pronounced if one took into account the probable sexual overtones of many figurative addresses not spoken in explicitly romantic contexts, the likelihood that some of the contextless fragments are in fact spoken by lovers, and the fact that adjectives used to lovers are somewhat different from those used elsewhere, since they often modify figurative nouns (as *festus* above, or *amoena* in the quotation with which this chapter began; adjectives used in other contexts normally modify the addressee's name, a kinship term, or another word denoting a human being, as in the daughter's addresses quoted above).

Terence's usage on this point is especially informative, since it has been observed (Lilja 1965*b*: 82; cf. above, pp. 43–4) that Terence's language often seems to be less inventive and more in keeping with non-literary rules of usage than that of Plautus (who provides most of the examples on which the above figures are based). Terence, when putting terms of affection into the mouths of lovers, always uses figurative nouns, while in non-romantic contexts he does so only 7% of the time.[39]

This distinction between romantic nouns and non-romantic adjectives can even be seen in the use of different forms of the same word. Olympio imagines his bride calling him *mea festivitas* 'my delightfulness', an address which elsewhere as well is used exclusively of romantic affection (e.g. Pl. *Cas.* 577, *Poen.* 389); conversely, the related adjective *festivus* is used to humans only in the address *o pater mi festivissime* 'O my most delightful father' addressed by a son to his father.[40]

Indeed, when such figurative addresses are used in comedy they normally carry a presumption of romantic affection. In the *Truculentus*, Plautus describes a meeting between a courtesan and a young man who has decided to break off his relationship with her and marry. She greets him with an affectionate *Quid agitur, voluptas mea?* 'How are things going, my pleasure?' (860), and he replies *non 'voluptas', aufer nugas, nil ego nunc de*

---

[39] Romance: only at *Eu.* 95, 456, *Hau.* 406; other: *An.* 685 (noun), *An.* 846, *Ph.* 853, *Ad.* 556, 911, 983, etc.

[40] Ter. *Ad.* 983; the adjective is also used to a door at Pl. *Cur.* 88.

istac re ago 'not "pleasure", stop that nonsense, I'm not having anything to do with that sort of thing now' (861). At the end of the conversation he takes his leave with *bene vale, Phronesium* 'fare well, Phronesium' (881), and the courtesan, who has by no means given up hope of winning him back, says sadly *iam me tuom oculum non vocas?* 'don't you call me your eye any more?' (881). The youth capitulates and agrees to continue both the endearments and the relationship in secret, replying *id quoque interatim furtim nomen commemorabitur . . . operae ubi mi erit, ad te venero* 'that name too will be mentioned secretly from time to time . . . I'll come to you when I can' (882–3).

In this passage the use of figurative terms of endearment symbolizes the relationship itself; if the courtesan can persuade the youth to use endearments, she has won him back as her lover. Something similar can be seen in the *Asinaria*, when a slave forces his desperate master to beseech him for money and his master's beloved courtesan to kiss him. It is no accident that along with the kisses she is asked to provide terms of endearment. When the courtesan responds with *da, meus ocellus, mea rosa, mi anime, mea voluptas, Leonida, argentum mihi, ne nos diiunge amantis* 'Leonida, my eye, my rose, my soul, my pleasure, give me the money, don't separate us lovers' (664–5), he increases his demands to *dic me igitur tuom passerculum, gallinam, coturnicem, agnellum, haedillum me tuom dic esse vel vitellum, prehende auriculis, compara labella cum labellis* 'So call me your little sparrow, your chicken, your quail, your little lamb, say that I am your little kid or little calf, hold me by the ears, put your lips against mine' (666–8).

It is notable that most of the terms of endearment requested by Leonida do not appear in Table 4, or indeed anywhere else in Latin literature, while those actually used by the courtesan are all attested elsewhere. Although we have observed that endearments based on animal names (such as those produced by Leonida) were probably more common than the literary evidence suggests, in most cases one is able to find at least an indirect attestation of a term's use, and the lack of any such corroboration here is suspicious. Leonida's speech seems in fact to fit a pattern of humorous Plautine exaggeration also found in the passage quoted at the start of this chapter: a string of endearments begins with perfectly plausible addresses such

as *mea voluptas* 'my pleasure' and then progresses into absurd-
ities such as *mea colustra, meu' molliculus caseus* 'my colostrum,
my soft little cheese' for humorous effect (cf. Maurach 1988:
99). Like *gallina* 'chicken' in the *Asinaria*, these absurd terms
are open to interpretation as less than fully complimentary, and
it would be a mistake to assume on the basis of the Plautine
evidence that they were ever used as endearments elsewhere in
Latin.

The correlation between figurative nouns and romance is
sufficiently strong that when such addresses are used between
two men in comedy, they can lead listeners to assume a
homosexual relationship. In the *Casina*, Lysidamus is exceptionally pleased with his bailiff and addresses him as *voluptas
mea* 'my pleasure' (453); an eavesdropper comments *quae
voluptas tua?* 'What's this? Your pleasure?' and rapidly concludes from Lysidamus' words and actions that there is more to
the relationship than he had previously suspected.

In classical and later Latin there is still a certain tendency for
affectionate addresses between lovers to use figurative nouns
more often than affectionate addresses without a romantic
element, but the distinction is less pronounced than in early
Latin.[41] This change is partly linked to the increased use of
terms such as *decus* 'honour', *gaudium* 'joy', *gloria* 'glory', and
spes 'hope', which are not always romantic even in comedy (if
they occur at all). However, the growth of these terms is by no
means the whole story, for even *voluptas*, which is highly
romantic in comedy, loses many of its connotations in later
Latin. When Vergil has Evander bid farewell to his beloved son
Pallas with *care puer, mea sola et sera voluptas* 'dear boy, my
late-born, my only pleasure' (*A*. 8. 581), there is clearly no
more suggestion of romance than in Cicero's address to his son
as *spes reliqua nostra, Cicero* 'Cicero, our remaining hope'
(*Fam*. 14. 4. 6).

A number of these figurative addresses have distribution
patterns which suggest some type of gender bias in their
usage. The only case in which such a gender difference can
be securely proven is *anime (mi)* '(my) mind, soul', which has

---

[41] In the later empire, Christian writers use abstract nouns freely with no
romantic overtones; see O'Brien (1930: 1–71).

been recognized as women's language since Donatus (on Ter. *An.* 685; cf. Adams 1984: 71). While male speakers do occasionally use the term (Pl. *Mos.* 336; Ter. *Hau.* 406), women form a large majority of the users despite the fact that in the works where it occurs most of the dialogue is spoken by men. A number of other terms, such as *lux* 'light', *vita* 'life', *decus* 'honour', and *gloria* 'glory', seem to be used primarily by men, but this distinction could be due to the prevalence of male speakers in the genres in which they occur.

Particularly difficult is the case of *anima* 'soul, life'. In the Vindolanda tablets, most of which represent correspondence between men, the address *anima mea* occurs twice, both times in the small group of letters written by one woman to another (*Tab. Vindol. II* 291. 12, 292. b back). This pattern suggests that *anima* was an address more likely to be used by women than by men, a theory which can be supported by women's use of the term in Phaedrus (3. 1. 5) and Apuleius (*Met.* 5. 6), as well as by the considerably later use of *animae meae* among women in the *Peregrinatio Aetheriae* (19. 19). On the other hand, these examples are numerically outweighed by Cicero's use of the address in letters to his wife and daughter (*Fam.* 14. 14. 2, 14. 18. 1) and Marcus Aurelius' use of it to Fronto (Fro. 30. 13, 40. 8, 51. 17, 56. 4). Adams argues that *anima* belongs to women's language nevertheless, dismissing the apparent counter-evidence on the grounds that 'endearments associated particularly with women may be used between the sexes' and 'Marcus Aurelius seems deliberately to have used highly emotive language which might have been appropriately used by or to a woman' (1995: 120; cf. 1984: 71–2).

Such an argument seems to reformulate the definition of 'women's language' to mean language that can be used in any situation except in unemotional interaction between two men. This formulation has something to be said for it—Latin, like any other language, had more and less emotional registers, and it is not implausible that particularly emotional language was used more between the sexes than between two men, nor is it implausible that women used or were regularly depicted as using such language more than men. At the same time, it is important to note the difference between such 'women's language' and the type to which *anime* belongs: *anime* was clearly used by women more often than by men, whatever their emotions or addressees, and the same is not true of *anima*.

Additional information on the use of *anima* can be found in graffiti and inscriptions, but it is less helpful than it might be, since in most cases the gender of the writer is unknown. Such evidence does, however, show that *anima* could be used to a wide variety of addressees: women,[42] men and boys,[43] and people of unspecified gender (*ILS* 8610, 8612).[44] A number of these examples are probably written by males, but most of the contexts are in some sense emotional. It is also possible that *anima* was used differently in funerary inscriptions and in addresses to living people, since in the former case the addressee had literally become only an *anima*.

Roman lovers seem on occasion to have used Greek nouns of endearment to address one another. Martial rebukes a woman as follows:

> Cum tibi non Ephesos nec sit Rhodos aut Mitylene,
> > sed domus in vico, Laelia, Patricio,
> deque coloratis numquam lita mater Etruscis,
> > durus Aricina de regione pater;
> κύριέ μου, μέλι μου, ψυχή μου congeris usque,
> > pro pudor! Hersiliae civis et Egeriae.
> lectulus has voces, nec lectulus audiat omnis,
> > sed quem lascivo stravit amica viro.
> > > > > > (10. 68)

Though your home is not Ephesus, Rhodes, or Mytilene, but in Patrician Street, Laelia, and though your mother, who was never smeared with make-up, is descended from the bronzed Etruscans, and your harsh father from the region of Aricia, you are continually piling up κύριέ μου, μέλι μου, ψυχή μου ['my lord, my honey, my soul'], for

---

[42] *CIL* iv. 2413h; *EDH* 001979, 008905 (dedicated by a man), 002460 (dedicated by a man).

[43] *CIL* iv. 4783, 4239 (*animula*); *ILS* 1768 (dedicated by a man) 9440 (dedicated by a couple); *EDH* 022740, 027951 (dedicated by a couple), 023187.

[44] Further examples can be found in later periods; note particularly the frequency of *anima dulcis/dulcis anima* on cups, plates, and glass medallions (Morey and Ferrari 1959, numbers 3, 15, 18, 20, 26, 48, 90, 109, 115, 292, 310, 426; *anima bona* at 411).

shame! And you a compatriot of Hersilea and Egeria! These words
should be confined to bed, and not every bed, but one which a
girlfriend makes up for her lusty man.

Juvenal complains that women not only speak too much Greek
in general, but that they even

> . . . concumbent Graece. dones tamen ista puellis:
> tune etiam, quam sextus et octogesimus annus
> pulsat, adhuc Graece? non est hic sermo pudicus
> in vetula. quoties lascivum intervenit illud
> ζωὴ καὶ ψυχή, modo sub lodice loquendis
> uteris in turba.
>
> (6. 191–6)

. . . go to bed in Greek. Even so, one could pardon that in girls, but do
you who are battered by your eighty-sixth year still speak Greek?
This language is not decent for an old woman. Every time you
produce that lusty ζωὴ καὶ ψυχή ['life and soul'], you are using in
public words that should be spoken only under a blanket.

It thus looks as though addresses made up of Greek nouns of
endearment were not uncommon in amatory language,[45] and

---

[45] Cf. Kaimio (1979: 170–1, 192–3); Pabón (1939). Though the evidence
quoted above is all from the imperial period, Lucretius (4. 1160–9) indicates
that a similar custom probably existed in the classical period. His testimony is,
however, difficult to evaluate for our purposes, since he is probably thinking
of referential rather than address usage: *nigra melichrus est, immunda et fetida
acosmos, | caesia Palladium, nervosa et lignea dorcas, | parvula, pumilio,
chariton mia, tota merum sal, | magna atque immanis cataplexis plenaque
honoris. | balba loqui non quit, traulizi, muta pudens est;| at flagrans odiosa
loquacula Lampadium fit. | ischnon eromenion tum fit, cum vivere non quit | prae
macie; rhadine verost iam mortua tussi. | at tumida et mammosa Ceres est ipsa ab
Iaccho, | simula Silena ac saturast, labeosa philema.* '[A man calls his love]
μελίχρους ["honey-skinned"] if she is dark, ἄκοσμος ["unadorned"] if she is
dirty and stinks, "little Athena" if she has grey eyes, δορκάς ["gazelle"] if she
is sinewy and wooden. If she is short and dwarfish, she becomes χαρίτων μία
["one of the graces"] or "all pure fun"; if she is huge and frightful, κατάπληξις
["stunner"] and "full of dignity". A stammerer who cannot speak τραυλίζει
["lisps"], and a mute woman is "restrained", while a hot-tempered, tiresome
gossip becomes λαμπάδιον ["a little torch"]. When she is too thin to live, she
becomes ἰσχνὸν ἐρωμένιον ["a slight little darling"], and if she is already dead
from coughing, she is ῥαδινή ["slender"]. But the swollen and buxom is
"Ceres herself nursing Iacchus", the snub-nosed is a she-Silenus or a she-
satyr, the thick-lipped φίλημα ["a kiss"].' There are (referential) Greek
parallels for most of the Greek in this passage; see R. D. Brown (1987:

that they were sometimes also used more generally, though this could reflect badly on those who used them. Direct attestation of such usage is rare, as is only to be expected given its register, but Marcus Aurelius addresses Fronto (to whom he frequently uses Latin terms of endearment) with μέγα πρᾶγμα (27. 22).

What is surprising about these Greek endearments is that many of them are not paralleled in Greek sources. It is of course impossible to prove that a given term of address did not exist in Greek, but many other terms of endearment are in fact attested; as Greek writers such as the novelists were not reticent about describing the type of situation in which we would expect to find these addresses, their absence is puzzling. As far as I can tell, neither μέλι μου nor μέλι in any other combination is attested as an address in Greek, and the same is true of μέγα πρᾶγμα and πρᾶγμα in other combinations.[46] Ζωή is so attested in literature only once to my knowledge, and that indirectly and in a source so late that it may well be a Latin borrowing (Heliodorus 8. 6. 4, in conjunction with φῶς and ψυχή). Ψυχή is sometimes used as an endearment, but it is very rare until a late period.[47] Κύριε, of course, is a common form of address in later Greek, but it is not usually a term of endearment.[48] Moreover, these Greek endearments are frequently qualified by μου, although possessives are very rarely used with vocatives in classical and Hellenistic Greek; the modern Greek use of μου with addresses is thought to have been

128–31, 280–94); Ernout and Robin (1962: ii. 295–7); Munro (1886–1928: ii. 277–8). It used to be thought (Bailey 1947: iii. 1310–1) that Lucretius used so many Greek words here because he was translating a Greek original, but this explanation is now rejected in favour of the view that Lucretius is accurately representing the use of Greek in Roman amatory language (R. D. Brown 1987: 281; Boyancé 1956: 125; but cf. Sedley 1998: 49–51). It has also been suggested that Lucretius' words may be women's names, not endearments (Colin 1955: 863–72), but this view is no longer in favour (R. D. Brown 1987: 281–2).

[46] Μέγα πρᾶγμα is, however, occasionally used to refer to people in Greek; see Van den Hout (1999: 70).

[47] Fridberg (1912: 12); Dickey (1996: 186–7). There is also a Pompeian graffito which reads ψυχή· ζωή· ἡ μῆτερ (CIL iv. 2317); the words may not be addresses here, but the resemblance to Juvenal's quotation is striking.

[48] For a possible example, see Grenfell (1896: 2, 4–5).

borrowed from Latin during the empire (Svennung 1958: 245; Wackernagel 1908: 151).

The Greek endearments quoted by Latin authors presumably represent Italian or Roman Greek rather than Attic or Koine (cf. Shipp 1953; Kaimio 1979: 301–2, 315). It is notable that all of these terms, while they may not fit what we know of the Greek address system, do fit the Latin address system beautifully if translated literally into Latin. Μέλι μου becomes the well-attested *meum mel*, ζωή becomes (*mea*) *vita*, ψυχή μου *anima mea* (or perhaps *mi anime*), and κύριέ μου is the amatory *domine* discussed in Chapter 2. Even μέγα πρᾶγμα is paralleled in the *maxima res* found in Fronto's correspondence.[49] One is thus inclined to suspect that when Romans of the imperial period addressed one another with Greek endearments, they were really translating their own address system into Greek.[50]

---

[49] Fro. 250. 6; cf. also from the same century *magna res*, not as a vocative, at *ILS* 1078.

[50] It is also possible that the Greek use of φιλότης as an endearment is behind the *meus amor* which Marcus Aurelius once uses to Fronto (63. 10; but cf. Verg. *Ecl.* 7. 21). Zilliacus (1949: 64), however, suggests that the Christian address *amor* may be derived from Greek ἀγάπη.

5

Insults

Agrippa Marce et quod in medio est   (Sen. *Con.* 2. 4. 13)
Marcus Agrippa, and what is in between.

Trium litterarum homo   (Pl. *Aul.* 325)
Man of three letters.

B O T H of the above addresses are insults, though it is not easy
for modern readers to understand why.[1] Many Latin insults are
hard to understand in one way or another, and perhaps as a
result the scholarly study of insults began at an earlier period
than that of most address forms. Unfortunately the different
works on insults tend to be isolated from each other, due in
part to the extreme obscurity of some of the publications
involved, and this has led to some duplication of effort. In
order to alleviate this problem in the future, I am providing
here a much fuller summary of previous research than is
offered in other chapters.

The first modern work devoted specifically to ancient insults
was published by Christoph Meisner in 1752. Meisner's essay
consists of a glossary of Greek and Latin insults, arranged in
alphabetical order, and examines the lexical meaning of the
various terms and the reasons why they might have been used
as insults. The words treated form only a tiny fraction of the
insult system of either language, and the study is of course
based on eighteenth-century textual resources and etymological knowledge. Nevertheless it is still of some use because
of the relatively thorough discussion it offers of many terms.

The next work on the subject was not published until 1892.

---

[1] Agrippa tried to avoid the use of his gentilicium (middle name) *Vipsanius*,
which indicated his low birth (cf. Syme 1958: 185–6), and the three letters
referred to by Plautus are *F*, *U*, and *R*, which spell 'thief' and were branded
on the faces of slaves who stole.

Its author, Gustav Hoffmann, aimed to supplement and expand Meisner's work, though as he himself recognized, his own collection of insults is far from complete (Hoffmann 1892: 3). This work contains far more entries than does Meisner's, for both Greek and Latin, and discussion is facilitated by grouping the insults according to semantic category rather than alphabetically. The discussion of lexical meanings is less extensive than Meisner's, but there is more consideration of the different contexts in which the insults are used.

Already by Hoffmann's time the corpus of insults being discussed was getting unmanageably large, and as a result later authors have all used a more restricted pool of literature. The first to take this step was Hammer (1906), who studied the insults used by Cicero in an attempt to prove that a high proportion of them came from the language of comedy (i.e. low-register language). Such a goal also required consideration of the insults of comedy (both Greek and Roman), but only in so far as these insults are repeated in Cicero's works and with little consideration of meaning or usage. Hammer was much more inclusive in scope than his predecessors and indeed than most of his followers, considering not only nouns but also a variety of rude and derogatory phrases; his work is still valuable as a collection of the Ciceronian data, and he was largely correct about the register of many Ciceronian insults.

Shortly afterwards came Müller's examination of the insults of comedy, which is made up of separate articles on Greek and Latin (Müller 1913*a* and *b*). Müller's work is essentially a list of references, with indication of speaker and addressee (insults are classified by the dyads in which they occur); he engages in virtually no discussion or analysis.

J. B. Hofmann's *Lateinische Umgangssprache* then devoted a brief section to low-register insults (Hofmann 1951: 85–9). As we shall see, many Latin insults do not belong to the low register, but Hofmann makes some interesting generalizations about those which do.

In the late 1950s three discussions of Latin insults were published independently. The first was Reimers's 1957 dissertation, a valuable work which remains the most thorough study of the corpus of Plautine insults. Reimers examined virtually all types of Plautine insults, organizing them by the type of ill-will being expressed (threats, accusations of cowardice, etc.). The work contains many interesting observations (not all of them accurate) but was regrettably ignored by the authors of later works on this subject because it was never published.[2]

A year later J. Svennung published a brief account of nouns used metaphorically as insults (Svennung 1958: 112–17), but his contribution consists primarily of a list of the nouns involved. More important was Miniconi's 1958 article, which offered an improvement on earlier literature in that it provided a discussion and analysis of the insult system of Roman comedy, rather than a list. Unfortunately much of the theoretical framework of that discussion is no longer considered valid.

A few years later came Nisbet's examination of Roman invective (1961: 192–7). While this study is excellent within the limits it sets, it is very brief and is geared to explaining a specific work (Cicero's *In Pisonem*) rather than Latin usage in general.

In 1965 two important works appeared independently. Saara Lilja's treatise (1965*b*) has a narrow focus, being concerned only with Roman comedy. Perhaps for that reason, her work is arguably the best study of Latin insults, being full of discussion, argument, and ideas as well as including a full list of references for comic insults. She classifies terms largely by semantic field and provides some illuminating discussions of lexical meaning. Ilona Opelt's book is by far the largest and most complete study of Latin insults, covering a wide range of literature (though graffiti and other non-literary evidence are ignored) and in consequence including far more terms than any other author. Opelt classifies insults by the types of strife in which they occur, meaning that the discussion of a single term can be fragmented and that it is difficult to tell which terms are unique and which common. She makes a number of valuable

[2] Cf. complaints of Lilja (1965*b*: 8). Future researchers on this topic should note that there is now a microfilm of this dissertation in the library of the Institute for Advanced Study in Princeton (almost certainly the only copy outside Germany). I would like to express my heartfelt thanks to the Institute librarians, especially Pat Bernard, Marcia Tucker, and James Fein, for the extraordinary efforts they made to locate and obtain this work.

points, however, and there is no doubt that hers is at present the definitive work on Latin insults as a whole. The book was widely reviewed for a number of years after publication, and some of the reviews (e.g. Nisbet 1967) contain useful corrections and additions.

There are also a number of articles on individual insults, as well as briefer discussions in commentaries; these cannot be listed here, but references to them can normally be found in Opelt's discussion of the words in question.

Previous work on Latin insults has thus provided us with the corpus of insults involved, their lexical meanings, the contexts in which they are used, and some interesting observations on the workings of the insult system and the concepts which a Roman found insulting. What is still lacking is a systematic discussion of the relative offensiveness of different terms and the registers to which they belong, along with a study of the principles governing the division of Latin insults by register and offensiveness. What made a Latin insult more or less rude? What made it more or less acceptable in different social circles? Did these factors change over time?

This chapter does not constitute such a work, but merely a preliminary to it. A study of forms of address is not a good context in which to undertake an examination of Latin insults; insults form a large subject and deserve books of their own. Moreover, while in many areas of the Latin language a real distinction between vocative and non-vocative usage can be observed, making it profitable to study vocatives as isolated from other uses of the same words, such a distinction is much less apparent for Latin insults: I cannot find any difference in meaning between, for example, *sceleste* and *scelestus es*. In this area, therefore, my address data are not adequate, and all conclusions based on them must be regarded as tentative.

As a result, the aim of this chapter is to explain the usage of vocative insults as part of the Latin address system and as they relate to other parts of that system, and to point the way for a more complete study of register and offensiveness by showing what sort of information insults can yield. The data examined include over 1,300 individual insults,[3] representing 477 differ-

---

[3] This figure cannot be precise, since the division into individual insults of

ent words and phrases, 149 of which occur often enough to be considered probably part of the Latin address system (cf. p. 305).

Previous studies of Latin insults have classified the terms by interlocutors, context, and lexical meaning; these different approaches reflect the two components of an insult's social meaning, register and offensiveness, and the simplest approach to insults, lexical meaning. The social meaning of an insult, like that of any other form of address, is not simply determined by its lexical meaning; this is evident both from the fact that some words with offensive lexical meanings are not insults when used as terms of address (e.g. Icelandic *rassgat* (Braun 1988: 254), which means 'anus' but functions as a term of endearment) and from the fact that the same address can have different social meanings in different cultures which share the same language (e.g. the difference in calling someone a 'bloody fool' in Britain and America). It is often the case that words with certain types of lexical meaning are more likely to become insults, or more likely to become particularly offensive insults, than are other words, but most such rules are language-specific: one must learn from the insults which objects and characteristics were considered particularly offensive to the Romans, rather than trying to fit their language into our own cultural assumptions. Lexical meaning is also distinct from register, for one of the most obvious examples of register differences is the use of different words in different registers to designate the same things, such as parts of the body.

Register and offensiveness are not equivalent concepts, either. An insult from a low register may always be particularly offensive when used in a context where a higher register of language is expected, but that does not mean that it is not possible to be extremely offensive while remaining entirely in the high register. Indeed, there exists a number of books with titles like *Shakespeare's Insults: Educating your Wit* (Hill and Öttchen 1991) or *Honourable Insults: A Century of Political Invective* (Knight 1990) which provide examples of particularly crushing high-register insults and suggest that such terms can be far more effective than anything from a low register. In a

a complex address like *ultima Lageae stirpis perituraque proles, degener incestae sceptris cessure sorori* (Luc. 8. 692–3) is bound to be somewhat arbitrary.

setting where the low register is appropriate, as well, it is possible to be more or less offensive while remaining within that register; thus in English some four-letter Anglo-Saxon words are more offensive than others, though all belong to the language of the school corridor rather than that of polite adult conversation.

The register of an insult governs where, by whom, and to whom it can be used; register can thus be determined in Latin by examining the settings in which a given term occurs. As there are 149 terms which seem to be part of the Latin address system and which therefore presumably belonged to a specific register or registers, it is not possible to discuss here all the settings in which each is used. Instead, a few words will be examined in order to give an idea of the principles used (cf. also the discussion of register on pp. 13–17, 32–4), and register judgements for the others will then appear without comment-ary in Table 5. Like most languages, Latin had a wide range of registers, with subtle distinctions among them. The division into high, middle, and low registers employed here is thus an oversimplification, and more detailed information on usage, when it can be ascertained, will be found in the Glossary.

Among the most popular Latin insults are those belonging to the *scelus* family: *scelus* 'crime', *scelerum caput* 'head of crimes',[4] *sceleste* 'guilty', and *scelerate* 'guilty'. *Scelus* itself appears to be a term belonging largely to the world of slaves and is, with one exception, confined to comedy. It is spoken by slaves 39% of the time, always to another slave or to a *leno*; a further 13% of the time it is used by low-status characters such as a parasite, *meretrix*, or *leno*. When used by a respect-able free man (48% of cases) it is normally addressed to a slave, or failing that to a parasite, *leno*, etc.; it only once occurs between respectable free men. That one occurrence is Cicero's use of *scelus* to his enemy Piso in a very heated passage (*Pis.* 56), in which it is probable that Cicero was prepared to descend to a low register of language in order to

---

[4] I follow for convenience the traditional view that *scelerum* in this phrase is the genitive plural of *scelus* (cf. *OLD* s.v.), but there is an interesting alternative view, based partly on a reinterpretation of Pl. *Ps.* 817, that the word in fact comes from an adjective *scelerus* (J. N. Adams, personal communication).

make a point about the low level of his opponent. *Scelus* is thus easily assignable to the low register.

Scelerum caput is even simpler; it is used as a vocative only in Plautus and only by or to slaves, so it belongs to the low register as well. This is true despite its resemblance to the high-register Greek insult κακὴ κεφαλή 'bad head' (of which it is probably not a translation, since the Greek insult apparently did not occur in comedies).[5]

Sceleste poses more of a problem, because in addition to its frequent use in comedy the term appears in Catullus and the *Appendix Vergiliana*, both places in which the average register of language is higher than in comedy (though both do provide examples of very low-register language on occasion). In comedy, however, the term is frequently (48% of the time) used by slaves, parasites, etc., and when it is used by respectable people the addressee is always a slave, cook, etc.[6] Moreover, the citation from the *Appendix Vergiliana* comes from the *Priapeum 'quid hoc novi est'* (19) and is addressed by the author to his penis, and the two instances in Catullus come from poems which are not the most elevated of his works.[7] All of this suggests that *sceleste* is a fairly low-register insult, and the isolated occurrence in Phaedrus (4. 11. 7) of the term spoken by a disembodied voice is not enough to change this classification.

One might conclude from these three terms that lexical factors are at work here, so any insult formed from this stem will belong to the low register. *Scelerate*, however, seems to be different. This term is rarely found in comedy (only Pl. *Per.* 275, though it is there used by a slave) and also occurs in Cicero, Quintilian, Ovid, Martial, Petronius, and the *Ilias Latina*. In Petronius the speaker is a priestess (137.1), and in Ovid the term is used repeatedly by heroines to their faithless lovers (*Ep.* 2. 17, 7. 133, 12. 19, etc.), normally a high-register setting in Latin poetry. Martial uses the term complainingly to

---

[5] On the use of 'head' in insults and endearments see Van Hook (1949); Nisbet and Hubbard (1970: 282); Lyne (1978: 192).

[6] The one possible exception is Plaut. *Am.* frag. 17, where the addressee is uncertain.

[7] 8, which uses colloquialisms such as *bella* (cf. Hofmann 1951: 142), and 15, which insults a man who in poem 16 receives a group of clearly low-register insults.

a schoolmaster (9. 68. 1), while the *Ilias Latina* puts it in the mouth of the epic hero Diomedes (557). In such a situation one is forced to conclude that the term *scelerate* covers a range of registers, including the high one and perhaps also the low one. This makes its social meaning very different from that of the low-register *sceleste*, although the lexical meanings of the two terms are not significantly different and although *scelestus* can appear in high-register language when not being used as an address.

It is also possible for a term to belong exclusively to the high register, and such appears to be the case with *saeve*. This vocative does not occur in comedy, nor in prose except for pseudo-Quintilian; it is basically confined to classical and later poetry. The poets put it in the mouths of heroes and heroines such as Oedipus (Sen. *Phoen.* 34), Jocasta (Stat. *Theb.* 7. 516, etc.), Theseus (Sen. *Phaed.* 1204), Nestor (Ov. *Met.* 12. 296), Remus (Ov. *Fast.* 5. 469), and the goddess Diana (Stat. *Theb.* 9. 715), and the contexts in which it is used tend to be dignified, as Propertius' complaint to Isis (2. 33a. 19).

The process of examining insults for register judgements can shed light on the tendencies of individual authors. Cicero, despite the normally elevated tone of his speeches, was capable of using insults of any register (cf. Hammer 1906; Opelt 1965: 21). In this he differs from the characters of Seneca's tragedies, who never descend to low-register insults whatever the emergency. The low-register (as determined by the criteria suggested above and on pp. 32–4) insults employed by Cicero include *asine* 'ass', *belua* 'beast', *caenum* 'filth', *canis* 'dog', *carnifex* 'executioner', *fugitive* 'runaway', *furcifer* 'one punished with the *furca*', *labes* 'disaster, disgrace', *lutum* 'dirt', and *monstrum* 'monster'[8] in addition to *scelus*; high-register insults include *amens* 'insane', *furiose* 'mad', *hostis* 'enemy', *nefande* 'wicked', *oblite* 'forgetful', *superbe* 'proud', and *vecors* 'mad',[9] and mid-register insults also occur. The low-register insults are most often found in the *In Pisonem*, but they can also appear elsewhere, and thus one cannot make assumptions about the register of a vocative insult merely because it occurs in Cicero or even in a particular work of Cicero.

---

[8] e.g. *Pis.* 73, 1, 13, 23, 10, *Deiot.* 21, *Vat.* 15, *Pis.* 56, 62, 31.

[9] *Pis.* 21, *Phil.* 13. 39, *Vat.* 26, *Dom.* 133, *Pis.* 62, *Luc.* 94, *Pis.* 21.

Cicero knew all the registers of the address system and moved among them for effect, and often one needs to know the register of a term from other sources in order to be able to understand the force of Cicero's usage.

The other main factor in the address meaning of an insult is offensiveness. Since offensiveness relates to the extent to which the speaker wishes to injure the addressee, it can be determined by examining the temperature of the debate in which an insult is used and the relationship of speaker and addressee (a master is more likely to deliver a really offensive insult to his slave than the slave is to his master, for example). Such judgements are much more subjective than those about register, and in consequence labels of offensiveness are more difficult to assign with confidence than those of register. For many insults I have been unable to make a judgement on offensiveness (where I have been able to do so, it can be found in the Glossary), though I think this would be possible if one examined non-vocative as well as vocative uses.

In some cases, however, it is clear that an insult was very offensive. *Furcifer* 'one punished with the *furca*', for example, is a popular low-register insult most frequently used for castigating slaves in comedy. There it is employed by a slave threatening to torture another slave (Pl. *Cas.* 139), a youth berating a *leno* for theft (Pl. *Poen.* 784), a slave abusing a *leno* for all he is worth (Pl. *Ps.* 361), etc. Elsewhere it is also used for castigating slaves (e.g. Hor. *S.* 2. 7. 22) or freedmen (e.g. Sen. *Con.* 7. 6. 4), and Cicero uses it to his opponents in moments of particular anger (e.g. *Pis.* 14).

Perfide 'treacherous', a high-register term, also seems to be a strong insult. This term is frequently used by women angry with former lovers, as Dido (e.g. Verg. *A.* 4. 305; Ov. *Ep.* 7. 79) or Medea (Ov. *Ep.* 12. 37). It is also employed by the dying Polynices to his hated brother Eteocles (Stat. *Theb.* 11. 569), by Philomela to Tereus when he rapes her (Ov. *Met.* 6. 539), and by Hermes to an old peasant who has broken a promise to the god (Ov. *Met.* 2. 704).

Improbe 'not good', on the other hand, seems to be a much milder word. While it too can be used by deserted women (e.g. Ov. *Ep.* 10. 77), it is more often employed in milder contexts, as one singer's challenge to another (Calp. *Ecl.* 6. 19), Helen's

half-hearted rebuke to Paris for his seduction attempt (Ov. *Ep.*
17. 77), or an author's rebuke to a character who is generally
portrayed in a favourable light (Parthenopaeus, Stat. *Theb.* 9.
744). The mildness of *improbe* is also suggested by its position
at the beginning of a crescendo of insults in Cicero (*Quinct.* 56).

Once one has examined the insults which were part of the
address system and determined their register and offensiveness, is it possible to make generalizations about the factors
which insults of each type have in common, so as to be able to
determine with accuracy the register and offensiveness of terms
which occur less often? It is clear that Romans did on occasion
use unique insults that were not part of the normal address
system; when this occurred, could the recipients of such insults
tell how offended they should be?

   And what about the situation in literature? A literary term
does not always belong to a high register (cf. p. 16). Suppose
that the author of an English novel were to invent two insults,
both of which were longer and more imaginative than the
insults normally occurring in speech, and give one to a prince
arguing with another prince, and the other to a beggar fighting
with another beggar. If the two insults involved were 'you son
of an AIDS-ridden piece of cat's diarrhoea blasted to bits by a
drunken postal worker' and 'you secret supporter of Hitler
with so little education that not even the Communist Party
would have you as a member' few native English speakers
would have any trouble working out which one was spoken by
the beggar and which by the prince. Yet neither of these insults
contains any words which are particularly high- or low-register
in their lexical meanings, and neither uses any of the standard
English insulting words which are easily classifiable by register.
English speakers sense that these two insults belong to different
registers not because they recognize the specific words in them
as belonging to different registers, but because there is a kind of
underlying grammar of insults in English, by which certain
semantic categories (such as excrement and the addressee's
parentage) normally belong to low-register insults, while others
(such as education and morality) normally belong to a higher
register. There are exceptions to these rules, of course, just as
irregular verbs are exceptions to another type of grammatical

Table 5. *Insults*

Latin	Translation	Number of occurrences	Low	Mid.	High
Amator	lover	8	x?	x?	x?
Amens	insane	2			x?
Amentissime	very insane	11		x?	
Animose	bold	3			x
Asine	ass	3	x		
Asper	harsh	2			x
Audacissime	very bold	7	x	x	
Audax	bold	7	x	x	x
Avare	greedy	4	x?	x?	x?
Barbare	foreign, uncivilized	9		x	x
Belua	beast	4	x		
Bucco	dolt	3	x?		
Caece	blind	2			x
Caenum	filth	2	x		
Cana	white-haired	2	x	x	
Canis	dog	2	x		
Carnifex	executioner	15	x		
Cinaede	catamite	14	x		
Credule	credulous	2			x
Crudelis	cruel	30+		x	x
Crudelissime	very cruel	5		x?	
Cruente	bloody	2			x
Cucule	cuckoo	2	x		
Cunne	female genitalia	4	x?		
Dedecus	disgrace	4		x	x
Degener	inferior, degenerate	5			x
Demens	insane	30			x
Difficilis	troublesome	2			x
Dire	dreadful	5			x
Dure	hard, harsh	20			x
Durior	harder	2			x
Edax	greedy, devouring	4	x		
Enervis	feeble	2			x
Excetra	watersnake	2	x		
Fallax	deceitful, treacherous	7			x
False	false, unfaithful	4	x?	x?	x?
Fatue	foolish	4		x	
Feles	marten	2	x		
Ferox	fierce	8+			x
Ferrea	made of iron	2			x
Flagitium hominis	disgrace of a man	2	x?		

Table 5 (*cont.*):

Latin	Translation	Number of occurrences	Register Low	Mid.	High
Foedissime	very foul	2	x?	x?	x?
Fugitive	runaway	6	x		
Fur	thief	11	x		
Furcifer	one punished with the *furca*	22	x		
Furia	fury	2	x?		
Furibunde	distraught, furious	2			x
Furiose	mad	9		x	x
Gurges	whirlpool, abyss	2		x?	
Hostis	enemy	4		x?	x?
Ignare	ignorant	2			x
Ignave	lazy, cowardly	12	x	x	x
Ignavissime	very lazy, very cowardly	3	x?	x?	x?
Illecebra	enticement	2	x?		
Illex	lawless	2	x		
Immemor	forgetful	4			x
Immitis	pitiless	2			x
Impia	impious	7			x
Importuna	troublesome, perverse	2		x?	
Impotentissime	very powerless	4			
Improbe	not good, etc.	53	x	x	x
Impudens	shameless	11	x		
Impudentissime	very shameless	3		x?	
Impudice	unchaste	3	x?		
Impurate	vile	3	x?	x?	
Impure	foul	8	x	x	
Impurissime	very foul	3	x	x	
Inepte	foolish	15	x	x	x
Iners	idle, lazy, worthless	8			x
Infide	treacherous, faithless	2			x
Ingrate	ungrateful	19		x	x
Ingratissime	most ungrateful	6		x	
Inimice	hateful	17	x?	x?	x?
Insane	crazy	14	x	x	x
Insanissime	very crazy	2	x		
Insipiens	unwise	2	x		
Invide	envious, hostile	8	x	x	x
Invidiose	odious, envious	3	x	x	x
Invisum	hateful	2			x
Labes	disaster, disgrace	3	x?		

Latin	Translation	Number of occurrences	Register		
			Low	Mid.	High
Larva	devil	2			
Lascive	naughty, lascivious	2		x	x
Latro	bandit	2	x		
Lente	slow	6			x
Levis	light, fleet, fickle, insubstantial	2			x
Levissime	very flighty	2		x	
Livide	jealous, spiteful	3			
Lutum	dirt	3	x		
Machinator	contriver	2			x
Male conciliate	badly bought	2	x		
Malus	bad	7	x	x	x
Mastigia	one who deserves a whipping	8	x		
Metuende	to be feared (sarcastic)	2 +			x
Minimi preti	of least value, cheapest	3	x	x	
Moleste	annoying	2		x?	
Monstrum	monster	2	x		
Moriture	about to die	3			x
Nefande	wicked	7		x	x
Nequissime	worthless	6	x	x	
Nihili	of nothing	3	x		
Nocentissime	very guilty	2			
Nugator	joker	5		x	
Oblite	forgetful	12			x?
Odiose	hateful	2			x
Parricida	murderer, traitor	11	x		x
Pauper	poor	5			x
Peior	worse	2			x
Perdite	lost	2			x
Perditissime	most desperate	2			
Perfide	treacherous, faithless	40 +			x
Periture	about to perish	3			x
Periure	perjured	4	x		x
Periurissime	most perjured	3	x		
Perverse	perverse	2			x?
Pessime	worst	26	x	x	x
Pestis	plague	2	x?		
Piger	sluggish	2			x
Praedo	brigand	4	x	x	x
Putide	rotten	8		x?	
Rapax	rapacious	2	x		
Raptor	robber, rapist	4			x?

Table 5 (*cont*.):

Latin	Translation	Number of occurrences	Register Low	Mid.	High
Sacrilege	sacrilegious	4	x	x?	x?
Saeve	savage	32+			x
Saevissime	very savage	4+		x	x
Scelerate	guilty	21	x	x	x
Scelerum caput	head of crimes	4	x		
Sceleste	guilty	28	x		
Scelus	crime	23	x		
Segnis	sluggish, lazy	4			x
Serve	slave	2	x	x	
Severe	strict, stern	2			x
Stolide	stupid	4	x		
Stulte	stupid	30	x	x	x
Stultissime	very stupid	9	x	x	
Subdole	treacherous	2	x		
Temerari	reckless	5			x
Timide	timid	2			x
Timidissime	very timid	2			x
Trifurcifer	triple *furcifer*	2	x		
Tyranne	tyrant	4			
Vecors	mad	2			x?
Venefice	poisoner	5	x		
Verbero	one who deserves a beating	25	x		
Verpe	circumcised, erect penis*	4	x		
Vervex	wether	2	x		
Vesane	mad	7			x
Vilis	cheap, worthless	2			x
Violente	violent	7			x
Vipera	viper	3			
Vorago	chasm	2		x?	

* For this sense see Adams (1982: 37–8) and Kay (1985: 258).

Note: 'x' indicates a definite attribution, 'x?' a tentative one. Where Register column is blank, I was unable to determine register (though it may be that the insult clearly does *not* belong to one of the registers). Passages in which the word is used in a non-insulting sense are not included.

rule, but the rules hold true often enough to be useful to native speakers. This insult grammar explains how a newly invented insult, even if it is invented by the author of a literary work and displays more imagination and literary flair than most insults one hears, can be immediately recognizable as belonging to a low or to a high register. Offensiveness as well as register seems to be encoded in the grammar, for English speakers have no trouble recognizing that 'you semiliterate truck driver' is less offensive than either of the insults quoted above.

Was there a similar insult 'grammar' in Latin? When a Roman author invented insults, did he differentiate between the type of insult invented for a character normally characterized by low-register language and those invented for characters who used high-register language, and could his audience appreciate the distinction? If so, we should be able to find traces of those rules in our data. Specifically, we would expect to find among the insults in Table 5 some semantic categories which seem to belong to the low register and others which seem to belong to the high register. We could then test the rules derived from these insults against the rarer insults, many of them unique, which do not appear in the table. If Roman authors were following specific rules in constructing these insults, a consistent relationship between contexts requiring certain registers and semantic categories associated with those registers should emerge.

In fact, such a relationship does exist, even in our relatively limited sample of data. Insults in Table 5 with lexical meanings referring to punishments all belong exclusively to the low register: *mastigia, furcifer, trifurcifer, verbero*. This may be because they refer to the world of the slave and thus in origin would naturally be used primarily by and to slaves. Less reason is apparent, however, for the fact that words referring to animals are also exclusively low-register (cf. Hofmann 1951: 88): *asine, belua, canis, cucule, excetra, feles, monstrum, vervex* (the only exception in Table 5 is *vipera*, the register of which is uncertain). When we test these generalizations against the rarer insults, our hypotheses are largely confirmed, for rare and unique insults referring to punishments or to animals tend to come from contexts which appear to be low-register: *carcer* 'prison' (Ter. *Ph.* 373, slave to parasite), *carnuficium cribrum* 'hangman's sieve' (Pl. *Mos.* 55, slave to slave), *catenarum colone* 'chain-farmer' (Pl. *As.* 298, slave to slave), *compedium tritor* 'shackle-rubber' (Pl. *Per.* 420, *leno* to slave), *crux* 'crucifix' (Pl. *Per.* 795, *leno* to slave), *gymnasium flagri* 'whip's gymnasium' (Pl. *As.* 297, slave to slave), *stimulorum seges* 'crop of goads' (Pl. *Aul.* 45, *senex* to slave), *stimulorum tritor* 'goad-rubber' (Pl. *Per.* 795, *leno* to slave), *suduculum flagri* 'whip's whipping-post' (Pl. *Per.* 419, *leno* to slave), *ulmitriba* 'wearing out elm rods' (Pl. *Per.* 279, slave to slave), *verberabilissume* 'very ready for a beating' (Pl. *Aul.* 633, *senex* to slave), *verbereum caput* 'head composed of blows' (Pl. *Per.* 184, slave to slave), *virgarum lascivia* 'sport of switches' (Pl. *As.* 298, slave to slave); *accipiter* 'hawk' (Pl. *Per.* 409, slave to *leno*), *anser* 'goose' (*CIL* iv. 8870, graffito), *culex* 'gnat' (Pl. *Cas.* 239, wife to *senex*), *lumbrice* 'worm' (Pl. *Aul.* 628, *senex* to slave), *milua* 'she-kite' (Petr. 75. 6, man to wife), *morticine* 'animal carrion' (Pl. *Per.* 283, slave to slave), *mule* 'mule' (Catul. 83. 3, author to Lesbia's husband), *mus* 'mouse' (Petr. 58. 4, freedman to boy). The only clear exceptions I found are *animal* 'animal' (Sen. *Dial.* 9. 11. 5, fortune to bad men) and *pecus* 'farm animal' (Hor. *Ep.* 1. 19. 19, author to his imitators).

Words referring to slowness and laziness might be expected to come from the world of the slave as well, but those in Table 5 in fact belong to the high register: *segnis*, *piger*, *lente*, *iners*, with *ignave* and *ignavissime* apparently common to all registers. Also normally from the high register are various forms of cruelty, for example, pride, ingratitude, harshness, or violence: *violente*, *severe*, *saeve*, *dure*, *durior*, *immitis*, *difficilis*, *cruente*, *asper*, *ferox*, *ferrea*; belonging both to the high and to the middle register are *crudelis*, *ingrate*, and *saevissime*, while in the middle register are *crudelissime* and *ingratissime*. On the other side, references to the addressee's fear, helplessness, harmlessness, or impending death also belong to the high register: *timide*, *timidissime*, *perdite*, *periture*, *metuende* (sarcastic), *moriture*, *enervis*, *credule*, with *perditissime* and *impotentissime* being uncertain.

Once again, most of the rarer insults from these semantic categories seem also to belong to the high register: *cruore semper laeta cognato* 'always delighting in kindred bloodshed' (Sen. *Oed.* 627, Laius to Creon etc.), *exitiose* 'destructive'

(Mart. 6. 21. 4, Venus to poet), *immansuetissime* 'most savage' (Ov. *Ep*. 18. 37, Leander to wind), *mactator senum* 'butcherer of old men' (Sen. *Tro*. 1002, Hecuba to Pyrrhus), *noxia* 'harmful' (Luc. 8. 823, author to place), *omnium amicorum interfector* 'killer of all your friends' (Sen. *Apoc*. 13. 6, friend to Claudius), *proterve* 'violent' (Ov. *Ep*. 11. 16, Canace to wind), *truces* 'savage' (Luc. 7. 231, author to characters); *bis capti* 'twice-captured' (Verg. *A*. 9. 599, enemies in battle), *dature supplicia* 'about to pay the penalty' (Stat. *Theb*. 12. 780–1, enemies in battle), *impotens* 'helpless' ([Quint.] *Decl*. 5. 2, speaker to opponent), *inrise* 'laughable' (Verg. *A*. 7. 425, 'priestess' to Turnus), *iugulate* 'murdered' (Prop. 2. 33b. 29, author to character), *orbature parentes* 'about to make your parents childless' (Stat. *Theb*. 9. 780, enemies in battle), *pauci* 'few' (Stat. *Theb*. 2. 668, enemies in battle), *pavidissime* 'very frightened' (Sil. 10. 65, Paulus to Metellus), *trepidum* 'nervous' (Sen. *Dial*. 9. 11. 5), *vane* '[acting] in vain' (Sil. 2. 315, Hanno to Hannibal), *vanissime* '[acting] very much in vain' (Juv. 14. 211, author to bad fathers). The only likely exception in my data is *immanissimum* 'most savage' (Cic. *Pis*. 31, orator to opponent).

It thus seems that Roman authors followed identifiable rules in constructing insults of specific registers, and that we can recover those rules to some extent. At the same time, not all semantic categories can be divided by register, nor can the registers of all Latin insults be explained by membership in such categories. Another approach is a grammatical division into nouns and adjectives. In some sense such a division is impossible, since many 'adjectives' are used substantively as insults and some nouns are used in apposition in what is virtually an adjectival function. Nevertheless, some of the words used as insults are essentially adjectives (e.g. *lentus* 'slow') and others are essentially nouns (e.g. *scelus* 'crime'). Using this distinction of normal grammatical function, one can observe from Table 5 that the strictly low-register insults are predominantly nouns (67%), strictly high-register insults are almost never nouns (only 4%), and the others fall in between (21% nouns).

What is it about nouns that causes them to belong to the low register? One could argue that Plautus simply had a preference for nouns as addresses, and thus that the preponderance of Plautine data in the low register has made what was simply an idiosyncrasy seem like an issue of register. Yet the data do not support this explanation: of those low-register insults in Table 5 which are attested in Plautus, 22 are nouns and 14 are adjectives; of those which are attested elsewhere, 23 are nouns and 11 adjectives.[10] It thus looks as though the tendency for low-register insults to be nouns explains Plautus' tendency to use nominal insults, rather than vice versa.

Perhaps a clue to the register division can be gained by looking at those nouns which do appear as high-register insults. These are *machinator* and *raptor*, both of which have a lexical meaning referring to a human being; of the 30 low-register nouns, only 11 normally refer to humans in their lexical meanings. This distinction is connected to a factor mentioned earlier, that insults comparing addressees to animals belong to the low register, but it also extends to words such as *scelus*, *lutum*, and *labes* which have nothing to do with animals.

A further distinction can be found between *machinator* and *raptor* and those low-register nouns which do refer to humans. *Machinator* and *raptor* accuse the addressee of specific misdeeds, and they are both used in contexts in which an accusation of those particular misdeeds is in fact relevant and believable. The low-register nouns, however, are often used in situations where they cannot be taken so literally (cf. Hofmann 1951: 86). *Carnifex*, for example, is a popular term but is almost never addressed to an actual executioner in my data, nor to those accused of having been a member of that profession. Likewise *venefice* is not an indication that the addressee is really suspected of being a poisoner, and the addressees of *fugitive* are not in fact runaways.

This difference between the more literal use of high-register insults and the less literal use of low-register ones seems to apply to adjectives as well as nouns. The low-register terms *sceleste* and *illex* are not taken as serious indictments of criminal activity, for example, while the high-register adjectives *perfide* and *saeve* are normally applied only to those who have actually acted in a faithless or cruel manner.

---

[10] See the Glossary for the authors in which each insult is attested.

In fact, this distinction of literalness seems to be the most important divider between high- and low-register Latin insults. This importance is shown not only by the consistency with which it applies (high-register insults are used literally far more often than low-register ones) but also by the existence of insults which can belong to different registers depending on how they are used. *Parricida*, for example, is normally a high-register rebuke used to men accused of murder or treason;[11] when it is applied more generally, to people who are not actually accused of such crimes, it seems to belong to the low register (Pl. *Ps.* 362). Likewise *periure* can be used like *perfide* as a high-register term for faithless lovers and the like (Ov. *Fast.* 3. 473; Prop. 1. 8a. 17, etc.), but it can also be a more generally applicable insult, in which case it has a low register (Pl. *Ps.* 363). A similar pattern appears with *monstrum*, which is a high-register non-insulting address used to monsters in Seneca (*Phaed.* 1204) but a low-register insult when used to people (Cic. *Pis.* 31; Ter. *Eu.* 860), and with *sacrilege*, which is of uncertain register when used as a rebuke to those committing sacrilege (Ov. *Am.* 1. 7. 28; Sen. *Con.* 8. 1) and low-register when used as a more general insult (Ter. *Eu.* 829; Pl. *Ps.* 363).

How should one describe this distinction? A few decades ago one might have said that the higher registers of the Latin insult system were more precise in usage, finding the correct word for each of the addressee's flaws, while the lower ones were imprecise and used the same insults for every flaw; now one might be more likely to speak of the high register as being literal and the low register as metaphorical.[12] Both formulations contain a certain amount of truth, but whichever one prefers, it is important to keep in mind that each register clearly had the capacity to produce a wide range of insults, and that one cannot understand the Latin insult system properly without taking into account all its different registers.

---

[11] Calp. *Decl.* 4; Sen. *Oed.* 1002; Curt. 8. 8. 17, etc.

[12] If one ignores the issue of non-vocative insult usage, one can also describe the distinction as one between address and referential meaning: at the higher registers, Latin vocative insults are used in a fashion closely connected to their lexical, non-insult meanings, while at the lower registers this connection is less apparent.

As we have already observed, the offensiveness of insults is harder to determine than their register. One might assume that since offensiveness is a question of intensity, it should be related to the presence or absence of intensifying prefixes and suffixes. In some cases this relationship appears to work: the Plautine prefixes used to form strengthened insults like *terve-nefice* 'triple poisoner' and *trifurcifer* 'triple *furcifer*' seem to add force, as is shown by the insult *non fur, sed trifur* 'not thief, but triple thief' (Pl. *Aul.* 633).[13]

The addition of a superlative suffix, however, does not necessarily produce a more offensive insult. It looks as though superlatives can be either more or less offensive than positives or can remain at the same level of strength. Thus for example *stulte* is a fairly mild term used by lovers in gentle rebukes (Prop. 2. 21. 18, etc.), by Athena in an encouraging remark to Martial (6. 10. 12), or by a matron giving advice to a friend (Pl. *Cas.* 204). *Stultissime* on the other hand seems considerably stronger and is used for example by Cicero expressing scorn for Antony (*Phil.* 2. 29) or Verres (*Ver.* 1. 102), though it can also occur in milder settings (e.g. Petr. 10. 1). A similar strengthening effect can be detected between *perdite* and *perditissime* and between *ignave* and *ignavissime*.

On the other hand, *impure* seems to be a strong insult, used by slaves and youths castigating a *leno* (Pl. *Per.* 408, *Ps.* 366). The superlative *impurissime* seems somewhat milder, being used by Cicero to express moderate anger (*Vat.* 26). With still other pairs, such as *ingrate* and *ingratissime*, *periure* and *periurissime*, and *crudelis* and *crudelissime*, I have not been able to find a clear difference between the offensiveness of positive and superlative forms.[14]

A lack of difference in intensity, however, does not imply a lack of any difference. The main distinction between degrees of comparison seems to be genre-dependent and is related to the pattern found among terms of endearment (pp. 134–9): prose

[13] It must be admitted that this is the only passage which indicates a clear difference in vocative usage, but there are no counter-examples; see Marx (1959: 153).

[14] Lilja (1965*b*: 19–20) notes that for referential as well as vocative insult usage, there is no clear distinction between the intensity of positives and superlatives in comedy.

texts contain a much higher percentage of superlatives than do poetic texts. Because superlatives are in general rarer as insults than as endearments, however, the figures for insults are less dramatic. Prose authors use superlatives 40% of the time and positives 60% for vocative insults, comic poets have 22% superlatives, and classical and later poets only 6%. Cicero, however, uses 67% superlatives, well above the average for prose in general. Comparatives are basically confined to classical and later poetry, as is the case among terms of endearment.

This difference in genre probably accounts for the fact that positives, comparatives, and superlatives sometimes seem to belong to different registers and/or have different uses. Thus *periure* and *periurissime* can both be low-register strong insults (e.g. Pl. *Ps.* 351, 363), but *periure* can also be a high-register rebuke for faithless lovers etc. (e.g. Prop. 1. 8a. 17); *perditissime* is a fairly strong insult and does not belong to the high register (e.g. Cic. *Ver.* 3. 65), but *perdite* is high-register and can simply be a warning (e.g. V. Fl. 4. 140).[15]

Another factor which might be expected to influence relative offensiveness is the lexical meaning of an insult. Thus in English, for example, sexual insults tend to be more offensive than non-sexual ones, though the distinction is not absolute. In Latin, sexual insults also appear to be highly offensive, as are most insults referring to crimes (*fur*, *parricida*, *sacrilege*, *scelus*, *venefice*, etc.) and punishments (*furcifer*, *mastigia*, *verbero*, etc.) Ingratitude is also grounds for a fairly strong insult in Latin (*ingrate*, *ingratissime*). On the other hand, accusations of ignorance and stupidity (*stulte*, *inepte*, *insipiens*, *fatue*, *ignare*, *bucco*, *credule*) often seem to be milder than we might expect. Again, a more complete study could probably tell us much about Roman cultural assumptions and the extent to which Latin speakers valued different characteristics.

It has been suggested that there is a grammatical distinction in offensiveness, so that 'abstract nouns, as terms of abuse, are stronger than the corresponding adjectives'.[16] No proof has

---

[15] It is notable, however, that many of the differences in offensiveness between positive and superlative noted above cannot be so explained, as they occur within a single author or genre.
[16] Lilja (1965b: 36), following a much less general suggestion in Hofmann (1951: 87); Opelt (1965: 21) makes a similar point.

been offered for this claim, and I can neither prove nor
disprove it. It seems likely, however, that the difference is
really one of register, not offensiveness.

Now that we have reconstructed as much as we can of the
grammar of Latin insults, to what extent is it possible to
predict the effect of other insults which were not considered
in making these statements? We have already seen that
generalizations about lexical meaning and register can allow
us to predict the register of less common insults, but in fact we
can now go further than that. Suppose for example we found,
out of context, the address *homo omnium scelerum flagitiorum-
que documentum* 'man [who is] a model of all crimes and
disgraces': although it does not fall into any of the semantic
categories discussed earlier, we could be fairly confident that it
belonged to the low register because of the noun *documentum*
'model', addressed metaphorically to a person; we could also
assume that it would have been very offensive, because of the
reference to crimes. So it is reassuring to check the context of
this insult and see that it is used by Cicero to Clodius in an
expression of outrage (Cic. *Dom.* 126) and was thus probably
intended both to be very offensive and to belong to the low
register.

We could then take another example, *o scelere vincens omne
femineum genus, o maius ausa matre monstrifera malum genetrice
peior* 'O surpassing all the female race in crime, O [you who]
dared a greater wrong than your monster-bearing mother,
[who are] worse than your mother'. This time the insult
appears to be literal rather than metaphorical and thus probably belongs to the high register; at the same time the reference
to crimes suggests considerable offensiveness. So it would
confirm our hypothesis to see that the address is delivered by
a furious and horrified Hippolytus to Phaedra in Seneca's
tragedy (*Phaed.* 687–9) and was probably therefore both
high-register and strong. In both of these cases most readers
of this book probably knew at once what type of insults these
were, for a grammar of insults is bound to be internalized to
some extent in anyone with a good knowledge of Latin
literature, but they would probably not have been able to
explain how they knew. The insult grammar must have been

internalized to a much greater extent in the Romans, and therefore a more detailed examination of it should be capable of predicting the effect of insults that a Roman would have understood even without context but that would confuse most modern readers.

6

Other Addresses

Sic Venus et Veneris contra sic filius orsus:
'nulla tuarum audita mihi neque visa sororum,
o quam te memorem, virgo? namque haud tibi vultus
mortalis, nec vox hominem sonat; o dea certe . . .'

(Verg. *A*. 1. 325–8)

Thus spoke Venus, and Venus' son began his reply thus:
'I have neither heard nor seen any of your sisters, O how
shall I address you, girl? For your face is not mortal, nor
does your voice sound human; O certainly a goddess . . .'

THE preceding chapters have covered the most important types of address for individuals in Latin, but many others exist as well: none of the terms used in the above passage belongs to the types already discussed. Some very common addresses are used primarily for groups, and some others are used only to non-human entities; these will be discussed in Chapters 12 and 13. There are, however, also some other types of address used to individual humans, and it is these that form the topic of this chapter.

One such address type is that conveying pity. Expressions of pity have something in common both with insults and with expressions of affection; they are by nature marked addresses, expressing the speaker's feelings at a given time, rather than the standard term within any given dyad. The nature of the feeling expressed, however, is less obvious here than in the case of insults or expressions of affection. Terms of pity are formed from two roots, the first providing *infelix* 'unhappy' and *infelicissime* 'very unhappy' and the second *miser* 'wretched', *miserrime* 'very wretched', *miserande* 'pitiable', and *miselle* 'poor little'. There is some difference in address meaning among the different forms built on each root, but apparently none between the two roots.

Miser and *infelix* can both express real sympathy for someone who is suffering or has suffered. Thus Catullus addresses
his dead brother with *miser indigne frater adempte mihi*
'wretched brother, unjustly snatched away from me' (101. 6),
while Thisbe bewails her dead lover Pyramus with *infelix* (Ov.
Met. 4. 149). Almost as often, however, these addresses are
used in a completely unsympathetic sense, conveying contempt
or scorn for someone who is not obviously deserving of pity.
Thus Cicero, in the midst of a torrent of invective directed at
his hated enemy Piso, also includes the address *infelix* (*Pis.* 78),
and he similarly attacks Antony with *miser* (*Phil.* 2. 16). This
difference in meaning has nothing to do with date, genre, or
authorship, for both senses can occur within the works of a
single author: Statius uses *miser* to express pity for Amphiaraus
(*Theb.* 6. 383) and scorn for Hippomedon (*Theb.* 9. 342).

   In still other passages, these addresses are used for warnings
or exhortations, in situations where the addressees are indeed
deserving of pity for their future suffering but may be unaware
of this fact. The vocatives seem to add potency to warnings or
exhortations by pointing out the danger of not heeding the
speaker's words (cf. Opelt 1965: 120). Thus after the apparent
departure of the Greeks from Troy, Laocoon addresses the
happy Trojans as *o miseri* (Verg. *A*. 2. 42), while Ovid exclaims
to his character Cephalus, who is about to kill his wife Procris
by accident, *quid facis, infelix?* 'what are you doing, unhappy
one?' (*Ars* 3. 735). In a less friendly vein, the boxing tyrant
Amycus addresses his opponent Pollux, whom he forces to
fight and intends to kill, as *infelix . . . puer* 'unhappy boy' (V. Fl.
4. 240).

   These passages seem to provide the link between the seem-
ingly unrelated meanings of sympathy and scorn. *Miser* or
infelix is used to express sympathy for someone who is
suffering, and hence as a friendly warning to someone who
will soon be suffering. It can thus also be used in a less friendly
way to intimidate someone by threatening him with future
suffering, or to point out his present contemptible status.
Basically, the use of *miser* or *infelix* indicates that the addressee
is in a position to deserve sympathy from his friends, but it
does not imply that any sympathy is necessarily forthcoming
from the speaker, nor that the addressee thinks himself to be

deserving of pity. In fact an addressee's ignorance of his state can make him even more suited to this address, for Cicero says to Antony *o miser cum re, tum hoc ipso quod non sentis quam miser es* 'O wretched not only because of your circumstances, but also for the very reason that you have no idea how wretched you are' (*Phil.* 13. 34).

The superlatives *miserrime* and *infelicissime*, like the superlatives of insults and expressions of affection, are used in prose a much higher percentage of the time than are the positives. The superlatives seem to be used only for pity, not for scorn, but they do not appear to differ in sense from the positives when these are used to express pity. Thus in one late declamation a man addresses his beloved dead son both as *miserrime fili* 'very wretched son' ([Quint.] *Decl.* 6. 21) and as *miser* (6. 22) without any perceptible difference in tone, but of these two terms only *misera* is used to the speaker's rather less beloved wife (6. 8). *Miserande*, like the superlatives, expresses only sympathy, but *miselle* again expresses both sympathy and scorn.

Thus the Latin address system contains some terms which merge the notions of sympathy and scorn, and others which apparently distinguish them. In Greek the address usage of terms of pity suggests that these two emotions may have been inextricably linked in that culture (Dickey 1996: 161–5), but such was apparently not the case for the Romans. At the same time, the Romans seem to have connected the two emotions more than we do, and this difference may point to a diachronic development of social attitudes to the unfortunate.

A peculiarity of usage of the pity terms is also notable. In poetry, perhaps for metrical reasons,[1] virtually the only plural term of pity in use is *miseri*. When *infelix* is used to plural addressees in poetry, it forms a collective singular instead of a plural. Thus Vergil uses *o miserae* to the Trojan women (*A.* 5. 623), but a little later *o gens infelix* 'O unhappy race' (624–5).

A very different type of address is that formed from words identifying the addressee by age and gender ('man', 'woman', 'boy', 'girl', etc). Such terms are much more important in the

---

[1] *Miserrimi* and *infelicissimi* are both almost impossible in a hexameter, while *infelices* consists of four long syllables and is thus not ideal.

Latin address system than in that of English, and they can convey a wide variety of meanings. In our data (which may be biased on this point because of the preponderance of men in literature), the most common such addresses are those meaning 'man', that is, *vir* and *homo*.[2] In referential usage, *homo* normally means a human being of either gender, while *vir* refers specifically to an adult male. In address usage, however, the singular *homo* is restricted to adult male addressees just as thoroughly as is *vir*; that this is a rule of the address system rather than an accident of survival is shown by a passage in Plautus in which a male slave and his mistress are greeted together with *mi homo et mea mulier* 'my human being and my woman' (*Cist.* 723).[3] The difference between the two addresses must therefore be sought elsewhere.

When *vir* and *homo* are used in the singular as vocatives, unmodified or modified only by *mi*, they have distinctly different functions. *Vir* under such circumstances is almost always a kinship term meaning 'husband',[4] in which case it is normally used with *mi*, perhaps to distinguish it more clearly from the non-kinship usage, which virtually never takes *mi*. Unmodified *vir* used other than by a woman to her husband is rare and occurs only when a contrast between male and female is being stressed, as *quisquis ades . . . vir mulierque* 'you, whoever is present, man or woman' (Tib. 2. 2. 2) or *laese vir a domina, laesa puella viro* 'man injured by your lady-love, girl injured by your man' (Ov. *Rem.* 608). *Homo* as well, though it does not mean 'husband', is very often used by women (and occurs only in comedy) when unmodified. It can be a polite address to a strange man, a somewhat surprised address to a known man, or an impolite address to the speaker's husband.[5]

---

[2] On these words see Santoro L'Hoir (1992) and Jocelyn (1973: 33–5), but note that some of their generalizations, e.g. that *vir* 'is always coupled with positive adjectives' (Santoro L'Hoir 1992: 10), are incorrect (cf. n. 7 below).

[3] This passage is sometimes thought to exemplify a rare pre-classical referential usage of *homo* for 'male' (cf. Lewis and Short 1879 s.v.), but it is more likely to exemplify vocative use, given that all the singular vocative uses of *homo* are addressed to adult males, and that Greek ἄνθρωπε shows exactly the same restriction to adult males in the vocative case (Dickey 1996: 152).

[4] e.g. Pl. *Am.* 502, *Cas.* 586, etc.; Ter. *Hau.* 622, *Hec.* 235, etc.; Ov. *Ep.* 9. 168; V. Fl. 8. 415.

[5] e.g. strange: Pl. *Epid.* 640, *Per.* 620, *Cist.* 719. Known: Ter. *An.* 721,

The unmodified usage is, however, less common for both words than the use of *vir* and *homo* as part of longer vocative phrases, often consisting of strings of complimentary or insulting adjectives. In such addresses the words *vir* and *homo* seem to have no meaning in themselves but serve merely as pegs onto which the more expressive adjectives are attached; they can thus be used either for positive or for negative adjectives, as *homo stultissime et amentissime* (Cic. *Ver.* 1. 102) or *vir optime mihique carissime Brute* (Cic. *Fam.* 11. 21. 3). These addresses are also restricted to adult males, and the addressees are normally known to the speaker, in contrast with the frequent usage of unmodified *homo* to strangers.

In referential usage, *homo* is found with both positive and negative adjectives, the two occurring in roughly equal proportion.[6] Referential *vir* is also used with both types of adjective in some authors, but Cicero almost always uses it with positive adjectives.[7] The address usage of *vir* resembles its referential use; Cicero uses it only with positive adjectives, never negative ones, and other authors prefer positive adjectives but also use some negative ones, as *vir venefice* 'poisoner man' (Pl. *Rud.* 1112) or *vir inepte* 'foolish man' (Mart. 1. 68. 8). *Homo*, on the other hand, is more prone to negative modifiers in address than in referential usage, being used negatively 69% of the time in our data. In comedy, though *homo* is frequently part of insults,[8] it is also used in genuine praise[9] and can even be part of requested flattery: thus one of Plautus' characters commands a parasite *dic hominem lepidissumum esse me* 'say that I am a very charming man' (*Men.* 147), and the parasite responds obediently *dico: homo lepidissume* 'I say it: very charming man'. In

Ad. 336, *Eu.* 756; Pl. *Bac.* 1155, *Epid.* 575. Husband: Pl. *Cas.* 266; Ter. *Hau.* 1004. Cf. Woytek (1982: 365).

[6] e.g. 52% of examples of modified *homo* in Plautus take a positive adjective, while 54% of examples of nominative *homo* modified by an adjective in Cicero have a positive adjective (sample restricted to the nominative due to its large size: 252 examples).

[7] In Cicero, 98% of nominative modified examples have a positive adjective (exceptions: *Clu.* 175, *Pis.* 54, *Tusc.* 2. 53, *Sen.* 1); in Plautus, only 64% of modified examples take a positive adjective.

[8] Pl. *Bac.* 1163, *Epid.* 333, *Men.* 487; Ter. *Ad.* 218, *Eu.* 239.

[9] Pl. *Cur.* 120a, *Ps.* 323; Ter. *Ph.* 853.

Plautus' day, then, there can have been nothing inherently negative about the address *homo*.

Cicero, however, rarely uses a positive adjective to modify the vocative *homo*, and when he does, the address is always sarcastic. Thus he calls Verres *sancte homo ac religiose* 'holy and devout man' (*Ver.* 5. 49) and Antony *homo diserte* 'eloquent man' (*Phil.* 2. 8) but more often employs the outright insults *homo audacissime* 'very bold man', *homo amentissime* 'most insane man', etc.[10] Other classical and post-classical authors use *homo* less often as an address; most appear to use it negatively,[11] but Marcus Aurelius in his letters to Fronto uses the vocative only with positive adjectives and in contexts of genuine praise,[12] showing that in his day, as in Plautus', there was nothing inherently negative about the address. Cicero's apparent negative usage of the vocative may have been characteristic of his style or of the Latin of his day, but if the latter, the feature did not last.

Both *vir* and *homo* are used somewhat differently in the plural from the singular usage we have so far examined. *Viri* and *homines* are more often used alone than with modifiers, but if modifiers do appear, they are always positive in the case of *viri* and frequently positive in the case of *homines*, even in Cicero.[13] *Viri* can be applied to any group of men, provided all members of the group are male, but it is particularly used to armies. *Homines* on the other hand can be addressed to a group of mixed gender, like the audience of a play (Pl. *Cist.* 678), or to humanity in general (Ov. *Rem.* 69). The plural address usage of these words thus shows a stronger connection to the referential usage than does the singular.

While *vir* and *homo* identify addressees as being adult males, some other addresses identify males as not yet adult. The most common of these words is *puer* 'boy' (or *puere*), which has a

---

[10] e.g. *Phil.* 2. 43, *Ver.* 3. 141, 4. 19, 5. 11.

[11] e.g. *homo stultissime*, Petr. 10. 1, 65. 5; *homo crudelissime*, Sen. *Apoc.* 13. 6; *homo inepte*, Gel. 1. 10. 2.

[12] *Suavissime*, Fro. 2. 17; *carissime*, 30. 12; *amicissime*, 34. 23, 61. 1; *rarissime*, 34. 15, 34. 23; *desiderantissime*, 30. 11; *iucundissime*, 27. 22; *honestissime*, 34. 14. Fronto does not use the vocative *homo* in return.

[13] e.g. *homines meo quidem iudicio acutissimi*, Cic. *Leg.* 2. 52; *homines amicissimi ac prudentissimi*, Cic. *Rep.* 1. 70.

complex address usage. Like Greek παῖ 'boy',[14] it is used both
to children and to slaves, and the two uses need to be
considered separately. Most commonly, *puer* is used as an
address for boys and young men of free birth. The addressee
may be named or nameless, known or unknown to the speaker,
and either related or unrelated; the most frequent use of *puer*,
however, is as an address to known, named boys unrelated to
the speaker. The addressee may be a baby, a boy, or a youth
just old enough to enter battle, like Vergil's Pallas.[15] In such
uses *puer* is a friendly address, normally indicating the kind of
generalized fondness that adults feel for the young. It is often
modified by terms of affection (*care puer* 'dear boy', Sil. 6. 537),
pity (*miserande puer* 'pitiable boy', Verg. *A.* 6. 882), or praise
(*fortunate puer* 'fortunate boy', Verg. *Ecl.* 5. 49). The speaker is
normally older than the addressee, but this need not always be
the case, for Vergil has Iulus address Euryalus as *venerande
puer* 'venerable boy' (*A.* 9. 276), and Ovid describes Narcissus
addressing his own reflection as *puer* (*Met.* 3. 454, 500).

Puer is also a popular address from men to boys as love
objects. Such addresses sometimes use *puer* alone[16] but more
often include a complimentary adjective, as *o formose puer* 'O
good-looking boy' (Verg. *Ecl.* 2. 17, 2. 45) or *puer o dulcissime* 'O
very sweet boy' (Mart. 9. 36. 7). Pseudo-Sulpicia also uses *caste
puer* 'pure boy' to her beloved Cerinthus ([Tib.] 3. 9. 20), and
the nymph Salamacis, who pursues Hermaphroditus, addresses
him as *puer* (Ov. *Met.* 4. 320); the address is rare from female
lovers, however, and these two passages have in common not
only the youth of the males but also the unusual assertiveness of
the women. The amatory use of *puer* may lie behind the
frequent use of the term as an address to Cupid in poetry.[17]

[14] Other parallels for this dual usage include French *garçon* for waiters and
the use of 'boy' for black men by some white Americans (Ervin-Tripp 1969:
229; Frank and Anshen 1983: 51–3).

[15] e.g. babies: Ov. *Met.* 2. 643; Verg. *Ecl.* 4. 18; Stat. *Theb.* 1. 582, 7. 98;
Calp. *Decl.* 51. Little boys: Verg. *A.* 3. 487; Sil. 4. 130; Stat. *Silv.* 3. 4. 36;
Sen. *Tro.* 508, 799. Older boys: Verg. *A.* 9. 656; Ov. *Met.* 4. 320; Stat. *Silv.* 5.
2. 51, *Ach.* 1. 252; Sil. 1. 112; Sen. *Her. F.* 1231. Youths: Ter. *Ad.* 940; Verg.
A. 8. 581, 10. 825, 11. 42, 12. 435; Ov. *Fast.* 1. 367; Stat. *Theb.* 9. 744.

[16] Verg. *A.* 9. 217; Tib. 1. 4. 83, 1. 8. 67.

[17] Alone at Tib. 2. 6. 5; Ov. *Am.* 1. 1. 13, 2. 9. 35, *Ars* 2. 15. Modified at
Catul. 64. 95; Ov. *Am.* 1. 1. 5, 3. 15. 15, *Rem* 11, *Met.* 1. 456.

Towards the upper end of the acceptable age limit for address with *puer*, the term may have been somewhat insulting. Cicero quotes a letter from Antony to Octavian in which the future emperor is addressed as *o puer, qui omnia nomini debes* 'O boy, you who owe everything to your name' (*Phil.* 13. 24); this is clearly not meant as a compliment, but it is notable that Cicero singles out the word *puer* in particular for comment, saying

Puerum appellat quem non modo virum sed etiam fortissimum virum sensit et sentiet. Est istuc quidem nomen aetatis, sed ab eo minime usurpandum qui suam amentiam puero praebet ad gloriam.

He calls a boy someone whom he has felt to be, and will feel to be, not only a man but a very strong man. Such a name is indeed appropriate to his age, but it most certainly ought not to be used by one who offers his own insanity to increase the boy's glory.

In other words, *puer* was an appropriate address to a 20-year-old (Octavian's age at the time), but not when the 20-year-old had a solid record of deeds behind him, nor when the speaker was inferior to him.[18] A similar insulting tone can be found in the *puer* with which the young heroes Pollux and Parthenopaeus are addressed by their enemies in battle (V. Fl. 4. 240; Stat. *Theb.* 9. 780).

Elsewhere in Latin, however, we find *puer* used in comparable situations without any negative implications. The young Scipio is fairly accomplished and 23 years old when he is called *puer* not only by the ghost of the Sibyl and by the personification of Pleasure, but also by a mortal priestess (Sil. 13. 503, 15. 46, 13. 758). Horace portrays himself as a young man being addressed as *puer* by an older friend, without any insulting overtones (*S.* 2. 1. 60), and Persius has a slave address his master, a young man old enough to marry, as *puer* (5. 167, 169). Statius portrays Tydeus as pleading with a comrade, calling him *o primis puer inclyte bellis Arcas* 'O boy Arcas, famous in your first wars' (*Theb.* 8. 743–4), which suggests that

[18] In reference, *puer* is frequently used of Octavian at this period, even by Cicero himself; the future emperor resented this usage, but it was clearly considered appropriate to his age (cf. McCarthy 1931; Shackleton Bailey 1977: ii. 495; Cic. *Phil.* 4. 3). Cicero uses *puer* in reference even for men as old as 30: *Fam.* 2. 15. 4; see Shackleton Bailey (1977: i. 427).

the addressee had made a name for himself as a warrior and could still be called *puer*. It thus looks as though *puer* used to a young man acting as an adult could be insulting but was not necessarily so.

In Greek, the address παî is not normally used to free adults except by the addressee's parents, but they can use the term even to middle-aged addressees (Dickey 1996: 68). In Latin there is no evidence for such a parental privilege; *puer* is in any case not as common an address from parents to children as Greek παî, but it does not seem to be used at all to adult children.[19]

Puer can also be used to address slaves, both by free men and by other slaves.[20] In such usage it almost always stands alone, in contrast to the frequent modifiers found with *puer* to boys, and is normally employed in a demand or order to a nameless servant. In comedy, where slaves are frequently important figures and are constantly addressed, the named slaves who function as real characters are virtually never called *puer*, while nameless, mute attendants are frequently so addressed in orders.[21] There are, however, two exceptional cases in which *puer* is used to named slaves. In one passage it is used to slaves who are unknown to the speaker and whom he must therefore treat as nameless,[22] and in the other the boy slave Paegnium is addressed as *puere* by characters who certainly know his name (Pl. *Per.* 771, 792). This latter use is presumably possible because Paegnium is a boy as well as a slave, and whereas named slaves are not called *puer*, named boys are frequently so addressed.

The evidence of later authors, though more scattered than that in comedy, follows the same pattern. Both poets and prose writers use unmodified *puer* in orders to nameless slaves,[23] and

[19] The term is occasionally used to apparently full-grown divinities by their fathers (Stat. *Theb.* 7. 7, 7. 196), but as divinities are ageless this does not show that the same usage could occur among humans.

[20] e.g. Pl. *Mos.* 947, *Per.* 792; *pace* Sonnenschein (1907: 97). Cf. Nisbet and Hubbard (1970: 421–2); Leary (1996: 232).

[21] e.g. Pl. *Ps.* 170, *Mos.* 308, *Bac.* 577; Ter. *Ph.* 152, *An.* 84, *Hec.* 719.

[22] Pl. *Mos.* 939–91; note, however, that unknown slaves are not always so addressed (cf. p. 254).

[23] e.g. Pers. 6. 69; Hor. *Carm.* 3. 19. 10; [Tib.] 3. 6. 62; Apul. *Met.* 10. 16; Cic. *De Orat.* 2. 247; Prop. 3. 23. 23; Ov. *Tr.* 5. 5. 11; Stat. *Silv.* 1. 5. 10; Mart. 4. 10. 3.

when the address is used to named slaves, those slaves are boys.[24] In reality, all Roman slaves had names, but a rich owner may not always have bothered to learn the names of all his slaves, or to care which one fulfilled a particular request; the use of *puer* in orders thus need not be a purely literary construct.

The plural *pueri* is also common and is normally used like the singular, whether to nameless slaves or to boys,[25] though it is apparently never modified by adjectives. On occasion, however, *pueri* can also be used to a group of adult men by their military superior. Vergil's Aeneas so addresses some of his men (*A.* 5. 349), as does a bandit chief in Apuleius (*Met.* 3. 5). The address is authoritative but does not seem to be insulting and can even be used in encouragement.

The addresses *adulescens* 'young person' and *iuvenis* 'young man' overlap in age with *puer*. In contrast to *puer*, *adulescens* is never used by parents to their own children except in the highly artificial setting of nameless children in the declamations.[26] When *adulescens* is used in its normal function, to a young man unrelated to the speaker, it seems to be neutral in tone. It is used, for example, by an old man trying to calm a younger comrade (Petr. 90. 5), by a woman to her lover in anger (Petr. 129. 6), and by a famous grammarian in a patronizing remark to Gellius (Gel. 20. 10. 2). It is possible that the term has a negative sense when used to addressees close to the speaker (e.g. the lover and sons in the declamations), but the evidence is inconclusive on this point. Many of the addressees receiving *adulescens* are strangers whose names the speakers do not know,[27] but there is no apparent difference in usage between such passages and those with known addressees. The speaker is often older than the addressee, but this need not be the case, for Plautus has a youth use the address to his (unrecognized) twin brother (*Men.* 1079). The precise ages of

[24] Mart. 1. 88. 7, 9. 93. 1, 11. 6. 9.
[25] e.g. slaves: Pl. *As.* 829, 906; Pers. 1. 113; Hor. *Carm.* 1. 19. 14. Boys: Tib. 1. 4. 61; Hor. *Carm.* 1. 21. 2; Juv. 12. 83; Verg. *Ecl.* 3. 93, 6. 24.
[26] e.g. Quint. *Decl.* 367. 3; Sen. *Con.* 10. 3. 15; Calp. *Decl.* 9.
[27] e.g. Pl. *Bac.* 587, *Rud.* 118, *Men.* 494, 1021; [Cic.] *Rhet. Her.* 4. 14; *ILLRP* 821.

most of the addressees cannot be determined, but they all seem to be youths and younger adults and therefore capable of being referred to as *adulescentes*.

Iuvenis in referential usage is often said to be applied to men older than *adulescentes* but younger than *senes* 'old men', that is, roughly from ages 20 to 45. Axelson (1948), however, suggests that the difference between *iuvenis* and *adulescens* is primarily one of tone, with *adulescens* being the standard prose term for 'young man' during the Republic and *iuvenis* starting as a poetic alternative and then overtaking *adulescens* in prose during the empire. Our data support Axelson's stylistic distinction but also have an age component. In terms of the addressees' ages *iuvenis* overlaps with both *adulescens* and *puer*, being used to young addressees such as Vergil's Lausus (*A.* 10. 793, addressed as *puer* 10. 825), Statius' Menoeceus (*Theb.* 10. 662, addressed as *puer* 10. 696), and Silius' Scipio (13. 435, addressed as *puer* by the same speaker at 13. 758). The youngest recipient of *iuvenis* whose age can be verified is 16 years old and normally called *puer* (Stat. *Silv.* 5. 2. 97). At the same time *iuvenis* is also used to men too old for the addresses *puer* and *adulescens*, as Menecrates, who is stated to be the father of three children (Stat. *Silv.* 4. 8. 14), or Hannibal in the middle of the second Punic war (Sil. 10. 366). The difference is clearly acknowledged in [Ovid], where Sappho calls Phaon *o nec adhuc iuvenis, nec iam puer* 'O you who are not yet a young man, but no longer a boy' (*Ep.* 15. 93), but equally clearly not always observed. In practice, most of the addressees of *iuvenis* are young men old enough to go into battle or otherwise act independently, but well below the age at which they could be addressed with *senex*. The speaker is often older, but by no means always: Medea uses the term to Jason (V. Fl. 7. 11), Hero to Leander (Ov. *Ep.* 19. 181), and Manto to Menoeceus (Stat. *Theb.* 10. 662). I know of no examples, however, in which the speaker of *iuvenis* is significantly younger than the addressee.

Like *adulescens*, *iuvenis* is virtually never used to the speaker's own child except to nameless sons in the declamations. Unlike *adulescens*, however, it is not common in use to unknown men either; the normal usage of *iuvenis* is as an address to young men known by but unrelated to the speaker.

The speaker is often a divinity,[28] the author in his own voice,[29] or a narrator addressing a character in his narration.[30] Adjectives modifying this address tend to express praise, or more rarely affection or sympathy,[31] and when used without modifiers it still tends to occur in positive contexts, except in the declamations. *Iuvenis* thus seems to be a courteous and somewhat distant, formal address belonging to the high and middle registers of language. It is quite different in tone from the neutral or possibly sometimes negative, low- and middle-register address *adulescens*.

The plural *iuvenes* is used to the speaker's own children more freely than the singular, often modified by *mei* 'my'.[32] Otherwise the plural is normally unmodified and can be used to a wide range of groups, provided the addressees are all male and more or less adult, by any type of speaker.

Terms indicating that the addressee is old are much less common than those stressing youth. The Latin address system has two such terms for males, *senex* and its comparative *senior* 'older'. In our data, *senex* is much more common than *senior* and is normally used to old men unrelated to the speaker, whether or not he knows them (though like the terms expressing youth it can be used to nameless relatives in the declamations, as [Quint.] *Decl.* 17. 15, 17). *Senex* seems to be a neutral address, for it is found with both positive and negative modifiers[33] and occurs in both positive and negative contexts when unmodified.[34] The speaker is often younger than the addressee, but as with other terms expressing age this is not a necessary restriction, for the term is also used from one old

---

[28] Venus, Ov. *Met.* 10. 545; Jupiter, Sil. 6. 601; heavenly voice, Sil. 10. 366; river-god, Ov. *Met.* 8. 880; Cupid, Stat. *Silv.* 1. 2. 90.

[29] Ov. *Met.* 8. 459; Stat. *Silv.* 5. 2. 97.

[30] Stat. *Silv.* 1. 2. 90, *Theb.* 7. 280.

[31] e.g. *magnanime*, Stat. *Theb.* 10. 662; *memorande*, Verg. *A.* 10. 793; *fortissime*, V. Fl. 7. 11; *carissime*, Ov. *Pont.* 2. 3. 55; *infelicissime*, Quint. *Decl.* 315. 22.

[32] Liv. 40. 4. 14; Sen. *Con.* 1 pr. 6, *Suas.* 6. 16.

[33] *Fortunate*, Verg. *Ecl.* 1. 46; *facunde*, Ov. *Met.* 12. 178; *optime*, Pl. *Bac.* 1170; *dis inimice*, Hor. *S.* 2. 3. 123; *minimi preti*, Pl. *Bac.* 444; *odiose*, Ov. *Rem.* 471.

[34] e.g. positive at Pl. *Rud.* 742, 773; negative at Pl. *Rud.* 782, 789.

man to another (Pl. *Mer.* 305; Sen. *Con.* 2. 3. 7). The addressee, however, is always an old man.

Despite the esteem often shown to elders in Roman society, *senex* is not a term of respect. Although it can be used in positive or negative contexts, the positive ones often express sympathy (Sen. *Con.* 10. 5. 7; Sen. *Tro.* 133) or are used by speakers much more important and powerful than the addressee.[35] The negative contexts tend to be expressions of scorn and contempt, as a philosopher addressing an old miser (Hor. *S.* 2. 3. 123) or a father condemning his son's teacher (Pl. *Bac.* 444), rather than the kind of anger felt for an equal or superior. Thus it seems that *senex* is normally a somewhat condescending address stressing the feebleness of old age, though this meaning is not always present when the term is used to unknown elders (presumably because there were few other ways to address these men; cf. Chapter 9).[36]

Senior, however, is much more respectful.[37] It is used almost exclusively in deferential contexts and when modified tends to take expressions of respect like *placidissime* 'very kind' (Stat. *Silv.* 3. 3. 43) and *mitissime* 'very mild' (Stat. *Silv.* 3. 3. 208). Perhaps for this reason, it can be used to the speaker's father and to other respected elders as *senex* cannot.[38] *Senior* is much rarer than *senex* in our data, but in late antiquity it became very common as a respectful address and ultimately produced words for 'Mr' in a number of Romance languages, as well as English 'sir' (Svennung 1958: 346–58, 366–72). The difference between *senex* and *senior* is paralleled to some extent by the referential usage of the terms 'old' and 'older' in some current varieties of English; the two are not interchangeable in, for example, 'Our senator is concerned about the problems facing older Americans' and 'Jack doesn't like old people'.

Parallel to these words identifying male addressees are terms identifying females. Such addresses, however, seem to be

[35] Jupiter to Philemon, Ov. *Met.* 8. 704; Jason to Phineus, V. Fl. 4. 538.

[36] Examples of apparently respectful use to unknown men include Pl. *Mer.* 503, *Rud.* 627; Ter. *An.* 788.

[37] Although it is formally a comparative, *senior* when used as an address (and sometimes in referential use as well) lacks any comparative sense; cf. Bömer (1969–86: v. 278).

[38] Ov. *Ep.* 9. 165; Sen. *Her. F.* 1032; cf. Bömer (1969–86: vi. 172).

fundamentally different from those used for men, in that while
a term like *puer* or *senex* does identify the addressee as male,
that identification seems to be less important in the mind of the
speaker, when context permits us to judge, than the identification of him as being old or young. Terms for women, on the
other hand, seem to stress the gender of the addressee more
strongly, so that age sometimes appears to be a secondary
consideration. Thus while the terms we have just examined
can be used by either male or female speakers, many of the
terms for women are employed primarily or exclusively by
men.

The main addresses in this category[39] are *mulier* 'woman',
femina 'woman', *matrona* 'matron', *virgo* 'girl, virgin', *puella*
'girl', *nupta* 'wife', and *anus* 'old woman'; *materfamilias* 'mistress of the household', *adulescentula* 'little girl', and *innuptae*
'unmarried girls' also occur, but rarely. The age of female
addressees is thus defined as much by marital status as by
chronology.[40]

The most common of these words is *mulier*, which can be
used to addressees ranging in age from unmarried girls (Pl.
Rud. 1151) to fairly old women (Pl. *Epid.* 601), whether free
(Pl. *Am.* 729) or slaves (Pl. *Mil.* 1057). When *mulier* is
addressed to women not very close to the speaker, the term
has no particular emotive force; it is used when the speaker is
being polite, kind, or affectionate[41] as well as in rude contexts.[42]
The positive uses, however, are not really respectful, tending
rather to express a rough sort of friendliness or pity, and the
term does not belong to a high register: it occurs in poetry
(apart from comedy) only when the poet seems to be descend-
ing to a lower register in order to be rude.[43] If, however, the

---

[39] For discussions of the referential use of these words, see Adams (1972,
1983: 344–8); Watson (1983); Axelson (1945: 53–8, 1948: 16–17); Lyne (1978:
135); Santoro L'Hoir (1992).

[40] Compare the English use of 'Miss' to an unmarried adult woman; in
German, age overrules marital status and such women are addressed as *Frau*
rather than *Fräulein*.

[41] e.g. Pl. *Men.* 418, *Epid.* 601, *Mer.* 522; Sen. *Con.* 2. 4. 4; Gel. 12. 1. 5.

[42] e.g. Pl. *Truc.* 265, *Mil.* 433; Sen. *Con.* 2. 4. 5; Cic. *Cael.* 35, 53; Hor.
Epod. 12. 1.

[43] Also once in a religious formula, Tib. 2. 2. 2.

addressee is the speaker's wife, lover, relative, or otherwise close to him, *mulier* is used almost exclusively in negative contexts.[44] The speaker of *mulier* is always male when the address is used to a known woman; strangers, however, may be addressed as *mulier* by women as well as by men. Latin *mulier* is thus very different from Greek γύναι 'woman', which is a perfectly neutral address used by members of both sexes and occurring freely in respectful speeches and high-register settings (Dickey 1996: 86–7).

Virgo, in contrast, belongs to a much higher register than *mulier* and is never found as an address in prose during our period.[45] Unlike *mulier*, *virgo* can be used by humans to address goddesses,[46] which shows that it conveys considerable respect. It is almost always used in positive contexts, usually ones of respect and admiration, as Turnus expressing gratitude to Camilla (Verg. *A*. 11. 508) or Aeneas addressing the Sibyl (Verg. *A*. 6. 104). There are also some negative uses, but these occur in high-register contexts and are not actually rude as are many cases of *mulier*.[47] *Virgo* can also be used to the speaker's relatives without negative connotations.[48] Perhaps the clearest indication of the usage of this address comes from the pseudo-Vergilian *Ciris*, in which Scylla's nurse normally addresses the girl with the intimate and affectionate *alumna* 'nursling' (224, 311, 324, 331, 338) but switches to the more formal *virgo* when performing a sacred ritual (372, 373).

In referential usage *virgo* normally designates a young, unmarried woman of free birth and respectable morals; in some genres, the word is occasionally used of girls who are not virgins in the English sense of the word (Watson 1983). The address usage does not seem to differ significantly from this referential use, though in our data all women addressed as *virgo* are virgins or are presumed by the speaker to be such. Most addressees are young, but the term is also frequently used

[44] e.g. Pl. *Poen.* 1305, *Am.* 729, *Men.* 802; Ter. *Hec.* 214; Sen. *Con.* 9. 6. 6; Prop. 3. 24. 1; Cic. *Cael.* 33.

[45] It is, however, so used by Christian writers; see O'Brien (1930: 87).

[46] Diana, Verg. *A*. 11. 557; Nemesis, Catul. 66. 71; Athena, Mart. 6. 10. 9; Clio, V. Fl. 3. 15.

[47] Verg. *A*. 7. 318; Prop. 4. 4. 92; Sen. *Ag.* 981.

[48] Sen. *Phoen.* 50; Pl. *Per.* 336; Ov. *Met.* 13. 523; Stat. *Theb.* 5. 279, 10. 597.

to address the Sibyl,[49] who can be very old. The restriction to virgins means that husbands and lovers do not use this address to the women they love, but it can be employed in courtship.[50] The speaker is frequently female, in sharp contrast to the use of *mulier*.[51] In comedy, where unknown women are usually addressed as *mulier*, freeborn virgins unknown to the speaker are more often called *virgo* (Pl. *Per.* 610, *Cur.* 487); although *virgo* is never used to the genuine female slaves in Plautine comedy, freeborn women so addressed can be disguised as slaves (see p. 244). *Virgo* is often modified with a term that is descriptive rather than obviously positive or negative and can thus form a sort of periphrastic patronymic, as *Latonia virgo* to Diana (Verg. *A.* 11. 557) or *Schoeneia virgo* to Atalanta (Ov. *Tr.* 2. 399). It can also be used with words that identify the addressee in other ways, as *virgo dextra caesa parentis* 'girl slain by your father's right hand' ([Sen.] *Oct.* 296), *patrona virgo* 'virgin patroness' (Catul. 1. 9), or *virgo Tegeaea* 'girl from Tegea' (Ov. *Fast.* 2. 167).

Puella has many similarities to *virgo*. It is occasionally used to goddesses (Tib. 2. 5. 114), though not as often as is *virgo*; it must have been somewhat flattering when so used, for Juvenal, after addressing the Muses as *puellae Pierides*, prays *prosit mihi vos dixisse puellas* 'may it profit me that I called you girls' (4. 35–6; cf. Townend 1973: 154). *Puella* can also receive the same types of descriptive modifiers as *virgo*; thus Sappho is called *Lesbi puella* ([Ov.] *Ep.* 15. 100) and Hero *Sesti puella* (Ov. *Ep.* 18. 2). This vocative belongs, however, to a less elevated level of language and is found in prose as well as poetry. Lacking *virgo*'s implications of free birth and sexual purity, *puella* is used not only to virgins (Ov. *Ep.* 20. 28) but also frequently to non-virgins; unlike *virgo*, however, it is restricted to young addressees (though they may be married, as at Sen. *Con.* 2. 2. 3). *Puella*'s best-known usage is that from a lover to the object of his affections, whether she is named or unnamed,[52] but it is not really a very frequent address in this sense, in comparison to other terms used by lovers. *Puella* is almost never used by

---

[49] Five times, e.g. Verg. *A.* 6. 104; Sil. 13. 520.
[50] Ov. *Ep.* 20. 14, *Met.* 1. 589; V. Fl. 7. 499.
[51] Verg. *A.* 11. 536; Ov. *Met.* 13. 740, *Fast.* 2. 167; V. Fl. 2. 127.
[52] e.g. Lesbia, Catul. 8. 12; Hero, Ov. *Ep.* 18. 168; Sappho, [Ov.] *Ep.* 15.

women and is not addressed to the speaker's relatives except in the artificial situation of nameless relatives.[53]

Like *virgo, puella* is a polite address, but it seems to be polite in a different way: whereas *virgo* indicates respect for the addressee, *puella* indicates that the addressee possesses a certain physical attractiveness, though not necessarily one leading to sexual interest on the part of the speaker (the term can be used by fathers). Another difference in meaning between the two terms comes in their use to unknown girls. Here *virgo* is a very polite greeting and is usually accompanied by an attempt to learn the addressee's name.[54] *Puella* is also polite, but less so, and the speaker of this address is much less likely to try to learn the addressee's name, perhaps because he seems less likely to be interested in her as an individual.[55]

Other words for women are considerably rarer, so that it is difficult to be certain exactly how they are used. *Femina* seems to be the equivalent of *mulier* in a higher register; it tends to be found in elevated forms of poetry and appears to be a neutral term.[56] It lacks the negative sense of *mulier* when used to close relatives, however; the one occurrence of *femina* in comedy is occasioned by a joke requiring a word meaning 'woman' usable in a compliment from a man to his sister.[57] *Matrona* seems to be another high-register, neutral substitute for *mulier*,[58] while *anus* is a neutral term for older women[59] and *nupta* an address for brides and young wives.[60] The plurals of all of these words tend to be used like the singulars, except that *mulieres* is not necessarily negative in address to relatives, probably because in the plural there are fewer alternatives for address.[61]

100; unnamed at Prop. 3. 20. 10; Tib. 2. 4. 6; Ov. *Am.* 2. 5. 4. On the extent of the sexual sense of *puella* see Adams (1983: 344–8); Watson (1983: 136).

[53] e.g. Cic. *Div.* 1. 104; Quint. *Decl.* 299. 6; Sen. *Con.* 1. 6. 3, 8. 6.

[54] e.g. Verg. *A.* 1. 327 (cf. p. 186); Ov. *Met.* 13. 918; V. Fl. 2. 468.

[55] Apul. *Met.* 6. 30; Pl. *Rud.* 1148.

[56] Ov. *Met.* 1. 351, 8. 433; [Verg.] *Cat.* 13. 17; Sen. *Apoc.* 3. 1; NB also *ILLRP* 934. The referential usage is similar; see Axelson (1945: 53–7). Cf. Adams (1972: 234–42).

[57] Pl. *Aul.* 135; he calls her *optuma femina*, and she denies that there can be any such thing.   [58] Ov. *Met.* 14. 832; Mart. 3. 68. 1, 7. 35. 7.

[59] Pl. *Cur.* 120; Sen. *Tro.* 1059.

[60] Pl. *Cas.* 816; Ov. *Fast.* 2. 425, 794; Catul. 61. 144.

[61] Pl. *Rud.* 1209, *Poen.* 1251, 1356.

Another type of address is that identifying the addressee by his or her occupation, social role, or current activity, rather than via the less flexible characteristics of age and gender. Such words are of course extremely common in addresses to large groups, who often have little in common apart from their current occupation: thus *iudices* 'jurymen' is the most common address in our data, occurring over a thousand times.[62] In the singular, however, this type of address is comparatively rare. One situation in which it occurs is when the author of an inscription or literary work speaks directly to the reader or some other hypothetical audience; as the author cannot know anything about this audience, the choice of addresses is sharply limited, and most of those used elsewhere in the address system are excluded.[63]

More frequent than the use by authors in their own voices, however, is the use of such generic terms by characters in the work concerned to addressees with very little individual identity. Such terms are often characteristic of the declamations; thus *dives* 'rich man' normally occurs in hypothetical court cases in which one litigant is identified only by his wealth (e.g. Sen. *Con.* 10. 1. 1), while *accusator* 'accuser' is often used to nameless opponents (e.g. Quint. *Decl.* 310. 7). Outside the declamations, this type of address is used primarily in orders to subordinates. Livy describes one of the magistrates judging Publius Horatius rendering his decision thus: *'Publi Horati, tibi perduellionem iudico' inquit 'i, lictor, colliga manus'* '"Publius Horatius, I find you guilty of treason", he said; "Lictor, go and bind his hands"' (1. 26. 7), marking the order to an otherwise unidentified lictor with the address *lictor*. In general, terms like *praeco* 'herald', *signifer* 'standard-bearer', *tibicen* 'piper', *vigil* 'sentry', *vilice* 'bailiff', and *lictor* 'lictor' are used in orders to characters whose only relevant feature is their role as herald, etc.[64] This usage is essentially the same as that of *puer* to slaves: it is conditional upon the addressee's having no real identity, and to a certain extent it is used to let the reader of a literary text know that a servant is being addressed. Whether lictors

---

[62] See Ch. 12 for a discussion of these group addresses.

[63] See Ch. 9 for a discussion of the addresses used in such circumstances.

[64] e.g. Pl. *Poen.* 11; Liv. 5. 55. 2; Pl. *St.* 758; Stat. *Theb.* 10. 492; Hor. *Ep.* 1. 14. 1; Liv. 8. 7. 19.

and the like were actually addressed as *lictor* in real life is not a question our data can answer.

Less often such generic terms are addressed to individuals who are nameless for some other reason. *Medice* 'doctor' can be used to address a nameless doctor (Pl. *Men.* 946), and *commilito* 'fellow-soldier' from one soldier to another (Petr. 82. 3).

It is also possible for terms of this type to be used to addressees with distinct identities and known names. Brothel-keepers in comedy, for example, are frequently addressed as *leno* 'brothel-keeper', an address which is often derogatory in tone (p. 237). Learned men of the imperial period are even more frequently addressed as *magister* 'teacher', a term which conveys respect (Fro. 78. 11). Less common, but in the same vein, are terms such as *advena* 'visitor' (addressed to foreigners), *auctor* 'maker', *augur* 'seer', *bellator* 'warrior', *censor* 'censor', *custos* 'guardian', *miles* 'soldier', *poeta* 'poet', *praetor* 'praetor', *sacerdos* 'priest, priestess', *vates* 'prophet', *vicine* 'neighbour', and *victor* 'conqueror'.[65] In general, such addresses seem to be used either as weak insults or as expressions of mild respect, depending on the term and on the context; it appears that generic terms are neutral when used to identify a nameless addressee, but marked when used to someone who could have been addressed by name.

One group of such terms, that expressing the relationship between nurses and their charges, is especially interesting. Children of both genders were looked after by servants in the ancient world, and in Greek comedy there is a specific address, τρόφιμε 'nursling', for use by servants to young men they had helped raise. In Latin, however, the relationship between servants and children is normally reflected in the address system only when both parties are female; it is striking that equivalents of τρόφιμε are almost never used for males in Latin, even in texts translated from Greek originals which must have contained τρόφιμε.[66]

---

[65] e.g. Ov. *Ep.* 17. 5; Stat. *Silv.* 4. 6. 108; Hor. *S.* 2. 5. 22; Pl. *Cur.* 553; Mart. 6. 4. 1; Ter. *Ph.* 287; Pl. *Poen.* 1372; Prop. 2. 26b. 24; Cic. *Ver.* 1. 142; Stat. *Theb.* 4. 626; Ov. *Am.* 3. 9. 41; Pl. *Mos.* 1031; Prop. 4. 1. 117.

[66] In addition to Roman comedy, note Pers. 5. 167, where the vocative *puer* may conceal an original τρόφιμε; cf. *ere* in another rendition of the same scene

Nutrix 'nurse', *altrix* 'nurse', and *nutricula* 'little nurse' are used primarily by girls and women to their nurses.[67] As nurses are normally (though not always) nameless, such terms appear to resemble the use of *puer* and other terms to nameless servants, but the difference is that, unlike the recipients of *puer*, nameless nurses are often important characters whose words and actions are crucial to the development of a story. The part of the nurse in Seneca's *Phaedra*, for example, is a major one, and yet she is never given a name. As a result, words for 'nurse' can also be used (in literature) to address a nurse by someone other than the person nursed: Hippolytus calls Phaedra's nurse *o fida nutrix* 'O faithful nurse' (*Phaed.* 432), and the chorus addresses her as *altrix* (358). Thus the speaker of these terms can be of either gender, but the actual person nursed is virtually always female. The basic term seems to be *nutrix*; *altrix* is an elegant Senecan variant, and *nutricula* is an affectionate diminutive (e.g. [Verg.] *Ciris* 277; cf. Lyne 1978: 208).

Alumna 'nursling' is used by nurses to the girls and women they care for. There is a stronger link between *nutrix* and *alumna* than between almost any other pair of Latin vocatives, for nearly all the dyads in which *alumna* is used in one direction also offer examples of *nutrix* in the other direction. Thus Phaedra's nurse calls Phaedra *alumna* and is addressed as *nutrix* and *altrix* in return (Sen. *Phaed.* 178, 251, 255), Medea's nurse uses *alumna* and is called *nutrix* (Sen. *Med.* 158, 568), Deianira's nurse says *alumna* and receives *altrix* ([Sen.] *Her. O.* 276, 396), Scylla's nurse uses *alumna* and receives *nutrix* and *nutricula* ([Verg.] *Ciris* e.g. 224, 262, 257), etc. The addressees of *alumna* have names, and the use of this address instead of the name seems to convey intimacy and affection on the part of the nurse. *Alumna* can also be used with a genitive, like the periphrastic uses of kinship terms; in this usage the masculine *alumne* is also found. In such cases the addressee is

at Hor. *S.* 2. 3. 265. At Pl. *Mer.* 809 the MSS contain the address *alumne*, but the text is corrupt, and apart from that passage *alumne* is used only periphrastically with genitives (only at Mart. 1. 76. 2, 12. 60. 1; cf. Citroni 1975: 242) and indirectly (Suet. *Cal.* 13).

[67] e.g. Pl. *Aul.* 691; Ov. *Ep.* 19. 41; Sen. *Med.* 568, *Phaed.* 251; [Verg.] *Ciris* 257.

rarely human, and the word in the genitive is not the name of an actual nurse, for one would not identify someone by who her servants were: Martial's birthday is called *Martis alumne dies* 'day [which is] the nursling of Mars' (12. 60. 1) and ants *terrae omniparentis agiles alumnae* 'busy nurslings of all-nurturing earth'.[68]

Still another type of address is the ethnic. For our purposes, 'ethnic' is a broad category consisting of any word normally used to describe the inhabitants (or former inhabitants) of a given place, whether that word is in theory derived from the name of a city, as *Romani*, or of a distant ancestor, as *Teucri*. The latter category can be difficult to separate from the patronymics (see below); the criteria used here are that words with a distinctive patronymic ending, such as *Dardanidae*, have all been classified as patronymics, and ones without such an ending are considered ethnics if they normally identify a group of citizens rather than an individual.

Ethnics are used frequently in both singular and plural. The plural usage will be examined more closely in Chapter 12, but at this point we need to note some general features. Plural ethnics are common as addresses in Latin; they can be used either by a speaker who is a compatriot of the addressees or by a foreigner. Thus Livy has both a Roman (35. 49. 9) and an Achaean leader (32. 20. 3) address the Achaeans as *Achaei* in public speeches. In principle, plural ethnics seem to be register-neutral addresses, but in practice some are confined to the poetic registers because they apply only to groups normally discussed in poetic texts, while others refer to more recent federations and so appear only in historical works. Thus *Danai* is used only to address the Greek army before Troy, presumably in imitation of Homer (e.g. Prop. 4. 1. 53), and *Rutuli* is used only to Turnus' army in the *Aeneid* (e.g. 12. 229), while the use of *Aetoli* for members of the Aetolian League is found only in Livy (e.g. 31. 29. 4). Notable is the relative scarcity of examples of *Romani*, which is normally replaced by *Quirites* (cf. p. 286); in the singular, however, only *Romane* occurs as an ethnic for Romans.

[68] Apul. *Met.* 6. 10; cf. *aquai dulcis alumnae* to frogs at Cic. *Div.* 1. 15, and Pease (1973: 87–8).

With most types of address the singular can be considered the basic usage from which the plural may or may not deviate, but in the case of ethnics the reverse appears to be true. In our data plurals are not significantly more common than singular ethnic addresses, but as we shall see many of the singular ethnics belong to types of address which probably did not exist outside poetry; in ordinary language the plural was probably the more common and the basic form.

Singular ethnics,[69] apart from *Romane*, are virtually never used by a speaker who shares the addressee's nationality. One might be tempted to assume that this difference between *Romane* and other terms is due to the fact that most characters in Latin literature are Roman, so the chances of having two non-Romans address each other is statistically very small. Yet in fact non-Romans are very well represented in our data; none of the characters of Plautus or Terence is Roman, and Romans form a minority (at least in terms of addresses) in the works of Vergil, Ovid, Statius, and the younger Seneca, all of whom provide us with large quantities of data. In fact, only about half our singular ethnic addresses are spoken by Romans, even including those used by the (Roman) author in his own voice. Explanation of the difference must thus be sought elsewhere.

We can begin by examining addresses other than *Romane*. Such addresses can be adjectival, as *Troica . . . Vesta* 'Trojan Vesta' (Ov. *Met.* 15. 730–1) and *Tros . . . Aenea* 'Trojan Aeneas' (Verg. *A.* 6. 52), or substantives, as *Troiane* 'Trojan' (Ov. *Met.* 14. 110) and *perfide Poene* 'treacherous Carthaginian' (Ov. *Fast.* 6. 242). The adjectival uses are virtually always poetic; the use of ethnic adjectives was clearly one way of forming the varied and literary addresses preferred by classical poets. They are very often used as variational vocatives by the author in his own voice, in which context they cannot carry particular force. When used by other characters, however, adjectival ethnics virtually always appear in contexts where we would expect a particularly polite address, as for example

---

[69] On singular ethnics see Horsfall (2000: 193); Norden (1957: 338); Kroll and Lunelli (1980: 44–6); Löfstedt (1956: i. 15–17). Such ethnics sometimes have a religious flavour; see Austin (1977: 263). On collective singulars in general see pp. 294–6.

when a suppliant enemy pleads with Aeneas and addresses him
as *vir Troiane* 'Trojan man' (Verg. *A*. 10. 598), or when Apollo
addresses the Sibyl as *virgo Cumaea* 'Cumaean virgin' in an
attempt to win her love (Ov. *Met*. 14. 135), or often in prayers
to divinities. The one apparent exception, Jocasta's bitter
address to her exiled son Polynices as *rex Argive* 'Argive
king' (Stat. *Theb*. 7. 498), seems from the use of the (literally
inapplicable) title *rex* to be a sarcastic imitation of politeness
and therefore to confirm rather than refute the theory that
ethnic adjectives form polite addresses.

Substantive ethnics are somewhat different. These occur in
comedy and prose as well as in classical poetry, but they are
less often used in prayers, and they seem to be less polite than
the adjectives. Like adjectives, substantive ethnics are often
used neutrally by the poet in his own voice (*Gnosia* for
Ariadne, [Tib.] 3. 6. 39). When used by other characters
they can occur in positive contexts, as when Meleager, pre-
senting Atalanta with the spoils of the Calydonian boar,
addresses her as *Nonacria* (Ov. *Met*. 8. 426), but often
appear in negative settings, as when Tydeus and Camilla
exult over dying enemies with *Thebane* (Stat. *Theb*. 8. 473)
and *Tyrrhene* (Verg. *A*. 11. 686) respectively. The substantive
ethnic thus appears to be a neutral address. Often, as when the
term is used in battle scenes, the speaker may be unaware of
the addressee's name and simply using his or her most obvious
feature as an address; we have already seen several other
addresses which, though not neutral when used to known
addressees, become neutral under such circumstances. When
used in comedy and prose these terms are less common than in
classical poetry but also appear to be neutral addresses for
(often unknown) foreigners.[70]

In poetry, substantive ethnics have an additional function
not found with the adjectives, namely that of a collective
singular address to a whole nation. Such vocatives are normally
used in the poet's own voice and are less common than the use
to individuals; they seem on the whole to be variational
vocatives and thus neutral in tone. Silius describes the muster-
ing of Hannibal's army:

[70] Pl. *Poen*. 1410; Sen. *Con*. 10. 5. 1; Fro. 158. 3.

> Nec Cerretani, quondam Tirynthia castra,
> aut Vasco insuetus galeae ferre arma morati,
> non quae Dardanios post vidit Ilerda furores
> nec qui Massageten monstrans feritate parentem
> cornipedis fusa satiaris, Concane, vena.
>
> (3. 357–61)

Nor were the Cerretani, who once shared Hercules' war-camp, nor was Vasco, unaccustomed to the helmet, slow to bear arms; nor was Ilerda, which later saw Dardanian frenzy, nor you, Concanian, who are nourished by bleeding your steed, thus revealing by your savagery your Massagetan ancestry.

Lucan (1. 441–2) similarly describes the Treviri and Ligurians with *tu quoque laetatus converti proelia, Trevir, et nunc tonse Ligur . . .* 'you too rejoiced that the battle turned, Trevir, and you Ligurian, now shaven', while Ovid threatens the Parthian people with *Parthe, dabis poenas* 'Parthian, you shall pay the penalty'.[71]

   The address *Romane* is different from other ethnics, in that it can be used by speakers having the same nationality as the addressee. Most such uses, however, are examples of the collective singular sense just described. Thus Horace admonishes his countrymen,

> Delicta maiorum immeritus lues,
> Romane, donec templa refeceris
>   aedesque labentes deorum et
>   foeda nigro simulacra fumo.   (*Carm.* 3. 6. 1–4)

Though guiltless, Roman, you will atone for your ancestors' faults, until you rebuild the decaying temples and shrines of the gods and their statues foul with black smoke.

while Vergil's Anchises advises future Romans with *tu regere imperio populos, Romane, memento* 'you, Roman, remember to rule nations with your power' (*A.* 6. 851). The collective singular use of *Romane* seems to appear in prose as well, for Livy quotes a Samnite leader using *Romane* in a context where it is virtually impossible to pick out an individual he could be addressing.[72] This collective usage is proportionately more

---

[71] *Ars* 1. 179; other examples include Ov. *Fast.* 5. 593, 6. 467; Luc. 1. 430.
[72] 9. 1. 7; other examples at Sil. 7. 95, 9. 346; [Ov.] *Epic. Drusi* 19;

frequent for *Romane* than for other substantive ethnics, and
indeed the word is rarely used to an individual; when it is so
used, it is spoken exclusively by non-Romans like the other
substantive ethnics. The most informative example of such
use[73] is found in Lucan, who describes an old Egyptian priest
explaining divine mysteries to Julius Caesar; the priest begins
by using the address *Caesar* (10. 194, 263) but switches to
Romane when comparing Caesar to kings of other lands with
similar curiosity (268). Like other substantive ethnics, *Romane*
appears to be neutral in tone.

When *Romane* is used adjectivally, a usage much less
common than the substantive one, it is normally spoken by a
Roman. The adjective often modifies a collective noun referring to a group of people, as *Romana iuventus* 'Roman youth'
(Ov. *Ars* 1. 459), *Romane Cluenti* 'Roman Cluentius' (for the
family of the Cluentii, Verg. *A.* 5. 123), or *miles Romane*
'Roman soldier'.[74] Use to individuals is rare (the only example
I can find, Luc. 8. 676, certainly lacks the courtesy associated
with other adjectival ethnics—see below). As the speakers are
normally as Roman as the addressees, these addresses do not
have the identifying function of other ethnics but rather seem
to stress some ideal of Roman-ness. Thus Pompey exhorts his
men with *o vere Romana manus* 'O truly Roman band' (Luc. 2.
532), while Lucan expresses his disgust at behaviour unbecom-
ing a Roman soldier with

> Degener atque operae miles Romane secundae,
> Pompei diro sacrum caput ense recidis,
> ut non ipse feras?   (8. 676–8)

Degenerate Roman soldier acting as a mere henchman, are you
cutting off the sacred head of Pompey with your abominable
sword—for someone else to carry?

Closely related to ethnics in function are addresses derived not
from the name of a place but from that of a person, such as
patronymics. Most such addresses are in fact patronymics in

Hor. *S.* 1. 4. 85; Ov. *Fast.* 4. 119; probably also Ov. *Fast.* 4. 259, 6. 77, *Met.*
15. 637; Liv. 5. 16. 9.

[73] Others at Luc. 5. 131, 195.

[74] Probably for the twelfth legion, V. Fl. 6. 55; *miles* is very often used as a
collective singular, see pp. 291–2.

the strict sense of the term, that is, words derived from the name of the addressee's father, like *Anchisiade* for Aeneas (Verg. *A*. 6. 348). There is, however, no difference in form or function between these and addresses derived from the name of the grandfather (*Alcide* for Hercules, Ov. *Ep*. 9. 75) or even more distant ancestors, and thus these different types will all be referred to as 'patronymics' in this section for ease of presentation. They are strictly poetic forms; the patronymic suffixes with which they are formed are not even part of the Latin language, but rather belong to Greek, and the names to which they are attached normally come from the Greek mythological tradition as well. Heroes of Roman history may be addressed with patronymics when they appear in epic poetry, but in such cases the ancestor alluded to must be distant enough to belong to the epic tradition, as when Silius uses the address *Dardanide* to Scipio (16. 191).

Patronymics, in this broad sense of the term, are normally singular as addresses; plurals are possible only when the addressees are closely related to one another (*Atridae*, Sen. *Tro*. 596) or the ancestor mentioned is very far removed (*Dardanidae*, Verg. *A*. 3. 94).[75] The addresses can be used to divinities and when addressed to humans are normally courteous, whether singular or plural, adjectival or substantive. Thus Apollo addresses his beloved, dying Hyacinth as *Oebalide* (Ov. *Met*. 10. 196), a woman in distress appeals to Theseus for help with *belliger Aegide* 'warlike son of Aegeus' (Stat. *Theb*. 12. 546), and Jason politely greets Aeetes with *rex Hyperionide* 'king, son of Hyperion' (V. Fl. 5. 471). In a few passages patronymic addresses appear in hostile contexts, but in those passages the speakers are using elegant language to express their hostility, and the elegance required seems to make them willing to use an address which is normally courteous. Thus Laodamia angrily addresses Paris as *Dyspari Priamide* (Ov. *Ep*. 13. 43), using the Homeric vocative Δύσπαρι (cf. *Iliad* 3. 39), while Medea is crushingly polite to her husband with *optime quondam Aesonide* 'son of Aeson, formerly the best' (V. Fl. 8. 441–2). The hostile oracle which addresses Aeneas and his men as *Laomedontiadae* is a special case because of the disastrous

---

[75] The extended use of *Aeneadae* for a group of Trojans, only one of whom is the son of Aeneas (Verg. *A*. 9. 235), appears to be unique.

associations of the name Laomedon (Verg. *A*. 3. 248). It thus
seems likely that the patronymic is an inherently courteous
form of address, though the evidence is not completely con-
clusive; that it is a high-register, poetic address with no role in
non-literary language is certain, given its non-Latin formation
and the texts in which it appears. Patronymics are disproportionately frequent in addresses to women.

Non-patronymic adjectives derived from personal or group
names are also sometimes used as addresses. These adjectives,
which do not use patronymic suffixes, give no indication of the
exact relationship between the addressee and the person from
whose name the adjective is derived; the connection is normally
made by an accompanying noun. Thus Trojans, formerly
companions of Hector, can be addressed as *Hectorei socii*
'Hectorean comrades' (Verg. *A*. 5. 190; cf. Williams 1960:
83–4), while Theseus' wife Phaedra can be called *Thesea
coniunx* 'Thesean wife' (Sen. *Phaed*. 129). Such addresses are
rare, ad hoc formations which occur only in poetry and are too
infrequent to have acquired any particular address meaning.[76]

It is also possible, though even rarer, for a proper name
which does not in fact belong to the addressee to be used as an
address. Such vocatives are also constructed ad hoc; they are
not, however, always poetic. One way such addresses can be
used is for a man (or men) to be addressed with the feminine
form of his (or their) name; thus Cicero quotes a teasing
address of *Egilia mea* to a man named Egilius (*De Orat*. 2.
277; cf. Leeman *et al*. 1981–96: iii. 315), while Ovid describes
an enemy taunting Caeneus with the address *Caeni* (Ov. *Met*.
12. 470) and Vergil provides the insult *o vere Phrygiae, neque
enim Phryges* 'O really Phrygian women, for you are not
Phrygian men' (*A*. 9. 617; cf. Hardie 1994: 196). It is also
possible to use the name of a deity or famous human to another
addressee and by so doing to suggest that the addressee shares
the outstanding qualities of the person whose name is taken.
Thus Plautus uses *mi Achilles* in flattery to a soldier (*Mil*.
1054a) and *Thales* to a slave in mockery of his cleverness (*Rud*.
1003), Phaedrus calls a strict reader *lector Cato* (4. 7. 21), and
Varro uses the address *Faustule* (the name of a famous

---

[76] Cf. Löfstedt (1956: i. 110–24); Kroll and Lunelli (1980: 44–6).

shepherd) for Atticus, who has just been discussing sheep (*R.* 2. 3. 1).

There are also several hundred other words which are used as addresses in our data, and undoubtedly thousands more which were so used once but do not survive. Yet these words make little difference to our understanding of the address system, for they are rare or unique as addresses and thus have address meanings immediately obvious from their lexical meanings. Virtually any Latin noun, adjective, or participle can be used as an address alone or in combination with other words, and if one considers relative clauses having vocatives as antecedents to be parts of addresses, any word at all can be employed in address. The use of such ad hoc addresses is most frequent in poetry, but no literary genre is entirely devoid of it; the usage was probably less common in non-literary language but is likely to have occurred occasionally there as well. Such terms can be neutral in tone if they merely serve to describe an addressee for the purpose of identification, but in practice they are more frequently used to express some sort of judgement of the addressee and so can convey whatever emotion the speaker wishes; we have in fact already examined those with lexical meanings which make them clearly insults or terms of affection. Other words may not be positive or negative in themselves but can still convey a specific emotion in context. Thus Lucan has Caesar address an elderly priest with *o sacris devote senex, quodque arguit aetas non neglecte deis* 'O old man devoted to sacred rites, and, as your age reveals, not neglected by the gods' (10. 176–7), while Vergil describes Aeneas addressing Dido as *o sola infandos Troiae miserata labores* 'O you who alone took pity on the unspeakable sufferings of Troy' (*A.* 1. 597). Such flexibility is of course not peculiar to the Latin address system; I know of no language in which it is not possible to some extent.

7

The Use of *mi* and *o*

interea haec soror
quam dixi ad flammam accessit inprudentius,
sati' cum periclo. ibi tum exanimatus Pamphilus
bene dissimulatum amorem et celatum indicat:
adcurrit; mediam mulierem complectitur:
'mea Glycerium,' inquit 'quid agis? quor te is perditum?'
tum illa, ut consuetum facile amorem cerneres,
reiecit se in eum flens quam familiariter!

(Ter. An. 129–36)

In the meantime, the sister I mentioned approached the funeral pyre carelessly and rather dangerously. Then Pamphilus, terrified, revealed the love he had previously so well concealed: he ran to the woman and put his arms around her waist, saying 'My Glycerium, what are you doing? Why are you endangering yourself?' Then with what intimacy did she throw herself weeping upon him, so that you could easily see their long-established love!

LATIN vocatives may be preceded or followed by a word meaning 'my' (*mi*, *mea*, *meum*, *meus*, *mei*, or *meae*) or 'our' (*noster*). Historically, the masculine singular *mi* is probably not a vocative of the possessive adjective *meus* 'my', but rather a genitive/dative of the pronoun *ego* 'I'; thus Latin *gnate mi* 'my son' is equivalent to Greek τέκνον μοι 'son to me'.[1] By the time of our earliest texts, however, *mi* is already restricted to the masculine singular (a limitation virtually impossible for a pronoun), and *meus* has acquired additional vocative forms *mea*, *meum*, etc. for other numbers and genders; *mi* is thus treated as a vocative already in Plautus. Throughout the period of our study *mi* functioned as a vocative when joined with another word in the

---

[1] For discussions of the etymology and original sense of *mi*, see Wackernagel (1908: 151–2, 1926–8: 76–7, 81); Svennung (1958: 246–8); Leumann (1977: 463); Dickey (forthcoming).

vocative, and it was generally perceived to be distinct from the dative *mi* (= *mihi*), which occurs in many of the same texts.

In the second century AD, however, it is sometimes impossible to distinguish dative from vocative *mi*. The emperor Marcus Aurelius certainly uses the vocative *mi* in some passages, as *rescribere non sustineo, mi Fronto carissime* 'I cannot put off replying, my dearest Fronto' (54. 20), and plainly uses the dative *mi* in others, as *semper mi vale, animus meus* (35. 3) 'always fare well for me, my soul'. He is also fond of ending his letters with formulae like *vale mihi Fronto carissime et iucundissime mihi* 'fare well for me, dearest Fronto and most pleasant to me' (38. 22), which makes it virtually impossible to determine the status of *mi* in passages like *vale mi Fronto carissime et amicissime* 'fare well [for me?], [my?] dearest and friendliest Fronto' (36. 25).[2] Fortunately, such ambiguities are not common and do not affect our data significantly.[3] Another peculiarity of the imperial period is that the masculine *mi* begins to be used for feminine and plural vocatives as well as masculine singular ones,[4] though this usage remains rare throughout the period of our study.

Mi and other vocatives from *meus* (henceforth *mi* will be used to stand for any form of *meus* used as a vocative; *noster* will be discussed below, p. 224) are often described as intimate forms of address, and intimacy is certainly an important factor in their use. Thus Cicero in his letters to his brother Quintus attaches *mi* to every vocative (24 examples), while in those to his close friend Atticus he uses *mi* with 74% of the vocatives (34 examples), and in letters to his more distant friend Marcus Brutus he uses *mi* with only 15% of the vocatives (20 examples). Men with whom Cicero was not actually on intimate terms, and even those whom he disliked, are also addressed with *mi* in letters when Cicero is trying to give an impression of closeness

---

[2] Cf. Van den Hout (1999: 6–7): at this period *vale mi*[*hi*] + vocative 'seems to have become a colloquial formula in which the difference between the vocative and the dative has disappeared'.

[3] For similar, though more soluble, difficulties in Plautus, cf. Gratwick (1993: 154); Enk (1932: ii. 187).

[4] *Mi hospites*, Petr. 116. 4; *mi soror*, Apul. *Met.* 5. 16; *mi parens*, Apul. *Met.* 4. 26; *mi coniux*, Apul. *Met.* 8. 8; *mi erilis*, Apul. *Met.* 4. 27, 9. 16. *Mi* as a masculine plural also occurs in Plautus but is there thought to have a different explanation (see Bulhart 1952: 914. 7–10).

and affection, as M. Terentius Varro (*Fam.* 9. 8. 2), Julius Caesar (*Fam.* 7. 5. 3), and even the triumvir Antony (*Att.* 14. 13b. 3); non-intimates also use *mi* to Cicero in the same way, as M. Aemilius Lepidus (*Fam.* 10. 34a. 2).[5]

Intimacy, however, is not the only factor affecting the use of *mi*. While Cicero and his correspondents use *mi* with 80% of the 228 vocatives in the corpus of Ciceronian letters (excluding quotations in letters of addresses spoken elsewhere), in Cicero's oratorical, rhetorical, and philosophical works the figure for *mi* is less than 1%. Although many of the men addressed in Cicero's other works are less close to him than those addressed in the letters, the difference in the use of *mi* cannot be explained by the change of addressees, for not all of the addressees are different. Cicero's brother Quintus, for example, who always receives *mi* in letters, is addressed by his brother 29 times in other works, only once with *mi* (*De Orat.* 1. 23). Atticus, who in letters is given *mi* 74% of the time, in other works never receives *mi*, though he is addressed by Cicero 35 times, and Marcus Brutus receives *mi* in just one of Cicero's 70 addresses to him in the rhetorical and philosophical works (*Brut.* 187).

The normal assumption is thus that *mi* is informal in tone, too informal to be used in literary works. Adams has indeed concluded from the Ciceronian evidence that *mi* must have been an element normally attached to vocatives in ordinary conversation (1978: 162). Yet *mi* appears with only 1% of the vocatives in the Pompeian graffiti, with few of the vocatives in the Vindolanda tablets,[6] and with only 3% of the vocatives in Petronius, whose language is generally acknowledged to be much closer to the conversational style than that of most Latin authors. Plautus and Terence use *mi* more frequently, with 16% and 10% of their vocatives respectively, but this is still far less

[5] For more detail on Cicero's use of *mi* to particular individuals, see Adams (1978: 162–3).

[6] There are only 2 strongly probable cases of the possessive (*Tab Vindol. II* 291. 13, 292. b back); 3 more (242. 4, 247. 2, 288. 4) are preceded by *vale* and may be datives. That the *mi* in *vale mi* is a dative at Vindolanda is suggested by the phrase *vale mi soror* on an unpublished tablet (Vind. inv. no. 93. 1309; I am grateful to J. N. Adams for telling me about this tablet), though it is barely possible that this *mi* could be a feminine vocative (see above). It is also possible to read *vale mi* at 255. 14, though the editors prefer *valeas*, and in some fragmentary tablets *mi* may have been lost.

than the figures for Cicero's letters. Since Petronius wrote approximately a century after Cicero and the writers of the Vindolanda tablets came half a century after that, it is possible that diachronic change can account for the differences; the low incidence at Pompeii remains peculiar, however, since some of the Pompeian evidence was already old when Vesuvius erupted in AD 79.

Further complicating the issue is the fact that there are three texts, in addition to Cicero's letters, which make frequent use of *mi*: the epistles to and from Fronto, Seneca, and Pliny. In the first of these collections, *mi* is used with 48% of the 242 vocatives; in the second, with 51% of the 89 vocatives (excluding those not directed to the recipient of the letters, Lucilius), and in the third, though Pliny never uses *mi* himself, to any correspondent, Trajan uses *mi* with 75% of his 20 vocatives to Pliny.

It is notable that Pliny's letters were edited for publication, while Seneca's are literary productions, composed for publication and decorated with the veneer of linguistic informality traditionally applied to philosophical dialogues.[7] If *mi* was normally used with vocatives in conversation but omitted in literature because of its unacceptable informality, it should not be so much more common in these collections than in the works of Plautus, Terence, and Petronius. Nor is it likely that Seneca's frequent use of *mi* is simply part of an attempt to make his letters sound like ordinary conversation, for in his dialogues, which are also literary works with a very similar veneer of conversational language, *mi* is used with only one of the 54 vocatives (5. 23. 8).

It seems likely that the use of *mi* does not correlate primarily with the conversational register, but with the epistolary genre: *mi* was regularly attached to vocatives in letters but was much less frequently used in speech. Additional evidence in favour of this theory is provided by the use of *mi* in quotations of spoken and written communication. Suetonius quotes numerous addresses allegedly spoken by one character to another, and in none of these addresses is *mi* ever used. He also quotes eleven addresses from letters, of which nine (82%) include *mi*. The

---

[7] Sherwin-White (1966: 2–14); Griffin (1976: 416–19); Russell (1974: 74).

difference between epistolary and spoken style can be seen
most clearly in Suetonius' portrayal of addresses from Augustus to his wife Livia, for while in letters she is always *mea Livia*
(*Cl.* 4. 1, 4. 4, 4. 6), in speech she is simply *Livia* even in
Augustus' dying farewell (*Aug.* 99. 1).

Cicero, likewise, occasionally quotes a conversation or letter
in a speech, and sometimes these quotations include vocatives.
Whether Cicero quoted accurately cannot now be determined,
but if he did not, he certainly took care to provide verisimilitude, for the quotations use a register of language notably
different from, and lower than, the surrounding oration (cf.
quid tu 'guess what?' in the conversation quoted on p. 59).
When Cicero quotes in an oration something which was originally spoken, he never uses *mi* with vocatives, however friendly
the interaction;[8] when he quotes a letter, he does not use *mi*
when the tone is unfriendly (*Phil.* 13. 24, *bis*) but does use the
possessive when the context is affectionate (*Ver.* 3. 155).
Cicero's evidence is thus less substantial than that of Suetonius
but clearly points in the same direction.

It thus appears that the epistolary genre is a major factor
determining the use of *mi*: vocatives in letters are likely to have
mi attached, while those in other situations use *mi* much less
often (rarely in literature; in conversation perhaps 15% of the
time in early Latin, probably less often by the first century AD).
Even within the genre of the letter, however, *mi* is far from
obligatory. It is an element of positive politeness (cf. p. 17)
and may therefore be omitted not only where no friendship
exists and no politeness is intended (e.g. Cic. *Fam.* 11. 3. 1,
Brutus and Cassius to Antony), but also in respectful contexts,
when affection does exist but negative politeness is more
appropriate (e.g. Cic. *Fam.* 8. 16. 1, Caelius to Cicero). Thus
Pliny does not use *mi* to Trajan, but Trajan uses it in return.
Fronto's much more intimate relationship with his emperor is
reflected in the fact that Fronto does frequently use *mi* to

---

[8] Quotations of vocatives in casual, apparently friendly speech: *Clu.* 71, 72,
Cael. 36 (between siblings), *Ver.* 1. 66, 133, *Planc.* 33 (*bis*); of other spoken
communication: *Catil.* 1. 27, *Cael.* 33, *Mil.* 60, *Ver.* 3. 62, 4. 32, *Pis.* 59, *Dom.*
133 (*bis*). Quotations in Cicero's letters of casual, friendly addresses spoken
elsewhere once use *mi* (*Fam.* 9. 14. 3 = *Att.* 14. 17a. 3) but otherwise do not
(*Att.* 5. 1. 3, 15. 11. 1; *Fam.* 4. 5. 4).

Marcus Aurelius, as well as receiving this address—though he receives *mi* more often than he uses it, and though he does not apply *mi* to Antoninus Pius or to Lucius Verus (both of whom use *mi* to him). In the case of men like Brutus and Atticus to whom Cicero sometimes uses *mi* in his letters and sometimes does not, there is certainly no suggestion of rudeness in the addresses which omit *mi*. The addresses with *mi* convey more positive politeness, and the ones without it more negative politeness, the overall balance between the two reflecting the nature of the relationship more accurately than does any one individual address.

It is, however, striking that letters preserved on papyri and at Vindolanda so rarely include *mi*. Many of these letters are addressed to superiors or do not represent friendly communication; it is unsurprising that such documents do not use a possessive that indicates positive politeness. A significant minority, however, are addressed to relatives, friends, or inferiors in contexts where Cicero's usage would lead us to expect *mi*. Of course, the absence of *mi* from these documents is no more problematic for our explanation of *mi* as an epistolary element than for the traditional view of *mi* as conversational; in fact, it does not seem to point to any system which can be reconciled with the evidence of other sources. Two hypotheses might serve to explain it, but at present no really satisfactory solution to the problem can be given.

One possible explanation[9] is that, since the anomalous letters seem to come from military contexts, the absence of *mi* stems from a military culture favouring unemotional language. In favour of this explanation is the fact that the only two examples of the possessive at Vindolanda come from the very small group of letters written by non-soldiers (*Tab Vindol. II* 291. 13, 292. b back). The idea of a specifically military address characteristic is not a new one; it is periodically suggested that *frater* 'brother' may have had a military use.[10] I have not, however, been able to verify this characteristic of *frater*, since this address is also widely used in non-military contexts (cf. pp. 123–5); a further complication is that *frater*, with its implications of familial affection, points military language in

[9] I am grateful to J. N. Adams for suggesting this explanation.
[10] e.g. Kepartová (1986); MacMullen (1984: 443); Cugusi (1992: ii. 16).

the opposite direction from that suggested by the avoidance of *mi*. Moreover, some of the papyrus letters, though written by soldiers, are addressed to close relatives and seem in other respects to use the standard familial address system, which might not be compatible with military language (*P. Mich.* viii. 467, 468).

Another possibility is that in the imperial period *mi* became an elite epistolary form whose use indicated a relatively high status and level of education. In favour of this explanation is the fact that the only address from a man of high rank that I have found in documents of our period employs *mi* (*CEL* 85. 2); this theory also explains the absence of *mi* to members of a soldier's family more easily than does the military hypothesis. The two examples of the possessive used by non-elite writers at Vindolanda, which are both part of the set phrase *anima mea* 'my soul', could be argued to differ from the normal epistolary use of *mi* with the addressee's name and as such may not be counter-evidence to this theory. Such a status-based restriction on usage is unlikely to have existed in the classical period, however, for apart from the numerous examples from people of varying social status preserved in the works of Cicero, there is a letter of *c*.23 BC in which one ordinary citizen uses *mi* to another (*CEL* 8. 7). While a status distinction could have arisen in the post-classical period as a result of the classicizing education offered the elite, Latin epistolary conventions are normally fairly consistent across different social levels in our period (cf. Keyes 1935: 42–4; Cugusi 1983), and this consistency would make the evolution of such a distinction somewhat surprising.

Whatever the explanation, it seems likely that the letters which do not use *mi* reflect some sort of cultural difference from the ones that do; as such they are equally problematic for any explanation of the meaning and function of *mi*.

What of the examples of *mi* which occur in contexts other than letters? Though these are less frequent than those in letters, they are not rare, and their usage is governed by principles similar to, but not identical with, those we have seen in letters. *Mi* is normally a mark of intimacy, but while in letters the intimacy involved can be that between friends or those who pretend to be friends, elsewhere it is more likely to be the intimacy between lovers or very close relatives. Thus Cicero, who so rarely addresses his brother or friends with *mi* in his philosophical or rhetorical works, does introduce *mi* into these works when portraying himself in conversation with his son. Cicero uses *mi* with 57% of the addresses to his son in these writings (14 examples), and he portrays the younger Cicero as using *mi* to him 100% of the time (only at *Part.* 1, 140). He also tends to use *mi* when describing other addresses between parents and their children; thus a story about Aemilius Paulus and his little daughter told in the *De Divinatione* contains three vocatives, all of which have *mi* (1. 103), and an address to Spurius Carvilius from his mother also uses *mi* (*De Orat.* 2. 249). Other close relatives may on occasion also receive *mi* (*Div.* 1. 104), and the possessive is very occasionally used between friends (*Brut.* 253).

Our largest body of non-epistolary evidence for the use of *mi* comes from comedy, a genre in which the use of *mi* is dependent on a number of factors besides intimacy. It has been observed that in both Plautus and Terence vocatives with *mi* are more likely to occur in the speech of women than in that of men (e.g. Adams 1984: 68–73; Hofmann 1951: 138, 1985: 294–6), and also that *mi* is more likely to occur at particularly significant and emotionally intense moments (Köhm 1905: 179 and *passim*; Ferger 1889: 14–20). The most common usage of *mi* in comedy is as an attachment to addresses between relatives, though relatives are not always addressed using *mi*; *mi* used to relatives normally expresses particular closeness and affection but can also be more neutral in tone, particularly if the speaker is female. This intimate tone explains why *mi* to relatives is much more often attached to kinship terms or to terms of endearment than to names.

Mi is also frequently used in comedy to address lovers and people to whom the speaker has some kind of romantic attachment or interest, though not all addresses to lovers are so qualified. Male characters virtually never use *mea* to an unrelated woman unless they have a romantic interest in her, and this restriction is illustrated in a young man's address to two girls, the first of whom he loves, as *tu, mea Palaestra et Ampelisca* (Pl. *Rud.* 878). The passage quoted at the start of

this chapter also suggests that a man's use of *mea* to address a
woman could be taken as evidence that he was her lover;
Donatus comments on it *'mea' quasi amator . . . dixit* 'he said
"my" as her lover'. *Mi* to lovers of both sexes tends to be used
for particular affection and intimacy, and in consequence it is
attached to expressions of endearment more often than to
names.

Mi in comedy can also be used to addressees who are
neither relatives nor lovers, though in such contexts it is
comparatively rare. It tends to be attached to special expressions of affection or gratitude, important greetings, pleas, and
other speeches calling for an unusually high level of positive
politeness.[11] In such contexts it may be used by members of
either sex, but if the speaker is male, the addressee is almost
never female.[12] It is also possible for *mi* to be attached to
neutral addresses which do not seem to require significant
amounts of positive politeness, but in such cases the speaker
is almost always female.[13] Thus only women use addresses
like *mi senex* 'my old man' or *mi homo* 'my man' as polite
greetings to unknown men,[14] and only women attach *mi* to
their associates' names or titles in unemotional contexts.[15]
Occasionally, women may use *mea* alone, or *mea tu* 'my you'
alone, in the same way as *mi* + name;[16] these forms are never
used by men in comedy. Another gender-based usage difference is that, in comedy, women tend to use the possessive
before a noun, while men may place it before or after (cf.
Gratwick 1993: 154; Maurach 1988: 155; Hofmann 1951:
138).

Outside comedy, evidence for the non-epistolary use of *mi* is
scarcer, owing to its informal register. Nevertheless one can see
that the word is most often used with vocatives addressed to
lovers and relatives and continues to carry a sense of intimacy

[11] e.g. Pl. *Poen.* 421, *St.* 583, *Cur.* 305, *Bac.* 880, *As.* 689, *Trin.* 1072.
[12] Exceptions only at *Poen.* 365–7, 380 (plea on behalf of a lover), 392–4
(punning on loving addresses).
[13] Exceptions only at Pl. *Cas.* 646 (imitating an address spoken by a
woman), *Per.* 850 (in jest).
[14] e.g. Pl. *Cist.* 719, *Mer.* 503, *Per.* 620, *Epid.* 640.
[15] e.g. Pl. *Mos.* 343, *Cur.* 137, *Cist.* 22; Ter. *Hau.* 731.
[16] Pl. *Mil.* 1263, *Mos.* 346; Ter. *Eu.* 664, *Ad.* 289; cf. Donatus on Ter. *Eu.*
656; Adams (1984: 71); Hofmann (1951: 138).

and affection when so employed.[17] At all periods, women can also use the possessive more widely to their friends and associates, conveying a certain positive politeness and sometimes considerable affection, but no deep intimacy.[18] This wider use of *mi* is rare for male speakers during the Republic but becomes more common in the imperial period.[19]

It has been argued that *mi* might have a tendency to be used particularly often to women as well as by them; Cicero quotes the address *Egilia mea* as a taunt against a man named Egilius (*De Orat.* 2. 277), and it is suggested that *mea* is used here because it makes the address sound like one that would be used to a woman (Adams 1984: 52, 72–3). This interpretation seems to overlook the difference in usage between lovers, relatives, and others: in every genre of Latin literature, *mi* is used to relatives and lovers (both male and female) proportionately far more often than to addressees in any other category. Since in Latin literature women appear as lovers and relatives far more often than in other capacities, the tendency of *mi* to be used to these groups makes female addressees appear disproportionately often. But when the addressee is neither a relative nor a lover, use of *mea* by men to women is very rare. We have already seen that men in comedy very rarely use *mi/mea* to unrelated women in whom they do not have a romantic interest, and outside comedy, as far as I know, the avoidance of such addresses is complete (at least as concerns human beings), in both epistolary and non-epistolary genres. Cicero's *Egilia mea* must thus be explained otherwise; perhaps the speaker is feigning romantic interest in Egilius as part of the taunt.

There are other peculiarities of *mi*, including the occasional use of the nominative for the vocative and, in poetry, an apparent difference in usage between the masculine singular *mi* and other vocatives from *meus*. These peculiarities have a stylistic rather than a sociolinguistic basis and are beyond the

---

[17] e.g. Prop. 1. 18. 5; Tib. 1. 1. 57; Catul. 5. 1, 10. 25; Ov. *Am.* 1. 4. 25, *Met.* 13. 521; Apul. *Met.* 5. 16; V. Fl. 5. 677.

[18] e.g. Ov. *Met.* 10. 442, *Am.* 1. 8. 23; Petr. 131. 7; V. Fl. 6. 499; Apul. *Met.* 2. 20, 9. 16; *ILS* 8175.

[19] e.g. Var. *R.* 3. 2. 18; Catul. 13. 1; Petr. 90. 5, 116. 4; Sen. *Dial.* 5. 23. 8; Gel. 20. 1. 27; Apul. *Met.* 1. 6.

scope of the present work; they are treated elsewhere (Dickey forthcoming).

The possessive *noster*, which has a lexical meaning similar to that of *mi*, is used very differently. *Noster* is much rarer than *mi*; Cicero uses it with 2% of the addresses in his letters, and less than 1% of the addresses in his other works. It seems to be slightly informal in tone, but less informal than *mi*, and it does not appear to be disproportionately common in the epistolary genre as is *mi*. Cicero sometimes uses *noster* in letters and dialogues with addresses from men to unrelated male friends,[20] and he also very occasionally uses it to an opponent (*Div.* 2. 108, *Dom.* 47). Varro too uses the possessive between male friends in the *Res Rusticae*.[21] Plautus and Terence use *noster* with some friendly addresses, normally between men at least one of whom is a slave,[22] and the term is used elsewhere to divinities (e.g. Verg. *Ecl.* 7. 21).

The friendly nature of addresses with *noster* is shown by a passage of Terence in which an old man determines to change his ways and *blande dicere* 'speak pleasantly'; the first thing he does is to greet a slave with *o Syre noster, salve* 'O our Syrus, greetings', and he then comments that he has made a good beginning with the unaccustomed *o noster* (*Ad.* 878–85). This is not a context in which a man would be expected to use *mi* in comedy; it is friendly, but not emotional, as *mi* normally would be when spoken by a male to someone who was neither a relative nor a lover. Indeed addresses with *noster* generally have low emotional intensity; this difference from *mi* is probably connected to the fact that *noster* lacks the tendency of *mi* to be used with lovers and relatives. It is also used primarily by and to males, in contrast to *mi*, which in some contexts is used primarily by females. The plural element in the lexical meaning of *noster* does not prevent the address's being used in situations where only speaker and addressee are present (e.g. Pl. *St.* 705; Ter. *Ad.* 831).

---

[20] *Att.* 2. 16. 3, 8. 11. 3, *Leg.* 1. 1, 1. 4, *Fam.* 16. 7. 2, 16. 9. 4, *Fin.* 5. 71, 5. 94.

[21] 2. 1. 6, 2. 3. 1, 2. 11. 12, 3. 14. 1 (*bis*), 3. 17. 10.

[22] Pl. *Mil.* 1139, *St.* 705; Ter. *An.* 846, *Ph.* 609, *Ad.* 831, 883, 961.

Another word which can be attached to vocatives but is not an address in its own right is the particle *o*, which occurs nearly 800 times in our sample.[23] As the usage of this particle has been discussed fairly thoroughly elsewhere,[24] an exhaustive invest-igation of its usage is not needed here. A few basic principles, however, will be given.

Latin *o* is related to the Greek vocative particle ὦ in two different ways. The two particles are descended from a common ancestor, causing some original similarity in their usage, and in addition the Greek use of ὦ influenced the meaning of *o* in literary Latin. Despite these connections, however, Latin and Greek uses of the vocative particle are fundamentally different. In Greek the frequency and rules of usage for ὦ fluctuate wildly from one author to the next, and there does not seem to be an overall governing principle behind its use or omission; nevertheless it is likely that in the classical period most addresses in conversational Attic were preceded by this particle (Dickey 1996: 199–206). In Latin the use of the vocative particle was governed by a few fairly consistent rules, and throughout our period it was far rarer than classical Greek ὦ.

Cicero uses *o* with only 2% of his vocatives, and in his works the vocative particle has two distinct functions. The first and most common is to make vocatives more emphatic and emo-tional. In Cicero's works, 52% of all examples of *o* occur with insults, terms of pity, or expressions of affection, although this group of emotional addresses accounts for only 4% of Cicero's total vocatives. This emotional force, which applies to the majority of Cicero's uses of *o*, is probably connected to the fact that the vocative *o* can be only partially separated in Latin from the *o* accompanying exclamations. It is not, however, the case that all vocatives with *o* are particularly emotional, nor that all emotional vocatives have *o*; the pairing of *o* and emotion is a strong tendency rather than a firm rule.

[23] Exact figures are not possible, since in some cases one cannot determine whether an *o* near a vocative is really a vocative particle or not.

[24] Ellendt (1840: ii. 33–4); Ferger (1889: 20–5); Wackernagel (1926–8: i. 312); Hofmann (1951: 20–1); Svennung (1958: 270, 414); Hofmann and Szantyr (1965: 26); Goold (1965: 32); Wieland (1968); Ross (1969: 49–53); Petersmann (1977: 59, 108); Nisbet and Hubbard (1978: 109); Lepre (1985: 993–4).

The second main function of *o* in Cicero is to make an
address sound Greek. Thus Cicero remarks

Est enim, ut scis, quasi in extrema pagina Phaedri his ipsis verbis
loquens Socrates: Adulescens etiam nunc, o Phaedre, Isocrates est
. . . (*Orat.* 41)

For on almost the last page of [Plato's] *Phaedrus*, as you know,
Socrates appears speaking these very words: O Phaedrus, Isocrates
is still a youth now . . .

Here Cicero is quoting words originally written in Greek. The
address in the original is ὦ Φαῖδρε (*Phaedrus* 278e), and Cicero
keeps the Greek use of the vocative particle when he translates
the passage into Latin. This Greek use of *o* can also be found
elsewhere in Cicero's works, not only in direct translations but
also on other occasions where Cicero represents an address as
having been used between two Greek speakers.[25]

Most other prose authors seem to use *o* about as often as
Cicero does and with the same functions.[26] The Greek use of
the vocative particle is particularly visible in the *Asclepius*
formerly attributed to Apuleius, which is a translation from
the Greek and in which nearly all the vocatives have *o*.[27] Varro,
exceptionally among prose authors, uses the particle with 23%
of his vocatives in the *Res Rusticae*, often with addresses which
do not seem especially emotional.[28] It is likely that most of
Varro's examples of *o* are imitations of Greek usage, since the
Res Rusticae is a didactic dialogue written before Cicero's
dialogues existed to provide a Latin model. As such it would
inevitably have been heavily influenced by Greek didactic
dialogues such as those of Plato and Xenophon, in which ὦ is
used with more than 90% of addresses.

[25] e.g. *o Damocle* (*Tusc.* 5. 61), *o Socrate* (*frag. phil.* A 4. 1 = Garbarino
1984: 84), *o Protagora et Socrates* (*frag. phil.* A 4. 2 = Garbarino 1984: 84);
perhaps also *o fortunate* . . . *adulescens* (*Arch.* 24).

[26] The particle is extremely rare in non-literary texts such as graffiti,
inscriptions, and letters, but it seems to follow the Ciceronian rules when it
does occur.

[27] On the authorship and Greek original of this work see Nock (1945),
Wigtil (1984), and Harrison (2000: 12–13). Other probable cases of Greek *o* in
Latin are *o Lacedaemonii* (Sen. *Suas.* 2. 1), *o philosophe* (Gel. 19. 1. 8), *o iuvenis*
(Fro. 139. 20).

[28] *R.* 2. 2. 1, 2. 3. 1, 3. 14. 1 (*bis*), 3. 16. 9, 3. 17. 10.

In comedy *o* is used slightly more often than in most prose; Plautus attaches it to 4% of his vocatives and Terence to 6% of his. In many cases the addresses involved are especially emotional but, as in prose, not all emotional addresses have *o*. It is possible that when *o* is used with less emphatic addresses in comedy, Greek influence is at work.[29]

In high-register poetry the situation is somewhat different. Only Tibullus, Propertius, and Martial use *o* as infrequently as the comedians and prose writers. Ovid uses it 9% of the time and Vergil 16% of the time, and almost all the other poets fall within this range of 9% to 16%. In the preserved fragments of Ennius, however, *o* is attached to 36% of the vocatives. Ennius is probably following Greek practice, for many of his vocatives with *o* occur in Greek contexts and at least one can be shown to be a translation of a Homeric address with ὦ.[30]

If the preserved fragments of Ennius give an accurate picture of the frequency of *o* in Ennius' works as a whole, it was much higher than in contemporary comedy. Perhaps Ennius followed his models more closely in this respect than the comedians did theirs, or perhaps ὦ occurred more often in the type of Greek poetry Ennius imitated than in the comedians' models.[31] Ennius had a great influence on later high-register poetry, and it is likely that the relatively frequent use of *o* in poetry, as compared to contemporary prose, is due in part to this influence: Ennius' use made *o* sound elevated and poetic as well as Greek and emotional. In classical poetry *o* is often used to mark emotion, but there are many passages in which its usage is very difficult to justify on such grounds alone, and in which there is no clear evidence of imitation of Greek. Rather, the particle seems to be

---

[29] In Greek, the vocative particle is much less common in Menander than in Aristophanes or Plato, but Menander's use of ὦ with 12% of his vocatives still represents more extensive usage than that of most Latin comedy or prose.

[30] *O genitor noster, Saturnie, maxime divom* (*Ann.* 444) = ὦ πάτερ ἡμέτερε Κρονίδη, ὕπατε κρειόντων (*Iliad* 8. 31, etc.)

[31] As most of New Comedy is lost, no definite statements on the use of ὦ in that genre can be made, but Menander's use of ὦ with only 12% of his vocatives suggests that the frequency was fairly low by Greek standards. Homer is also sparing in his use of ὦ, which occurs only 10% of the time in his works, but the Attic tragedians use ὦ much more often (Dickey 1996: 201).

used for its elevated, poetic register, a register it may have derived from Ennius' usage.[32]

There also seems to be another motivation for attaching *o* to addresses in classical poetry. The Latin poets were fond of long and complex addresses involving many words not in the vocative case, as *o saepe mecum tempus in ultimum deducte Bruto militiae duce* 'O you who were often led with me into the final extremity when Brutus was the leader of our troops' (Hor. *Carm.* 2. 7. 1–2) or *o, nisi te virtus opera ad maiora tulisset, in partem ventura chori Tritonia nostri* 'O Tritonia, who would have come to be part of our chorus if virtue had not called you to greater tasks'.[33] Such addresses are extremely rare in prose and comedy and were almost certainly absent from non-literary Latin of the period (cf. pp. 32–4), so they were not entirely easy for a listener to follow and understand, particularly when the non-vocative words began the address. The addition of *o* to the start of such a phrase alerted the audience that it was an address and thus made it possible for poets to construct very intricate addresses without sacrificing clarity. Sometimes the poets even used the vocative force of *o* to make an address out of a relative clause which could not, strictly speaking, be a vocative phrase at all, as *o qui pendentia parvo aera cibo celas, moderator harundinis* 'O controller of the fishing rod, you who hide the hanging fishhook with a little bait',[34] or *o qui res hominumque deumque aeternis regis imperiis et fulmine terres* 'O you who rule the affairs of gods and men with eternal power and terrify them with the thunderbolt' (Verg. *A.* 1. 229–30).

A further factor affecting the use of *o* is avoidance of hiatus. In Greek this consideration arises only in certain authors, but in Latin most writers, regardless of genre,[35] seem to avoid using *o* directly in front of a vocative beginning with a vowel.

---

[32] Cf. Svennung (1958: 267). It is, however, possible that the influence here ascribed to Ennius should rather be attributed to the whole group of early Latin high-register poets. The fragments of other such poets contain too few vocatives to give meaningful statistics, but *o* seems to be fairly common among the vocatives that do survive. Most of these poets based their works on Greek models, and it is very likely that, like Ennius, they adopted the Greek use of ὦ to some extent.

[33] Ov. *Met.* 5. 269–70; cf. Bömer (1969–86: ii. 290–1).

[34] Ov. *Met.* 8. 855–6; cf. Bömer (1969–86: iv. 264–5).

[35] Exceptions: Propertius, Varro.

Only 3% of the examples of *o* in our data occur in such contexts, although about 20% of Latin vocatives begin with vowels.[36]

In Latin, then, *o* was probably not common in conversational language; if prose and comedy are reliable guides on this point, it was probably attached only to especially emotional addresses. In literature it could be used in imitation of Greek style as well as to express emotion, and in classical and silver Latin poetry it could also be used as a poetic feature and for clarity in front of long or syntactically difficult addresses.

[36] This is an estimate based on words included in the Glossary.

PART II

Interactions

8

Addresses between Known People without any Special Attachment to One Another

> Quod te nomine iam tuo saluto,
> quem regem et dominum prius vocabam,
> ne me dixeris esse contumacem.
>
> (Mart. 2. 68. 1–3)
>
> Do not call me disobedient because I now greet you by your name, when I used to call you 'patron' and 'master'.

W E have so far investigated the ways in which all of the major elements of the Latin address system were used, and it is now time to turn to the question of how these different terms interacted with one another. What was the normal way for a Roman to address his brother, his patron, or his slave? Were there differences in the way men and women were addressed? When more than one type of address was common for a given type of interaction, was there any difference in meaning between the two? These and similar questions form the focus of the second part of this work.

In the Latin address system, most types of interaction follow a broadly similar pattern, and a few types show more radical differences. The addresses which are most distinct are those not spoken to individual humans (i.e. addresses to groups and to animals), those spoken to people to whom the speaker has a close emotional attachment (i.e. relatives, spouses, and lovers), and those spoken to strangers. Such interactions will be treated in subsequent chapters; for the present we shall restrict our examination to addresses to known individuals unrelated to the speaker and without any romantic attachment to him or her.

The most common address situation in Latin literature is an interaction between two unrelated adult men who know each other. Such interactions occur nearly 5,000 times in our data, and in the vast majority of them names alone are used in address (including names with *mi* 'my', which are largely restricted to letters). Deviation from the standard address by name alone is confined to three types of situation: those in which the interaction is emotionally charged and the speaker has something particular to communicate by his address, those in which there is a significant status difference or power imbalance between speaker and addressee, and those in which a poet replaces a normal address with a specifically poetic one for the sake of elegant variation. This last category is found only in high-register poetry and accounts for less than 5% of all addresses between known, unrelated adult men; it includes patronymics, ethnics, *iuvenis* 'young man', and various periphrases. It will not be discussed further here as it has little bearing on the fundamental rules of the address system.

About the first category of exceptions little can be said here; these are the marked addresses, which derive their force by being exceptions to the rule. They consist of terms of affection, insults, and terms of pity (in declining order of frequency) and have been discussed in Part I. Non-name addresses of the second type, those conditioned by status differences and power imbalances, are not necessarily marked; they can be used habitually and without any special emotion.

As we saw in Chapter 1, even address by name to Roman men was a complex affair governed by address rules which took into account not only the formality of the setting but also, in some cases, the status of the addressee. Some of the status distinctions encoded within the naming system seem to have been observed primarily by Cicero.

One of the most significant status differences in Rome was that between slaves and free men, but this factor does not have as much effect on the address system as one might expect. Slaves addressing free men who are not their masters, and therefore do not have direct power over them, use names and the same other addresses that a free man would use. When addressing their masters, however, while slaves may still use names[1] or other terms, they have the additional option of *ere*

---

[1] Exactly which name is not clear; for arguments that it was the praenomen, see p. 66. I suspect that it was actually the cognomen.

'master'. Most of the evidence for addresses from slaves to
their masters comes from comedy, but elsewhere as well both
names and *ere* are possible.[2] I can detect little difference in tone
between names and *ere*, though one would expect the latter to
be more deferential; the two occur with roughly equal frequency, and in a number of passages both terms are used
within the same dyad without appreciable differences.[3]

Romans addressing slaves seem to use the same addresses as
they would to a free man. Slaves who have names are typically
addressed by name in Roman comedy (it makes no difference
whether the speaker is the slave's master, another free man, or
a fellow slave), and they are never addressed with *puer* 'boy'
unless they are actually boys. That this distinction reflects
Roman practice and was not borrowed from the original
Greek of the plays is shown by the repeated use of παî 'boy'
to adult, named slaves in Menander.[4] Outside comedy the
evidence for address to slaves is not abundant, but that
which does exist suggests that, in contrast to Greek practice,
named, known slaves were regularly addressed by name in
Rome.[5]

Ovid advises suitors to win over the slaves of the woman they
are pursuing; techniques for doing this include addressing
them by name.[6] This passage could be taken to suggest that
slaves were not normally addressed by name by non-suitors,
but such an inference is not necessary. Ovid's advice probably
has a close relationship to the advice one often hears today that
one should address by name one's clients, prospective clients,
and other people one wishes to exploit: the speaker is in a
position where he might well not bother to learn the names of
his potential victims, although it would be a natural part of his
address system for him to use those names in address if he did
know them.

Cicero produces a hypothetical example of cross-examination

---

[2] e.g. Hor. *S.* 2. 3. 265; Petr. 74. 7; Sen. *Con.* 10. 5. 26.

[3] e.g. Pl. *Am.* 570, 578, 583, 590, *Cur.* 146, 181, *Poen.* 205, 248, 280, 297,
Ps. 4, 35, 231, 383; Ter. *An.* 503, 508, *Hau.* 591, 593. Occasionally *ere* is
combined with a name: Pl. *Mos.* 447–8, *Trin.* 617.

[4] e.g. *Dyscolus* 82, 401, 551, 959.

[5] e.g. [Cic.] *Rhet. Her.* 4. 63; Hor. *Ep.* 1. 7. 52; Ov. *Am.* 2. 2. 1; Petr. 36. 6,
69. 5, 70. 10, 77. 7, 78. 2; Mart. 5. 64. 1–2, 9. 92. 2.

[6] *Ars* 2. 253; cf. Donatus on Ter. *Ad.* 891.

of a slave, which begins '*Heus tu, Rufio,*' *verbi causa* . . . 'Hey
you, Rufio (to invent a name) . . .' (*Mil.* 60). It is notable that
even though the slave is hypothetical, and therefore nameless,
Cicero does not use the *puer* normally given to unnamed slaves
of any age (cf. pp. 253–4), but rather invents a name and
comments upon this invention. For the sake of his argument
here,[7] Cicero needs to use an address which would be employed
by a speaker previously acquainted with the addressee, and it is
this need that leads him to invent the name *Rufio* rather than
using *puer*. This passage is thus further evidence that known
slaves were addressed by name in Cicero's day.

Address by name would not, however, have meant a complete lack of distinction between addresses to slaves and to free
men, for the two groups had very different naming conventions. While Roman citizens bore two or more names, normally
ones which came from a restricted pool of recognizably Roman
names, most slaves had only one, and that single name was
often immediately identifiable as servile. Several passages in
literature suggest that slaves resented the social stigma of their
naming system, and that new freedmen (who received a Roman
praenomen and gentilicium upon being freed, retaining the
original slave name as a cognomen) wanted to receive addresses
indicating their free status. Martial ridicules a former slave for
wanting to be addressed with the traditional Roman cognomen
Cinna rather than with his old name *Cinname* (6. 17), while
Persius comments upon a freedman who is constantly flattered
by address with his new praenomen, *Marce*, rather than his old
name, *Dama* (5. 81; cf. p. 65).

Like free men, slaves are also addressed with terms other
than names, and in comedy they both use and receive insults
notably more often than do most types of free man. Comic
invective is of course a dramatic ploy, so there is no necessary
correlation between the frequency of insults in comedy and
that in real life, but it is nevertheless not improbable that the
disproportionately high frequency of insults used to slaves has
some counterpart in reality. Free men could, however, receive
insults as well, as Cicero makes abundantly clear in the *In
Pisonem*. The high proportion of comic insults used by slaves to

---

[7] Cicero is ridiculing the value of testimony produced when a slave owned
by a party to the prosecution is examined on behalf of the prosecution.

other slaves and to free but low-status characters such as parasites and brothel-keepers may also reflect reality, although Cicero's use of insults in a formal speech shows that such language did not necessarily debase its speaker.

Another feature of comic language which may reflect status distinctions is the tendency for male brothel-keepers to be addressed as *leno* 'brothel-keeper' even when their names are known.[8] This type of address is unusual in Latin; normally (at least until the second century of the empire) terms describing the addressee's occupation are used as addresses only when more standard terms, such as names, are unavailable. Male brothel-keepers are the only type of character to receive such occupational addresses with any frequency when names could be used instead, and the usage occurs only in comedy.[9] It is possible that this address was borrowed from Greek along with the scenes in which it occurs, but no evidence can be adduced in favour of such borrowing. The equivalent Greek address πορνοβοσκέ is unattested, but since the preserved fragments of Greek comedy rarely include addresses to brothel-keepers, the lack of attestation may not reflect Greek practice. The usage in Latin seems generally to be derogatory, though *leno* can be used in contexts which do not otherwise appear uncivil (e.g. Pl. *Poen.* 698, *Cur.* 455).

At the other end of the social spectrum, interactions involving emperors may also use special address patterns. Emperors speaking to ordinary citizens use the same forms of address as any other citizen would use—chiefly names, but also other

---

[8] e.g. Pl. *Cur.* 525, 715, *Poen.* 751, 798; cf. Martin (1976: 131).

[9] Donatus (on Ter. *Ad.* 210) argues that this usage is part of a larger pattern whereby occupational terms denoting dishonourable occupations are used as less polite alternatives to address by name, while those denoting honourable professions are used as more polite addresses. This theory is in some respects correct (cf. p. 204), but in early Latin its application is very limited. Donatus' formulation probably reflects the address usage of his own time, in which non-name addresses had become much more common than in earlier forms of Latin (see below). In comedy, *leno* is not always impolite, while Donatus' other example, *miles* 'warrior', is not really an example of a dishonourable profession in the Republican period; the examples he gives of honourable occupations (*imperator, orator, philosophus*) either do not occur as addresses in extant comedy or are not used as he describes (cf. Pl. *Rud.* 986, *Mil.* 1160). Donatus' use of this system to make *nutrix* an honourable address (on Ter. *Ad.* 288) is likewise suspect.

terms such as indications of affection or esteem.[10] Citizens addressing emperors normally use titles such as *Caesar*, *Auguste*, or *imperator* 'commander', and/or words of praise, affection, or respect. Aside from the conventions restricting some titles to certain registers (for which see pp. 100–4), the only rule of address to emperors seems to be that the address should be flattering. A wide variety of terms occurs, including virtually any positive term that could be used to a Roman man (except *ere*); thus emperors may even be addressed as *pater* 'father' or with endearments such as *care* 'dear' or *dulcissime* 'sweetest'.[11] Emperors are also addressed by name, without any lack of respect,[12] though this usage is relatively rare (unless one counts *Caesar* as a name). Dead, deified emperors are addressed with *dive* and a name.[13]

There are thus certain similarities between the addresses at the bottom of the social scale and those at the top. In both cases a superior speaking to an inferior uses essentially the same addresses that another member of the inferior's class would use, and in both cases an inferior speaking to a superior has the option of using special titles or of employing address by name as he would to a member of his own class, without communicating any disrespect.

In between these two social extremes distinctions of power or status are much less likely to be reflected in address, though such reflection is possible. Kings can be addressed with titles such as *rex* (cf. p. 106), but they are also frequently addressed by name or with other terms.[14] Powerful men protecting or helping the less powerful may be addressed as *patrone* 'patron', *rex* 'patron', or *domine* 'master' (cf. pp. 106–7), but at least in the classical period names are more common in address to

[10] e.g. Plin. *Ep. Tra.* 10. 16. 1, 10. 97. 1; Fro. 38. 12, 85. 20; Tac. *Ann.* 2. 38, 4. 40.

[11] e.g. Calp. *Ecl.* 4. 146; Stat. *Silv.* 5. 1. 167; [Verg.] *Eleg. Maec.* 171; Fro. 87. 2.

[12] e.g. *pater Traiane*, Plin. *Pan.* 89. 2; *Caesar Traiane*, Mart. 10. 34. 1; *Nero*, Tac. *Ann.* 16. 22; *Nero Caesar*, Sen. *Cl.* 1. 1. 1, 2. 1. 1; *Antonine*, Fro. 87. 12; *Luci*, Fro. 119. 7; *Marce*, Fro. 20. 8; *Traiane*, *ILS* 1046a.

[13] e.g. *dive Iuli*, V. Max. 1. 6. 13; *dive Nerva*, Plin. *Pan.* 89. 1; *dive Claudi*, Sen. *Apoc.* 10. 4.

[14] e.g. Ov. *Pont.* 2. 9. 5; Liv. 33. 13. 6, 35. 19. 3; Curt. 6. 10. 11; Sen. *Suas.* 1. 1, etc.; Sen. *Ep.* 120. 6.

patrons.[15] Military commanders are often addressed as *imperator* 'commander', but they too frequently receive names.[16] In the imperial period *magister* 'teacher' could be used as a respectful address to learned men (see p. 204), but again names were also possible.[17]

We have seen (p. 45) that during the imperial period there seems to have been a major change in the address system, as polite addresses such as *domine, frater*, etc. replaced names in many interactions. This change had little impact on the literary address system but fundamentally altered the non-literary one. In the first century BC free men do not seem to have used titles or other status-based addresses to one another with any appreciable frequency; in Cicero's letters, for example, out of 210 addresses between unrelated adult men, 95% use the name alone, and fewer than 1% use a title. Yet by the end of the first century AD Martial could have patrons who objected to being addressed by name rather than with *domine* (pp. 1, 233). Martial's fears, which he expresses repeatedly (cf. p. 91), belie the fact that the vast majority of the addresses in his works use the name alone. At that period, apparently, the address system of conversational language had changed to make more use of titles and reflect status distinctions more fully, while the literary address system, adhering to the classical model, to some extent failed to follow that change.

The earlier, more egalitarian address system was very similar to that in use in classical Greece, where free men very rarely used titles. The later system went on to develop even more status-based variation than is apparent in the second century, eventually producing a complex and frequently used set of titles and a very stratified late Latin address system in which address by name alone probably played a very minor role.

We have seen that Cicero appears to have made status distinctions in his address system which were not observed by all other Romans, distinctions that involved the use of different names rather than titles. Is it possible that Cicero,

[15] e.g. Hor. *Carm.* 2. 17. 3, etc., *Ep.* 1. 9. 1; Cic. *Fam.* 7. 29. 1; Mart. 1. 82. 9.

[16] e.g. [Caes.] *Afr.* 45. 2 (with comment on the lack of the address *imperator*); Luc. 1. 373, etc.; Tac. *Ann.* 1. 22; [Quint.] *Decl.* 3. 3, etc.

[17] e.g. Fro. 2. 13, 28. 16, 36. 25, 38. 12, 43. 3.

in creating these distinctions, was reacting to the same impulse toward greater status differentiation in the address system that caused the majority of his countrymen to begin using titles among themselves?

We have so far considered only interactions in which both parties are adult males. Contrary to what we might expect, the presence of adult females as speakers and/or addressees makes little difference to the major rules of the address system. Women normally address men by name, just as men do, and they are normally addressed by name as well. This situation differs sharply from classical Greek practice, in which respectable women were normally addressed as γύναι 'woman' rather than by name (Dickey 1996: 243). In Greece, the names of respectable living women were not even mentioned in public by free men, and it has been suggested that the Roman comedians made some effort to adhere to this custom when adapting Greek plays (Schaps 1977; Sommerstein 1980). Outside comedy, however, Romans use women's names freely. The women so addressed in prose include such respectable characters as Cremutia Marcia, one of Seneca's dedicatees (*Dial.* 6. 1. 1, etc.), and Scintilla, the wife of an important guest at Trimalchio's dinner (Petr. 69. 2). Poets also use names to Roman matrons of unimpeachable reputation,[18] and even matrons in comedy are addressed by name under certain circumstances.[19]

As in the case of slaves, address by name to Republican women was not entirely the same as address by name to free Roman men, since women had a very different name system (see p. 73). In the imperial period, part of this difference was eliminated by the introduction of female cognomina, but the two genders did not develop identical naming conventions until long after our period.

Addresses from women to men seem to reflect status in the same way as those between two men. Like men, women use the same addresses to known slaves as to free men (i.e. normally names), but with a somewhat higher percentage of insults to

[18] e.g. Stat. *Silv.* 5. 1. 3; Mart. 12. 52. 3; Juv. 6. 167; [Sen.] *Oct.* 769; Luc. 5. 726.

[19] e.g. Pl. *As.* 855, *Cas.* 171, 541; Ter. *Ad.* 511, *Ph.* 1046.

slaves than to free men.[20] Female slaves can address their masters by name or with *ere* 'master'[21] but, like male slaves, do not use titles to men who are not their masters. They also seem to use insults more often than do free women, but there is not enough evidence to be certain on this point. Women, like men, use names, titles, and other polite terms to emperors, monarchs, and other high-status men.[22]

A parallelism with male addresses is also found in addresses to women, whether the speaker is male or female. Maidservants, like male slaves, are addressed by name or other terms, especially insults;[23] if they are nurses, they may also be addressed as *nutrix* or *altrix* 'nurse' and address their female charges as *alumna* 'foster-child' (see pp. 204–5). Slaves of either gender can address their mistresses by name or with *era* 'mistress',[24] the exact equivalent of *ere*, but they do not use titles to other free women. Women in positions of power, such as queens or patronesses, are normally addressed by name but can also receive terms of praise or the title *regina* 'queen'.[25] Women belonging to the imperial family, however, are not called *regina*.[26]

This similarity between male and female addresses does not extend to all areas of the address system. As we shall see (cf. pp. 244–5, 254, 264, 267, 269), in some types of interactions involving strangers, relatives, and young people differences can be found between the genders. In addition, there are a few gender-based peculiarities of address which apply in any type

[20] e.g. Pl. *Men.* 736, *Mil.* 366, *Truc.* 286; Ter. *Ad.* 320, 323, *An.* 790, *Eu.* 941; Ov. *Met.* 9. 569.

[21] e.g. Pl. *Am.* 1076, *Cas.* 632, *Poen.* 1127, *Truc.* 836; Ov. *Met.* 10. 464.

[22] e.g. Stat. *Silv.* 4. 3. 139, *Theb.* 5. 29, *Ach.* 1. 350; Curt. 3. 12. 24.

[23] e.g. Pl. *Aul.* 41, *Cas.* 644–5, *Cist.* 637, *Mer.* 808, *Mil.* 1248, *Rud.* 336; Ter. *An.* 481, *Eu.* 500, 704, 861, 1017, *Ph.* 739; Petr. 128. 3; Apul. *Met.* 1. 23, 2. 24.

[24] e.g. Pl. *Cas.* 311, *Cist.* 695, *Mer.* 683, *St.* 331; Ter. *Ad.* 295, 329, *Eu.* 834, 851; Sen. *Med.* 426, 892; Phaed. Appendix Perottina 15. 15. If the slave is male, *era* is much more common than names in comedy.

[25] e.g. Curt. 3. 12. 25; Sen. *Dial.* 6. 4. 3, *Ag.* 203, *Phoen.* 387, *Her. F.* 641; Ov. *Met.* 11. 389, *Pont.* 3. 4. 96; Verg. *A.* 2. 3; Catul. 66. 89; Mart. 6. 13. 1, 10. 64. 1; [Ov.] *Epic. Drusi* 3; [Sen.] *Oct.* 219–20, 932–4.

[26] Emperors, of course, were not normally addressed as *rex* 'king' either; there is only one example of such an address in our data (Stat. *Silv.* 4. 1. 46; cf. p. 106).

of interaction. Women are more likely than men to receive patronymics (p. 212) and addresses identifying them as someone's spouse or parent (pp. 114-15), but much less likely to receive terms for spouses in a transferred or extended sense (p. 117). Unlike those of men, their names are almost never modified by *mea* 'my' in address by men other than relatives and lovers (pp. 221–2). They can be addressed as *mulier* 'woman', often in rebukes, without modifiers in a way that men do not normally receive *vir* 'man' (p. 199). *Puella* 'girl' as an address to an adult is flattering, whereas *puer* 'boy' in similar circumstances can be insulting (pp. 193, 201–2). Some words which in their referential meaning apply to both genders are restricted in address primarily or exclusively to males (*adulescens* 'young person', *advena* 'visitor', *amicus* 'friend' (p. 150), *amicissimus* 'very friendly', *comes* 'companion' (p. 150), *hospes* 'guest, host, foreigner' (p. 150), *homo* 'human being' (p. 189), *iucund(issim)us* '(very) delightful', *quisquis es* 'whoever you are', *socii* 'comrades')[27] or to females (*almus* 'nurturing', *alumnus* 'nursling' (pp. 204–5), *deus* 'god', *impius* 'impious', *malus* 'bad', *socius* 'partner' (p. 150)). In addition, some addresses are used primarily or exclusively by male speakers (*formose* 'good-looking' (p. 143), *iucund(issim)e* '(very) delightful') or by female speakers (*anime* 'mind, soul' (p. 157), *animule* 'little soul', *pulcher* 'beautiful', *pulcherrime* 'very beautiful' (p. 143), and in some contexts *mi* 'my' (p. 222)).

It thus looks as though the basic structure of the address system was the same for both males and females, but that the details of that system were by no means identical for the two genders. Clearly the differences in the address system can tell us something about Roman perceptions of gender, but at the same time this information must be used with caution. We have already seen some examples of apparent gender differences in our data which probably did not really exist in the Latin language (p. 144), and it is possible that some of the differences listed here are also illusory. In addition, not all of these distinctions result from sociolinguistic factors. *Deus, impius, socius*, and a few rarer terms such as *egregius, pius,* and *regius* are avoided in the masculine singular vocative for phonological and stylistic reasons, since for most of our period Romans seem to

[27] For further information, see the Glossary entries for these words.

have disliked forming vocatives in -*e* on words with a nominative in -*eus* or -*ius* (see Dickey 2000, forthcoming).

We can, however, tentatively suggest that the address system shows that marital status and the identity of the addressee's spouse, children, and other relatives were more relevant in the case of females than in the case of males. The avoidance of *mea* and of transferred or extended terms for spouses may reveal a need on the part of male speakers to avoid being misinterpreted when speaking to women. The difference between *puer* and *puella* suggests that Romans may have valued youthfulness more in women and maturity more in men. The restriction of *homo* to male addressees is part of a larger pattern of address usage betraying the implicit assumption that adult maleness is a 'normal' state and any deviation from that state is remarkable (see p. 255). Many of the gender differences, however, are difficult to explain in cultural terms: why do women use *pulcher* and *pulcherrime* where men use *formose*? Both in terms of these obscurities and in terms of the further insights which could be gained by pursuing the more obvious cultural connections, this is an area of the address system that would amply reward further study.

So far we have considered only addresses to adults. Addresses to children and young people follow a similar pattern but make less use of names than those to adults. Most addresses to and from children occur in the context of the family and will therefore be treated in Chapter 10; the present discussion concerns only non-relatives.

In contrast to slaves, who can be called *puer* only when unknown or nameless, boys and young men are addressed freely as *puer*; youths may also be called *adulescens* and *iuvenis*. The connotations and age limits of these addresses have already been discussed (pp. 191–7). Names can also be used to address boys and young men and are usable from a very young age (e.g. Stat. *Theb.* 5. 609), but they are not a common form of address until a young man is old enough to act as an adult. The exception to this rule is slave boys, who are more often addressed by name than as *puer*;[28] it may be that this tendency

[28] e.g. Pl. *Mil.* 843, *Per.* 195, *St.* 332; Stat. *Silv.* 2. 6. 81; Mart. 1. 88. 1, 7. 15. 5.

is related to the use of *puer* as a general address for unknown
and nameless slaves of all ages and reflects a desire to address
the boy concerned as an individual, rather than as a slave. It is
difficult, however, to see any difference in tone between the two
types of address, provided the addressee is not yet an adult (cf.
the use of both at Martial 9. 93 and 11. 6). Boys and young men
can also receive insults, terms of praise and affection, and other
addresses used to adults; such characters are rarely quoted in
our sources, but when they do speak, they seem to use the same
addresses that an adult would use.

The evidence for addresses to girls is much thinner than
that for boys, particularly outside the family; the youngest
group of females about which we can speak is that of young
women old enough to marry. There is some evidence that
when such women were of free birth, they were not addressed
by name by people other than relatives, lovers, or would-be
lovers. In comedy freeborn virgins are not normally addressed at all by men other than relatives and lovers, and
when they do receive addresses they tend to be masquerading
as slaves. Nevertheless the use of *virgo* 'virgin' to such
women is revealing. *Virgo* in comedy is used exclusively to
freeborn virgins, though in one case the speaker is unaware
that the addressee is in fact freeborn (Pl. *Cur.* 487). There is
one extended passage in which a free virgin, disguised as a
captive for sale, is questioned by a man who knows her real
identity. He consistently addresses her with *virgo*, despite her
telling him her assumed name (Pl. *Per.* 610, 617, 640) and
continues this form of address when the need for deception is
over (673). In later poetry unmarried women are frequently
called *virgo* by both men and women;[29] they can be addressed
by name as well, but such addresses are rare from unrelated
men who are not romantically involved with them.[30] I have
found no unambiguous evidence for address to virgins in
prose.

It thus seems that there may have been a tendency (though
not an absolute rule) in at least early Latin for men other than

[29] e.g. Verg. *A.* 6. 104, 7. 318, 11. 508, 536; Prop. 4. 4. 92; Ov. *Met.* 2. 426,
13. 483, 14. 570, *Tr.* 2. 399, *Fast.* 2. 167; Sen. *Ag.* 981.

[30] e.g. Sen. *Ag.* 924, *Tro.* 367; Ov. *Ars* 3. 2; names are more common from
unrelated women, e.g. Ov. *Met.* 10. 730, *Fast.* 4. 452; Sen. *Ag.* 691, 952.

relatives, lovers, and suitors to avoid addressing young unmarried women by name and to use *virgo* as the unmarked address instead. Boys and youths could also be addressed by terms indicating their age rather than by name, but their names were not avoided in address like those of young women.

9

Addresses to Strangers and Nameless Characters

o dea (namque mihi nec, quae sis, dicere promptum est,
et liquet esse deam), duc, o duc . . .

(Ov. Met. 14. 841–2)

O goddess (for it is not easy to say who you are, but it is
clear that you are a goddess), lead, O lead me . . .

T HE fact that names play such a major part in the classical
Latin address system means that addresses directed to
unknown or nameless people are very different from those
used in normal interactions. Of course, nameless people did
not exist in Rome, but they do exist in virtually every genre of
Latin literature and thus provide an identifiable and not
insignificant part of the literary address system. Moreover,
examination of the addresses to unknown and to nameless
characters reveals that in most cases address to the nameless
ones follows the same pattern as address to the unknown ones.
Such agreement is only to be expected, since the two situations
caused the same problems for a speaker of Latin. In most cases,
therefore, nameless addressees can provide us with additional
data on addresses to unknown addressees, and as a result the
two categories will be discussed together, except in contexts
where the treatment of nameless addressees can be observed to
differ.[1]

There are several different types of situation in which
unknown or nameless people may be addressed. Sometimes a
speaker simply needs to talk to a stranger whose name he or she
does not know, as when Aeneas addresses the disguised Venus
with o quam te memorem, virgo 'O how should I address you,

---

[1] The declamations contain a number of logically impossible interactions,
such as fathers addressing nameless sons, and it is these situations which
account for the majority of deviations.

girl?' (Verg. *A*. 1. 327). Sometimes an address is directed to a person or people not positively identifiable by the speaker, as Martial's address of *quisquis habes* 'you, whoever has it' to the thief who stole his cloak (8. 48. 3), and sometimes the addressee is hypothetical, as when Persius addresses a character in a dialogue with *quisquis es, o modo quem ex adverso dicere feci* 'whoever you are whom I just made speak on the opposite side' (1. 44). In addition, a nameless addressee can be a minor character in a literary work to whom it is not worth assigning a name when some other form of address will be clearer to the audience, as when Horace includes in an epode the aside to a slave *capaciores adfer huc, puer, scyphos* 'bring bigger cups here, boy' (*Epod*. 9. 33).

These different situations pose problems which overlap but are not identical. In many cases strangers do not, strictly speaking, need to be addressed at all; Venus would have known whom Aeneas was talking to even if he had not used the term *virgo*. They are often addressed not for the sake of clarity, but out of politeness, and in consequence the address used tends to be governed less by a need for identification than by the rules of polite address. Unidentified addressees and minor characters, on the other hand, less often require polite treatment but frequently need an address that will make it clear whom the speaker is talking to. Hypothetical interlocutors seem to fall in between these two groups.

A lack of names is only relevant in situations which normally call for address by name. When a speaker is angry enough with a stranger to use a direct insult, or when he or she needs to use a term of praise or pity, there is no difference between address to characters with and without names in Latin. As we have seen, however, such emotional addresses are the exception rather than the rule; in most situations names are used if they are known, and as a result addresses to unnamed characters are normally different from those to named characters. Insults, terms of pity, and terms of praise which could easily have been used to a named character are not discussed in this chapter.

The most common type of address used to an unknown or nameless character is a simple descriptive term. Thus Catullus' wedding hymn contains addresses to the bride, the groom, and the groom's former lover; these characters are normally addressed as *nupta* 'bride' (61. 144), *marite* 'husband' (e.g. 61. 135, 184), and *concubine* 'lover' (e.g. 61. 125, 130) respectively. Similarly Horace addresses sailors with *nauta* 'sailor' (*Carm.* 1. 28. 23), Plautus has a doctor addressed as *medice* 'doctor' (*Men.* 946) and a stranger in a cloak as *chlamydate* 'cloaked' (*Ps.* 1139), Phaedrus addresses misers with *avare* 'miser' (4. 20. 18), and military officers address nameless or generic subordinates with terms like *miles* 'soldier' (Curt. 8. 4. 17), *signifer* 'stand-ard-bearer' (V. Max. 1. 5. 1), or *centurio* 'centurion' (Liv. 45. 39. 15).

All of the addresses just quoted serve a practical function: they identify the addressees. Such a function is common for descriptive addresses; for example, when Martial writes

> Baiano procul a lacu, monemus,
> piscator, fuge, ne nocens recedas.   (4. 30. 1–2)

Fisherman, we warn you, flee far from the lake at Baiae, lest guilty you depart.

the address conveys the essential information that not everyone is being warned to avoid the lake, only those who want to fish in it.

Often, however, the practical function of a descriptive address is less immediately obvious. Such is particularly the case when generic vocatives are used to address anyone who happens to read the text in which the address occurs. This type of address often employs the terms *lector* 'reader' or *viator* 'traveller',[2] words which cannot be used to named dedicatees, but only to an unknown future reader. *Viator* is used when the work in question is thought of as an inscription (even if it is found in a literary collection),[3] and *lector* is used mainly to the readers of books but also occasionally of inscriptions.[4] Thus

---

[2] *Amice* 'friend' (e.g. *ILS* 6192) and *hospes* 'foreigner, guest' are also used (cf. p. 149), as are other terms. On more general issues concerning address to the readers of an inscription see Lattimore (1942: 230–7) and Courtney (1995: 214–15); on *lector* see also Citroni (1975: 16) and Kay (1985: 101); on *viator* Cugusi (1996: 193).

[3] e.g. *ILLRP* 797, 985, *ILS* 1961, 2783, 2792, 5150, 5299, 5301, 6881, 7710, etc. Cf. the Greek use of ὁδῖτα and παριών 'traveller' in similar contexts (Dickey 1996: 149; Lattimore 1942: 230–7).

[4] e.g. Ov. *Tr.* 5. 1. 66; Phaed. 2 *pr.* 11; Mart. 9 *pr.* 12, 11. 108. 2; *ILS* 6068, 7542.

Ovid concludes one of his poems with *iure tibi grates, candide lector, ago* 'I justly give thanks, kind reader, to you' (*Tr.* 4. 10. 132), while one of Martial's epigrams begins,

> Marmora parva quidem sed non cessura, viator,
> Mausoli saxis pyramidumque legis.
>
> (10. 63. 1–2)

Traveller, the marble blocks you are reading, though small, will not yield to the stones of Mausolus or of the pyramids.

Although these terms do not single out one particular group of people as addressees, they do make it clear to every hearer or reader that he or she is being addressed, and thus they can be seen as having some practical function.

Both *lector* and *viator* are consistently singular as addresses (cf. p. 296), despite the fact that the authors who use them clearly expect to have more than one reader. The reason might be that the process of reading is seen as an act of individual interaction with the text, but in fact this collective singular is also used in address to groups of people who are not necessarily envisioned as readers of the text. Thus Vergil advises,

> cape saxa manu, cape robora, pastor,
> tollentemque minas et sibila colla tumentem
> deice.[5]

Seize stones in your hand, seize clubs, shepherd, and as it raises up its threats and puffs out its hissing neck, strike it down.

while Martial counsels

> Si vicina tibi Nomento rura coluntur,
> ad villam moneo, rustice, ligna feras. (13. 15)

If you inhabit rural areas near Nomentum, countryman, I advise you to carry wood to your house.

This tendency towards collective address to unknown, hypothetical people is probably related to the use of the singular ethnic (pp. 207–10) and the collective singular *miles* (p. 291, cf. p. 295). As in those two cases, however, the frequent use of the singular does not preclude the use of the plural on occasion as well (e.g. *agricolae*, Verg. *G.* 2. 36).

[5] *G.* 3. 420–2; see Horsfall (1995: 95–8) and Schiesaro (1993: 136–8).

Sometimes descriptive addresses are used in situations where no practical need for identification exists, when the passage would be equally comprehensible without any vocative at all. Cicero is said to have greeted his assassin with *ego vero consisto, . . . accede, veterane, et, si hoc saltim potes recte facere, incide cervicem* 'I indeed am stopping here; approach, veteran, and sever my neck, if you can do even that properly' (Sen. *Suas*. 6. 18). In similarly unambiguous situations Alexander addresses a soldier who had been sitting on his throne with *miles* (Curt. 8. 4. 17), a pair of Plautine slaves address an old man as *senex* 'old man' (*Mos*. 940), and a Plautine youth addresses an unfamiliar parasite as *adulescens* 'young person' (*Men*. 494). Ovid (*Met*. 2. 699) and Calpurnius Siculus (*Ecl*. 7. 40) both use *rustice* 'peasant' for addresses to strange peasants in contexts where clarity is not an issue. An extreme example is Accius' *quis tu es, mortalis* 'who are you, mortal?' (*trag*. 228), in which the description provided by the address is so general that it could hardly have been used to identify anyone.

The use of such addresses in places where they serve no practical purpose suggests that one of the rules of the Latin address system was that addresses should be used, particularly at the beginning of interactions. Their omission would have sounded hostile or ill-mannered (cf. Adams 1978: 163). This rule in fact applies to the whole of the address system, not merely to unnamed characters. Its most common manifestation is of course address by name, which can on occasion be used for clarity but more often occurs in contexts where identification is not an issue. Cicero's letters, for example, are normally addressed to a single person, and that person is clearly identified by the formula at the beginning of the letter. The hundreds of vocatives which occur in these letters (and in those of Fronto, Seneca, and Pliny) are therefore, from a merely practical point of view, superfluous and are used only because of conventions about the need for addresses. The same is true of most of the group addresses which occur in oratory, such as *patres conscripti* 'enrolled fathers' or *iudices* 'jurors'; the orator uses them not to indicate that he is speaking to the audience, but for emphasis and as a mark of courtesy towards that audience (cf. p. 284).

These conventions are very similar to those at work in

classical Greek (cf. Dickey 1996: 193–4) and may not seem obviously different from English practice. In some situations addresses are almost obligatory in English: formal speeches normally begin with an address to the audience (e.g. 'ladies and gentlemen'), letters almost always begin with an address to the recipient (e.g. 'Dear Aunt Sarah'), and introductions usually require an address to each of the parties being introduced (e.g. 'Barbara, I'd like you to meet John Smith. John, this is Barbara Owen'). Yet in modern English this need for addresses is largely restricted to certain contexts. Formal speeches may begin with an address, but it is most unusual for 'ladies and gentlemen' to be repeated at intervals throughout a speech like Cicero's *patres conscripti*. Similarly, although letters almost always begin with an address, they rarely contain further addresses within their texts. And if John Smith, having been introduced to Barbara Owen, proceeds to address her as 'Barbara' repeatedly in the course of their conversation, he will label himself as belonging to a particular subgroup of English speakers and may succeed in alienating his interlocutor, depending on the group to which she herself belongs.

The compulsion towards the use of addresses seems in general to have been much stronger in Latin than it is in contemporary English, although in a few specific contexts (such as the beginnings of letters) English speakers are more likely than Latin speakers to use addresses. The area of the address system in which this difference is most notable is that of unnamed addressees. In modern English there is rarely a social necessity to address people whose names are unknown, though on occasion, if one needs to get the attention of a stranger, there may be a practical necessity for such an address. As a result, unknown people are addressed with descriptive terms only in order to identify them and get their attention: 'you there in the red shirt' can be the functional equivalent of Martial's *piscator* or Plautus' *chlamydate*, but not of Accius' *mortalis*. Moreover, it cannot be the social equivalent of any of these Latin phrases, because descriptive addresses in modern English tend to sound impolite, while in Latin they are normally courteous or neutral in tone (barring a few exceptions like *leno* 'brothel-keeper').

One occasion on which the use of addresses to strangers is

sanctioned by the rules of English usage is in polite speech to
an identified addressee with whom the speaker has specific,
limited business (such as asking directions, collecting a fare,
etc.). Under such circumstances, though they are far from
obligatory, terms of respect or affection such as 'sir', 'dear',
or 'love' (depending on the setting and the region in which the
interaction takes place) can be used. The apparent rudeness of
descriptive addresses can also lead to the use of these polite
terms to get the attention of an addressee, as 'Sir! You dropped
your wallet!' shouted in a crowded railway station where 'you
with the red hair' might actually be a more efficient means of
identification. When a descriptive address is unavoidable, as for
a photographer arranging subjects for a group picture, specifically polite words may be introduced into it, as 'gentleman in
the blue jacket'. This tendency to give strangers addresses
which are especially polite when used to known addressees is
found in many modern languages, but it is largely absent from
classical Latin (see pp. 255–6 for exceptions), as from classical
Greek (cf. Dickey 1996: 257–8).

In most circumstances, however, addresses to strangers are
not socially necessary in English, whereas in Latin they are.
Two English-speaking men meeting for the first time are much
more likely to say 'Hi, I'm Bob Jones.' 'I'm Jim Morris.
Pleased to meet you', than they are to say 'Hi, soldier (or
'old man', 'young man', 'human being', 'jeans-wearer', 'whoever you are', etc.), I'm Bob Jones'. When two Romans met for
the first time, they could of course ask each other's names, but
they would very often use an address to do so, as *adulescens,
quaeso hercle eloquere tuom mihi nomen, nisi piget* 'young man,
please by Hercules tell me your name, if you don't mind' (Pl.
Men. 1066), or *quis tu es, mulier, quae me insueto nuncupasti
nomine?* 'who are you, woman, who called me by an unfamiliar
name?' (Pac. *trag.* 239), or *quod, virgo, tibi nomenque genusque,
quae sors ista, doce* 'instruct me, girl, what your name and
family is, and what this fate of yours' (V. Fl. 2. 468–9).

Sometimes the request for the name almost becomes an
address in itself. Thus we find *o qui vocare* 'O how are you
addressed' (Ter. *Ad.* 891) used as if it were a vocative. A
similar type of address can be made out of the fact that a
character is nameless; phrases such as *quisquis es* 'whoever you

are' are not strictly speaking vocatives, but they can be used as if they were.[6] Thus we find statements like Pallas' greeting to Aeneas:

> 'egredere o quicumque es' ait 'coramque parentem
> adloquere ac nostris succede penatibus hospes.'
>
> (Verg. *A*. 8. 122–3)

'disembark,' he said, 'O whoever you are, and speak to my father face to face and enter our house as a guest.'

The most common such phrase is *quisquis es*, but many others occur, such as *quidquid est nomen tibi* 'whatever your name is' (Pl. *Ps*. 639) and *quaecumque es* 'whoever you (f.) are' (Stat. *Theb*. 5. 20). The fact that addresses of this type are often used in the context of polite greetings shows that they have none of the dismissive connotations their English equivalents might lead us to expect. Such addresses seem to be acceptable in polite language in Latin partly because the use of addresses is so much more important for polite speech in Latin than it is in English, and therefore there is a greater need for them.

An additional complication is the choice of characteristics on which descriptions are based. In English, on the rare occasions when descriptive addresses are used to strangers, they are usually formed from aspects of physical appearance, but in Latin this obvious route is rarely taken; addresses such as *chlamydate* are the exception rather than the rule. In Latin, the selection of characteristics for use in address seems to have been governed partly by address rules and partly by the authors' needs for clarity. When an author was addressing a person who could only be usefully identified by one feature, that feature would form the address, as in the examples of *piscator*, *marite*, *lector*, etc. quoted above. In this category also fall the standard use of *praeco* 'herald' and *lictor* 'lictor' to give orders to heralds and lictors, who are normally nameless in Roman literature,[7] and the ubiquitous use of *puer* for nameless slaves.[8]

---

[6] Cf. Ferger's (1889: 12) classification of *quisquis es* as the *vocativus anonymus*.

[7] e.g. Liv. 1. 26. 11, 24. 8. 20, 26. 16. 3; Sen. *Con*. 9. 2. 3; Pl. *Poen*. 11.

[8] e.g. Pl. *As*. 891, *Mer*. 930; Ter. *An*. 84, *Ph*. 152; Cic. *De Orat*. 2. 247;

In other cases, when the address is used because of the sociolinguistic need for an address rather than in order to make the situation clear to an audience, most Roman authors seem to follow a rough hierarchy of features usable for descriptive addresses. At the top of this hierarchy are age and gender. Unknown boys are normally addressed as *puer*, young men as *adulescens* 'young person' or (less often) *iuvenis* 'young man', and old men as *senex* 'old man'.[9] Unnamed women are normally called *mulier* 'woman',[10] while young women may also be called *virgo* or *puella*.[11] Next in order of usefulness comes the division between slaves and free men: slaves of either gender are often addressed by their age and gender as if they were free, but unknown male slaves may also be called *puer*.[12] Other characteristics may be used instead of these, but the terms just listed are (at least for strangers who can be described with one of them) significantly more common than other addresses.

Given this pattern, one would expect mature men to be addressed as *vir* 'man', but such address is very rare. In comedy, women frequently address unknown men with *mi homo* 'my human being';[13] that this address is exclusively male and viewed as contrasting with *mulier* is shown by the address *mi homo et mea mulier* spoken by one Plautine woman (*Cist.* 723; cf. p. 189). In addition, the address *adulescens* seems to be used more broadly of unknown men than for those who can be addressed by name; it can be used to men who are not

---

Hor. *Carm.* 1. 38. 1, 3. 14. 17; Prop. 3. 23. 23; [Tib.] 3. 6. 62; Ov. *Tr.* 5. 5. 11; Pers. 5. 126, 6. 69; Stat. *Silv.* 1. 5. 10; Mart. 4. 10. 3, 11. 11. 1; Apul. *Met.* 9. 33, 10. 16. Cf. pp. 194–5.

[9] e.g. *puer*: Verg. *Ecl.* 4. 18; Ov. *Met.* 3. 454; Sen. *Con.* 9. 5. 5; *adulescens*: Pl. *Mil.* 1297; Ter. *Hec.* 803; Liv. 29. 1. 8; *iuvenis*: Ov. *Met.* 6. 331; Quint. *Decl.* 306. 8; Apul. *Met.* 2. 23; *senex*: Pl. *Mos.* 940, *Trin.* 871; Ter. *An.* 788.

[10] e.g. Pl. *Men.* 710; Ter. *An.* 742; Pac. *trag.* 239; Sen. *Con.* 2. 4. 6; Quint. *Decl.* 388. 22.

[11] e.g. Pl. *Cur.* 487, *Rud.* 1148; Ov. *Met.* 13. 917; V. Fl. 2. 468; Sen. *Con.* 1. 2. 3; Mart. 11. 16. 8.

[12] e.g. *adulescens*: Pl. *Cist.* 731, *Men.* 1021, *Rud.* 941; *senex*: Sen. *Con.* 10. 5. 7; *mulier*: Pl. *Cist.* 704, 747; Quint. *Decl.* 338. 31; *puer(e)*: Pl. *Mos.* 947, 949, 965.

[13] e.g. Pl. *Per.* 620, *Epid.* 640; Ter. *Ph.* 1005.

otherwise characterized as especially young, and so it fills part of the gap left by the lack of *vir*.[14]

Outside comedy adult male strangers are most often addressed with a term describing not their age and gender, but their status as strangers. We have already seen the use of *quisquis es* and similar phrases as addresses, and the address *hospes* 'guest, foreigner' is also fairly frequent in such circumstances. *Hospes* is probably friendlier than most other addresses used to strangers, but its use does not imply that the speaker intends to offer the addressee any hospitality.[15] *Hospes* is used exclusively for men, and there is no feminine equivalent of it; phrases like *quisquis es* can be used for either gender but are much more common for men than for women.

In terms of the address system, then, the most important aspect of a stranger who is not an adult man is usually his or her deviation from the state of adult maleness, while the most important feature of an adult male stranger is usually that he is a stranger. If, however, a particular individual has some other feature that is more striking or more relevant in context, that feature can be used to form an address instead.

In addition to the addresses we have so far examined, there are a few terms which are favoured for showing particular politeness to unknown or nameless Romans. There seem to be more such terms for women than for men, perhaps because the standard address for unknown women, *mulier*, is often derogatory when used to known women and would therefore have sounded less polite than the descriptive addresses used to men. Older women can be called *mater* 'mother';[16] *erilis* 'related to a master', *parens* 'parent', and *regina* 'queen' also occur as respectful addresses to unknown women.[17] On a number of occasions strange women are addressed as *dea* 'goddess' or *diva* 'goddess', when the speaker assumes (or pretends to assume) that they are goddesses in disguise;[18] it is

[14] e.g. Pl. *Men.* 285, 498, *Trin.* 871, *Per.* 579, *Ps.* 615, 1141, *Rud.* 1303.

[15] e.g. Cic. *Brut.* 172; Prop. 4. 1. 1; Ov. *Met.* 2. 695, 4. 639; Liv. 1. 45. 6.

[16] e.g. Pl. *Rud.* 263; Ov. *Fast.* 4. 513. *Pater* is also usable for strange men but is less consistently polite (e.g. Pl. *Mos.* 952, *Rud.* 103, *Trin.* 878); cf. p. 121.

[17] Apul. *Met.* 4. 27, 4. 26; V. Fl. 5. 385.

[18] e.g. Verg. *A.* 1. 328 (echoing Homer, *Od.* 6. 149); Stat. *Theb.* 4. 753.

probable that such addresses were not used outside literature. On the other hand, *domine* 'master', as an address for men whose names the speaker has forgotten, is not directly represented in literary sources but seems to have existed outside them (cf. p. 88).

Addresses between Relatives

iam dominum appellat, iam nomina sanguinis odit:
Byblida iam mavult quam se vocet ille sororem.

(Ov. *Met.* 9. 466–7)

Now she calls him 'master', now she hates kinship terms,
now she prefers him to call her 'Byblis' rather than
'sister'.

I N this passage Ovid describes how the girl Byblis, who
developed an incestuous passion for her brother, began by
her use of address to reveal her feelings even before she herself
was fully aware of them. Byblis tries to move away from
specifically familial addresses, thus providing us with important clues to how sisters were normally addressed. In this
chapter we shall examine the way Romans addressed their
siblings and other people who were related to them by blood
or marriage (except spouses, who are discussed in Chapter 11).[1]
   We can begin with addresses to siblings. Ovid suggests that
in such contexts both names and kinship terms were possible,
and other evidence corroborates this view. One of the best
documented fraternal relationships is that between Marcus
Tullius Cicero and his brother Quintus Tullius Cicero,
whom Cicero often refers to as *Quintus frater* 'brother Quintus'. The address *Quinte frater* is also found in Cicero's works,
but other forms of address from Cicero to Quintus are much
more common.
   Cicero's letters to his brother provide a range of different

---

[1] For general information on the familial structure underlying these
address terms, see Treggiari (1991), Bannon (1997), Rawson and Weaver
(1997), Dixon (1988, 1992), Hallett (1984), Bettini (1986: 13–123), Kertzer
and Saller (1991), Bradley (1991), Rawson (1991), and Saller (1994). Harrod
(1909) provides much interesting information on the way relatives are
described in sepulchral inscriptions; his findings do not entirely match
mine (see p. 130).

addresses, and a certain pattern emerges. Although the headings of these letters invariably refer to Quintus as *Q. fratri*, the vocative *Quinte frater* never occurs in a letter. The most common address is *mi frater* 'my brother' alone, which occurs fifteen times;[2] combinations of *mi frater* with affectionate superlatives occur eight times.[3] On one occasion only is Quintus' name used, in *mi Quinte* (*Q. fr.* 2. 15. 2), but the one example of a letter from Quintus to Marcus Cicero containing an address uses *mi Marce* (*Fam.* 16. 16. 1).

In the letters, then, *frater* is much more common than names, and the combination of *frater* with a name is unknown. A different picture emerges from Cicero's other works. *De Legibus*, for example, is a dialogue among Cicero, Quintus, and their friend Atticus. In it, Cicero's addresses to Quintus make much more use of names than do those in the letters; *Quinte* occurs fifteen times,[4] *Quinte frater* once (3. 26), *frater* once (3. 26), and *optume et dulcissume frater* 'best and sweetest brother' once (3. 25). Quintus on the other hand never uses names to address his brother, only *frater* alone (thirteen times);[5] this difference is caused by the fact that Cicero avoids putting his own name into the mouths of characters in his dialogues, whether as an address or as a form of reference.[6]

De Divinatione, the other dialogue containing fraternal addresses, presents a very similar pattern. Quintus never addresses his brother in this work, but Cicero addresses Quintus eight times, seven times as *Quinte*[7] and once as *Quinte frater* (2. 150).

The difference between the addresses in the letters and those in the dialogues is striking. It is possible that it could be due to a difference in date; the letters range in date from 60 to 54 BC,

---

[2] *Q. fr.* 1. 3. 1 (*tris*), 1. 3. 10, 1. 4. 1, 2. 3. 7 (*bis*), 2. 5. 5, 2. 6. 3, 2. 6. 4, 2. 15. 1, 2. 16. 5, 3. 1. 25, 3. 5. 4, 3. 7. 4.

[3] *Q. fr.* 2. 6. 4, 2. 7. 2, 2. 15. 2, 3. 4. 6, 3. 5. 4, 3. 5. 9, 3. 6. 6, 3. 7. 9.

[4] 1. 5, 12, 18, 57, 58, 2. 7, 9, 12, 18, 43, 3. 12, 17, 23, 33, 39.

[5] 1. 5, 18, 52, 56, 2. 8, 11, 17, 43, 69, 3. 12, 19, 28, 34.

[6] Dickey (1997a). Shackleton Bailey (1996: 11) suggests that the difference results from a feeling that a younger brother should not use the praenomen to the elder one. There is, however, no other evidence for such a restriction of the praenomen, and Quintus' use of Marcus Cicero's praenomen in address at *Fam.* 16. 16. 1 is strong evidence against it.

[7] 1. 10, 11, 2. 8, 13, 100, 101, 136.

but the dialogues were probably written later, perhaps only a short time before Cicero's death in 43. On the other hand, if Cicero's custom of addressing his brother as *mi frater* had remained stable over the fifteen years represented by the letters, it is unlikely that he would have changed to *Quinte* less than ten years later. It seems more plausible that the difference in genre is responsible for the shift. The dialogues are supposed to represent informal conversations, but they are nevertheless literary works, designed for publication in a way that Cicero's letters are not and thus intended to be intelligible to a wider public. This requirement of intelligibility includes a need to make it clear who is speaking to whom. One of the reasons to include vocatives in dialogues at all is to provide a reminder of who the characters are and which one is currently speaking, and for that purpose *frater* is not a very useful vocative, since it could be used by and to either brother; there would thus have been an incentive to replace it with names. It is therefore likely that Cicero in conversational usage followed the practice he used in the letters, rather than that of the dialogues, and addressed his brother as (*mi*) *frater*[8] more often than as (*mi*) *Quinte*.

In two works the address *Quinte frater*, which is rare in these dialogues and does not occur in the letters, plays a more prominent role. The only address to Quintus in Cicero's speeches occurs in the *Pro Milone*, where Cicero brings his family's debt to Milo into his argument:

Quid respondebo liberis meis qui te [i.e. Milonem] parentem alterum putant? quid tibi, Quinte frater, qui nunc abes, consorti mecum temporum illorum? (102).

What shall I reply to my children, who think of you [Milo] as a second father? What shall I say to you, brother Quintus, who shared that time with me, though now you are absent?

This address is clearly not aimed at Quintus; as Cicero tells us, his brother is not even present. It is aimed at the jurors and at future readers of the published version of the speech, for whose sake the addressee needs to be explicitly identified. Since Cicero had only one brother, *frater* might in theory have

---

[8] For the extent to which *mi* would have been used outside the epistolary genre, see Ch. 7.

been identification enough, but he could probably not rely on the audience's having detailed knowledge of his family.

De Oratore makes more extensive use of the address *Quinte frater*. Quintus is not a character in this dialogue, but rather the dedicatee. The normal way of indicating a dedication in the ancient world was to include an address to the dedicatee at the beginning of the work; often this address was repeated at the beginning of each book, and sometimes it was reiterated within books as well. In this case there are seven addresses to the dedicatee, one at the start of each book and the rest scattered within the books. The three addresses at the start of books all use the same vocative: *Quinte frater* (1. 1, 2. 1, 3. 1). Those within books are more varied, using (*mi*) *frater* (1. 4, 23), *carissime frater atque optime* 'dearest and best brother' (2. 10), and *Quinte frater* (3. 13). The books of *De Oratore* are long, and these addresses within books usually occur within the first 5% of each book. There is thus a relatively short gap between the addresses at the beginnings of books and the ones within books, but a much larger gap between these addresses and those at the beginnings of the subsequent books.

It looks as though Cicero deliberately uses *Quinte frater* for the more obligatory dedicatory vocatives at the start of each book in an effort to make it clear who the dedicatee is. Since a dedication is meant to be an honour, it is important that the dedicatee's name be expressed in a fashion that unambiguously identifies him or her, and in both Latin and Greek this is sometimes done at the expense of adherence to the normal rules of address. Cicero thus employs *Quinte frater* where necessary: at the beginning of each book it has been a long time since he last addressed his brother, and the reader might well need reminding. But when Cicero provides another vocative shortly thereafter, he is free to use something aimed more at Quintus himself and less at the reader, who can be expected to remember the dedicatee's identity for a page or two.[9] Hence

[9] A similar pattern of difference between initial dedicatory vocatives and subsequent ones can be seen in some other authors. The dedicatee of the *Ad Herennium* is first called *C. Herenni* (1. 1) and later *Herenni* (4. 69), and Scribonius Largus addresses his dedicatee first as *Cai Iuli Calliste* (*pr.*) and then as *mi Calliste* (271). Columella tends to use *Publi Silvine* at the start of books (e.g. 1 *pr.* 2, 2. 1. 1, 3. 1. 1) and *Silvine* within them (e.g. 2. 2. 1, 3. 3. 14,

the use of vocatives much closer to those in the letters; this again suggests that the avoidance of *frater* in the other dialogues was due more to issues of clarity than to any concerns about register.

It thus seems that Cicero's normal way of addressing his brother in private was to use *frater*, often combined with an affectionate adjective, or (less often) to use the praenomen. *Quinte frater* was an artificial construct employed primarily to identify the addressee to a third party, and considerations of clarity often led to the use of *Quinte* more than *frater* in literary works.

Evidence from other sources largely confirms this picture of fraternal address and suggests that it applies not only to addresses between two brothers, but also to those to or from sisters. In prose authors, addresses to siblings often use *frater* or *soror* 'sister',[10] but names also occur,[11] and literary dedications to brothers use either names alone or, once, a name combined with *frater*.[12] The fact that this combination is so rare outside Cicero's works and used in prose only for dedications supports our theory that it is an artificial construction.

3. 7. 1), but the tendency is by no means absolute (e.g. 3. 8. 1, 9. 16. 2, 10. 1. 1). Seneca's dedicatory addresses suggest that for him the difference may not be based simply on clarity, for he has a tendency to use terms such as *Lucili virorum optime* (*Nat.* 1 *pr.* 1, 3 *pr.* 1, 4 *pr.* 1, 6. 1. 1), *Liberalis virorum optime* (*Cl.* 2. 1. 1, 6. 1. 1), and *Nero Caesar* (*Ben.* 1. 1. 1, 2. 1. 1) at the start of books, alternating with addresses such as *Lucili* (*Nat.* 2. 59. 6, 4 *pr.* 3, 6. 32. 9, etc.), *Liberalis* (*Cl.* 2. 6. 1, 6. 6. 1, etc.), and *Caesar* (*Ben.* 1. 1. 5, 1. 11. 2, 2. 2. 1) within books. Seneca could be making a distinction of formality between initial and subsequent dedicatory vocatives, and such a distinction could be related to the tendency in Cicero's speeches for an addressee to receive double names the first time he is addressed and single names later (see pp. 51–2). Yet for other authors formality seems a less plausible explanation than clarity, and in any case it is common, when the dedicatee is addressed by a single name which provides adequate identification in itself, for the same address to be used to dedicatees throughout a work (e.g. *Brute* in Cic. *Tusc.*, *Fin.*, *Orat.*; *Marcia* in Sen. *Dial.* 6).

[10] e.g. *frater*: Liv. 2. 46. 6, 40. 9. 8; Sal. *Jug.* 14. 22; Sen. *Con.* 6. 1, 7. 5. 2; Quint. *Decl.* 287. 4; [Quint.] *Decl.* 5. 21; *ILS* 2793; *soror*: Cic. *Cael.* 36; Sen. *Con.* 7. 6. 2; Apul. *Met.* 5. 16.

[11] To brothers: only Liv. 37. 7. 8, 40. 12. 9, 40. 15. 2. To sisters: only Apul. *Met.* 5. 14 (perhaps for clarity, as there are three sisters involved).

[12] Sen. *Dial.* 3. 1. 1, 4. 1. 1, 5. 1. 1, 5. 39. 1, 7. 1. 1.

There is some evidence for the use of *puer* 'boy' for a very young brother in the declamations (Sen. *Con.* 7. 5. 1, 2), and at a later period *domine* 'master' was probably used to address brothers. It is notable that whereas the name used by Cicero to address his brother is always the praenomen, Seneca consistently uses the cognomen. The difference is probably due to the new imperial custom of giving sons individual cognomina (see p. 48); Cicero could not easily use his brother's cognomen in a dedication, as it was the same as his own (cf. Salomies 1987: 255). It is unclear whether Seneca and other men of his age would have used cognomina to address their brothers in private conversation as well as in dedications, or whether they in fact retained the intimate use of the praenomen when alone.

In comedy, the situation is somewhat different. Plautus normally uses (*mi*) *frater* or (*mea*) *soror* between siblings,[13] but Terence (who depicts such addresses only between brothers) normally uses names.[14] The difference between Plautus and Terence, as we shall see, is part of a larger pattern which has several possible explanations. It is possible that the use of names is less common when a female is involved than in addresses between brothers, but this point cannot be established with certainty because of the lack of sisters in Terence. In early Latin *germane/a* 'sibling' may also be used as a kinship term (though not alone as a self-standing address), and it looks as though both *frater* and *germane* may be seen by Terence as emotive addresses.[15] Thus in the *Adelphoe* the two older brothers, who are not overflowing with love for one another, always address each other by name, while the two younger ones, who have a much closer relationship, use names most of the time and *frater* or *germane* in moments of happy affection. Similarly in the *Phormio*, *frater* is used for the one fraternal address which occurs at a genuinely happy moment, and names are used for the others. Affectionate adjectives are less common

[13] *Frater*: 18 times, e.g. *Aul.* 120, *Cur.* 658, *Men.* 1154, *St.* 531; *soror*: 46 times, e.g. *Aul.* 141, *Cur.* 657, *Bac.* 101, *Poen.* 300, *St.* 147; name (between two brothers) at *St.* 528; *germane* at *Men.* 1125; *germana* at *Poen.* 329.

[14] Names: 32 times, e.g. *Ph.* 567, 577, *Ad.* 60, 80; *frater* at *Eu.* 1051, *Ph.* 895, *Ad.* 256; *germane* at *Ad.* 269.

[15] On the meaning of *germanus*, cf. Del Rio (1939) and Meyer (1929).

in comedy than in Cicero's addresses to his brother, but they do occur (e.g. Pl. *Men.* 1132).

In classical and post-classical poetry siblings usually address each other with *frater*, *soror*, or *germane/a*, often as part of larger and more complex phrases involving insults or expressions of praise; names are less frequently used, and other addresses (mostly expressions of praise or blame) occur occasionally.[16]

Thus, except for Terence (whose evidence will be discussed below), Latin authors appear largely to agree on the use of addresses to siblings. Sisters and brothers normally address each other with the kinship terms *frater* and *soror*, but names are possible as well, as is *germane* in poetry. We can conclude from this that in ordinary conversation both names and *frater/soror* were possible, but the latter were probably more common; in some circumstances they may also have been more affectionate. Endearments, insults, and other emotive addresses are also possible. It does not look as though the ages of the siblings affect address usage, but one cannot be certain, since most of the speakers and addressees are adults or young adults.

Another common type of familial address is that from parents to children. Here again Cicero provides some of the most important evidence. Cicero only once addresses his children individually in a letter,[17] and there he says *mea carissima filiola et spes reliqua nostra, Cicero* 'my dearest little daughter and Cicero, our remaining hope' (*Fam.* 14. 4. 6). Even without other letters, the distinction between an address by name to the

---

[16] e.g. *frater*: Catul. 68. 21, 101. 2; Verg. *A.* 12. 883; Ov. *Fast.* 4. 852; Sen. *Thy.* 521; Sil. 15. 749; Stat. *Theb.* 11. 364; Mart. 1. 36. 6; V. Fl. 2. 602; *ILS* 1046a; *soror*: Verg. *A.* 4. 47, 12. 676; Sil. 8. 168; Stat. *Theb.* 8. 627; V. Fl. 6. 483, 8. 277; *germane*: Ov. *Met.* 5. 13; Sen. *Ag.* 914, *Thy.* 970; *Ilias* 273; Luc. 9. 123; Sil. 5. 372; Stat. *Theb.* 1. 223, 11. 367, 11. 548; *germana*: Verg. *A.* 4. 478, 12. 679; Ov. *Met.* 6. 613, 9. 382; Sil. 8. 181, 17. 348; Stat. *Theb.* 9. 650, 11. 76; V. Fl. 8. 271; names: Verg. *A.* 4. 9, 12. 872; Ov. *Met.* 9. 149, *Ep.* 7. 191; Sen. *Ag.* 917; *Thy.* 513; Sil. 4. 823, 9. 112, 17. 261; other: Verg. *A.* 4. 492; Sen. *Ag.* 910; Sil. 8. 169; Stat. *Theb.* 11. 372.

[17] Cicero's daughter Tullia and his wife Terentia are sometimes addressed together with *animae meae* (*Fam.* 14. 18. 1) or *meae carissimae animae* (*Fam.* 14. 14. 2).

son and a kinship term to the daughter is probably worth taking seriously, for the same distinction is found in Propertius. There a mother is depicted addressing her two sons as *tu, Lepide, et tu, Paulle* 'you, Lepidus, and you, Paullus' (4. 11. 63) and then turning to her daughter with *filia* 'daughter' (67). Cicero was not averse to using his daughter's name, and in the heading of this letter she is included as *Tulliolae*, but address seems to have posed special difficulties.

The majority of Cicero's addresses to his son Marcus Tullius Cicero come from *De Officiis*, a philosophical treatise dedicated to the younger Cicero. *De Officiis* contains twelve addresses to the dedicatee, six in the form *Marce fili* 'son Marcus' and six in the form *mi Cicero*. The address at the very beginning of each book is always *Marce fili* (1. 1, 2. 1, 3. 1); in each case there is also another address a few paragraphs later, and that one is always *mi Cicero* (1. 3, 2. 8, 3. 5). At the very end of the work, the conclusion is indicated by another pair of addresses, again *Marce fili* followed almost immediately by *mi Cicero* (3. 121). Vocatives within the various books can appear in either form (1. 15, 1. 78, 2. 44, 3. 33).

This pattern bears a striking resemblance to the alternation between *Quinte frater* and *frater* to the dedicatee of *De Oratore*. As a result, if *Quinte frater* is an artificial construct and *frater* is Cicero's habitual address to his brother, it is likely that *Marce fili* is also artificial and that *Cicero* is the address the orator normally used to his son. The need for clear identification of the dedicatee was if anything more important in the case of Cicero's son than in that of his brother, for Cicero's son was less well known, being only 21 and a student at the time of the *De Officiis*.

There is also a dialogue in which Cicero and his son are both characters, *Partitiones Oratoriae*; in this work Cicero always calls his son *mi Cicero* (1, 140). This address does not aid clarity, since Cicero is a name shared by both interlocutors while *fili* is applicable only to one of them; as a result, these addresses are more likely to reflect Cicero's conversational usage than are the examples of *Quinte* in *De Legibus* and *De Divinatione*.

It thus looks as though Cicero normally addressed his son as (*mi*) *Cicero*; the fact that the *mi* is always attached to this address in non-epistolary contexts, whereas it is virtually never attached to *Quinte*, makes it likely that Cicero normally used *mi* with this address in conversation. It is striking that the name Cicero uses to his son is the cognomen rather than the prae-nomen always given to Quintus; this address would not have been practical if Cicero had had more than one son and is thus unlikely to be the way that the orator was addressed by his own parents. Cicero typically refers to his son by cognomen as well, and Adams suggests that this choice of names reflects Cicero's pride in the fact that his own rise in status had ennobled his son and allowed him admission to the ranks of people known by their cognomina.[18] The fact that the dedicatory formula is *Marce fili* rather than *Cicero fili* is another piece of evidence in favour of its artificiality and suggests that it is modelled on a standard pattern rather than being a spontaneous creation of Cicero's; this pattern can be traced back at least as far as Cato (see below).

When Cicero quotes parent–child addresses from other families, the praenomen is normally used for sons (*Publi*, *Rep.* 6. 15; *mi Spuri*, *De Orat.* 2. 249), but when the birth father of the younger Scipio Africanus urges his son to follow in the footsteps of his adoptive grandfather, he addresses his son by the cognomen of his son's adopted family, *Scipio* (*Rep.* 6. 16). Only one daughter is addressed, and she is called both *mea filia* and *mea Tertia* (*Div.* 1. 103).

If Cicero's practice is to address sons by name and daughters with *filia* or a name, other authors show a very different system. One can discount the numerous parent–child addresses in the declamations, since these are always addressed to nameless children and thus cannot use names; sons are there addressed interchangeably as *fili*, *iuvenis* 'young man', and *adulescens* 'young person', and daughters as *filia* and *puella* 'girl'.[19] We cannot, however, ignore the fact that prose authors other than Cicero normally use *fili* to named sons,[20] as well as the more expected *filia* to daughters.[21] Indeed on the one occasion that

---

[18] (1978: 159); but note the counter-arguments of Salomies (1987: 260).
[19] e.g. Quint. *Decl.* 299. 6, 315. 22, 23, 25; [Quint.] *Decl.* 10. 7, 12, 13, 19.
[20] *Fili* at Liv. 23. 9. 1, 24. 44. 10; V. Max. 2. 2. 4, 7. 2. ext. 10; Gel. 13. 4. 2. Names at Sal. *Jug.* 10. 1, 7, 8 (perhaps for clarity, as there are three sons).
[21] Liv. 3. 48. 5; Sen. *Dial.* 6. 22. 6, 6. 26. 2. The latter, spoken by the

Livy depicts a parent addressing a son by name, that address is surely meant to emphasize the uniqueness of the situation: the consul Manlius, condemning his victorious son to death for disobeying military orders, uses both his names and calls him *T. Manli* (8. 7. 15). The formality of this address stresses the fact that the father is acting not as father but as consul.

Equivalents of Cicero's *Marce fili* can be found in the elder Seneca, who calls a dedicatee *Mela, fili carissime* 'dearest son Mela' (*Con.* 2 *pr.* 3) and quotes Cato as addressing his son with *Marce fili* (*Con.* 1 *pr.* 9); the address *Lagge fili* is also to be found on a funerary inscription (*ILS* 8147), and *fili Gerio* occurs in a comic dialogue preserved on a late mosaic (Daviault *et al.* 1987: 56). Cato himself used the vocative *Marce fili* in dedicating works to his son.[22] The combination of name and *fili* in these addresses is likely to be artificial, but the shift between praenomen in Cato's address to cognomen in Seneca's is probably authentic and reflects the rise of individual cognomina just as does the equivalent change in dedications to brothers (cf. Salomies 1987: 257–9).

Fili is rarely found in any type of poetry;[23] the standard kinship terms for addressing sons and daughters in comedy and later poetry are (*g*)*nate* 'son' and (*g*)*nata* 'daughter', though *filia* is also used. In Plautus, daughters normally receive kinship terms and are never addressed by name, while sons are usually called *gnate* but may also receive names;[24] *mi* is common with the kinship terms but never used with the names. There does not seem to be any difference in tone between names and *gnate* (cf. *As.* 830 and 833), nor between *gnata* and *filia* for girls. In Terence, on the other hand, both sons and daughters are addressed by name more often than with kinship terms,[25] and there is some evidence for

dedicatee's father, contrast with the *Marcia* which Seneca himself uses to her (6. 1. 1 *et passim*).

[22] *Libri ad Marcum filium*, frag. 1, 6, 14 (Jordan 1860: 77, 78, 80).

[23] Cf. p. 113; exceptions include Catul. 33. 2, 37. 18; Andr. frag. 2; Pomponius (emended to *filia* in Courtney 1993: 109); Phaed. *Fabulae Novae* 5. 5.

[24] *Gnata*: *Men.* 834, *Per.* 740, *Rud.* 1179, *Trin.* 1, etc.; *filia*: *Men.* 822, 844, *Rud.* 742, 1173; *gnate*: *As.* 830, *Aul.* 694, *Capt.* 1021, *Mer.* 367, *Trin.* 281, etc.; names: *As.* 833, *Mer.* 963, 1010.

[25] *Gnata*: *Hec.* 318; *gnate*: *Hec.* 352, 456, 577, 605, 606, *Hau.* 843, 1028,

a difference in tone between the two types of address. The two
uses of names to a daughter may be explicable by the fact that
her father is angry at her (*Hec.* 243, 623), and in three dyads a
change between the two forms of address to sons may suggest
that *gnate* expresses greater closeness than a name;[26] this
added closeness might explain why mothers use *gnate* proportionately more often than do fathers in Terence. As in
Plautus, *gnate* and *gnata* are usually accompanied by *mi* or *mea*
in Terence; there are also two instances of a mother using *mi*
with a name. Occasionally in comedy a son is called *puer* 'boy'
or a daughter *mulier* 'woman', apparently as a less affectionate
alternative to the standard addresses (Ter. *Ad.* 940; Pl. *Men.*
802).

Terence's divergence from Plautus in his use of names to
sons and daughters, and his tendency to make a distinction in
meaning between address by name and address by kinship
term, must be related to the parallel developments he exhibits
in address to brothers. In the case of address to sons, the
simplest explanation is that Terence is reflecting the development of the Latin address system of his day, revealing one step
in the chronological progression from Plautus to Cicero. Yet in
the case of daughters, and in that of brothers, there is no other
evidence that such a chronological progression in fact occurred.
Perhaps it did occur, and then kinship terms came back into
fashion before the classical period. It could also be that
Terence's use of names was influenced by his Greek models,
for Menander uses names regularly to brothers, frequently to
sons, and on occasion to daughters (Dickey 1996: 220, 227).

In other types of poetry, the standard address is *nate/nata*,
but names are not infrequent, both for sons and for daughters.[27] When sons have Roman names, both praenomina and

1060, 1065; names: *Hau.* 105, 209, 1057, *Hec.* 482, 585, 602, *An.* 254, *Ad.*
564, etc.

[26] *Hec.* 456 vs. 482, 484, 613, 620, 650, 671; *Hau.* 105 vs. 843; *Hau.* 1028,
1057, 1060.

[27] *Nate*: 109 examples, e.g. Verg. *A.* 8. 613, 10. 846; Ov. *Met.* 1. 769, *Ars*
2. 63; Sen. *Her. F.* 918, *Tro.* 503; Sil. 1. 109, 6. 584; *nata*: 28 examples, e.g.
Enn. *Ann.* 44; Ov. *Met.* 1. 482, 13. 521; Sen. *Tro.* 967, *Phoen.* 38; Stat. *Theb.*
3. 712, 11. 706; V. Fl. 7. 550, 8. 145; names to sons: 32 examples, e.g. Verg.
A. 9. 481, 11. 169; Ov. *Met.* 8. 204; Sen. *Ag.* 941; Luc. 3. 745; Stat. *Theb.* 9.
356; names to daughters: 10 examples, e.g. Hor. *Carm.* 3. 27. 57; [Verg.] *Ciris*

cognomina occur.[28] Daughters may also be called *filia*, and the non-kinship terms *puer* and *virgo* 'girl' (but not *puella* or *mulier*) are not uncommon in address by parents.[29] When the same parent uses more than one type of address to the same daughter, *filia*, *nata*, and names are apparently interchangeable,[30] but *virgo* sometimes seems to have a different tone from *nata* (the only address with which it is contrasted) and to emphasize the relationship less strongly.[31]

In the case of sons, little difference can be found between names and *nate*,[32] but *puer* seems on occasion to be used as a more emotional alternative. Thus Vergil's Evander uses *puer* to Pallas only at the highly emotional climax of his farewell to the youth (*A.* 8. 581), preferring names or *nate* elsewhere (8. 569, 11. 152, 169), while Seneca's Andromache normally uses *nate* to Astyanax and switches to *puer* only for the last address before she gives him up (*Tro.* 503, 556, 562, 799). Ovid uses both *nate* and *Phaethon* from the sun to Phaethon, alternating apparently for the sake of variation, but then switches to *puer* for the father's last warning to his doomed son.[33] This extra emotional force probably comes from *puer*'s emphasis on the addressee's youth; although many recipients of *puer*, such as Pallas, Menoeceus, and Aristaeus (Ov. *Fast.* 1. 367), are old

296; Ov. *Met.* 6. 503, *Fast.* 4. 483; Sen. *Tro.* 61. On the tone of *nate* see Fasce (1987).

[28] Praenomina: Hor. *S.* 2. 3. 171, 173; Luc. 9. 85 (all of these sons lack cognomina); cognomina: Prop. 4. 11. 63; [Ov.] *Epic. Drusi* 157, 162.

[29] *Filia*: Prop. 4. 11. 67; Ov. *Met.* 1. 481, *Fast.* 4. 456, 483; *puer*: 24 examples, e.g. Ov. *Fast.* 1. 367; Sen. *Tro.* 799; Stat. *Theb.* 12. 85; V. Fl. 1. 718; also to an adopted son at Ter. *Ad.* 940; *virgo*: 7 examples, e.g. Ov. *Met.* 13. 523; Sen. *Phoen.* 50; Stat. *Theb.* 10. 597, 11. 612.

[30] Cf. Ov. *Fast.* 4. 483, *Met.* 1. 481–2; [Verg.] *Ciris* 295, 296, 306.

[31] Cf. Ov. *Met.* 13. 494–5, 521, 523; Sen. *Phoen.* 2, 38, 43, 50, 94, 103, 229, 306; Stat. *Theb.* 11. 612, 706; I can detect no difference in meaning at Stat. *Theb.* 4. 546, 584, 10. 597.

[32] Cf. Verg. *A.* 9. 481, 492; Ov. *Met.* 5. 365, 366. There may be some difference at Ov. *Ars* 2. 63, 93, 94, 95, but cf. *Met.* 8. 204, 231, 232, 233.

[33] *Met.* 2. 34, 52, 54, 89, 99, 127. Cf. also Aeneas and Iulus (Verg. *A.* 11. 58, 12. 435) and Thetis and Achilles (Stat. *Ach.* 1. 252, 256, 273, 320, 340). Sometimes an alternation between *puer* and other terms seems to carry no special emotional weight: Pelias and Acastus (V. Fl. 1. 713, 718), Creon and Menoeceus (Stat. *Theb.* 10. 691, 695, 696, 11. 284, 12. 74, 85, 88), Hannibal and his father (Sil. 1. 109, 112).

enough to function as adults, the term is never applied to
Aeneas and Hercules, men who are frequently addressed by
their parents in Latin literature[34] but who are simply too old
and too competent to receive *puer*. *Nate*, on the other hand, is
used to sons of any age, from babies[35] to adults, while names
are used only to adults and children old enough to bear names.

How might the conflicting evidence of Plautus, Terence,
other poets, Cicero, and other prose writers reflect conversational usage? Cicero and Terence normally address sons by
name, Plautus and other poets prefer *(g)nate*, and other prose
writers prefer *fili*. *Nate* and *nata* seem to be strictly poetic
terms except in early Latin; the words are not common in prose
even in cases other than the vocative. Thus, while it is perfectly
possible that parents in Plautus' day normally called their sons
gnate, it is virtually certain that this was no longer the case by
the classical period. It seems most likely that the standard
address for sons changed from kinship terms to names by the
time of Cicero, and then changed back to a new kinship term,
fili, shortly afterwards. Poets would thus be using an archaic
address pattern with no basis in contemporary conversational
language. Daughters were probably addressed primarily by
kinship terms at all periods, though one of the kinship terms
used to them, *(g)nata*, went out of use in non-literary language
before the classical period.

In all types of literature it is also possible to address sons and
daughters with other terms, such as expressions of affection,
pity, or anger. Such addresses are especially common in poetry.
When parents address several children at once, names become
unwieldy; they are sometimes used to address two sons, but
never for larger groups. Prose writers tend to use *filii* or *iuvenes*
'young men' for groups of children, while poets prefer *nati* and
pueri.[36] Masculine terms, as usual in Latin, are used for groups
of mixed gender.

[34] 15 times each, always with *nate*, e.g. Verg. *A*. 2. 594, 704; Sen. *Her. F.*
622, *Her. O.* 1341.

[35] e.g. Ov. *Ep*. 11. 115; Sil. 4. 815; Stat. *Theb*. 6. 139.

[36] *Filii*: Cic. *Sen*. 79; *iuvenes*: Sen. *Suas*. 6. 16, *Con*. 1 *pr*. 6, 9, 19, 9. 3. 7;
Liv. 40. 4. 14; *nati*: Ov. *Met*. 6. 209; Sen. *Med*. 845, *Thy*. 1002; Luc. 9. 87; Sil.
8. 346; Stat. *Theb*. 3. 151; *pueri*: Hor. *S*. 2. 2. 127; Prop. 4. 11. 87; Juv. 14.
180; Sen. *Con*. 4. 6, 9. 3. 3; *liberi*: Sen. *Her. F.* 1227; *gnatae*: Ov. *Met*. 7. 346;
mulieres: Pl. *Poen*. 1251.

Addresses from children to parents are much more consistent
than those in the other direction: at all periods and in all genres
the standard address from sons or daughters of any age to their
parents is *pater* 'father' to fathers, *mater* 'mother' to mothers,
and *parentes* 'parents' to both parents.[37] In poetry (other than
comedy), *genitor* 'father', *genetrix* 'mother', and *parens* 'parent'
(used to both fathers and mothers) also occur not infrequently,
and *senex* 'old man' is occasionally used to fathers in the
declamations.[38] *Senex* is not very respectful, but I can find no
difference in meaning among the other terms.[39] At a subliterary
level, *domine* 'master' was also used to fathers, and probably
domina to mothers (see pp. 85–8). Expressions of endearment,
insult, praise, or the like may be joined to the kinship term, and
sometimes such expressions occur alone, though this is less
common for parents as addressees than for children.

On a few occasions names are used to address parents,
usually in conjunction with a kinship term. Addresses such as
Micipsa pater, which Sallust quotes a foreign envoy as deliver-
ing in the course of a speech to the Roman Senate (*Jug.* 14. 9),
and *pater Druse*, which Tacitus includes in a speech by
Germanicus to the army (*Ann.* 1. 43), seem to be formed on
the same principle as the *Quinte frater* Cicero uses under
similar circumstances: the address is not intended for the
benefit of the addressee (who is absent in the first case and
dead in the second), but for that of an audience for whom he
must be clearly identified. These addresses are not inauthentic,
in the sense that absent relatives probably were so addressed in
formal speeches when need arose. Nevertheless they do not

---

[37] *Pater*: 331 examples, e.g. Pl. *Men.* 775; Ter. *Ad.* 643; Cic. *Part.* 1, *Rep.*
6. 15; Verg. *A.* 6. 863; Hor. *Carm.* 3. 27. 34; Sen. *Phoen.* 190; Suet. *Tit.* 5. 3;
P. Mich. viii. 467. 4; *mater*: 95 examples, e.g. Pl. *As.* 507; Enn. *trag.* 38; Ter.
Hec. 355; Hor. *S.* 2. 3. 62; Ov. *Met.* 2. 361; Sen. *Con.* 8. 1; Sen. *Dial.* 12. 19. 3,
Tro. 792; *parentes*: Pl. *Rud.* 1144; Ov. *Met.* 13. 880; [Sen.] *Her. O.* 215. Cf.
Moseley (1926: 71–3); Bettini (1986: 18–26).

[38] *Genitor*: Verg. *A.* 2. 657; Ov. *Met.* 1. 486; Stat. *Silv.* 5. 3. 3, etc.; *genetrix*:
Ov. *Met.* 1. 757; Sen. *Phaed.* 115; Stat. *Theb.* 9. 891, etc.; *parens*: Verg. *A.* 5.
80; Sen. *Phoen.* 403; V. Fl. 2. 293, etc.; *senex*: Sen. *Con.* 1. 1. 8; [Quint.] *Decl.*
17. 15, 17.

[39] Cf. Verg. *A.* 2. 657, 707, 717, 3. 710, 5. 80, 6. 695, 698, 719, 863; Ov. *Ep.*
11. 101, 102; Sen. *Her. F.* 626, 638, 1189, 1192, 1245, 1269, *Oed.* 323, 328,
353, *Phoen.* 182, 190, 215; V. Fl. 2. 250, 290, 293.

show that names could be used in actual interaction with a parent. In this category also belong the *Fronto pater* and *genetrix Flaccilla* used by Martial to identify his parents (5. 34. 1), the *Cyrene mater* given by Vergil to Aristaeus (*G.* 4. 321), the *mater Scribonia* assigned by Propertius to a dead woman (4. 11. 55), the *Althaea mater* [Seneca] gives Deianira (*Her. O.* 954), the *Vorapte pater* of Valerius Flaccus' Gesander (6. 288), and the *Nise pater* of Ovid's Scylla (*Met.* 8. 126).

The combination of name and kinship term is only once used to a parent who is actually present, when Ovid's Phaethon addresses the sun as *Phoebe pater* (*Met.* 2. 36). This address is clearly intended to reflect Phaethon's uncertainty about his right to use the address *pater*. Names are also sometimes used without a kinship term, but in such cases the parent addressed is never known to be present. Sometimes this type of address is significant, as Myrrha's use of *Cinyra* to her father (Ov. *Met.* 10. 380), for whom she feels an incestuous passion that makes kinship terms as unwelcome to her as they are to Byblis in the quotation with which this chapter begins. Similarly, the use of *Magne* by a son to the dead Pompey emphasizes the father's achievements because of the honorific nature of this cognomen (Luc. 9. 157).

Other examples are not intended to carry such significance but are motivated by external circumstances, as when a rhetor composing a speech as if by a son to his father forgets to use the address that would be appropriate to the son and uses the one appropriate to an advocate instead (Sen. *Con.* 9. 1. 6, 8), when a mother giving her son a message for his father uses an address appropriate to her rather than to him (Sen. *Tro.* 805), or when a man's apostrophe to his supposedly absent father by name is dramatically necessary so that the returning father can recognize his son (Sil. 9. 111). I can find only three addresses by name to parents which cannot easily be explained in such a way.[40] It thus seems that parents were probably not addressed by name in conversational Latin, but that an absent parent could occasionally be addressed by name in speeches and literary works for clarity or dramatic effect.

[40] *Iuppiter*, [Sen.] *Her. O.* 87, 1138 (probably influenced by the language of prayer); *Aeeta*, V. Fl. 8. 11. *Marce* at *ILS* 1768 is the result of the need for identification in a funerary address.

In comedy, there is a clear alternation between *pater* and *mater* without *mi*, used for ordinary interactions, and *mi pater* and *mea mater*, used for greater emotion. This correlation between *mi* and emotion cannot be found with every type of address in comedy, but it is certainly applicable to these words. Thus in Plautus' *Stichus* two affectionate daughters greet their father with *mi pater* (90), but then back off to *pater* when he is less affectionate in return;[41] likewise in the *Trinummus*, *mi pater* is used in a recognition scene (1180) but *pater* elsewhere (e.g. 1181, 1183). In the *Aulularia* a son addresses his mother with *mater mea* at the most intense moments of his plea for help (685, 690, 692) but as *mater* the rest of the time (682, 684, 696). In Terence's *Hecyra*, Pamphilus uses *mea mater* to his mother at moments of greater emotion (353, 358) and *mater* both at such moments and elsewhere (355, 590); similarly he uses *mi pater* to greet his father at 455 but *pater* elsewhere (486, 494, 612, 655). Sometimes, as in the last example, there is a correlation between the use of *mi* to a parent and that of kinship terms to a child: Pamphilus' father addresses him as *gnate mi* at 456 but as *Pamphile* at 482, 484, 613, 620, 650, and 671.

More distant relatives are less well represented in our data, but for a number of types of relationship there is enough evidence to draw some conclusions about address. Most frequently addressed are in-laws, who figure in all major literary genres. Cicero addresses his own son-in-law as *mi Dolabella* in letters,[42] and elsewhere in prose and comedy fathers-in-law and mothers-in-law normally address their sons-in-law by name;[43] this practice is probably attributable to conversational language as well. In high-register poetry, however, *gener* 'son-in-law' is used more frequently than names.[44] The name used can be either gentilicium or cognomen; in Cicero's *De Amicitia*,

---

[41] 91, 92, 95, 97, 100, 109, 111, 115, 131, 139.

[42] *Fam.* 9. 14. 1, 4, 8 (= *Att.* 14. 17a. 1, 4, 8), *Att.* 15. 14. 2.

[43] Names: Cic. *Amic.* 8, 9, 14, 37, 100, *Leg.* 1. 1, 3; Liv. 1. 41. 3; Pl. *Men.* 809, 825, *St.* 506; Ter. *Hec.* 382, 389, 395, 456 (NB the contrast with *gnate mi* from the youth's father), 504, 635, 664; other: Pl. *Men.* 819; Tac. *Ann.* 16. 35; Fro. 176. 10.

[44] Name: Ov. *Met.* 6. 497; *gener*: Ov. *Met.* 6. 496; Stat. *Theb.* 11. 433; cf. [Sen.] *Her. O.* 1437; both: V. Fl. 7. 38.

Laelius addresses one of his sons-in-law with his cognomen, *Scaevola* (8, 14, 37), and the other (who did not have a cognomen) with his gentilicium, *Fanni* (9); he then addresses both together with praenomen and gentilicium: *C. Fanni et tu Q. Muci* (100). In another dialogue, Cicero has Atticus address his son-in-law Quintus Cicero with his praenomen *Quinte*, probably to avoid confusion with the orator, who is also present (*Leg.* 1. 1, 3). Daughters-in-law are rarely addressed, and little can be said about addresses to them except that *nurus* 'daughter-in-law' does not occur.[45]

The reverse of this relationship is somewhat more complex (as, in fact, in modern English), but it is very likely that in Latin the usual address to a father-in-law was his name. Dolabella writes to Cicero as *mi Cicero* (*Fam.* 9. 9. 1) and *mi iucundissime Cicero* 'my very delightful Cicero' (*Fam.* 9. 9. 3), and elsewhere in prose and comedy names are standard[46] except in the declamations, where the addressees are nameless and fathers-in-law receive *socer* 'father-in-law' and *pater* 'father'.[47] In high-register poetry fathers-in-law are normally addressed as *socer* (also once with *pater*); mothers-in-law receive names or *genetrix* 'mother'.[48] When names are used in prose, the cognomen is employed, or in its absence the gentilicium.

Poetic texts also provide a number of examples of address between a young man and the parents of the woman he intends to marry. In such circumstances the young man seems normally to be addressed by name and his prospective parents-in-law as *pater* and *mater*; *socer* is once used to a prospective father-in-law in a declamation.[49]

Brothers- and sisters-in-law are not well represented in prose and comedy, but when they occur, they usually address each

[45] Suet. *Tib.* 53. 1 (*filiola*); Sen. *Her. F.* 309, 439 (periphrases).
[46] Cic. *Leg.* 1. 1, *Amic.* 6, 8, 16, 32; Sen. *Dial.* 10. 1. 1; Pl. *St.* 508, 517; Ter. *Hec.* 480.
[47] Sen. *Con.* 2. 2. 3, 9, 10, 11; Quint. *Decl.* 280. 16.
[48] *Socer*: [Sen.] *Her. O.* 847; Stat. *Theb.* 3. 362, 9. 61, 11. 163, 188; *pater*: Stat. *Theb.* 11. 156; other: Stat. *Theb.* 3. 348–9; *genetrix*: Ov. *Met.* 9. 326; name: Sen. *Tro.* 969.
[49] Verg. *A.* 7. 596, 11. 410, 12. 13, 50, 56, 62, 74 (cf. Bettini 1979: 26, though I do not agree with his separation of Turnus' *mater* from his *pater*); Sen. *Con.* 2. 3. 9; V. Fl. 8. 350.

other by name.[50] In other poetry such addressees can receive names, patronymics, or any of a wide variety of expressions of affection, praise, anger, etc.[51] In a few passages, however, addresses are used which specifically acknowledge the relationship: *germane nostrae coniugis* 'sibling of our wife' from Oedipus to Creon (Sen. *Oed.* 210), *frater Amor* 'brother Amor' from Dido to Cupid (Ov. *Ep.* 7. 32).

Uncles pose a problem of definition.[52] Technically, in Latin, one's father's brother was a *patruus* 'paternal uncle', while this man's son (in our terms, one's first cousin) was a *frater patruelis* 'uncle-brother'. But the *frater* in *frater patruelis* was taken so literally that the son of one's *frater patruelis* (in our terms, one's first cousin once removed) could also refer to one as *patruus*. In Roman comedy both types of *patruus* (uncles and first cousins once removed) are addressed by their nephews with *patrue*;[53] that this was inherently an affectionate address is shown by the use of *patrue mi patruissime* 'my unclest uncle' as an endearment (Pl. *Poen.* 1197). Aunts and maternal uncles are represented only in classical and later poetry; they can be addressed by name, with various expressions of respect, or (rarely) with kinship terms such as *mater* and *matertera* 'aunt'.[54]

Nephews, nieces, and cousins are addressed by name or with terms indicating the relationship in comedy and other poetry; other types of address are also possible.[55] Grandparents are addressed with various kinship terms in poetry.[56] Grandchildren are addressed by name in prose (usually the cognomen, but once a praenomen), except for *puer* to nameless grandsons

[50] Cic. *Amic.* 25; Ter. *Ph.* 784, 813, 1011, 1014, 1024, 1031.

[51] e.g. Verg. *A.* 2. 282, 289; Ov. *Met.* 6. 539; Sen. *Tro.* 951; Stat. *Theb.* 3. 380, 11. 678.

[52] On uncles see further Guastella (1980); Saller (1997); Bettini (1986: 27–76).

[53] e.g. Pl. *Poen.* 1155, 1278, 1419; Ter. *Ph.* 254, 263, 270.

[54] e.g. Ov. *Met.* 3. 719–20; Stat. *Theb.* 11. 709, 737; V. Fl. 7. 217, 242, 248, 347. See Bettini (1979: 25–36, 1986: 77–117).

[55] Names: e.g. Pl. *Poen.* 1076; Ter. *Ph.* 154, 163, 173, 257; V. Fl. 1. 164; *fratris mei gnate*: Pl. *Poen.* 1196; *o mihi de fratris longe gratissime natis*: Ov. *Met.* 12. 586; *nata*: V. Fl. 7. 229; *soror*: Ov. *Met.* 1. 351; other: Pl. *Poen.* 1356; Cic. *Div.* 1. 104; Stat. *Theb.* 11. 270; V. Fl. 1. 175, etc.

[56] *Cognata* (Enn. *Ann.* 59), *genetrix patris nostri* (Enn. *Ann.* 58), *genitor* (Sen. *Med.* 33). Cf. also *Africane*, Cic. *Rep.* 6. 26.

in the declamations; in poetry they receive a variety of terms, including names and *nepos* 'grandson'.[57] Stepmothers receive various kinship terms,[58] and stepsons are addressed by name or with other terms.[59] This evidence is not sufficient to allow us to determine how such relatives were normally addressed.

[57] Cic. *Rep.* 6. 10, 12, 13; Sen. *Con.* 2. 4. 1, 9. 5. 1; Suet. *Cal.* 8. 4; Gel. 15. 7. 3; Enn. *Ann.* 60; Ov. *Fast.* 1. 521; [Sen.] *Her. O.* 1427–8; Stat. *Theb.* 5. 278, 279.

[58] *Mater* (Sen. *Phaed.* 608), *noverca* (Sen. *Con.* 7. 5. 9 (possibly transferred); [Sen.] *Her. O.* 1187, 1317).

[59] Sen. *Phaed.* 611, 646, 710, 1168; Sen. *Con.* 9. 5. 1; Suet. *Aug.* 51. 3, 71. 2, 3, 76. 2, *Tib.* 21. 4, 5; Apul. *Apol.* 100.

11

Addresses between Spouses and Others
with a Romantic Interest

cui me moribundam deseris hospes
(hoc solum nomen quoniam de coniuge restat)?

(Verg. A. 4. 323–4)

To what, guest (since this name alone is left from that of
husband), do you leave me when I am about to die?

Non dixit marite, id est, quia non vis dici maritus. Aeneas
enim et hospes fuerat et maritus, sed modo maritum se
negat, hospitem confitetur.

(Servius ad loc.)

She did not say 'husband', that is, because you do not
want to be called her husband. For Aeneas had been both
Dido's guest and her husband, but he now denies that he
is her husband and acknowledges that he is her guest.

WHEN Aeneas abandons Dido in Vergil's *Aeneid*, she complains that she can no longer call him *coniunx* 'spouse'. Servius,
commenting on this passage several centuries later, suggests
that the word Dido would have preferred to use was really
marite 'husband'. And had Plautus depicted this scene, Dido
would have been talking about the address *mi vir* 'my husband'. How were husbands, wives, and lovers really addressed
in Latin? Is the variation we see here due to genre, changes
over time, or both?

Part of the answer to these questions may be that in classical
Latin husbands were not normally addressed with kinship
terms at all, but rather by cognomen. While the evidence
from classical prose is not extensive, both Livy (1. 58. 7) and
Pliny (*Ep*. 3. 16. 6, 13) quote wives addressing their husbands
by name. *Marite* as an address between spouses appears only
from the second century AD and is used almost exclusively to

nameless husbands;[1] otherwise wives tend to use insults or
endearments in addressing their husbands in prose, though
domine 'master' seems also to have been used at some periods
(see p. 84).

Husbands addressing wives normally use names in prose,
except for the anomalous case of nameless wives in the
declamations. Cicero in letters to his wife uses her name,
endearments, and, once, *uxor* 'wife' combined with endearments;[2] other husbands show a similar distribution of addresses, except that names predominate more clearly and
insults are also an option.[3] *Domina* 'mistress' was probably
also fairly common in address to wives in the imperial period
(see p. 84). Nameless wives are often called *uxor*[4] but are even
more often addressed by other words such as transferred
kinship terms;[5] this varied address may be indirect evidence
that wives were normally addressed by name, so that *uxor*
could not convincingly be used as a standard address even in
the declamations.

It is likely that in conversational usage as well, husbands and
wives normally addressed each other by name, endearments, or
at some periods *domine/a*. This statement may not apply to
early Latin, since while names are not infrequently used to
spouses in Plautus and Terence,[6] (*mi*) *vir* and (*mea*) *uxor* (or
occasionally *uxorcula* 'little wife')[7] are more common; I cannot

---

[1] Apul. *Met.* 5. 6; [Quint.] *Decl.* 8. 5, 10. 6, 18. 17, 19. 6; *ILS* 8453; Alfius
Avitus frag. 1. The address appears much earlier in transferred sense: see
Glossary s.v.

[2] *Fam.* 14. 1. 5, 14. 2. 2, 3, 4, 14. 3. 1, 5, 14. 4. 1, 5, 6, 14. 5. 2, 14. 14. 2, 14.
18. 1.

[3] Cic. *Att.* 5. 1. 3; Var. *R.* 1 *pr.* 1; Petr. 47. 5, 75. 6, 9; Suet. *Aug.* 99. 1, *Cl.*
4. 1, 4, 6; Apul. *Apol.* 85, *Met.* 5. 5, 6, 12, 24, 8. 8; *ILS* 8395.

[4] e.g. [Cic.] *Rhet. Her.* 4. 65; Sen. *Con.* 2. 2. 1; Quint. *Decl.* 373. 3; [Quint.]
Decl. 6. 21.

[5] e.g. *noverca*, Sen. *Con.* 9. 6. 1, etc.; *puella*, Sen. *Con.* 1. 6. 3, etc.; *mulier*,
Sen. *Con.* 9. 6. 6, etc.; *mater*, [Quint.] *Decl.* 19. 9, etc. NB contrast between
uxor and *mater* at [Quint.] *Decl.* 19. 16.

[6] 16 times to wives and 8 times to husbands, e.g. Pl. *Am.* 540, 708; Ter.
Hau. 647, 1052.

[7] 30 times to wives and 17 times to husbands, e.g. Pl. *Am.* 522, 710; Ter.
Hau. 622, 879. Note the distinction in Ter. *Ph.* between Nausistrata's addresses
to her husband Chremes, which use only *mi vir* (991, 1002), and those to her
brother-in-law Demipho, which use only names (1011, 1024, 1031).

find a difference in meaning between these alternatives, though the addition of *mea* 'my' clearly makes a spousal address more affectionate. As with the case of children and siblings, spouses are addressed by name more often in Terence than in Plautus. Insults and endearments are also possible, as is *mulier* 'woman' from husbands who are displeased with their wives.[8] In classical and post-classical poetry husbands are most often addressed by name, frequently with *coniunx*, and rarely with *vir*;[9] wives are most often called *coniunx*, but not infrequently addressed by name or with *uxor*.[10] Endearments, insults, and terms of pity are also not uncommon in both directions. When Roman husbands are addressed by name, the name chosen is always the cognomen, as in prose; all of the examples come from a period at which the cognomen would have been the name used to sons and brothers as well (see pp. 262, 266).

It thus looks as though *uxor*, which appears in a variety of genres, was probably a genuine alternative to names in conversational language, while *coniunx*, which is almost entirely restricted to high-register poetry, was not (cf. Adams 1972: 252–5). *Vir* may also have been part of conversational language at an early period, and *marite* seems to be late as a spousal address. By Servius' time, however, *marite* may have been the natural address from wife to husband.

Spouses are different from the relatives discussed in Chapter 10 in that, in all genres, spouses are more likely to be addressed with emotive terms such as endearments or insults than are other relatives. When Cicero addresses his brother in letters, he normally uses *mi frater* 'my brother'; about a third of the time he joins endearments to this address, but endearments are never used by themselves to Quintus. Cicero's wife, on the other hand, is addressed with endearments more often than by

---

[8] e.g. Pl. *Am.* 729, *Cas.* 212; Ter. *Hec.* 214, 525. Cf. the use of *mulier* to daughters (p. 267).

[9] e.g. names: Verg. *G.* 4. 494; Prop. 4. 11. 1; Luc. 5. 763; *coniunx*: Verg. *A.* 2. 777; Sil. 6. 501; *vir*: Ov. *Ep.* 9. 168; V. Fl. 8. 415 only.

[10] e.g. *coniunx*: Verg. *A.* 11. 158; Ov. *Pont.* 3. 1. 31; Stat. *Silv.* 3. 5. 110; names: Ov. *Ep.* 7. 102; Juv. 1. 126; Sil. 2. 566; *uxor*: Ov. *Tr.* 1. 6. 3, *Ep.* 16. 304; Stat. *Silv.* 3. 5. 1.

name alone, and these endearments are frequently used as self-standing addresses, without the name or *uxor*. Moreover, while affectionate addresses used to Quintus are adjectives, those to Terentia are very frequently nouns (cf. pp. 154–7). These distinctions can be found in other authors as well, and in many genres insults as well as endearments are commonly used to spouses. Thus while it is possible to speak of a standard address to a wife or husband, the standard terms are used less frequently to spouses than to other family members.

The frequent use of emotional addresses rather than a standard term, and the use of endearments consisting of nouns rather than adjectives, are even more apparent in address to lovers and other people who have some level of romantic involvement but are not married. Such people are not of course addressed with terms like *vir* or *uxor*, but they frequently receive names, sometimes modified by *mi/mea*. In Petronius, who provides some of the best evidence for conversational usage on this point, a woman addresses a man with whom she is romantically involved with terms such as *iuvenis* 'young man' and *adulescens* 'young person' (127. 2, 129. 6), while he uses *domina* and *regina* 'queen' to her (128. 2, 130. 1); the man in this relationship is in a subordinate position, which may account for the inequality in address use. Homosexual lovers in Petronius use *frater*, *domine*, and names (86. 7, 91. 2, 8, 94. 10, 129. 1, 133. 1).

In comedy, where lovers are much more often addressed than in prose, both males and females frequently receive endearments, while names, which are also common, tend to be modified by *mi/mea*.[11] Men who are displeased with the objects of their affection can use *mulier* (as to a wife or daughter),[12] or in extreme cases insults.[13] Lovers in Terence are more likely to use names than those in Plautus, a tendency which is probably connected to Terence's more frequent use of names for spouses, siblings, sons, and daughters (see pp. 262, 266–7, 278).

In classical and post-classical poetry romantic addresses are

[11] e.g. Pl. *Cur.* 203, *Men.* 676, *Mos.* 297, *Per.* 763, *Rud.* 878, *Trin.* 245, *Truc.* 391, 529; Ter. *An.* 134, *Eu.* 456, 743, *Hau.* 406.

[12] Pl. *Truc.* 860, 926, *Poen.* 1305.

[13] Pl. *Truc.* 759, 762–3; Ter. *Eu.* 152.

very common and follow no set pattern. Names (usually without *mi/mea*) are frequent both from men to women and from women to men,[14] and so are endearments such as *mea vita* 'my life' and *mea lux* 'my light'. Insults are common when the speaker accuses the addressee of desertion or hard-heartedness, and terms of pity, transferred kinship terms, and other addresses also occur. There is also some evidence that *frater* and *soror* 'sister' could be romantic addresses (see p. 125). In homosexual relationships all of these possibilities are found, as is *puer* 'boy' to boys.[15]

The fact that a relationship is romantic is normally reflected in the address system in Latin, but there are many different ways in which it can reveal itself. Unmarried girls of free birth, who would normally be addressed as *virgo* 'girl, virgin' (see p. 244), are more likely to be addressed by name by men seeking their love;[16] in such circumstances the use of a name may be enough to signal romantic interest. In situations where names would be used even in the absence of such interest, a name may be modified by *mea* or *mi*, joined with endearments, or even replaced by endearments to make the speaker's feelings clear. We have already seen (p. 150) how Vergil's Dido uses *nate dea* 'born from a goddess' to Aeneas before she falls in love with him (*A.* 1. 615), then *hospes* 'guest' once her passion is aroused (1. 753), and then *hospes* again upon being deserted (4. 323), with an indication that she would have called him *coniunx* in between. Numerous other examples can be found throughout Latin literature of couples whose addresses change as their relationship progresses, as well as of individuals who use romantic or unromantic addresses as part of a struggle over the nature of a relationship.

Terence's *Hecyra* portrays a good-hearted courtesan who had to part from her lover Pamphilus when he married but who is generous enough to reconcile him with his wife when needed. She quotes herself as having addressed him as *mi Pamphile* before his marriage (824), but during the play itself

[14] e.g. 5 times from Sulpicia to Cerinthus, 26 times from Propertius to Cynthia.

[15] e.g. Catul. 48. 1; Verg. *Ecl.* 2. 6, 17; Ov. *Met.* 3. 477; Mart. 9. 36. 7, 11. 58. 1.

[16] e.g. Ter. *Hau.* 408; Ov. *Met.* 5. 625, 9. 744, *Am.* 3. 6. 61, *Ep.* 20. 109.

she always calls him *Pamphile* (855, 862, 864). In Plautus' *Bacchides*, two courtesans seduce a number of men, and in so doing they not only use endearments[17] but also suggest that the men use endearments in return (83). The men, being reluctant, prefer clearly non-romantic addresses such as *Bacchis* (53, 1118), *mulier* (52, 56), and *scelus* 'crime' (1176).[18]

In Ovid's *Heroides*, Helen writes a letter to Paris refusing his advances. She begins with *advena* 'visitor' (17. 5) and continues with *improbe* 'not good' (17. 77) and *infide* 'faithless' (17. 197) in firm refusals, but at the end, when she hints that she is not as resolute as she sounds, she uses *Pari* (17. 256). Here the progression is from positively unfriendly addresses to names, which in comparison seem a relatively welcoming type of address, even if not overtly romantic.

In Valerius Flaccus' *Argonautica*, Jason and Medea first meet as strangers, with Jason very much in need of help. He first addresses her as *regina* in a request (5. 385); later, once he knows who she is, he consistently calls her *virgo* (7. 415, 419, 499, 529, 8. 38), while she calls him *Thessale* 'Thessalian' (7. 437), *hospes* (7. 454, 8. 53), *Aesonide* 'son of Aeson' (8. 105), and *care* 'dear' (7. 533). If Medea's addresses are less reserved than Jason's (see p. 150 on *hospes*), this reflects Valerius' portrayal of Medea as the one in love. The only exception to Jason's use of *virgo* is when he promises to marry Medea, addressing her once as *coniunx* (7. 497) but then immediately returning to *virgo* (499). Once the two have eloped, however, the addresses change, and Medea uses both *vir* (8. 415) and *coniunx* (8. 419) as well as other terms (8. 441–2, 460).

In Apuleius' *Metamorphoses*, the narrator Lucius at first addresses the maidservant Photis in the same fashion as her master does, with her name alone (1. 24). Once he makes a decision to seduce her, however, the addresses change. He opens his bid by calling her *Fotis mea* (2. 7), followed once he has gained some ground with *mea festivitas* 'my delightfulness' (2. 10). Once he has achieved his end he continues with *Fotis mea* (2. 18) and, when making a request, *mea mellitula* 'my little honey' (3. 22).

---

[17] *Mi anime* (81), *senex optume quantumst in terra* (1170), *mea Pietas* (1176), *mel meum* (1197).

[18] Other examples from comedy are discussed on pp. 155 and 214.

There are thus many ways in which romantic affection can be indicated in Latin. None of these addresses is used exclusively for such affection, and some of them, such as names, are more often used in non-romantic contexts. It is the shift in address, the use of a term which is slightly warmer than might be expected in that context, which indicates romance, rather than the use of any particular term.

12

Addresses to Groups

Decimanos autem Romae cum ingentibus minis summo-
que etiam urbis periculo missionem et praemia flagi-
tantes, ardente tunc in Africa bello, neque adire
cunctatus est, quanquam deterrentibus amicis, neque
dimittere; sed una voce, qua Quirites eos pro militibus
appellarat, tam facile circumegit et flexit, ut ei milites esse
confestim responderint et quamvis recusantem ultro in
Africam sint secuti . . .[1]

When the war was raging in Africa, in Rome the men of
the tenth legion were demanding discharge and bonuses
with serious threats and posing a grave danger to the city,
but Caesar did not hesitate to approach them, against the
advice of his friends, and to disband them. Indeed he so
easily won them over with a single word, calling them
Quirites instead of 'soldiers', that they immediately
replied that they were soldiers and spontaneously followed him into Africa, even over his objections.

T H E skilful use of group addresses could be crucial to the
success and even the survival of a general speaking to his army,
a politician speaking to the citizen body, or an accused man
speaking to a jury. Yet in such situations the normal rules of
the Latin address system could not be applied, since address by
name or by other individual characteristics is impossible for
someone facing a large group. Group addresses thus had their
own set of rules, which in most cases were strictly adhered to; it
was this rigidity that made Caesar's address to his mutinous
soldiers so effective.

The rules of group address do not apply simply to all
vocatives that happen to be in the plural, for plural addresses
may be used to individuals (e.g. *meae deliciae*, Catul. 32. 2), and

---

[1] Suet. *Jul.* 70; cf. Tac. *Ann.* 1. 42; Appian, *BC* 2. 93; Butler *et al.* (1982:
130–1).

collective singular addresses may be used to large groups (e.g. *o gens infelix*, Verg. *A.* 5. 624–5). The rules apply rather to addresses spoken to groups large enough to be considered a group rather than a collection of individuals, a size which can vary but normally requires at least three addressees. Thus when Cicero depicts Cato addressing two younger men as *optimi adulescentes* 'excellent youths' (*Sen.* 39), he is not operating under the normal constraints affecting group addresses, since he can also make Cato use the nominal address *Laeli et Scipio* 'Laelius and Scipio', as he does elsewhere (*Sen.* 35). This chapter is concerned with the rules for addressing groups large enough to make address by individual names impossible.

One such group frequently addressed in Latin literature is the Roman Senate. For these addresses the term used is nearly always the formulaic *patres conscripti* 'enrolled fathers'. Cicero invariably uses this address in orations before the Senate (183 times, e.g. *Catil.* 1. 4), and other speakers whose speeches to the Senate are preserved either independently or in prose histories almost always use this address.[2] Most Senate speakers were of course Romans, but the historians also put *patres conscripti* into the mouths of foreigners addressing the Roman Senate,[3] showing that it was not perceived as a term restricted to 'insiders'. The formula could not normally be altered even by the addition of any further vocatives to it; thus Suetonius quotes the address *patres conscripti et tu Caesar*, delivered to the Senate and Tiberius, as flattery of the emperor (Suet. *De Oratoribus* 71 (p. 88 Re.)). As noted above (p. 101), the flattery here must consist in the addition of the emperor to the initial address to the Senate, which until the second century would normally stand alone regardless of the presence of the emperor or any other dignitary.[4]

---

[2] e.g. Pliny (14 times), Calpurnius Flaccus (5 times), Sallust (21 times), Tacitus (15 times), Livy (68 times), Suetonius (4 times). On the history and meaning of this term, which are disputed, see Mommsen (1864–79: i. 226–30, 254; 1887–8: iii. 837–40); Ihne (1865); Willems (1883: 187–9; 1885: i. 37–42, 640–53); Brassloff (1900); Wilkins (1929: 395); Brink (1971: 341); Gizewski (1997).

[3] e.g. Sal. *Jug.* 14. 1; Liv. 7. 30. 1, 28. 39. 1.

[4] There are, however, some other exceptions to this rule, e.g. *T. Manli vosque patres conscripti* (Liv. 8. 5. 3) and *Quirites vosque patres conscripti* (Liv. 8. 6. 6). The address to Catiline rather than the Senate at the start of Cicero's

Only two other types of address to the Senate occur in prose, and both are rare. One is the simple *patres* 'fathers'. This address occurs once in Tacitus, spoken by a woman in a brief and terrified plea (*Ann.* 16. 31), and twice in Livy, both times in brief interactions rather than formal speeches (2. 12. 5, 6. 35. 9); Sallust, most exceptionally, qualifies it to produce *grati patres* in a letter from Pompey to the Senate (*Hist.* 2. 98. 6). *Romani* is also used by Livy in a speech by foreign envoys who begin and end with the more usual *patres conscripti* (7. 30. 11, 17, 18). This evidence suggests that while in formal orations the address from a Roman to the Senate was invariably *patres conscripti*, it may also have been possible to use the shorter *patres* on occasion for brief, urgent communications. I would not venture to hypothesize about how foreign envoys normally addressed the Senate when they spoke in Latin.[5]

Poets, in sharp contrast to prose writers, never use the address *patres conscripti*, which although not impossible metrically was apparently stylistically unacceptable in epic. The only poets to report Senate speeches are Lucan and Silius. Lucan uses *patres* for addresses directed to the Senate when it is still functioning as a Senate (5. 21, 46), but after the defeat of Pompey he has that general address the forlorn remnants of the Senate as *comites* 'companions' (8. 262, 289). Silius, though portraying addresses to an intact and functional Senate, strays further from normal usage than does Lucan, for he does not even use *patres* to the Roman Senate, preferring a variety of alternative addresses such as *Curia* 'Senate' (2. 456), *belli iudex* 'judge of war' (2. 456), and *viri* 'men' (1. 651). It is clear that these poetic addresses do not reflect vocatives actually used to the Senate.

Latin literature contains very few examples of address to a senate other than the Roman one. Such bodies existed in a number of ancient states, and they undoubtedly had their own conventions of address in their own languages, but Latin authors show no sign of acquaintance with such conventions.

first Catilinarian oration is striking; it was probably intended to shock the audience and give an immediate sense of emergency.

[5] Sometimes, apparently, they did not use Latin; Greek in particular was used in Senate speeches at various periods, both with and without translation into Latin. See Kaimio (1979: 103–10); Willems (1885: ii. 488).

When depicting speeches delivered by Romans to a foreign
senate or council, Latin authors use the plural ethnic as an
address.[6] When depicting those spoken by a native of the
country concerned, Roman authors impose their own conventions and use *patres conscripti* or *patres* (Liv. 23. 12. 8; Sil. 2.
279). There are also a number of addresses from gods to the
heavenly senate; these use *patres conscripti* (Sen. *Apoc.* 9. 1 etc.)
or the parody *dei conscripti* 'enrolled gods' (Apul. *Met.* 6. 23).

Another group frequently addressed is the Roman people. In
speeches before a popular assembly, whether of the plebeians
or the populace as a whole, Roman orators used the address
Quirites 'Romans' as consistently as they used *patres conscripti*
to the Senate. Cicero uses only this term to address the
populace (169 times, e.g. *Catil.* 2. 1), and it is as a rule
employed in speeches before the Roman people preserved in
prose works.[7] Unlike *patres conscripti*, *Quirites* also appears in
poetry when speeches before the Roman people are portrayed
(Enn. *Ann.* 102; Ov. *Met.* 15. 600).

It is also possible, though less common, for the Roman
populace as a whole to be addressed in a context other than
an assembly: a poet may address his countrymen in his poem,
or an oracle may address the Roman nation, for example.
Under such circumstances the rules of address are more
flexible. *Quirites* may still be used,[8] but it is not common; the
most frequent address is the collective singular *Romane*, which
can be used by both Romans and foreigners (see pp. 209–10).
The plural *Romani* is very rare in addresses to the populace as a
whole, though it is occasionally used by oracles (Liv. 23. 11. 2).
Cives 'citizens' may also be used, especially in poetry (e.g.
[Cic.] *Rhet. Her.* 4. 66; Prop. 4. 1. 67; Luc. 1. 8), and various
forms of *populus* 'people' appear occasionally (see p. 295); other
addresses are very rare but possible.[9]

---

[6] *Tusculani*, Liv. 6. 26. 1; *Achaei*, Liv. 35. 49. 9; *Aetoli*, Liv. 31. 31. 18.

[7] e.g. Livy (57 times), Sallust (26 times), Gellius (10 times), Valerius
Maximus (7 times), Pliny (*Ep. Tra.* 10. 58. 7). On the origins and meaning
of this term see Kretschmer (1919; 1924: 136 n. 1); Walde and Hofmann
(1938–54: ii. 409); Koch (1960: 23–9); Ogilvie (1965: 79); Kraus (1994: 295).

[8] Ov. *Pont.* 4. 15. 11, *Fast.* 4. 187; Juv. 3. 60.

[9] e.g. *gens Veneris*, Sil. 12. 324; *miseri*, Luc. 7. 43.

Populaces other than the Roman one are also frequently addressed. When such address occurs before a popular assembly, the use of the plural ethnic is normal regardless of the nationality of the speaker, and *cives* is also possible.[10] As in the case of senatorial addresses, however, Latin authors may extend Roman practice to other nations, leading to the use of *Quirites* to assemblies which are not Roman.[11] In poetry the standard term for a non-Roman assembly is *cives* (e.g. Verg. *A.* 11. 243; Sil. 11. 160), but other terms are possible, including *viri* 'men' (Sil. 11. 194).

More often, a non-Roman populace is addressed in the abstract or at a distance. Under such circumstances *Quirites* is not used, nor is *cives*, probably because these terms do not adequately identify the addressees. In prose the normal address is the plural ethnic, whether or not the speaker is a member of the populace concerned; in poetry plural ethnics are also common, but a collective singular ethnic may be used as well when the speaker does not belong to the group he addresses.[12] Other types of address are possible but rare.

There is thus a significant difference between addresses used to the Roman populace and those to other peoples. If, however, the addressee is not the populace as a whole but rather an embassy or other group of citizens abroad, no such difference is observable. Such groups are normally addressed with a plural ethnic regardless of nationality;[13] in the case of non-Romans these addressees make up a relatively small percentage of all the recipients of this ethnic, but they are the normal addressees of *Romani*, which in contrast to the collective singular *Romane* does not normally designate the Roman populace as a whole. Another context in which addresses to Romans and non-Romans merge is cries for help; these can of course be

[10] e.g. *Achaei*, Liv. 41. 23. 5; *Campani*, Liv. 23. 3. 1; *Lacedaemonii*, Gel. 18. 3. 5; *Latini*, Verg. *A.* 11. 302; *cives*, Apul. *Met.* 3. 9. *Athenienses* in Quint. *Decl.* 323. 11, 339. 1, etc. may be influenced by knowledge of the actual practice of Greek orators.

[11] Pers. 4. 8; Quint. *Decl.* 253. 1, 254. 3, 4; Apul. *Met.* 2. 24, 3. 3, 3. 5, cf. also 8. 29.

[12] e.g. *Danai*, Ov. *Ep.* 13. 129; *Achaei*, Liv. 39. 37. 1; *Arabes*, Luc. 3. 247; *Concane*, Sil. 3. 361; *Arimaspe*, Luc. 3. 281; see pp. 207–9.

[13] e.g. *Romani*, Liv. 8. 23. 8, 21. 18. 4, 34. 24. 4, 42. 41. 13; *Lacedaemonii*, Liv. 39. 37. 4; *Aetoli*, Liv. 36. 28. 2; *Rhodii*, Liv. 45. 23. 7.

addressed to anyone, but often they are addressed to the
populace at large (that is, to those members of it who happen
to be within earshot), and in such circumstances the address of
choice seems to be *cives*, regardless of nationality.[14]

The Roman army is another common addressee, but one for
whom the rules of address are more difficult to establish. Livy
quotes many addresses from Roman commanders to their
armies, normally with the address *milites* 'soldiers' (e.g. 9. 23.
9, 22. 29. 8, 28. 27. 6) but occasionally with *iuvenes* 'young
men'[15] (3. 61. 7, 35. 35. 16, 45. 8. 6), *Romani* 'Romans' (1. 12.
7, 1. 28. 4), or the collective singular *miles* 'soldier' (10. 36. 8).
When Livy has soldiers address each other, they use *miles* (3.
27. 8) or *commilitones* 'fellow-soldiers', a term also so used in
the declamations.[16] That *commilitones* was particularly emotive
is suggested by the way Livy describes the speech Verginius
made to the army after being forced to slay his daughter to save
her from the decemvir Appius Claudius:

Supinas deinde tendens manus, commilitones appellans orabat ne
quod scelus Ap. Claudi esset sibi attribuerent neu se ut parricidam
liberum aversarentur.   (3. 50. 5)

Finally, raising his hands in supplication and addressing the men as
'fellow-soldiers', he pleaded with them not to blame him for Appius
Claudius' crime and not to shun him as the murderer of his children.

Livy's use of *milites* as the standard address from a commander to his men is seen also in Sallust (*Cat.* 58. 1 etc.) and
Frontinus (*Str.* 1. 12. 1), but Tacitus always uses *commilitones*
under such circumstances,[17] and his usage is supported by that
of the younger Seneca (*Ep.* 82. 22).

Of all Roman authors Caesar is the one who knew best how

[14] e.g. Cic. *Mil.* 77; Liv. 2. 55. 7; V. Max. 4. 1. 12; Pl. *Aul.* 406, *Cur.* 626,
Men. 1000. Appeals to the populace of Rome could also use *Quirites*, giving
rise to the verb *quiritare*; see Schulze (1918: 178–9) and Lintott (1999: 11–16).
This type of appeal is attested in Apul. *Met.* 8. 29, but in general *cives* is
preferred in our data.

[15] Or perhaps 'warriors'; cf. Adams (1999: 120).

[16] *Commilitones* spoken by someone other than the commander: Liv. 42. 34.
15, cf. 2. 55. 7 and Ogilvie (1965: 375); Sen. *Suas.* 1. 4; Quint. *Decl.* 315. 15.
On *commilitones* and other terms for soldiers cf. MacMullen (1984: 443–4).

[17] *Ag.* 33, *Hist.* 1. 29, 37, 83, etc.

to address an army, and though he never quotes his own addresses, Caesar is consistent about attributing *milites* rather than *commilitones* to other commanders.[18] When he mentions address from one soldier to the others, the manuscripts present both *milites* and *commilitones* as possibilities.[19] The only occasion on which Caesar certainly refers to the address *commilitones* is in a report that Labienus, having deserted to Pompey's side in the civil war and obtained from Pompey the captives from Caesar's side, called them *commilitones* tauntingly before executing them.[20]

Caesar's own practice may have been at variance with the one he attributes to other commanders, however, for Suetonius reports[21] that Caesar *nec milites eos pro contione, sed blandiore nomine commilitones appellabat* 'in assembly, he did not call the men "soldiers", but by the more flattering term "fellow-soldiers"'. In the passage quoted at the beginning of this chapter, however, Suetonius seems to assume that Caesar's normal address to his men was *milites*, and it may well be that Caesar used both terms.

Suetonius also comments on the use of *commilitones* elsewhere. Of Augustus he says:

neque post bella civilia aut in contione aut per edictum ullos militum commilitones appellabat, sed milites, ac ne a filiis quidem aut privignis suis imperio praeditis aliter appellari passus est, ambitiosius id existimans, quam aut ratio militaris aut temporum quies aut sua domusque suae maiestas postularet. (*Aug.* 25. 1)

After the civil wars he never in an assembly or edict called any of his troops 'fellow-soldiers', but rather 'soldiers', nor did he allow them to be addressed otherwise even by his sons or stepsons when they held military command, for he thought that this [i.e. the use of *commilitones*] indicated a desire for popularity that suited neither military discipline, the peacefulness of his times, nor his own dignity and that of his household.

[18] *Gal.* 6. 8. 4, 7. 38. 2, *Civ.* 2. 39. 2.
[19] *Gal.* 4. 25. 3; Meusel (1886: 276–7) argues in favour of *commilitones* because of the low rank of the speaker, but T. R. Holmes (1914: 159) doubts the validity of this argument.
[20] *Civ.* 3. 71. 4; that this was not Labienus' normal form of address is shown by the *milites* which Caesar attributes to him in a more normal context (*Gal.* 6. 8. 4).
[21] *Jul.* 67. 2; cf. Butler *et al.* (1982: 128).

Of Galba, slain by mutinous soldiers, he reports:

Sunt qui tradant, ad primum tumultum proclamasse eum: quid agitis
commilitones? Ego vester sum et vos mei; donativum etiam pollici-
tum.   (*Gal.* 20. 1)

There are those who say that at the beginning of the mutiny he
shouted, 'Fellow-soldiers, what are you doing? I am yours, and you
are mine', and that he promised them a largesse as well.

These passages suggest that the addresses used by commanders to their armies were in the process of change during the
late Republic and early empire. Caesar's use of *commilitones*
during the Republic is unusual enough to be worthy of comment, but so is Augustus' use of *milites* a few decades later, and
Suetonius implies that Augustus too used *commilitones* during
the civil wars. These differences, and those between Livy's
milites and Tacitus' *commilitones*, are probably best explained
by a change in address habits: during the Republic, the
standard address from a commander to a Roman army was
milites, while a member of that army, if he had occasion to
speak, used *milites* or *commilitones* to its other members. Once
the civil wars began and generals had to curry favour with their
troops, they began to use the more ingratiating *commilitones* as
well; indeed Caesar may be the man who started this practice.
Augustus clearly tried to end it once peace had been restored,
but the fact that Tacitus and other later authors regularly quote
addresses from commanders to their troops with *commilitones*
suggests that he was unsuccessful in the long run.

A few other addresses for armies are found in prose, but
these are rare. Cicero addresses live soldiers as *fortissimi viri*
'very brave men', *centuriones* 'centurions', and *milites* (*Mil.*
101), and eulogizes dead ones with *fortissumi, dum vixistis, nunc
vero etiam sanctissimi milites* 'soldiers, very brave while you
lived, but now very sacred as well' (*Phil.* 14. 33). Caesar has an
officer use *manipulares mei qui fuistis* 'you who were my troops'
to the men he formerly led (*Civ.* 3. 91. 2). Livy occasionally has
a commander modify *milites* with adjectives such as *Romani* (7.
36. 5) or *veteres* 'veteran' (26. 41. 23), and he also uses *Romani*
alone (1. 12. 7, 1. 28. 4). Sallust quotes Catiline addressing his
mob as *fortissumi viri* (*Cat.* 20. 9). Clearly such other addresses
were conceivable, but at the same time the convention of using

milites or *commilitones* was very strong, especially when the speaker was a commanding officer.

It was this convention which made deviant addresses to mutinous soldiers a powerful tool, for Caesar's use of *Quirites* rather than one of the accepted military addresses showed that he was treating the mutineers like a civilian assembly. Caesar was not the only general to use the conventions of military address to chastise mutineers, for Livy quotes Scipio Africanus rebuking his army by complaining that he does not know how to address them: he rejects first *cives*, on the grounds that they are not being loyal to their state, and then *milites*, on the grounds that they are insubordinate, finally proposing *hostes* 'enemies' as an alternative (28. 27. 3–4). Tacitus also quotes M. Antoninus Primus addressing the Praetorian guard as *pagani* 'civilians' with similar implications (*Hist.* 3. 24; cf. Wellesley 1972: 110).

As with other types of group address, the rules applicable to armies in prose are generally ignored by poets. Neither *milites* nor *commilitones* appears in poetry, perhaps because neither can be admitted into a hexameter. The collective singular *miles* 'soldier' is used frequently to address Roman armies,[22] but *commilito* 'fellow-soldier' is never so employed, perhaps for metrical reasons. Another popular poetic term for military address is *viri* 'men',[23] and *iuvenes* 'young men' is not infrequent.[24] A variety of rarer addresses also appear, as *socii* 'companions, allies' (e.g. Luc. 2. 483), *comites* 'companions' (Luc. 4. 516), and *cohortes* 'cohorts' (Luc. 3. 360).

Various expressions of praise and blame are also used for Roman armies in poetry, in contrast to the purely descriptive terms in prose: *o domitor mundi, rerum fortuna mearum, miles* 'O soldier, conqueror of the world, fortune of my affairs' (Luc. 7. 250–1), *ignavi* 'cowardly' (Luc. 2. 496). More subtle, but equally powerful, effects are produced by the use of *cives* 'citizens' in a plea for mercy from a Roman soldier to his Roman enemies in the civil war (Luc. 6. 230). Caesar's punitive address to his rebellious legionaries is given by Lucan as *ignavi . . . Quirites* (5. 358), and it is probable that Lucan added the

[22] e.g. Luc. 4. 273; Sil. 15. 444; V. Fl. 6. 55.
[23] e.g. Luc. 7. 738; Sil. 4. 405, 10. 8.
[24] e.g. Luc. 6. 155, 7. 318; Sil. 15. 659.

ignavi, which does not appear in prose sources, because the more flexible rules of group address in poetry made the point of the address more difficult to catch. Nearly all addresses to Roman armies in poetry are spoken by commanding officers, and when the speaker is someone else, there is no noticeable difference in address.

Non-Roman armies and military units are very frequently addressed in poetry but less often in prose. Prose authors tend to treat other armies like Roman ones for purposes of address; thus Frontinus, who has Roman commanders address their armies as *milites*, also gives this address to Greeks (*Str.* 1. 10. 1, 1. 12. 5, 4. 7. 6), while the younger Seneca, who uses *commilitones* for Romans, also has Leonidas use this term to a Greek army (*Ep.* 82. 21). Valerius Maximus consistently assigns *commilitones* to Greek commanders (3. 2 ext. 3, ext. 5). Curtius preserves the original difference between *milites* and *commilitones*, since he consistently has Alexander address his troops with *milites* (6. 3. 1, 5, 6, etc.) but also gives *commilitones* to the men themselves (6. 10. 8, 10. 6. 8). He also provides an address reminiscent of Caesar's *Quirites* when he has Alexander address his discharged army, in disgust, as *ingratissimi cives* 'most ungrateful citizens' (10. 2. 27). Plural ethnics are occasionally used, whether by a commander addressing an army of a different nationality (Liv. 1. 28. 7) or between compatriots (Sen. *Suas.* 2. 1, etc.). Other addresses also occur, including *pueri* 'boys' (Apul. *Met.* 3. 5) and *socii* (Liv. 21. 21. 3).

In poetry *cives* is not a reprimand, being used on several occasions to encourage non-Roman armies (e.g. Verg. *A.* 11. 459, 12. 572); *miles* also occurs but is less frequent to non-Roman than to Roman armies (e.g. Sil. 7. 531, 11. 241). The most common addresses from a commander to his own non-Roman army are *viri*, *socii*, and plural ethnics; *iuvenes* is also fairly frequent.[25] When the speaker is not a member of the army concerned, ethnics are the most common type of address, but *viri* and *iuvenes* can also occur.[26] Indeed the flexibility of

[25] e.g. *viri*: Stat. *Theb.* 7. 433; Verg. *A.* 9. 158; Sil. 7. 535; *socii*: Verg. *A.* 10. 369; Sil. 2. 44; Stat. *Theb.* 6. 809; ethnics: Stat. *Theb.* 10. 482; V. Fl. 8. 264; Verg. *A.* 12. 693; *iuvenes*: Verg. *A.* 9. 51; Stat. *Theb.* 10. 485; Sil. 6. 715.

[26] e.g. ethnics: Verg. *A.* 9. 428; Stat. *Theb.* 7. 523; Sil. 6. 500; *viri*: V. Fl. 4. 146; *iuvenes*: V. Fl. 4. 206.

viri is shown by its use to the same band of warriors, in the
same engagement, both by their own members and by an
enemy (Stat. *Theb.* 2. 535, 620). Other addresses, including
expressions of praise and blame, are used not infrequently both
to the speaker's own army and to others. There is thus no
major difference between address to Roman and to non-Roman
armies.

Another common object of group address is a jury. Juries are
addressed more often than any other group in Latin literature,
almost always with the address *iudices* 'jurors'. Cicero always
uses this address to juries (623 examples, e.g. *S. Rosc.* 1), while
other authors tend to use *iudices* (e.g. V. Max. 8. 5. 6; Calp.
Decl. 2, 4) but can also qualify it to produce *sanctissimi iudices*
'most sacred jurors';[27] only in pseudo-Quintilian have I found
alternative addresses, usually *sanctissimi viri* 'most sacred
men'.[28] Addresses to juries were thus some of the most
inflexible in the Latin address system.

Another group to be addressed is an audience, such as the
audience of a play. Plautus addresses his audience frequently,
nearly always with (*mei*) *spectatores* '(my) audience' (e.g. *As.* 1,
Am. 1146). The emperor Claudius addressed the audience at
the games as *domini* 'masters' (Suet. *Cl.* 21. 5), but as we have
seen (p. 89) this address was considered inappropriate.

A group of men all holding the same office can be addressed
by their common title of office. Such address is most common
with *tribuni* 'tribunes', *consules* 'consuls', and *pontifices* 'pontiffs'[29] but can also be used with other titles such as *decemviri*
(Liv. 3. 52. 6), *duces* 'leaders' (e.g. Sil. 11. 215), or *sacerdotes*
'priests' (Ov. *Fast.* 1. 719).

The groups so far considered are conceived of as being male,
even if they sometimes include women, but it is also possible to
address a group of women. Such groups are most often
addressed either with a plural ethnic or patronymic[30] or with

---

[27] Only at Calp. *Decl.* 13, 48; [Quint.] *Decl.* 8. 2, 8. 16, 16. 2.

[28] *Decl.* 14. 2, 16. 1 (*tris*), 16. 2, 17. 5, 17. 7, 17. 20.

[29] e.g. Liv. 2. 37. 6, 3. 17. 2; Plin. *Ep.* 7. 33. 8; Cic. *Agr.* 1. 26, *Dom.* 1; Ov.
Fast. 4. 630; Calp. *Decl.* 23.

[30] e.g. *Iliades*, Sen. *Tro.* 144; *Lemniades*, Stat. *Theb.* 5. 106; *Troades*, Ov.
Met. 13. 534; *Danaides*, Sen. *Med.* 749.

a word designating some type of female, as *virgines* 'virgins'
(e.g. Catul. 61. 224; Hor. *Carm.* 1. 21. 1), *puellae* 'girls' (e.g.
Ov. *Ars.* 3. 57; Mart. 12. 55. 1), *innuptae* 'unmarried girls' (e.g.
Prop. 3. 19. 25), *nuptae* 'brides' (e.g. Catul. 66. 87), *matres*
'mothers' (e.g. Verg. *A.* 5. 646; Quint. *Decl.* 246. 9), *matronae*
'matrons' (e.g. V. Max. 1. 8. 4), *mulieres* 'women' (e.g. Pl. *Ps.*
172), or *nurus* 'young wives' (Mart. 14. 59. 2). *Cives* and *comites*
are also sometimes addressed to groups of women (e.g. Verg.
A. 5. 671; Ov. *Met.* 3. 728). Other addresses, including
expressions of pity, praise, or condemnation, are not infrequent
for women, proportionately more so than for groups of men.

Groups of servants are sometimes addressed in poetry when
collective orders are given, but there is no fixed form of address
under such circumstances. Seneca in his tragedies prefers
famuli/ae 'attendants',[31] and other poets tend to use either
this term or *pueri/puellae* 'boys/girls'[32] but can on occasion
use other addresses, such as *servi* 'slaves' (Mart. 14. 79. 1). In
comedy such addresses are less common than one might
expect, and they follow no standard format; *pueri* (Pl. *As.*
906), *comites* (Pl. *Cas.* 165), *servi* (Pl. *Cist.* 649), and *satellites*
'attendants' (Pl. *Mil.* 78) all occur, but none are common.
From this evidence it is not possible to draw conclusions about
the address(es) normally used to groups of servants, though if
there was any prevalent term *pueri* seems the most likely
candidate.

The groups discussed here are far from the only groups
addressed in Latin literature; any gathering of people could in
theory be addressed as a group, and many were. But in other
contexts there is little evidence that group address was frequent
enough to have developed its own rules. The groups discussed
in this chapter represent the ones most often addressed in Latin
literature, and therefore the ones for whom a consistent pattern
of address could exist.

Some generalizations may be made about group addresses as a
whole, regardless of the group to which they are addressed.
While Latin authors very frequently use collective nouns such

---

[31] e.g. *Her. F.* 1053, *Med.* 188, *Phaed.* 387.

[32] e.g. *pueri*: Pers. 1. 113; Hor. *Carm.* 1. 19. 14; *puellae*: Ov. *Fast.* 2. 745;
famuli: Verg. *A.* 2. 712; Stat. *Theb.* 11. 306; *famulae*: Ov. *Met.* 4. 223.

as *senatus* 'Senate' or *populus* 'people' to refer to groups, in addressing these same groups they normally prefer plurals such as *patres conscripti* or *Quirites* (cf. E. Fraenkel 1957: 289 n. 1). Yet collective nouns do occur as addresses, and there are considerable differences among such nouns in the extent to which they can function as addresses, differences apparently unrelated to the frequency of their referential usage. Thus *populus* and *popule* are used in address on a number of occasions in both prose and poetry,[33] but as far as I know *senatus* is never used in address. In addition to *populus*, collectives used repeatedly in address are *turba* 'crowd',[34] *iuventus* 'youth',[35] *genus* 'race',[36] *manus* 'band',[37] and *domus* 'house'.[38] Rare collectives include *gens* 'clan', *proles* 'progeny', *pubes* 'youth', *civitas* 'state', *plebs* 'common people', *cohors* 'cohort', *sanguis* 'blood', *curia* 'Senate', *coetus* 'crowd', *orbis* 'world', and *propago* 'progeny'.[39] Most of these addresses are confined to poetry, and it is unlikely that any of them was used in non-literary language, but some of them occur with enough frequency to make it clear that they were an accepted part of the literary address system.

In addition to such inherently collective nouns, Latin authors also use other singular nouns as collective addresses on occasion. This usage is fairly common with *miles* (at least 20 examples) and ethnics (at least 13 examples);[40] it is also used

[33] Ov. *Fast.* 4. 731; [Cic.] *Oct.* 6; Liv. 1. 24. 7; Quint. *Decl.* 302. 5; [Quint.] *Decl.* 11. 11. Cf. Wackernagel (1912: 13–16); Löfstedt (1956: i. 98–9); E. Fraenkel (1957: 289 n. 1); Svennung (1958: 284–6); Ogilvie (1965: 111); Hofmann and Szantyr (1965: 24).

[34] Stat. *Theb.* 7. 282; Sen. *Tro.* 409; Ov. *Ep.* 9. 51, *Fast.* 1. 74, *Tr.* 5. 3. 47; Mart. 1. 42. 6, 7. 22. 2, *Sp.* 22. 12; Sil. 11. 395.

[35] Luc. 9. 256; Stat. *Theb.* 8. 600; Verg. *A.* 8. 499; Ov. *Ars* 1. 459, 2. 733.

[36] Catul. 64. 23; Sen. *Apoc.* 12. 3. 28, *Her. F.* 268; Ov. *Ars* 3. 87, *Met.* 15. 139.

[37] Luc. 2. 532; Sen. *Phaed.* 725; Verg. *A.* 10. 294; Sil. 1. 390; V. Fl. 4. 437.

[38] Sen. *Oed.* 627; Luc. 6. 819; Ov. *Fast.* 2. 225; Trag. incert. auct. 184.

[39] *Gens*: Sil. 12. 324; Mart. *Sp.* 33. 1; Verg. *A.* 5. 624; *proles*: Sen. *Her. F.* 268, *Oed.* 110; Ov. *Met.* 3. 531; *pubes*: Sen. *Ag.* 310; Sil. 10. 599; *civitas*: Quint. *Decl.* 315. 15; [Quint.] *Decl.* 19. 16; *plebs*: Hor. *Carm.* 3. 14. 1; Ov. *Ib.* 79; *cohors*: Sen. *Med.* 980; Stat. *Theb.* 12. 643; *sanguis*: Hor. *Ars* 292; Pers. 1. 61; *curia*: Sil. 2. 456; *coetus*: Catul. 46. 9; *orbis*: [Sen.] *Her. O.* 1332; *propago*: Sen. *Phoen.* 334.

[40] Neither of these figures can be exact, because in several passages the

sporadically with a large number of other words in poetry. In the case of these other words it is frequently difficult, and often unproductive, to attempt to distinguish between a singular used for a group and a singular used for an indefinite addressee. An inscription carrying an address to its reader as *viator* 'passer-by' is expected to have more than one reader and may even be read by several people at once. But the vocative, by convention, is never addressed to the group of readers, rather to each individual reader. In that case, how does one interpret addresses such as Propertius' *virgo, tale iter omne cave* (4. 8. 6) 'virgin, beware of every such route': as a collective address to girls in general, or as a singular address to a generic girl? What about Tibullus' *quisquis ades, lingua, vir mulierque, fave* (2. 2. 2) 'Whoever is present, man and woman, keep silent'? When Caesar gives an order to the new recruits in his legion with the singular *tiro rudis* 'raw recruit' (Luc. 5. 363), he is clearly speaking to more than one man, but could he be addressing each individually rather than the recruits as a group? Such questions cannot really be answered, except to note that these ambiguous addresses are sufficiently frequent in Latin poetry to be in themselves a recognizable part of the Latin address system (cf. p. 249).

An important difference between group addresses and those used to individuals is the tendency for purely descriptive terms to be used to groups, while individuals are more likely to receive expressions of respect, affection, contempt, or blame. This tendency is much more marked in prose than in poetry; in general, Latin poets tend to use more emotive and less formulaic addresses than prose writers and probably than ordinary speech, but this pattern is more pronounced in group address. Prose writers rarely use emotive addresses to groups, adhering instead to a strict set of conventions which are largely ignored in poetry. The lack of emotive addresses could be caused partly by the non-linguistic fact that a speaker is more likely to feel strong emotions towards an individual than towards a group, but this cannot entirely explain the striking disparity between group and individual address. Speeches such as exhortations to armies and pleas to juries do in theory allow

addressee could be either an individual or a group. On the general problem of collective singulars see Löfstedt (1956: i. 12–26).

plenty of scope for the expression of strong emotion, but in prose, and probably in actual delivery, such emotion was not conveyed by means of emotive addresses. It looks as though the formality of the contexts in which large groups were addressed normally precluded addresses other than those traditionally used in such formal settings. Thus prose writers have Caesar address his mutinous soldiers with the formulaic *Quirites* rather than with the more obviously emotive *ignavi . . . Quirites* given him by Lucan.

The fundamental difference between group address and that to individuals is indicated by the substantial number of terms which appear as addresses only to groups or which show differences in meaning or usage between singular and plural use. Details of individual words are given in the Glossary and will not be repeated here, but the words involved are: *aequales, cives, comites, commilitones, domus, duces, famulae, famuli, homines, hospites, innuptae, iudices, iuvenes, iuventus, liberi, magistri, manus, milites, miserrimi, mulieres, oculi, parentes, patres, pontifices, popule, proceres, propinqui, pueri, Quirites, reges, servi, socii, spectatores, turba, viri,* and all ethnics. A few of these words, like *popule* and *turba,* are restricted to groups by their lexical meaning, but in most cases the distinctions in address usage are not explicable by the lexical meaning. Moreover, the words in this list are not evenly distributed among the different categories of address: none are insults or terms of endearment, although these two categories of address between them make up the majority of terms in the Latin address system. It looks as though the primarily descriptive terms which were normally employed in address to groups developed separate address meanings in this context over time, while the more emotive ones which were less often used to groups failed to develop such independent meanings.

13

Addresses to and from Non-Humans

nuntiatum est . . . consulis Cn. Domiti bovem locutum
'Roma, cave tibi'. (Liv. 35. 21. 3–4)[1]

It was reported that the consul Gnaeus Domitius' ox said,
'Rome, be on guard.'

M O S T addresses in Latin literature are spoken by one human
being to another, but a substantial minority are directed
towards non-human entities such as cities, animals, or objects,
and a few are even spoken by non-humans. The largest group
of non-human addressees consists of divinities, but as noted in
the Introduction (p. 22), the language of prayer is excluded
from this study. Leaving aside the divinities, then, places form
the largest group of non-humans in our data. Some types of
place, particularly rivers, have resident spirits which may be
personified in human or semi-human form and act like humans
or divinities. When the spirit rather than the place seems to be
the object (or the speaker) of addresses, the addresses involved
have been included in other chapters as appropriate and are not
considered here.

Addresses to places are fairly common in poetry (cf. Kroll
and Lunelli 1980: 46), often as variational vocatives but also as
direct addresses by a character in the poem, though the speaker
is normally at a distance from the place addressed. Propertius,
whose works are fairly typical as far as address to places goes,
addresses places fourteen times in his own voice (*Troia*, 2. 3.
34; *Alba*, 3. 3. 3; *Corinthe*, 3. 5. 6; *Sparte*, 3. 14. 1; *Appia*
'Appian Way', 4. 8. 17; *Erythea* 'isle of Erythea', 4. 9. 2; *Roma*,
3. 1. 15, 3. 11. 36, 49, 3. 14. 34, 4. 1. 67; *conscia Roma* 'knowing
Rome', 1. 12. 2; *invisae magno cum crimine Baiae* 'hateful Baiae
with great guilt', 3. 18. 7; *Anio Tiburne* 'Anio, tributary of the

---

[1] This incident is also reported by Valerius Maximus, 1. 6. 5, there with the
words *Cave tibi, Roma*.

Tiber', 3. 22. 23) and also puts such addresses into the mouths
of Cleopatra (*Roma*, 3. 11. 55), Cynthia's epitaph (*Aniene*
'river Anio', 4. 7. 86), and a ghost (*vada lenta, paludes* 'slow-
moving shallows, swamps', 4. 11. 15; *Roma*, 4. 11. 37; *Africa*,
4. 11. 38). Addresses to places are found as early as Ennius
(*Roma, Ann.* 6) and also occur occasionally in prose: for
example, *Massilia* 'Marseilles', Cic. *Flac.* 63; *Roma*, Sen.
Con. 10. 4. 9.

As the above examples show, cities are the most common
type of place to be addressed. Unlike other places, cities can be
thought of as collections of people, and occasionally an address
to a city seems really to be directed to its citizens as a group.
Thus Seneca has Phaedra's nurse cry for help with *Adeste,
Athenae* (*Phaed.* 725), rather than the more usual *cives*. Such
addresses are rare, however, and occur only in elevated forms
of poetry.[2]

Places other than cities are also addressed freely. Rivers,
countries, and continents are the most frequent (e.g. *Rhene*
'Rhine', Ov. *Pont.* 3. 4. 88; *Nile*, Mart. 6. 80. 10; *Xanthe*, Ov.
Ep. 5. 31; *Africa*, Suet. *Jul.* 59; *Aegypte*, Luc. 8. 834; *Ponte*, Ov.
Tr. 5. 5. 32), but mountains, islands, and lakes may also receive
vocatives (e.g. *Cithaeron*, Sen. *Phoen.* 31; *Parnase*, Luc. 5. 78;
Corcyra, Luc. 2. 623; *Thrasymenne*, Sil. 1. 547). Other types of
place may also be addressed on occasion, as *Maxime Circe* (Ov.
Fast. 2. 392) and *Appia* 'Appian Way' (Mart. 9. 101. 1).

The majority of addresses to places use the place-name alone
as a vocative, but it is also possible to add virtually any word or
words that can be used to address humans. Thus we find *o
magna vasti Creta dominatrix freti* 'O great Crete, mistress of
the vast sea' (Sen. *Phaed.* 85), *Graecia fallax* 'treacherous
Greece' (V. Fl. 8. 275), *culta Bononia* 'refined Bologna'
(Mart. 3. 59. 1), *mitis Eleusin* 'kind Eleusis' (Stat. *Theb.* 2.
382), *Mantua, dives avis* 'Mantua, rich in ancestors' (Verg. *A.*
10. 201), and *Carthago parens* 'parent Carthage' (Sil. 4. 811).
Places can also be qualified by terms that would not be used to
humans, as *saxosa Caryste* 'rocky Carystus' (Stat. *Theb.* 7. 370)
or *bacchate Cithaeron* 'Cithaeron, scene of Bacchic revels' (Stat.
Theb. 4. 371).

[2] e.g. Ov. *Met.* 7. 507; Stat. *Theb.* 12. 562. On linguistic conflation of places
and their inhabitants see further Hahn (1957).

It is also possible to address places with generic terms rather than place-names. Thus Vergil has Aeneas address Italy with *fatis mihi debita tellus* 'land owed to me by the fates' (*A.* 7. 120), while Silius has Romans call Rome, and Carthaginians call Carthage, *patria* 'fatherland' (9. 646, 13. 15), Ovid has Cydippe address Delos as *insula* 'island' (*Ep.* 21. 85), and Cicero addresses Rome with *patria* (*Sest.* 45). Such generic terms are sometimes used in declamations in order to avoid the problem that the place has not been specified: e.g. *patria* (Calp. *Decl.* 7), *res publica* (Sen. *Con.* 1. 4. 1). The use of *terra* or *tellus* 'land' with an ethnic adjective is not uncommon in poetic addresses, as *Argiva tellus* (Sen. *Tro.* 277), *Pontica tellus* (Ov. *Pont.* 3. 1. 7), and *Attica terra* (Ov. *Pont.* 1. 3. 68).

Natural features other than places rarely have names, and as a result they are normally addressed with generic terms, sometimes modified with adjectives: *harena* 'sand' (Ov. *Fast.* 3. 472), *fluctus* 'waves' (Mart. 14. 181. 2), *felix rosa* 'fortunate rose' (Mart. 7. 89. 1), *caprifice* 'wild fig tree' (Prop. 4. 5. 76), *scirpe* 'bulrush' (Pl. *Rud.* 523), *rus* 'countryside' (Hor. *S.* 2. 6. 60), *silvae* 'woods' (Verg. *Ecl.* 8. 58), etc. The earth may be addressed with *terra* (e.g. Ov. *Ars* 3. 740) or *tellus* (e.g. Ov. *Met.* 1. 544). Winds, on the other hand, are often addressed by name, as *saeve Aquilo* 'savage Aquilo' (Prop. 3. 7. 71), *Borea* (Ov. *Ep.* 18. 39), or *Zephyre* (Apul. *Met.* 5. 27). The story of Cephalus, whose addresses to the breeze were mistaken for those to a lover, provides occasion for the more affectionate addresses *optima* and *gratissima* (Ov. *Met.* 7. 814, 839).

Animals[3] are often addressed in groups, in which case the plural of the generic term is normally used: *iuvenci* 'young cattle' (Verg. *Ecl.* 7. 44), *oves* 'sheep' (Verg. *Ecl.* 3. 94), *boves* 'cattle' (Prop. 4. 9. 16), *tauri* 'bulls' (Tib. 2. 5. 55), *capellae* 'goats' (Verg. *Ecl.* 1. 74), *aves* 'birds' (Ov. *Am.* 2. 6. 2), *formicae* 'ants' (Ov. *Fast.* 1. 685), *canes* 'dogs' (Pl. *Mos.* 850), etc. This generic address may be qualified by virtually any type of modifier and is sometimes replaced by other descriptive terms: *o celeres* 'O swift ones' (to birds, [Verg.] *Ciris* 195), *noctis equi* 'horses of night' (Ov. *Am.* 1. 13. 40), *piae volucres* 'pious fliers' (Ov. *Am.* 2. 6. 3), *o quicumque sub hac habitatis*

---

[3] On animal–human relations in antiquity see Dierauer (1977).

rupe, leones 'O whatever lions live under this rock' (Ov. *Met.*
4. 114).

Animals addressed individually may have names, though this
is not common. Three kinds of named animals exist in our
data: animals who according to legend were once human (e.g.
Philomela, Ov. *Am.* 2. 6. 7; *Procne*, [Verg.] *Ciris* 410), unique
monsters (e.g. *maxime Python*, Ov. *Met.* 1. 438; *Cerbere*, Ov.
Met. 9. 185), and some war-horses (only at Verg. *A.* 10. 861;
Sil. 4. 266, 16. 389, 426). It is notable that, apart from horses,
real animals do not seem to be addressed by name in Latin,
even when an individual animal is clearly a cherished pet.
Animals may be addressed by terms designating their species,
and/or with many of the terms used for humans. Thus Catullus
calls Lesbia's sparrow *passer, deliciae meae puellae* 'sparrow, my
girl's darling' (2. 1), Hippomedon calls Tydeus' horse *infelix
sonipes* 'unhappy steed' (Stat. *Theb.* 9. 212), Statius calls a
friend's parrot *psittace dux volucrum, domini facunda voluptas,
humanae sollers imitator, psittace, linguae* 'parrot, leader of the
birds, eloquent delight of your master, clever imitator of the
human voice, parrot' (*Silv.* 2. 4. 1–2), a girl relying on an ass to
escape her captors calls him *praesidium meae libertatis meaeque
salutis* 'protector of my liberty and of my safety',[4] an old
woman calls the same ass *quadrupes nequissime* 'worthless
quadruped' (Apul. *Met.* 7. 27), a farmer calls his hen *o bona
. . . ancilla et satis fecunda* 'O good and sufficiently fertile
handmaiden' (Apul. *Met.* 9. 33), and Medea calls the dragon
guarding the golden fleece *miserande* 'pitiable' (V. Fl. 8. 99).

Animals also appear in fables, in which they tend to speak
and act like humans; these animals may receive either generic
addresses or ones that would be appropriate to a human under
similar circumstances (barring of course terms like *homo* specific to humans). Thus one finds *lupe* 'wolf' (Phaed. 1. 1. 7),
canis 'dog' (Phaed. 3. 7. 26), *infelix* 'unhappy' (to a deer, Phaed.
2. 8. 6), *amice* 'friend' (to a dog, Phaed. 3. 7. 17; to a mouse,
Hor. *S.* 2. 6. 90), *stulte* 'stupid' (to a lamb, Phaed. 3. 15. 2),
frater 'brother' (to a boar, Phaed. 1. 29. 5), *bone* 'good' (to a
mouse, Hor. *S.* 2. 6. 95), etc.

Man-made objects also receive addresses in Latin. They are

---

[4] Apul. *Met.* 6. 28; cf. Hor. *Carm.* 1. 1. 2 and Nisbet and Hubbard (1970: 4).

normally addressed by the generic name for the object concerned, not infrequently qualified by various modifiers. Examples include *mea tibia* 'my pipes' (Verg. *Ecl.* 8. 21), *compedes* 'shackles' (Pl. *Capt.* 651), *dulces exuviae* 'sweet spoils' (Verg. *A.* 4. 651), *ianua* 'door' (Tib. 1. 2. 9), *libelle* 'little book' (Pers. 1. 120), *liber* 'book' (Hor. *Ep.* 1. 20. 1),[5] *spongia* 'sponge' (Apul. *Met.* 1. 13), *Iuli bibliotheca Martialis* 'library of Julius Martialis' (Mart. 7. 17. 12), *festivae fores* 'merry doors' (Pl. *Cur.* 88), *epistola* 'letter' (Stat. *Silv.* 4. 4. 1), *barbite* 'lute' (Hor. *Carm.* 1. 32. 4), *nummi* 'coins' (Juv. 5. 136), *pessuli* 'door-bolts' (Pl. *Cur.* 147), *grabattule . . . animo meo carissime* 'little camp-bed dearest to my soul' (Apul. *Met.* 1. 16), *centum miselli . . . quadrantes* 'hundred wretched pennies' (Mart. 3. 7. 1), *anime mi, Liberi lepos* 'my soul, pleasure of Bacchus' (to wine, Pl. *Cur.* 98), *o nata mecum consule Manlio* 'O born along with me in the consulship of Manlius' (to a jar of wine, Hor. *Carm.* 3. 21. 1), *invide . . . paries* 'hostile wall' (Ov. *Met.* 4. 73), etc. On the rare occasions when such an object has a name, it is addressed by name: the ship Argo is called *Argo* (V. Fl. 1. 648) and the Marcian aqueduct *Marcia* (Stat. *Silv.* 1. 3. 67).

Speakers may also address parts of the human body, normally but not always their own (cf. McKeown 1987– : ii. 178). The most commonly addressed body part is the hand or hands, which are normally addressed either in exhortation to some task or in condemnation of a deed already done. Thus Ovid calls his hands *sacrilegae . . . manus* in remorse for his assault on his beloved (*Am.* 1. 7. 28), Jocasta uses *dextra* 'right hand' in preparing to kill herself (Sen. *Oed.* 1038), and Lucan rebukes the hand that buried Pompey with *temeraria dextra* (8. 795). The tongue and eyes are also addressed on a number of occasions (e.g. *lingua* 'tongue', Mart. 11. 25. 2; *oculi* 'eyes', Calp. *Decl.* 43), and rare vocatives occur to other body parts (e.g. feet, Prop. 3. 21. 21; fists, Pl. *Am.* 302; penis, Ov. *Am.* 3. 7. 69).

Speakers may use a variety of terms to address the seat of their thoughts and feelings, a type of address that is normally found in elevated forms of poetry. By far the most common

---

[5] On addresses to books, which are not uncommon in Latin poetry, see Szelest (1996); Kay (1985: 52); Citroni (1975: 23).

such address is *anime* 'soul', which is frequently used by Senecan characters deliberating with themselves but is by no means confined to Seneca.[6] This usage is entirely distinct from that of (*mi*) *anime* as a term of affection (p. 157; see Glossary s.v.). Also possible are *mens* 'mind' (e.g. Sil. 12. 497; Pac. *trag.* 285) and various forms of *pectus* 'heart' (Sen. *Con.* 2. 3. 1; Sen. *Thy.* 920). These addresses are normally used alone but may also be qualified as appropriate.

Feelings and other abstractions can also be addressed, usually with generic terms but also with other words. The most popular such addressee is *dolor* 'pain', but *livor* 'envy', *fortuna* 'fortune', *pudor* 'modesty', *pietas* 'piety', *fama* 'fame', *senectus* 'old age', and *mors* 'death' also occur a number of times (see Glossary for details). This type of address is also used sporadically with a large number of other abstractions, such as *ira* 'anger' (Sen. *Her. F.* 75), *virtus* 'virtue' (Calp. *Decl.* 52), *longa vetustas* 'remote antiquity' (Stat. *Silv.* 4. 1. 28), *inpotentissima medicina* 'very ineffective art of medicine' ([Quint.] *Decl.* 8. 21), *ratio* 'reason' (Grat. 6), etc. Abstractions are sometimes personified as divinities and are then addressed in terms appropriate for deities.

It is also possible for the speaker of an address to be non-human. Such speakers are rare and are almost always divinities or animals (the latter usually in fables). They appear to use the same terms that a human would use.

Some generalizations can be made about addresses involving non-humans. Non-human addressees are to a large extent treated like humans: insults, terms of endearment, titles, and even kinship terms can be used to them as to humans. The only addresses they never receive are those designating the addressee specifically as human: *homo*, *vir*, *mulier*, etc. If non-human entities have names, they are addressed by name as a human would be; if they do not have names, they are normally addressed by the generic term which would be used to refer to them. These generic terms are used largely as names would be used to humans, except that in poetry generic terms for non-humans are less likely to have modifiers attached to them than

---

[6] e.g. Sen. *Ag.* 108, *Tro.* 613, *Med.* 41, *Oed.* 1024, *Phaed.* 112; Pac. *trag.* 284; Grat. 481; Catul. 63. 61; Prop. 2. 10. 11; Quint. *Decl.* 315. 22. See Tarrant (1976: 194–5); Bonner (1949: 69, 166).

are names. This discrepancy is probably due to a lack of addresses to non-human entities in conversational language. Poets appear to have made an effort to avoid addresses that sounded too normal and prosaic, resulting in a reduction of the percentage of unmodified personal names they used to humans (see p. 43). Since addresses to non-humans did not sound prosaic in any case, however, there was no need to change to a more elaborate type of address for non-humans.

GLOSSARY

T H I S glossary is intended both to provide facts and details on individual words, when they cannot be given in the main text, and to act as a self-standing resource for readers who would like a summary of a given word's usage. It includes only those addresses which, in my judgement, formed part of the Latin address system (both literary and non-literary), not every word which happens to occur in the vocative once or even twice. A term which is part of an address system has a predictable social meaning (or meanings); this is the only way that an addressee can know what the address is communicating. Rare and unique addresses, by contrast, gain their meaning not from their previous use as vocatives, but directly from their lexical meaning and the context in which they are delivered (cf. p. 13). To understand such addresses, therefore, one does not need to consult a study of the address system, but rather a dictionary and a text.

Determination on whether a word forms part of the address system is necessarily subjective, and I have tried to err on the side of inclusivity rather than exclusivity; the presence of a word in this glossary is thus no indication that it was common in Latin, that it existed in the non-literary language, or even that it was used by more than one author. In general the following guidelines have been used. Unique addresses are omitted unless there is evidence that they were used as vocatives more than once. Addresses occurring twice or more are normally included, but they may be excluded if all attestations are from repetition within the same passage, or if there are only a few attestations and they have unrelated meanings. Personal names are not included, even when they have the same form as addresses in more general use; thus the *magne* in *Magne Pompei* (V. Max. 5. 3. 5) and the *iuste* in *Iuste Fabi* (Tac. *Dial.* 1. 1) are excluded, as is *Maxime* when a cognomen (e.g. Ov. *Pont.* 1. 2. 1). Ethnics and place-names, however, are included if they occur reasonably often.

It is hoped that this glossary will be of use not only to those reading ancient literature, but also to those wishing to include addresses in their own written or spoken Latin. In recognition of the traditional prominence of Ciceronian Latin as a model for more recent writings, at least one of the glossary examples is taken from the prose works of Cicero whenever possible; if no example from Cicero is given but his name appears in the list of authors, Cicero does not use the address as other authors do.

The entries use the following format:

1. The word used as an address (in a standardized spelling for ease of reference, though occasionally a vocative is attested only with archaic spellings of the word), with all the endings it takes as an address in my data.

2. Translation of its referential meaning, or those of its referential meanings which appear to be most relevant to the address usage.

3. Its total number of occurrences in my data (the sign + after this number means that there are more occurrences of the term in prayers).

4. A brief description of its address usage, including an indication of whether adjectives are used adjectivally or sub-stantivally, if they show a marked preference ('Adj.' and 'Subst.'), and whether nouns are normally used alone or modified by adjectives (such rules are not absolute unless qualified by 'always').

5. An evaluation of whether the address belongs only to literary language ('Lit.') or to more general usage ('Gen.'), and a broad judgement on its register ('High', 'Mid.', 'Low'; 'Var.' = not restricted as to register).

6. A complete listing of the authors in which I found the address, excluding those using it only in prayers (the existence of such excluded authors is indicated by 'and prayers').

7. Two references to typical examples of the term's use (more than two are given when the usage cannot be adequately illustrated from two examples).

The following conventions have been adhered to:

1. Gender-neutral terms such as 'person' are used in the description of usage when there is no evidence for gender-

based restrictions on usage; the use of the word 'man' implies the exclusion of women, and vice versa.

2. Masculine and feminine versions of the same words are sometimes listed separately when there are differences in usage between the genders. Positive, comparative, and superlative forms of adjectives are always listed separately as their usage is normally distinct.

3. The term 'modified' means that the address is qualified by an adjective, genitive, dative, or any other type of grammatically dependent construction; when a word is stated to be 'unmodified', however, this designation does not exclude the use of *mi/mea* or of *o*, both of which may be used with words not normally modified in other ways.

4. 'Known' and 'unknown' refer to the prior acquaintance of the speaker with the addressee, not to the perspective of the reader.

5. 'Mistress' is used only in relation to slaves, not lovers.

For reasons of space, references to other discussions of these terms are not included. Most words listed, however, are discussed in the *TLL*, and in many cases the *OLD* entry is relevant as well. Many words are also treated by one or more of the works mentioned on pp. 20–1 and in the introductions to the individual chapters; O'Brien (1930), Opelt (1965), and Harrod (1909) are useful for a particularly large number of terms.

In the listing of references, the citation system normally follows that of the *Oxford Latin Dictionary*; exceptions to this policy are indicated in the list of editions on pp. 370–3. In the listing of authors, however, the omission of titles would in some cases lead to ambiguity if the *OLD* reference system were followed, and so that system is supplemented as follows: the abbreviations 'Sen.' and 'Plin.' are restricted to Seneca the younger and Pliny the younger respectively, while the elder authors of these names are indicated with 'Sen. S.' and 'Plin. S.' Calpurnius Siculus is listed as 'Calp. S.', and Calpurnius Flaccus as 'Calp. F.' 'Nov.' and 'Pompon.' always refer to poets. The designation [Verg.] is added for the works of the *Appendix Vergiliana*, and 'trag. frag.' and 'com. frag.' indicate unattributed fragments. Non-literary attestation is indicated by 'graf.' for material from Pompeii and Herculaneum, 'epist.' for papyrus letters, ostraca, and the Vindolanda tablets, and 'inscr.' for all other epigraphic material. In the case of Seneca the younger, as the language of his tragedies is markedly different from that of the prose works, a word found only in one type of his work is so indicated with '(trag.)' or '(prose)'; references to Cicero, Varro, and Apuleius are to prose works unless marked '(poetry)'. When an author's name is in round brackets, as (Cic.), the address is found only in works not actually written by the author concerned (e.g. in letters to Cicero contained in the Ciceronian corpus), while square brackets, as [Cic.], indicate that the vocative is found only in spurious works. If the term is found in both genuine and spurious works, no special mention is made of spurious ones, with the exception of Quintilian. For that author, because of the significant differences in style and date between the *Declamationes Minores* and *Declamationes Maiores* (see p. 27), these two are treated as separate authors, 'Quint.' and '[Quint.]'. (The *Institutio Oratoria* is also designated as 'Quint.' but virtually never referred to.)

Accusator, -es 'accuser (m.)': 6. Somewhat pejorative address from a person on trial, or someone acting on behalf of such a person, to the accuser(s), esp. in declamations. Lit.? Mid.   Cic., Quint., [Quint.]   Cic. *S. Rosc.* 58, Quint. *Decl.* 328. 9.

Achaei 'Achaeans': 6. Neutral term for groups of Achaeans in the historical period.   Gen. Var.?   Liv. Liv. 32. 20. 3, 35. 49. 9.

Achivi 'Achaeans': 6. Neutral term for the Greek army before Troy.   Lit. High (poetic).   Cic. (poetry), Ov., *Ilias.*   Ov. *Met.* 13. 136; *Ilias* 151.

Adempte 'taken away': 5. Used to a dead relative to express the speaker's grief.   Lit. High (poetic).   Catul., Ov.   Catul. 68. 20; Ov. *Ep.* 9. 166.

Adulescens, -es 'young person': 82. Neutral term for young men not particularly close to the speaker, especially strangers, in which case it is usable to adults. Also used as a somewhat negative address to close relatives and lovers. Addressees are always male. Usually unmodified; always unmodified when addressee is unknown.   Gen. Mid.

Pl., Ter., Pac., Cic., Liv., Sen. S., V. Max., Petr., Quint., Gel., Calp. F., [Quint.], inscr.   Pl. *Men.* 135, *Ps.* 1141; Cic. *Sen.* 39; Petr. 129. 6.   Cf. *adulescentula* (Pl. *Rud.* 416).

Advena, -ae 'visitor': 3. Neutral term for male visitors. Lit.? Mid.?   Pl., Ov., Stat.   Pl. *Aul.* 406; Ov. *Ep.* 17. 5.

Aequales 'age-mates': 3. Friendly term for a group of men or women the same age and gender as the speaker.   Lit.? High–mid.   Catul., Curt.   Catul. 62. 11; Curt. 7. 11. 8.

Aetoli 'Aetolians': 4. Neutral term for Aetolians in the historical period.   Gen. Var.?   Liv.   Liv. 31. 31. 18, 36. 28. 2.

Agricola, -ae 'farmer (m.)': 3. Neutral address for farmers in general.   Lit.? Mid.   Pl., Verg., Plin. S. Pl. *Rud.* 616; Verg. *G.* 2. 36.

Alme, -a 'nurturing': 6 +. Term of praise and great respect for goddesses or very exalted humans, usually female. Lit. High (poetic, cultic).   Verg., Ov., Stat., V. Fl., and prayers.   Verg. *A.* 6. 117; Ov. *Met.* 13. 759; V. Fl. 5. 551.

Altrix 'nurse (f.)': 6. Senecan variant of *nutrix*; similar usage but higher register.   Lit. High (poetic).   Sen. (trag.)   Sen. *Phaed.* 251, 358.

Alumna, -ae 'nursling (f.)': 18. Affectionate term used by a nurse to the girl or woman she cares for or cared for; also occasionally with a genitive in metaphorical sense to non-humans.   Gen.? Mid.   Cic. (poetry), [Verg.], Ov., Sen. (trag.), Sil., Apul.   Cic. *Div.* 1. 15; Ov. *Met.* 10. 442; Sen. *Med.* 158; Sil. 2. 531.

Alumne 'nursling (m.)': 2. Used with a genitive to describe an addressee's relationship with something parent-like. Lit.? Mid.?   Mart.   Mart. 1. 76. 2, 12. 60. 1; perhaps to be read also at Pl. *Mer.* 809.   Cf. Suet. *Cal.* 13.

Amate, -a 'beloved': 4. Term of affection, meaning dependent on context.   Lit. High (poetic).   Ov., Stat. Ov. *Pont.* 4. 12. 22; Stat. *Theb.* 2. 343.

Amator 'lover (m.)': 9 +. (1) Rebuke to an old man engaged in

inappropiate and illicit affairs. (2) Neutral address to people
who are lovers of someone or something (not the speaker).
Gen. Var.?   (1) Pl. (2) Ov. and prayers.   Pl. *As.*
921, *Mer.* 976; Ov. *Am.* 1. 8. 66.

Amens 'insane': 2. Rebuke for those who act wrongly. Subst.
Gen.? High?   Cic., Sen. (trag.)   Cic. *Pis.* 21;
Sen. *Ag.* 244.

Amentissime, -i 'very insane': 11. Fairly strong insult and
expression of scorn. Adj.   Gen. Mid.?   Cic.
Cic. *Phil.* 2. 42, *Pis.* 57.

Amica 'friend (f.)': 3. Complimentary term used by a male
lover to his beloved or the (female) object of his desire.
Gen. Low?   Pl.   Pl. *Poen.* 393, *Truc.* 917.

Amice, -i 'friend (m.)': 95. (1) In singular, affectionate address
usually from a man to a male friend, often used when names
are avoided but also frequently to named friends; in inscriptions it can be used to the reader. (2) Plural used by a man,
often an author in his own voice, to a specified or unspecified
group of male friends; in funerary inscriptions it can be used
to friends of the deceased or to readers in general.
Gen. Mid.   (1) Pl., Ter., Cic., Catul., Verg., Hor.,
Prop., Ov., Phaed., Petr., Pers., Mart., V. Fl., Fro., [Quint.],
inscr. (2) Pl., Pac., Hor., Prop., Liv., Ov., Sen. S., Petr.,
Curt., Quint., Stat., Tac., Juv., Suet., [Quint.], inscr.
(1) Pl. *Trin.* 48; Cic. *Fam.* 7. 29. 2; Ov. *Pont.* 4. 12. 1; *ILS*
6192; (2) Petr. 33. 1; Tac. *Ann.* 1. 43; *ILS* 1967, 8145.

Amicissime, -i 'very friendly': 7. Term of affection used by
men to valued male friends.   Gen. Mid.   Pl.,
Cic., Fro.   Cic. *Rep.* 1. 70; Fro. 34. 23.

Amoena 'pleasant': 2. Term of endearment for lovers.
Gen.? Low?   Pl.   Pl. *Poen.* 389, *St.* 736.
Cf. *amoenissumi* (Pl. *Cur.* 149).

Amoenitas 'pleasantness': 2. Term of endearment for lovers,
with *mea*.   Gen.? Low?   Pl.   Pl. *Cas.* 229,
Poen. 365.

Amor 'love': 3. Term of endearment.   Gen. Mid.
(Fro.), graf.   Fro. 63. 10; *CIL* iv. 5395, 8137.

Amplissime 'very great': 7. Honorific title in later Latin,
often used with *consul*.   Gen. High–mid.
(Fro.), Gel.   Fro. 31. 18; Gel. 1. 2. 6.

Ancilla 'maidservant': 3. Neutral address to a maidservant, normally modified.   Gen.? Mid.?   Pl., Apul. Pl. *Cas.* 647; Apul. *Met.* 6. 8.

Anima, -ae 'soul, life': 25. (1) Term of endearment, often with adjectives such as *dulcissima*. (2) Neutral address to souls, usually dead ones; always plural.   (1) Gen. Low–mid. (2) Lit. High.   (1) Cic., Phaed., (Fro.), Apul., graf., epist., inscr. (2) Verg., Sen. (trag.), Sil., Tac.   (1) Cic. *Fam.* 14. 14. 2; Fro. 30. 13; *Tab. Vindol. II* 291. 12; (2) Verg. *A.* 6. 669; Sen. *Med.* 743.   Cf. *animula* (Hadr. 3. 1; *CIL* iv. 4239). Also (as endearment) genitive after nouns such as *pars* (q.v.).

Anime, -us 'mind, soul': 53. (1) Term of endearment, usually from a woman to her lover, always with *mi*. (2) Neutral address to the speaker's own soul.   (1) Gen. Low. (2) Lit. High–mid.   (1) Pl., Ter., (Fro.) (2) Pac., Catul., Prop., Grat., Sen. S., Sen., Quint., [Quint.]   (1) Pl. *Men.* 182, *As.* 941; Fro. 35. 3; (2) Prop. 2. 10. 11; Sen. *Con.* 2. 3. 6; Sen. *Med.* 41.

Animose, -a 'bold': 3. Mild rebuke.   Lit. High (poetic). Ov., Sen. (trag.), Stat.   Ov. *Am.* 3. 1. 35; Sen. *Phoen.* 94.

Animule 'little soul': 2. Term of endearment for romantic love, with *mi*, used only by women.   Gen. Low. Pl.   Pl. *Cas.* 134, *Men.* 361.

Anus 'old woman': 4. Term for known old women.   ? Pl., Pompon., Sen. (trag.)   Pl. *Cur.* 120; Sen. *Tro.* 1059.

Arbor 'tree': 3. Neutral term for a tree.   Lit. High (poetic).   Hor., Stat., Mart.   Hor. *Carm.* 2. 13. 3; Mart. 9. 61. 19.

Asine 'ass': 4. Rebuke and expression of scorn; also once as a neutral address to an ass.   Gen. Low.   Ter., Cic., Apul., graf.   Ter. *Ad.* 935; Cic. *Pis.* 73; Apul. *Met.* 9. 30.

Asper, -a 'harsh': 2. Term for people who are abnormally harsh; not necessarily pejorative.   Lit. High. Verg., Suet.   Verg. *A.* 11. 664; Suet. *Tib.* 59. 1.

Athenae 'Athens': 4. Neutral address for the city of Athens and

its people.   Lit. Var.?   Pl., Ov., Sen. (trag.),
Stat.   Pl. *St.* 649; Ov. *Met.* 7. 507.

Atheniensis, -es 'Athenian': 10. Term for Athenians; normally plural.   ?   Sen. S., Quint.   Sen. *Con.*
10. 5. 1, 10. 5. 15; Quint. *Decl.* 339. 1.

Auctor 'maker, causer (m.)': 4+. Term for gods and other
makers and causers; takes genitive of thing made. Positive or
negative depending on genitive.   Lit. High (poetic).
Ov., Grat., Sen. (trag.), Stat.   Ov. *Met.* 9. 577; Stat.
Silv. 4. 6. 108.

Audacissime 'very bold': 7. Moderately strong insult and
rebuke for those who have displayed brazenness.   Gen.
Low–mid.   Pl., Ter., Cic.   Pl. *Aul.* 745; Cic.
Phil. 2. 43.

Audax 'bold': 7. Rebuke to someone acting too bold, normally
from a superior.   Gen. Var.   Naev., Pl., [Cic.],
Prop., Sen. (trag.), Juv.   Pl. *Men.* 1050; [Cic.] *Rhet.
Her.* 4. 65; Juv. 5. 74.   Cf. *ausa* (Sen. *Phaed.* 688);
audaciai columen (Pl. *Am.* 367).

Augur 'seer, interpreter': 3. Polite address to a seer of any
type.   Lit. High (poetic).   Hor., Ov., Stat.
Hor. *S.* 2. 5. 22; Ov. *Am.* 3. 5. 31.

Auguste 'Augustus': 22. With *Caesar*, used to address emperors in formal speeches; otherwise laudatory address for
emperors, esp. in poetry.   Gen. High.   Hor.,
Prop., Ov., Mart., Tac., Plin., Suet.   Hor. *Carm.* 4.
14. 3; Plin. *Pan.* 4. 3.

Aura, -ae 'breeze': 5. Neutral address to breezes.   Lit.?
High (poetic)?   [Verg.], Ov.   Ov. *Met.* 7. 813,
Ep. 15. 177.

Avare, -a 'greedy': 4. Moderate rebuke for those displaying
greed or avarice. Subst.   Gen. Var.?   Pl., Ov.,
Phaed., Mart.   Pl. *Per.* 687; Ov. *Am.* 3. 8. 22.

Avis, -es 'bird': 4. Neutral term for a bird or birds.   Lit.?
High (poetic)?   Ov., Luc.   Ov. *Fast.* 2. 249; Luc.
7. 834.

Barbare, -a 'foreign, uncivilized': 9. Term of opprobrium for
foreigners and for those acting in an uncivilized manner.
Subst.   Lit.? High–mid.   Caecil., Tib., Ov.,
Mart., V. Fl.   Ov. *Am.* 1. 7. 19; V. Fl. 8. 148.

Beate, -i 'happy': 6. Respectful and distant address, or statement of fact with no polite implications.   Lit. High
(poetic).   [Verg.], Hor., Prop., Stat.   Hor. *Carm.*
1. 4. 14; Prop. 2. 15. 2.

Bellator 'warrior': 3. Somewhat derogatory address for a
soldier from a civilian.   Gen.? Low.   Pl.
Pl. *Cur.* 553, *Truc.* 629.

Belle, -a 'pretty, nice': 2. Term of praise.   Gen. Var.
Pl., Laev.   Pl. *As.* 676; Laev. 20. Cf. *belliata* (Pl. *Rud.*
463); *belliatula* (Pl. *Cas.* 854).

Belua 'beast': 4. Moderately strong insult.   Gen. Low.
Pl., Ter., Cic.   Pl. *Rud.* 543; Cic. *Pis.* 1.   Cf.
bestia (Apul. *Met.* 2. 25).

Bone, -a, -i 'good': 49. (1) Term of genuine praise usable to
equals, superiors, and subordinates. (2) Used ironically to
show the speaker's superiority, in contexts ranging from
polite correction (esp. in philosophical contexts) to outright
anger. In both senses it is normally adjectival (and, in
comedy, usually qualifies *vir* and is addressed to slaves).
Gen. Var.   (1) Pl., Ter., Lucr., Verg., Catul., Hor.,
Ov., Pers., Stat., Fro., Apul., inscr. (2) Pl., Ter., Cic.,
Catul., Hor., Sil., Pers., Stat., Apul., Gel.   (1) Ter.
An. 846; Verg. *A.* 11. 344; Hor. *Carm.* 4. 5. 5, *Ep.* 2. 2. 37;
Apul. *Met.* 2. 24; *ILS* 8183; (2) Pl. *Capt.* 954; Cic. *Ver.* 5. 12;
Hor. *S.* 2. 3. 31; Gel. 5. 21. 6.

Bucco 'dolt': 3. Mild insult.   Gen. Low?   Apris.,
Pompon., graf.   Apris. *com.* 1; Pompon. *com.* 10; *CIL*
iv. 4720.

Cacator 'defecator': 9. Address to anyone who might foul the
area near an inscription.   Gen. Low.   Graf.
CIL iv. 3782, 6641.

Caece, -i 'blind': 3. Neutral address to a nameless blind man,
and rebuke for those blind in spirit. Subst.   Lit. High–
mid.   Sen. S., Luc.   Sen. *Con.* 10. 4. 4; Luc. 1.
87.

Caenum 'filth': 2. Strong insult.   Gen. Low.   Pl.,
Cic.   Pl. *Ps.* 366; Cic. *Pis.* 13.   Cf. Pl. *Per.* 407.

Caesar 'Caesar': 157. (1) As the inherited cognomen of Gaius
Julius Caesar and others, used like a cognomen (see Ch. 1);
these uses are not included in the figure 157. (2) As an

imperial address, very often used for current or future
emperors, mostly in formal speeches (where it can be
combined with *Auguste* or a name to give a slightly higher
register) and literary works.   Gen. High–mid.
(1) Cic., [Caes.], Catul., Gal., Sen. (prose), Luc. (2) Verg.,
Hor., Ov., Sen. S., V. Max., Calp. S., Vitr., Sen. (prose),
Luc., Quint., Mart., Tac., Juv., Plin., Suet., Fro., inscr.
(1) Cic. *De Orat.* 2. 98; Catul. 93. 1; (2) Hor. *Ep.* 2. 1. 4; Tac.
Ann. 1. 12; Suet. *Aug.* 58. 2; *ILS* 137.

Callide, -a 'clever, skilled': 2+. Term of praise.   Lit.
High (poetic)?   Hor., Stat., and prayers.   Hor.
Carm. 3. 11. 4; Stat. *Theb.* 2. 334.   Cf. *callidissime*
([Quint.] *Decl.* 11. 11).

Cana 'white-haired': 2. Address for the elderly, somewhat
derogatory.   Gen.? Low–mid.   Pl., Mart.
Pl. *Cas.* 239; Mart. 14. 27. 1.

Candide, -a 'kind, white, clear': 9+. Term of praise, usually
for gods, readers, and patrons, used in author's own voice.
Lit. High (poetic).   Hor., Ov., *Laus Pis.*, inscr., and
prayers.   Hor. *Epod.* 14. 5; Ov. *Tr.* 1. 11. 35.
Cf. *candidior* (Ov. *Met.* 13. 789).

Canis, -es 'dog': 6. (1) Neutral address for dogs. (2) Insult for
humans (probably strong).   (1) Gen. Mid. (2) Gen.
Low.   (1) Pl., Phaed., Priap. (2) Ter., Cic.   (1)
Pl. *Mos.* 850; Phaed. 3. 7. 26; (2) Ter. *Eu.* 803; Cic. *Pis.* 23.

Capellae 'goats': 4. Neutral term for absent goats (not a call).
?   Verg.   Verg. *Ecl.* 1. 74, 10. 77.

Caput 'head': 18. Combined with an adjective or genitive,
forms a base for a positive or negative address (esp. in
scelerum caput, q.v.). Probably general at early period and
literary later. Register varies by collocation.   Pl., Ter.,
Verg., Hor., Prop., Sen. (trag.), V. Fl.   Pl. *Per.* 184;
Prop. 4. 11. 55; Hor. *Epod.* 5. 74; Verg. *A.* 11. 361.

Care, -a 'dear': 52. General term of affection for relatives,
lovers, and friends (usually of equal or lower status).
Lit. High–mid.   Verg., Prop., Tib., Ov., Sen. (trag.),
Luc., Sil., Stat., Mart., V. Fl., Apul., inscr.   Verg. *A.*
8. 581; Ov. *Pont.* 4. 8. 89; Mart. 5. 20. 1.   Cf. *caritas*
(Fro. 34. 15).

Carior, -ius 'dearer': 3. Term of endearment; takes ablative of comparison.   Lit. High (poetic).   Ov., V. Fl. Ov. *Met.* 8. 405; V. Fl. 2. 404.   Cf. *care magis* (Verg. *A.* 5. 725).

Carissime, -a, -i, -ae 'very dear': 122. General term of mild affection, esp. for friends or acquaintances of equal or lower status.   Gen. Var.   Cic., Catul., Sal., Verg., Ov., Sen. S., Sen. (prose), Petr., Curt., Stat., Mart., Plin., Fro., Apul., Calp. F., Paul., [Quint.], epist., inscr.   Cic. *Q. fr.* 2. 6. 4; Plin. *Ep. Tra.* 10. 60. 2.

Carmina 'songs': 11. Address from a poet/singer to his own poetry/songs.   Lit. High (poetic).   Verg., Prop. Verg. *Ecl.* 8. 68; Prop. 2. 10. 11.

Carnifex 'executioner': 16. Strong insult normally used to male slaves; also very rarely as a neutral address to a nameless executioner.   Gen. Low.   Pl., Ter., Cic., Sen. S., Hyg. *Fab.*   Pl. *Am.* 588; Cic. *Pis.* 10; Sen. *Con.* 2. 3. 19.   Cf. *carnuficium cribrum* (Pl. *Mos.* 55).

Carthago 'Carthage': 11. Neutral address for Carthage. Lit. High?   Hor., Sil.   Hor. *Carm.* 3. 5. 39; Sil. 4. 811.

Caste, -a, -ae 'pure': 4+. Term of praise for the chaste, also used in mockery for the unchaste.   Lit. High–mid.? [Tib.], Mart., inscr., and prayers.   [Tib.] 3. 1. 23, 3. 9. 20; *ILS* 6261.   Cf. *castior* (Mart. 8. 46. 2).

Catelle 'puppy': 1. Term of endearment.   Gen.? Low? Hor. *S.* 2. 3. 259.   Cf. Pl. *As.* 693.

Caupo 'innkeeper': 6. Neutral address for named and nameless innkeepers.   Gen. Low?   Graf., inscr. *CIL* iv. 3502; *ILS* 8609.

Causidice, -i 'barrister (m.)': 2. Somewhat derogatory term for unnamed lawyers.   Lit. Mid.?   Sen. (prose), Mart.   Sen. *Apoc.* 12. 3. 28; Mart. 5. 33. 2.

Censor, -es 'censor': 3. Polite term for holders of the office of censor.   Lit. High?   [Cic.], Liv., Mart. [Cic.] *Rhet. Her.* 2. 41; Liv. 40. 46. 1; Mart. 6. 4. 1.

Cinaede 'catamite': 14. Strong insult. Adj.   Gen. Low. Pl., Catul., [Verg.], graf.   Pl. *As.* 627; Catul. 16. 2; *CIL* iv. 10086.

Cives 'citizens': 35. Term for an assembly of citizens, random bystanders, or almost any group of free men and/or women, normally spoken by a fellow-citizen. Generally positive. Sometimes with ethnic or other adjective.   Gen. Var. Pl., Enn., Pac., Cic., Verg., Hor., Prop., Liv., Phaed., V. Max., Sen. (trag.), Luc., Sil., Curt., Apul., [Quint.] Pl. *Cur.* 626; Cic. *Mil.* 77; Verg. *A.* 11. 243.

Clare, -a, -um 'famous': 8 +. Term of respect or general politeness.   Lit. High (poetic).   Sen. (trag.), Sil., Stat.   Sil. 12. 175; Stat. *Theb.* 7. 731.

Clarissime, -i 'very famous': 6. General polite address; in the imperial period, a title for those of senatorial rank (with *vir*; cf. Bang 1921: 77–81).   Gen. High–mid.   Cic., Laurea, Verg., Plin., Gel.   Cic. *Agr.* 2. 50; Verg. *A.* 5. 495; Plin. *Ep.* 9. 13. 19.

Cliens, -es 'client (m.)': 4. With genitive or other modifiers, address to someone who is a client (or is acting as such) in relation to the speaker or the person in the genitive. Lit. Mid.   Sen. S., Mart., Apul., graf.   Sen. *Con.* 5. 2; Mart. 12. 68. 1; *CIL* iv. 7668.

Cohors, -es 'troops': 4. Address from a military leader to his men, normally positive.   Lit. High (poetic). Catul., Sen. (trag.), Luc., Stat.   Luc. 3. 360; Stat. *Theb.* 12. 643.

Colone, -i 'inhabitant, colonist, farmer (m.)': 9. Neutral address to farmers, settlers, etc. in general or to unspecified individuals.   Lit. (Gen. in pl.?) Mid.?   Tib., Ov., *Priap.*, Calp. S., Mart., inscr.   Ov. *Fast.* 4. 407; *Priap.* 61. 1; *ILLRP* 1139.

Columba 'dove': 1. Term of endearment for lovers. Gen.? Low?   Pl. *Cas.* 138.   Cf. Pl. *As.* 693.

Columen 'keystone': 6. Term praising (or, less often, blaming) the addressee for being crucial to some person, thing, or group named in the genitive.   Gen.? Var.   Pl., Ter., Catul., Sen. (trag.), V. Max.   Pl. *Am.* 367; Catul. 64. 26; Sen. *Tro.* 124.

Comes, -tes 'companion': 25. (1) In singular, shows a male addressee's association with the speaker or someone else; usually with genitive. (2) In plural, mildly positive term used to the speaker's friends or subordinates of either gender, less often with genitive to another's associates.   (1) Lit.

High. (2) Gen. High–mid.   (1) [Cic.], Hor., Ov., Sen. (trag.), Sil., Mart., Hadr., Calp. F. (2) Pl., Catul., Hor., Ov., Sen. (trag.), Luc., Stat.   (1) Hor. *S.* 2. 6. 93; Sen. *Her. F.* 646; Mart. 10. 92. 1; (2) Catul. 28. 1; Ov. *Fast.* 4. 431; Stat. *Theb.* 4. 678.

Commilito, -es 'fellow soldier': 26. In sing., address from one soldier to another whose name is unknown; in plural (much more common), neutral address from a soldier to his comrades or ingratiating one from a commander to his men. Gen. Mid.   Liv., Sen. S., Phaed., V. Max., Sen. (prose), Petr., Curt., Quint., Tac., Suet., Apul., [Quint.] Petr. 82. 3; Curt. 6. 10. 8; Suet. *Gal.* 20. 1.

Commoditas 'convenience' (Tyrrell 1927: 219): 3. Term of praise for useful subordinates.   ?   Pl.   Pl. *Epid.* 614, *Poen.* 421.

Coniunx (fem. also **coniuga**) 'spouse': 78 +. (1) Address from husband to wife or wife to husband. (2) With genitive or adjective indicating object of relationship, address to anyone's wife (or occasionally husband). (3) Alone in transferred sense to the spouse of a person under discussion (rare).   Lit. High.   Catul, Verg., Tib., Ov., Sen. (trag.), *Ilias*, Luc., Sil., Stat., V. Fl., Apul., inscr., and prayers (usually in sense 2).   (1) Verg. *A.* 2. 519; Ov. *Met.* 9. 382; (2) [Sen.] *Her. O.* 950; (3) Catul. 61. 226; Luc. 7. 675.

Consul, -es 'consul': 16. Address from people of any rank to a consul, or in plural to both consuls. From the end of the 1st cent. AD takes a complimentary adjective, as *amplissime* or *clarissime*.   Gen. Mid.   Cic., Liv., Luc., Sil, Plin., (Fro.)   Cic. *Phil.* 2. 30; Liv. 9. 26. 19; Fro. 30. 12.

Cor 'heart': 3. Term of endearment for romantic love, with *meum*.   Gen. Low?   Pl.   Pl. *Bac.* 17, *Poen.* 367.   Cf. *corculum* (Pl. *Cas.* 836).

Corpora 'bodies': 3. With appropriate modifiers, term for a group of living or dead people.   Lit. High (poetic). Enn., Verg., Ov.   Enn. *trag.* 242; Ov. *Met.* 3. 58.

Credule 'credulous': 2. Mild rebuke for those holding unwise beliefs. Subst.   Lit. High (poetic).   Prop., Ov. Prop. 2. 25. 22; Ov. *Met.* 3. 432.

Crudelis, -es 'cruel': 30 +. Rebuke for those causing suffering, normally the speaker's suffering. Addressed often to loved ones who die, do not return the speaker's love, or act cruelly; also to more distant trouble-causers, occasionally including gods and inanimate objects.　　Gen.?　High–mid. Hor., Ov., Verg., Sen. (trag.), Luc., Stat., Mart., V. Fl., [Quint.]　　　　Hor. *Ep.* 1. 17. 61; Verg. *A.* 9. 483; Ov. *Met.* 3. 477, *Ars* 3. 581.　　　　Cf. *crudelior* (Prop. 1. 16. 17).

Crudelissime, -a 'very cruel': 5. Rebuke for those causing suffering. Adj.　　　Gen.?　Mid.?　　　　Sen. (prose), [Quint.]　　　Sen. *Apoc.* 13. 6; [Quint.] *Decl.* 18. 14.

Cruente 'bloody': 2. Address for harmful non-human entities. Subst.　　　Lit. High (poetic).　　　　Ov., Sen. (trag.) Ov. *Pont.* 4. 16. 48; Sen. *Phoen.* 34.

Cucule 'cuckoo': 2. Expression of contempt.　　　Gen. Low.　　Pl.　　　Pl. *Per.* 282, *Ps.* 96.

Culte, -a 'refined': 3. Term of praise, usually for poets. Lit. High (poetic)?　　　Ov., Mart.　　　Ov. *Am.* 3. 9. 66; Mart. 3. 59. 1.　　　　Cf. *exculte* (Ov. *Pont.* 4. 8. 1).

Cultor, -trix 'cultivator, worshipper': 4 +. With genitive of thing cultivated, forms laudatory addresses.　　　Lit. High (poetic).　　　Ov., Mart., and prayers.　　　Ov. *Tr.* 3. 14. 1; Mart. 5. 5. 1.

Cunne, -i 'female genitalia': 4. Rude address to lewd women or their genitalia.　　Gen.?　Low?　　　　Mart., graf. Mart. 6. 45. 1, 7. 35. 8; *CIL* iv. 3932.

Cura 'care': 11. Term of affection and/or praise, depending on modifiers, usually with *mea* or another possessive. Occasionally used neutrally to the abstraction Care.　　　Gen. High–mid.　　　Verg., Tib., Ov., Stat., Mart., V. Fl., Fro.　　　Verg. *A.* 3. 476; Ov. *Tr.* 2. 1. 1; Mart. 11. 26. 1; V. Fl. 6. 499.

Custos, -es 'guardian': 9 +. Address for men or women employed in guarding a person or thing; usually takes genitive of thing guarded. Meaning (frequently ironic) and register depend on context.　　　Lit. Var.　　　Pl., Enn., Ter., Cic., Hor., Ov., V. Max., V. Fl., and prayers. Enn. *trag.* 237; Cic. *Ver.* 5. 12; Hor. *Carm.* 4. 5. 2.

Danai 'Danaans': 7. Neutral term for the Greek army before

Troy.   Lit. High (poetic).   Verg., Prop., Ov.,
Ilias, Sen. (trag.)   Verg. *A.* 2. 117; Ov. *Ep.* 3. 127.

Dea 'goddess': 5 +. Very respectful address used by humans to
goddesses, also sometimes used less respectfully by one
divinity to another. In prayers it is general; otherwise literary
and high register (poetic).   Verg., Ov., Sil., and
prayers.   Verg. *A.* 1. 328; Ov. *Met.* 14. 841; Sil. 9. 473.

Decus, -a 'honour': 47 +. Term of praise, usable to anyone,
meaning often specified by genitives or other modifiers.
Gen. High–mid.   Pl., trag. frag., Lucr., Catul., Cic.
(poetry), Verg., Hor., Ov., Sen. S., Sen. (trag.), Luc., *Ilias*,
Laus Pis., Sil., Stat., Mart., V. Fl., Fro.   Verg. *A.* 11.
508; Hor. *Carm.* 1. 1. 2; Ov. *Ep.* 16. 273.

Dedecus 'disgrace': 4. Fairly strong insult; takes genitive of
the people or thing disgraced.   Gen. High–mid.
Cic., Phaed., *Ilias*, Apul.   Cic. *Pis.* 53; Phaed. 1. 21.
11.

Degener, -es 'inferior, degenerate': 5. Fairly strong rebuke to
those who fail to meet the standards of their predecessors.
Lit. High (poetic).   Luc., Stat.   Luc. 8. 676;
Stat. *Theb.* 10. 209.

Delicia, -ae 'delight': 9. Term of endearment, normally for
lovers; frequently in plural even to singular addressees;
usually with *mea, -ae.*   Gen. Mid.   Pl., Titin.,
Catul., graf.   Pl. *Truc.* 921; Catul. 32. 2.

Demens 'insane': 30. Moderately strong insult, also usable in
warnings or rebukes to men or women close to the speaker,
or to himself/herself. Subst.   Gen.? High.
Verg., Prop., Ov., Sen. S., V. Max., Sen. (trag.), Luc., Sil.,
Curt., Quint., Stat., Mart., V. Fl., Juv., [Quint.]
Verg. *A.* 11. 399; Sen. *Med.* 174.

Desiderantissime 'greatly desired': 4. Term of affection
between male friends.   Gen.? Mid.?   Fro.
Fro. 30. 11, 81. 7.   Cf. *desideratissima* (*Tab. Vindol. II*
292 b back).

Desiderium, -a 'desire': 3. Term of endearment, with *meum,*
-a.   Gen. Low–mid.   Cic., (Fro.)   Cic.
Fam. 14. 2. 2; Fro. 63. 21.   Cf. Petr. 139. 4.

Dextra 'right hand': 5. Term for a hand, normally the
speaker's own.   Lit. High (poetic).   Sen.

(trag.), Luc., Sil., Stat.　　　Sen. *Her. F.* 1281; Stat. *Theb.*
9. 548.

Dictator 'dictator': 3. Address from a military subordinate to a
Roman dictator.　　　Lit.?　Mid.　　　Liv., Sil.
Liv. 7. 13. 3; Sil. 8. 269.

Die, -a 'divine': 2. Term for deified humans or those related to
gods.　　　Lit. High (poetic).　　　Enn.　　Enn.
Ann. 60, 106.

Difficilis, -es 'troublesome': 2.　　　Rebuke for inanimate
objects causing trouble for the speaker. Adj.　　　Lit. High
(poetic).　　Tib., Ov.　　　Tib. 1. 2. 7; Ov. *Am.* 1.
12. 7.

Digne, -a 'worthy': 13. Usually a term of praise, but can also
be an insult, depending on modifiers; only used with a
specification of what the addressee is worthy of. Does not
have the self-standing positive sense of English 'worthy'.
Lit. High (poetic).　　　Hor., Prop., Ov., Sil., Stat., Mart.
Ov. *Met.* 1. 589; Sil. 15. 33.

Dignissime, -a, -i 'very worthy': 8. Usually a term of praise,
but can also be an insult, depending on modifiers; only used
with a specification of what the addressee is worthy of.
Lit.? High–mid.　　　Hor., Ov., Luc., *Laus Pis.*, Curt.,
Stat., Juv.　　　Ov. *Met.* 4. 320; Juv. 13. 33.

Dilecte, -a 'beloved': 8. Term of general, mild affection.
Lit. High (poetic).　　　Verg., Hor., Ov., Stat., Mart.,
V. Fl.　　　Hor. *Carm.* 2. 20. 7; Stat. *Silv.* 2. 1. 37.

Dire, -a 'dreadful': 5. Term for those who are dreadful or act
dreadfully, spoken either in anger or as a simple statement of
fact.　　　Lit. High (poetic).　　　Corn. Sev., Ov., Sen.
(trag.), Stat.　　　Ov. *Fast.* 2. 718; Stat. *Theb.* 12. 594.

Discipule, -i 'pupil (m.)': 2.　　　Patronizing address from a
more elevated scholar to a (supposedly) lesser one.
Gen.? Mid.　　　Cic., Gel.　　　Cic. *De Orat.* 2. 29; Gel.
15. 9. 9.

Diserte 'eloquent': 2. Term of praise for those good at
speaking or writing, may be used sarcastically.
Gen.? Mid.?　　　Cic., Mart.　　　Cic. *Phil.* 2. 8; Mart.
5. 59. 2.

Disertissime, -i 'most eloquent': 6. Term of praise for those
good at speaking or writing; may be used sarcastically.

Gen. Mid. Catul., Petr., Tac., (Fro). Petr. 96.
6; Fro. 13. 11.

Dive, -a 'god, goddess': 18 +. Respectful address for gods and deified rulers, or for humans mistaken for gods. Gen. High. Verg., Ov., V. Max., Sen., *Ilias*, Sil., Petr., Stat., Tac., Plin., and prayers. Ov. *Met.* 5. 261; Stat. *Theb.* 4. 753; Tac. *Ann.* 1. 43.

Dives, -tes 'rich': 13. Neutral term for nameless rich men in declamations. Lit. Mid. Verg., Sen. S., Quint., [Quint.] Sen. *Con.* 5. 5; Quint. *Decl.* 252. 18.

Divine, -a 'divine': 5. Polite or sarcastic address for those connected in some way to divinities. Gen. Mid. Pl., Verg., Liv., Juv. Verg. *Ecl.* 10. 17; Liv. 1. 36. 4.

Docte, -a, -ae 'learned': 13 +. Term of praise for the learned, esp. poets, and for anything having to do with song. Adj. Lit. High (poetic). [Verg.], Hor., Prop., Ov., Stat., Mart. Hor. *Ep.* 1. 19. 1; Ov. *Ars* 2. 425; Mart. 8. 73. 8. Cf. *doctior* (Catul. 35. 17); *praedocte* (Stat. *Silv.* 5. 3. 3).

Doctissime, -a 'very learned': 6. Term of praise for friends. Gen. Mid. [Verg.], Ov., (Fro.), Gel. Ov. *Pont.* 2. 5. 15; Fro. 13. 12.

Dolor 'pain, grief': 19. Term most often addressed to the speaker's grief or pain; also occasionally to grief in the abstract, or to a beloved person whose loss causes grief. Lit. High. Verg., Ov., Sen. (trag.), Luc., [Quint.] Verg. *A.* 10. 507; Sen. *Tro.* 107; Luc. 9. 70.

Domina 'mistress': 21 +. (1) Term of erotic endearment for lovers. (2) Term of respectful affection used to family members. (3) Generalized, polite address for equals and superiors, and from the 2nd cent. AD also for inferiors. (4) Occasionally used to goddesses (and perhaps to emperors' wives). Gen. (at first strictly non-literary, later more acceptable). Var. (1) Petr., graf. (2) inscr., *Dig.* (3) Petr., Apul., epist., inscr., graf.? (4) Prayers. (1) Petr. 130. 1; *CIL* iv. 8364; (2) *CIL* vi. 15106, 29026; *EDH* 002460; cf. Sen. frag. 13. 51; (3) Petr. 20. 1; Apul. *Met.* 2. 20.

Domine 'master': 217 +. (1) Term of erotic endearment used by a man or woman to a beloved boy or man. (2) Term of respectful affection used to family members, esp. fathers. (3)

Generalized, polite address for equals, superiors, and sometimes inferiors; often combined with kinship terms such as
frater. (4) Occasionally, in literature, by contamination
between address and referential use, a more strongly polite
address for superiors.   Gen. (at first strictly non-
literary, later more acceptable). Var.   (1) graf.? (2)
Fro., *Dig.*, inscr. (3) Petr., Quint., Mart., Plin., [Hyg.],
Fro., Apul., epist., inscr. (4) Mart.   (1) Cf. Ov. *Met.*
9. 466, *Am*. 3. 7. 11; (2) Fro. 176. 10; *ILS* 8377; *CIL* vi.
11252; cf. Mart. 1. 81; (3) Quint. *Inst.* 6. 3. 100; Fro. 105. 10;
Apul. *Met.* 2. 14; cf. Sen. *Ep.* 3. 1; (4) Mart. 8 *pr.* 1; cf. 2.
68. 2.

Domitor 'conqueror (m.)': 5. Complimentary address praising
a god or important man for his status as conquering or
controlling something (specified in the genitive). Does not
imply subordination of speaker to addressee.   Lit.
High (poetic).   Sen. (trag.), Luc., Mart.   [Sen.]
Her. O. 1989; Mart. 9. 5. 1.

Domus 'house, family': 6. With appropriate modifiers, term
for a family, *gens*, etc.   Lit. High (poetic).   Enn.,
trag. frag., Ov., Sen. (trag.), Luc., Sil.   Ov. *Fast.* 2.
225; Sen. *Oed.* 627.

Ductor 'leader (m.)': 14. Complimentary address praising an
important man for his status as leader of some group (often
specified in genitive). Does not imply subordination of
speaker to addressee.   Lit.   High   (poetic).
Verg., Sen. (trag.), Luc., Sil., Stat., V. Fl.   Verg. *A.* 8.
470; Sil. 13. 711.

Dulcior 'sweeter': 2. Term of affection for friendship or
romantic love; with ablative of comparison.   Lit.
High (poetic).   Ov., Luc.   Ov. *Tr.* 5. 4. 29;
Luc. 5. 739.

Dulcis, -e, -es 'sweet': 27 +. Term of sincere affection for
family, lovers, and friends. Adj.   Lit. High–mid.
Catul., Verg., Hor., Ov., Sen. (trag.), Pers., Stat., Mart.,
Apul., graf., inscr., and prayers.   Catul. 32. 1; Verg.
A. 2. 777; Hor. *Ep.* 1. 7. 12.   Cf. *dulciculus* (Pl. *Poen.*
390).

Dulcissime, -a 'very sweet': 59. Term of affection for family,

lovers, and friends. Adj.   Gen. Mid.   Cic.,
[Verg.], Hor., Stat., Mart., Fro., Apul., graf., inscr.
Cic. *Leg.* 3. 25; Hor. *S.* 1. 9. 4; Mart. 9. 36. 7.

Dure, -a, -i 'hard, harsh': 20. Rebuke for those causing
suffering, normally to the speaker. Often used to loved
ones who die, depart, do not return the speaker's love, or
act cruelly; also to more distant trouble-causers, and occasionally to those who do not cause trouble but are simply
tough.   Lit.? High (poetic).   Catul., Verg., Hor.,
Prop., Tib., Ov., Sen. (trag.), Luc., Sil., Stat., Mart., V. Fl.
Verg. *A.* 3. 94; Hor. *Carm.* 4. 1. 40; Luc. 5. 682; Sil. 6. 419;
Mart. 13. 70. 2.

Durior 'harder': 2. Rebuke for harshness; takes ablative of
comparison.   Lit. High (poetic).   Ov.   Ov.
Am. 1. 6. 62, *Tr.* 5. 1. 56.

Dux, -es 'leader': 26. (1) In singular, complimentary address
praising an important man or non-human for his/its status as
leader of something or some group (may be specified in
genitive). Does not imply subordination of speaker to addressee, though can be used by subordinates. Never alone,
often with complimentary adjectives. (2) In plural, complimentary address to a group of military officers or soldiers
from someone outside their command structure. Normally
alone.   (1) Gen. High–mid. (2) Lit. High–mid.?
(1) Cic., Verg., Hor., Ov., Sil., Stat., Mart., Suet., [Quint.]
(2) Luc., Sil., Stat.   (1) Cic. *Tusc.* 5. 5; Verg. *A.* 6. 562;
Hor. *Carm.* 4. 5. 5; Suet. *Tib.* 21. 4; (2) Sil. 11. 215; Stat.
Theb. 4. 599, 6. 168.

Edax 'greedy, devouring': 4. (1) Term of abuse for a slave,
implying greed for food. (2) Used metaphorically to abstracts
which cause destruction. Adj.   (1) Gen. Low. (2) Lit.
High.   (1) Pl. (2) Ov.   (1) Pl. *Per.* 421; (2) Ov.
Am. 1. 15. 1.

Egregie, -um, -ii 'excellent': 3. Term of praise. Adj.
Gen. Low.   Lit. High (in later Latin probably Gen.
Mid.).   Verg., Stat., Gel.   Stat. *Theb.* 10. 240;
Gel. 14. 5. 3.   Cf. *egregissime* (Gel. 14. 5. 3).

Enervis 'feeble': 2. Rebuke for inactivity and exhortation to
manly exertion. Subst.   Lit. High (poetic).   Sen.
(trag.)   Sen. *Thy.* 176, *Her. O.* 1721.

Equi 'horses': 3. Neutral address for a team of horses. Lit.? High (poetic)? Prop., Ov. Prop. 3. 4. 8; Ov. *Am.* 1. 13. 40.

Equites 'knights': 6. Neutral address to the Roman knights, always with *Romani*. Gen. Mid. Cic. Cic. *Sest.* 26, *Q. fr.* 2. 12. 2. Cf. *eques* (Prop. 3. 9. 1).

Era 'mistress': 18+. Polite address used by male or female slaves to their own mistresses. Gen. Low–mid. Pl., Ter., [Phaed.], Sen. (trag.), and prayers. Pl. *Cist.* 544; Sen. *Phaed.* 267.

Ere 'master': 49. Polite address used by male or female slaves to their own masters. Gen. Low–mid. Pl., Caecil., Ter., Turp., Hor., inscr. Pl. *Cas.* 632; Ter. *Eu.* 57; Hor. *S.* 2. 3. 265.

Erilis 'having to do with my master': 4. (1) Used substantively (with *mi*) as an ingratiating way for a low-class old woman to address another woman. Does not imply any actual power of addressee over speaker, but addressee seems to come from a slightly higher social class. (2) Used as an adjective qualifying *patria* to address a slave's home. ? (1) Apul. (2) Pl. (1) Apul. *Met.* 4. 27, 9. 16; (2) Pl. *St.* 650, *Bac.* 170.

Excetra 'watersnake': 2. Insult used in threats to female slaves. Gen.? Low. Pl. Pl. *Ps.* 218, *Cas.* 644.

Exoptate 'longed-for': 2. Expression of eager welcome. Non-romantic. Gen. Mid.? Pl. Pl. *Capt.* 1006, *Cur.* 306. Cf. *exoptatissume* (Pl. *Trin.* 1072).

Exspectate, -a 'eagerly awaited': 5. Strong term of affection for people whom the speaker has sorely missed. Gen.? Var.? Pl., Verg., V. Fl., graf. Pl. *Poen.* 1260; Verg. *A.* 2. 283.

Facunde, -a 'eloquent': 7. Term of praise for those good at speaking or writing. Lit. High (poetic). Ov., *Laus Pis.*, Stat., Mart. Ov. *Met.* 12. 178; *Laus Pis.* 32. Cf. *facundia* (Ov. *Pont.* 1. 2. 67).

Fallax 'deceitful, treacherous': 7. Rebuke for the treacherous in any respect, including lovers and non-human entities such as rivers. Lit. High (poetic). Ov., Sen. (trag.), Sil, Mart., V. Fl. Mart. 10. 26. 8, 11. 73. 5.

False, -a 'false, unfaithful': 4. Rebuke for unfaithful friends or spouses.   Gen. Var.?   Pl., Catul.   Pl. *Am.* 813; *Catul.* 30. 1.

Fama 'fame': 5. Neutral address to one's own fame or to Fame as an abstract.   Lit. High (poetic).   Prop., Ov., Sen. (trag.), Stat., Mart.   Prop. 4. 2. 19; Sen. *Phaed.* 252.

Famulae 'attendants (f.)': 3. Neutral term from a mistress giving orders to a group of nameless servants.   Lit. High (poetic).   Ov., Sen. (trag.)   Ov. *Met.* 4. 223; Sen. *Phaed.* 387.

Famuli 'attendants (m.)': 9. Neutral term normally used by a master giving orders to a group of nameless servants. Lit. High (poetic).   Trag. frag., Verg., Sen. (trag.), Luc., Stat.   Verg. *A.* 2. 712; Sen. *Ag.* 787.

Fatue 'foolish': 4. Mild insult. Subst.   Gen. Mid. Pl., Ter., Pompon., Apul.   Pl. *Am.* 1026; Ter. *Eu.* 604.

Feles 'marten': 2. Rebuke for pimps who prey upon girls; modified by *virginalis* or *virginaria*.   Gen.? Low. Pl.   Pl. *Rud.* 748, *Per.* 751.

Felix, -es 'happy': 22. Term of praise or envy, esp. for the dead or those distanced from the speaker. Often with ablative expressing grounds for happiness.   Lit. High (poetic).   Tic., Verg., Ov., Luc., *Laus Pis.*, Sil., Stat., Mart., graf., inscr.   Verg. *A.* 6. 669; Mart. 4. 75. 1.

Femina 'woman, female': 8. Term for women, perhaps rude unless modified with a positive word.   Lit. Var. Pl., [Verg.], Ov., Sen. (prose), Quint., inscr.   Ov. *Met.* 8. 433, 8. 704; *ILLRP* 934.

Ferox 'fierce': 8 +. Term for people, things, or divinities displaying ferocity or cruelty; sometimes insulting but sometimes a complaint or merely a statement of fact.   Lit.? High (poetic).   Verg., Ov., Sen. (trag.), Luc., and prayers.   Verg. *A.* 12. 895; Ov. *Ep.* 4. 165; Luc. 1. 30.

Ferrea 'made of iron': 2. Rebuke from lovers to women who cause them suffering. Subst.   Lit. High (poetic). Ov.   Ov. *Am.* 1. 14. 28, *Met.* 14. 721.

Festivitas 'delightfulness': 4. Term of endearment for lovers, with *mea*.   Gen. Low.   Pl., Apul.   Pl. *Cas.*

577; Apul. *Met.* 2. 10.   Cf. *festivae* (Pl. *Cur.* 88); *festus* (Pl. *Cas.* 137); *festivissime* (Ter. *Ad.* 983).

Fida, -us, -um, -i, -ae 'loyal': 12. Term of praise for loyal spouses, friends, followers, or servants. Adj.   Lit. High.   Enn., Ov., Sen. (trag.), Stat., Apul. Enn. *trag.* 237; Sen. *Tro.* 84, 453.   Cf. *fides* (Luc. 2. 243).

Fidelis, -e 'loyal': 2. Term of praise for loyal friends or servants.   Lit. High (poetic).   Hor., [Sen.] (trag.)   Hor. *Ep.* 2. 2. 1; [Sen.] *Her. O.* 570.

Fidelissime, -i 'very loyal': 4. Term of praise for loyal comrades or servants.   Gen.? Mid.?   Sen. S., Apul., [Quint.]   Apul. *Met.* 4. 7; [Quint.] *Decl.* 9. 21.

Fidissime, -a, -i 'very loyal': 15 +. Term of praise for loyal spouses, friends, followers, or servants.   Gen. Var. Cic., Verg., Ov., Luc., Sil., Curt., Stat., V. Fl.   Cic. *Fam.* 14. 4. 6; Ov. *Met.* 9. 569.

Fili, -ii 'son': 72. (1) Affectionate? address from a parent to his/her son. (2) In transferred sense to someone else's son. (3) In extended sense as a polite address to any younger man. Gen. (except 2). Mid.   (1) Cic., Liv., Sen. S., Phaed., V. Max., Quint., Fro., Apul., Gel., Calp. F., [Quint.], inscr. (2) Andr., Catul. (3) Fro., Apul., Gel., graf.?   (1) Cic. *Off.* 1. 1; Gel. 13. 4. 2; (2) Catul. 33. 2, 37. 18; Andr. 2; (3) Fro. 187. 14; Apul. *Met.* 4. 12.

Filia 'daughter': 19. Affectionate? address from a father or mother to his/her daughter, rarely in transferred or extended sense.   Gen. Mid.   Pl., Cic., Hor., Prop., Liv., Ov., V. Max., Sen. (prose), Quint., Apul., inscr., graf. Pl. *Men.* 822; Cic. *Div.* 1. 103; Prop. 4. 11. 67.   Cf. *filiola* (Cic. *Fam.* 14. 4. 6; Suet. *Tib.* 53. 1).

Flagitium hominis 'disgrace of a man': 2. Strong insult. Gen.? Low?   Pl.   Pl. *Men.* 489, 709.   Cf. *flagiti flagrantia* (Pl. *Rud.* 733), *flagitiorum documentum* (Cic. *Dom.* 126).

Foedissime, -um 'very foul': 2. Fairly strong insult. Gen. Var.?   Cic., Verg.   Cic. *Pis.* 31; Verg. *A.* 11. 392.

Formose, -a, -i, -ae 'good-looking': 15. Term used by a man to the object of his desire (male or female); occasionally also used generally to any physically attractive person, thing, or group. Lit.? High–mid.? Verg., Ov., *Buc. Eins.*, and prayers. Verg. *Ecl.* 7. 67; Ov. *Ep.* 16. 271, *Ars* 3. 417.

Fortis, -es 'strong, brave': 3. Term of praise for a group of men (plural or collective singular). Lit. High (poetic). Hor., Sen. (trag.) Hor. *Carm.* 1. 7. 30; Sen. *Med.* 980.

Fortissime, -a, -i 'very strong, very brave': 38. Term of praise for military heroes and those who can plausibly be flattered as such; used in both military and non-military contexts. Gen. High–mid. Cic., Sal., Verg., Ov., Sen. (prose), *Ilias*, Sil., Stat., V. Fl., Plin., Suet., Apul. Sal. *Cat.* 20. 9; Ov. *Ars* 2. 585; Sil. 13. 669.

Fortuna 'fortune': 9. Term for Fortune in general or for an individual's fortune. Gen. Mid.? Sen. S., Sen. (prose), Luc., Petr., Mart., Plin., [Quint.] Petr. 101. 1; Plin. *Ep.* 4. 11. 2.

Fortunate, -ae 'fortunate': 7. Term of praise or envy. Gen. Mid. Pl., Ter., Cic., Verg. Ter. *Hec.* 418; Cic. *Arch.* 24. Cf. *fortunatissime* (Ter. *Ph.* 504).

Frater, -es 'brother': 176. (1) Neutral or affectionate address from a man or woman to his/her brother. (2) Occasionally with a genitive to anyone's brother. (3) Occasionally in transferred sense to another's brother. (4) Often in extended sense as a flattering or mildly polite address for men not too distant in age and/or rank from the speaker. Gen. Var. (1) Pl., Ter., Cic., Catul., Sal., Verg., Prop., Liv., Ov., Sen. S., Sen., Sil., Quint., Stat., Mart., V. Fl., [Quint.], inscr. (2) Tib. (3) Sen. S., Sen. (trag.), V. Max., Quint. (4) Cic., Hor., Phaed., Calp. S., Petr., Mart., Juv., [Hyg.], Fro., Apul., epist., inscr. Unclassifiable: Afran., Pompon. (1) Pl. *Cur.* 697; Cic. *Q. fr.* 1. 4. 1; (2) Tib. 2. 5. 39; (3) V. Max. 5. 4. ext. 3; Quint. *Inst.* 9. 2. 20; (4) Cic. *Ver.* 3. 155; Fro. 176. 21.

Fugitive 'runaway': 6. Fairly strong insult. Gen. Low. Pl., Ter., Cic., Sen. S., inscr. Ter. *Ph.* 931; Cic. *Deiot.* 21. Cf. *fugax* (Pl. *Per.* 421).

Fur, -es 'thief': 16. (1) Strong insult often applied to men suspected of theft. (2) Neutral address to unspecified thieves. (1) Gen. Low. (2) Lit. Mid.? Pl.,

Lucil., Tib., *Priap.*, Mart., graf.   Pl. *Aul.* 326, 633;
Lucil. 775; Mart. 1. 66. 1.   Cf. *furuncule* (*CIL* iv.
1715, 1949); *furum optime balneariorum* (Catul. 33. 1); *furax*
(Pl. *Per.* 421); *trium litterarum homo* (Pl. *Aul.* 325).

Furcifer 'one punished with the *furca*': 22. Strong insult
normally used to male slaves.   Gen. Low.   Pl.,
Ter., Cic., Hor., Sen. S., Apul.   Pl. *Am.* 285; Cic. *Vat.*
15; Hor. *S.* 2. 7. 22.

Furia 'fury': 2. Strong insult.   Gen.? Low?   Cic.
Cic. *Pis.* 8, 91.

Furibunde, -a 'distraught, furious': 2. Insult for those unex-
pectedly acting wrongly and so causing serious trouble for
the speaker.   Lit. High (poetic).   Sen. (trag.),
Stat.   Sen. *Ag.* 981; Stat. *Theb.* 3. 272.

Furiose, -a 'mad': 9. Insult for those acting wrongly. Subst.
Lit.? High–mid.   Cic., Hor., Ov., Sen. (trag.), Mart.,
[Quint.]   Cic. *Phil.* 13. 39; Hor. *S.* 2. 3. 207; Sen. *Med.*
897.

Gaudium, -a 'joy': 7. Term of endearment, often in plural for
singular, usually with *meum/mea*.   Gen. Mid.
Pl., Verg., Phaed., Stat., Fro.   Pl. *Bac.* 18; Stat. *Theb.*
5. 610; Fro. 21. 10.   Cf. Ov. *Ep.* 19. 41.

Gemine, -a, -i, -ae 'twin': 5. Address to the speaker's own
twin, or more often in plural to two addressees who are twins
or closely connected to each other.   Lit. High–mid.?
Pl., Pac., Verg., Ov., Sil.   Pl. *Men.* 1125; Verg. *A.* 10.
390; Sil. 16. 87.

Gener 'son-in-law': 7. Address from a man or woman to his/
her son-in-law, or in transferred sense to another's son-in-
law.   Lit. High (poetic).   Catul., [Verg.], Ov.,
Stat., V. Fl.   Catul. 29. 24; Ov. *Met.* 6. 496.   Cf.
[Sen.] *Her. O.* 1437.

Generose, -a 'noble': 4. Term of praise for a noble man or
family, spoken at a distance rather than in the presence of the
addressee(s).   Lit. High (poetic).   Ov., Sen.
(trag.), Sil., Juv.   Ov. *Fast.* 2. 225; Juv. 6. 124.

Genetrix 'mother': 13 +. (1) Affectionate? address from sons
or daughters to their mothers. (2) With a genitive, to the
mother of anything. (3) Alone in extended sense to someone
in a position resembling mother to the speaker.   Lit.

High (poetic). (1) Verg., Ov., Sen. (trag.), Stat., Mart. (2) Enn., Ov. (3) Catul., Ov. Also used in prayers. (1) Verg. *A.* 9. 94; Sen. *Phaed.* 115; (2) Enn. *Ann.* 58; Ov. *Met.* 5. 490; (3) Catul. 63. 50; Ov. *Met.* 9. 326.

Genitor 'father': 64+. (1) Affectionate? address from sons or daughters to their fathers. (2) With a genitive to the father of anything. (3) Alone in transferred sense to the father of a person under discussion. (4) Alone in extended usage as a respectful and affectionate address to gods and important (usually older) men. Lit. High (poetic). (1) Enn., Verg., Ov., Sen. (trag.), Luc., Sil., Stat., V. Fl. (2) Sil., Stat. (3) Verg., Sen. (trag.) (4) Enn., Sen. (trag.), Sil., V. Fl. Unclassifiable: Acc. Also used in prayers. (1) Verg. *A.* 1. 237; V. Fl. 2. 290; (2) Sil. 13. 738; Stat. *Silv.* 1. 1. 74; (3) Verg. *A.* 7. 360; Sen. *Thy.* 429. (4) Enn. *Ann.* 108; Sil. 7. 737.

Gens, -es 'race, clan': 14. In singular, complimentary address to an individual or group, always modified with a genitive or adjective. In plural, elevated address to a group or to people in general. Lit. High. Verg., Sen. (trag.), Luc., Sil., Stat., Mart., [Quint.] Verg. *A.* 10. 228, 11. 252; Sil. 12. 324; Stat. *Silv.* 4. 3. 109.

Genus 'offspring, race': 15. Used with a modifier as a type of patronymic address to individuals or as an address to groups. Lit. High. Catul., Verg., Ov., Sen., V. Fl. Catul. 64. 23; Ov. *Ars* 3. 87; [Sen.] *Her. O.* 1485.

Germane, -a 'sibling, sharing both parents': 40. Affectionate? address from males or females to a brother or sister (including on occasion half-siblings). Subst. Lit.? High–mid.? Pl., Enn., Ter., Verg., Ov., Sen. (trag.), *Ilias*, Luc., Sil., Stat., V. Fl., Apul. Enn. *Ann.* 40; Ter. *Ad.* 269; Verg. *A.* 12. 679; Sen. *Ag.* 914.

Germanice 'conqueror of Germany': 18. Term used in polite address to someone holding the title *Germanicus*. Lit. High. Ov., Sil., Stat., Mart., inscr. Ov. *Fast.* 4. 81; Mart. 7. 61. 3.

Gloria 'glory': 12. Term of praise, usable to anyone; meaning often specified by modifiers. Lit. Mid.? Ov.,

Mart., V. Fl., Fro.   Ov. *Met.* 12. 530; Mart. 2. 90. 2;
V. Fl. 1. 77; Fro. 21. 10.

Grata, -um, -i 'pleasant, welcome': 6. General term of affection; tends to modify abstract nouns or objects, rather than
people directly.   Lit. High–mid.   Sal., Hor.,
Ov., Gracch., Mart.   Hor. *Carm.* 1. 32. 14; Mart. 11.
26. 1.

Gratissime, -a 'most pleasant, most welcome': 7. General
term of affection.   Gen.? Mid.   Verg., Ov.,
(Fro.)   Verg. *A.* 10. 607; Ov. *Met.* 14. 221; Fro. 45. 16.

Gurges 'whirlpool, abyss': 2. Rebuke for spendthrifts and
gluttons.   Gen.? Mid.?   Lucil., Cic.
Lucil. 1238; Cic. *Sest.* 111.

Heros, -es 'hero': 2. Laudatory term for mythical heroes,
always modified.   Lit. High (poetic).   Catul.,
Ov.   Catul. 64. 23; Ov. *Met.* 13. 644.

Homo, -es 'human being': 83. (1) In singular, unmodified,
used (normally by women) for adult men, often unknown;
frequently with *mi*. Polite unless used by a woman to her
husband. (2) In plural, unmodified, used neutrally by anyone
to groups of mixed gender or to humanity in general. (3) In
singular or plural, modified by a positive or negative word,
used by anyone to praise or blame an adult man or an all-
male group.   Gen. Mid. (1 a bit lower than others).
(1) Pl., Ter., Afran., Var. (poetry), inscr. (2) Pl., Ov., Quint.,
[Quint.] (3) Pl., Ter., Cic., [Sal.], Sen. (prose), Petr., Fro.,
Gel., epist., graf.   (1) Pl. *Cist.* 723; Ter. *Ad.* 336; (2)
Pl. *Cist.* 678; Ov. *Rem.* 69. (3) Pl. *Men.* 487; Cic. *Leg.* 2. 52,
Ver. 3. 75; Fro. 34. 23.

Honestissime 'very honourable': 2. Term of praise.   ?
(Fro.)   Fro. 34. 14, 68. 14.

Hospes, -ites 'guest, host, foreigner (m.)': 96. Friendly address to a man who comes from a different place from the
speaker, sometimes showing a *xenia* connection, or between
two compatriots abroad. Often from women to foreign men
who are not currently their lovers. Often to readers of an
inscription. Plural rarer and less warm than the singular.
Gen. Mid.   Pl., Enn., Acc., trag. frag., com. frag., Var.
(poetry), Cic., Catul., Verg., Prop., Liv., Ov., Luc., Petr.,

V. Fl., Hadr., graf., inscr.   Pl. *Rud.* 883; Cic. *Brut.*
172; Ov. *Met.* 10. 620; Petr. 116. 4.

Hostis 'enemy': 4. Insult to a state enemy or one who can be
protrayed as such, sometimes with genitive of the object of
enmity. Also occasionally as a neutral address to an enemy in
war.   Lit.?   High–mid.?   Cic., Verg., Dom.
Mars., Sen. (trag.), Stat.   Cic. *Vat.* 26; Verg. *A.* 10.
900; Stat. *Theb.* 11. 431.

Ianitor 'doorkeeper (m.)': 4. Term for nameless porters,
positive or negative according to modifiers. Not a call.
Lit. High.   Ov., Sil., Apul.   Ov. *Am.* 1. 6. 1; Sil.
2. 240.

Ianua 'door': 7. Term used by lover cajoling or blaming his
beloved's closed door.   Lit. High (poetic).
Catul., Prop., Tib., Ov.   Catul. 67. 14; Tib. 1. 2. 9.

Ignare 'ignorant': 2. Gentle rebuke for the ignorant, from
their friends.   Lit.? High (poetic).   Verg., Ov.
Verg. *A.* 3. 382; Ov. *Met.* 2. 100.

Ignave, -i 'lazy, cowardly': 12.   Rebuke and exhortation,
especially in military contexts. Subst.   Gen. Var.
Pl., Ter., Sen. (trag.), Luc., Stat.   Ter. *Eu.* 777; Luc.
2. 496.   Cf. *mea Ignavia* (Pl. *Per.* 850).

Ignavissime 'very lazy, very cowardly': 3. Strong insult.
Gen. Var.?   Pl., Ter., Sil.   Pl. *Men.* 924; Sil. 12.
236.

Illecebra 'enticement': 2.   Rebuke for prostitutes.
Gen.? Low?   Pl.   Pl. *Cist.* 321, *Truc.* 759.

Illex 'lawless': 2. Insult.   Gen.? Low.   Pl., Caecil.
Pl. *Per.* 408; Caecil. *com.* 60.

Immemor, -es 'forgetful': 5. Fairly strong rebuke to those
who let someone down, sometimes with a genitive of the
thing forgotten.   Lit. High.   Acc., Catul., Sen.
(trag.), Luc., [Quint.]   Catul. 30. 1; Luc. 4. 212.
Cf. *vix memor* (Cic. *Pis.* 62).

Immitis 'pitiless': 2. Rebuke for those who cause suffering.
Subst.   Lit. High.   Ov., Suet.   Ov. *Met.* 8.
110; Suet. *Tib.* 59. 1.

Imperator 'commander': 64. (1) Respectful address to a
Roman general of the Republican period, from his own
subordinates or others. (2) Respectful address to Roman

emperors from subordinates and others.   Gen. Low-mid.   (1) Pl., Cic., Caes., Catul., Sal., Liv., Sen. S., [Phaed.], Sen. (prose), V. Max., Calp. F., [Quint.] (2) Vitr., Quint., Plin. S., Plin., Suet., Fro.   (1) Caes. *Civ.* 3. 91. 3; Sal. *Cat.* 33. 1; (2) Suet. *Cl.* 21. 6; Fro. 164. 20.

Impia, -um 'impious': 7. Fairly strong rebuke for impiety or for cruel treatment of a lover. Subst.   Lit. High (poetic).   Prop., Ov., Sen. (trag.), Luc.   Prop. 2. 9. 20; Sen. *Ag.* 953; Luc. 5. 158. Cf. *inpientissime* (*Tab. Vindol. II* 311. 5).

Impiger 'energetic': 2. Term of praise for heroes.   Lit. High (poetic).   [Verg.], Tib.   [Verg.] *Eleg. Maec.* 69; Tib. 2. 5. 39.

Importuna 'troublesome, perverse': 2. Insult used to unchaste women.   Lit. Mid.?   Ov., Sen. S.   Ov. *Met.* 2. 475; Sen. *Con.* 1. 3. 1.   Cf. *importunissime* (Cic. *Ver.* 1. 113).

Impotentissime, -a 'very powerless': 4. Moderate insult. ?   [Quint.]   [Quint.] *Decl.* 5. 4, 8. 21.   Cf. *impotens* ([Quint.] *Decl.* 5. 2).

Improbe, -a 'not good': 53. Rebuke and insult, ranging from very mild to moderately strong. Subst.   Gen. Var. Pl., Cic., Lucr., Verg., Hor., Prop., Ov., Calp. S., Luc., Sil., Pers., Quint., Stat., Mart., Apul., [Quint.]   Pl. *Aul.* 53; Cic. *Quinct.* 56; Prop. 1. 3. 39.   Cf. *improbissime* (Cic. *Ver.* 1. 48).

Impudens 'shameless': 11. Strong insult. Subst.   Gen. Low.   Pl.   Pl. *Mil.* 1402, *Per.* 40.

Impudentissime 'very shameless': 3. Fairly strong insult. Gen. Mid.?   Cic., Sal., [Quint.]   Cic. *Ver.* 2. 40; Sal. *Hist.* 1. 77. 15.

Impudice 'unchaste': 3. Fairly strong insult. Subst. Gen. Low?   Pl., [Verg.]   Pl. *Ps.* 360; [Verg.] *Cat.* 13. 9.

Impurate, -a 'vile': 3. Moderate insult.   Gen. Low-mid.?   Pl., Apul.   Pl. *Aul.* 359; Apul. *Met.* 2. 25. Cf. *inpuratissume* (Pl. *Rud.* 751).

Impure 'foul': 8. Strong insult. Subst.   Gen. Low-mid. Pl., Luc.   Pl. *Bac.* 884; Luc. 8. 552.

Impurissime 'very foul': 3. Moderate insult.   Gen.

Low–mid.   Ter., Cic.   Ter. *Ph.* 372; Cic. *Vat.* 26.

Inclite, -a, -um 'famous': 22 +. Distant term of respect used for gods, the respected dead, rulers, dedicatees, and at a later period ordinary men.   Lit. High (poetic).   Acc., Lucr., Verg., Ov., Sen. (trag.), Sil., Stat.   Sil. 6. 579; Stat. *Theb.* 4. 610, *Ach.* 1. 775.

Indulgentissime 'very kind': 3. Term of praise. Adj. Gen.? Mid.?   Plin., [Quint.]   Plin. *Ep. Tra.* 10. 10. 2; [Quint.] *Decl.* 10. 13.

Inepte, -a 'foolish': 15. Mild to moderate rebuke, often but not always for those doing something silly. Subst.   Gen. Var.   Ter., Catul., Prop., Ov., Mart., Apul., Gel. Ter. *Ad.* 271; Catul. 12. 4.

Iners, -tes 'idle, lazy, powerless': 8. Rebuke for inactivity, often as an exhortation to action.   Lit. High (poetic). Catul., Verg., Sen. (trag.), Stat.   Catul. 61. 124; Verg. *A.* 11. 732; Sen. *Thy.* 176.

Infelicissime, -a 'very unhappy': 5. Expression of pity and sympathy. Adj.   Gen.? Mid.   Sen. S., Quint., [Quint.]   Quint. *Inst.* 8. 5. 21, *Decl.* 315. 22; [Quint.] *Decl.* 9. 5.

Infelix, -es 'unhappy': 66. Expression of pity and sympathy, scorn and contempt, or an intermediate emotion to an addressee who has or is claimed to have a reason to be miserable, whether or not he or she is actually unhappy. Plural very rare, prose only.   Gen. Var.   Pl., Caecil, Ter., Cic., Verg., Prop., Ov., Sen. S., Phaed., Sen., Luc., Sil., Quint., Stat., Mart., V. Fl., Juv., Apul., Calp. F., [Quint.]   Ter. *Ph.* 428; Cic. *Pis.* 78; Verg. *A.* 9. 390.

Infide 'treacherous, faithless': 2. Rebuke for those committing some treachery.   Lit. High (poetic).   Ov., [Sen.] (trag.)   Ov. *Ep.* 17. 197; [Sen.] *Her. O.* 514.

Ingrate, -a 'ungrateful': 19. Fairly strong rebuke for people who mistreat a benefactor (normally the speaker). Subst. Gen. Mid.–high.   Prop., Ov., Sen. S., V. Max., Sen. (trag.), Luc., Stat., Mart., Juv., [Quint.]   Ov. *Met.* 8. 119; Sen. *Con.* 5. 4.   Cf. *ingratifici* (Acc. *trag.* 365).

Ingratissime, -i 'very ungrateful': 6. Fairly strong rebuke for people who mistreat a benefactor.   Gen. Mid.

Cic., Sen. (prose), Curt., [Quint.]   Cic. *Phil*. 13. 41;
Curt. 10. 2. 27.

Inimice, -a 'hateful': 17. Unmodified, term for personal
enemies (esp. in declamations); with an indication (usually
dative) of who or what the addressee is hateful to, normally
an insulting address. Subst.   Lit.? Var.?   Pl.,
Hor., [Verg.], *Ilias*, Sil., Stat., [Quint.], graf.   Pl.
Poen. 393; Hor. *S*. 2. 3. 123; [Quint.] *Decl*. 7. 6.

Innuptae 'unmarried (f.)': 2. Term for girls.   Lit. High
(poetic).   Catul., Prop.   Catul. 62. 6; Prop. 3. 19.
25.

Insane, -a 'crazy': 14. Mild insult. Subst.   Gen. Var.
Pl., Ter., Cic., Hor., Prop., Sil., Pers.   Cic. *De Orat*. 2.
269; Hor. *S*. 2. 6. 29; Prop. 2. 20. 3.   Cf. *male sane* (Ov.
Am. 3. 7. 77).

Insanissime 'very crazy': 2. Insult for people who are acting
insane.   Gen.? Low?   Pl.   Pl. *Men*. 517,
819.

Insipiens 'unwise': 2. Affectionate admonishment for those
speaking or acting foolishly. Subst.   Gen. Low.
Pl.   Pl. *Bac*. 627, *Cas*. 209.

Insperate 'unexpected': 3. Strong term of affection and
unexpected joy used at reunions with lost relatives.
Gen.? Mid.?   Pl.   Pl. *Rud*. 1175, *Men*. 1132.
Cf. *insperatissume* (Pl. *Poen*. 1127).

Invicte 'invincible': 15 +. Term of praise for gods and heroes.
Gen.? High.   Enn., Verg., Hor., Sen. S., Sen. (trag.),
Sil., graf., inscr., and prayers.   Hor. *Epod*. 13. 12; Sen.
Con. 7. 7. 19; Sil. 17. 651.

Invide, -a 'envious, hostile': 8. Rebuke for the envious or those
obstructing happiness.   Gen.? Var.   Pl., Prop.,
Ov., graf., inscr.   Pl. *Per*. 409; Ov. *Met*. 4. 73, *Pont*. 4.
16. 1.

Invidiose, -a 'odious, envious': 3. Term of opprobrium.
Gen. Var.   Ov., graf.   Ov. *Met*. 15. 234; *CIL* iv.
3775, 8259.

Invisum, -ae 'hateful': 2. Moderate insult. Adj.   Lit.
High (poetic).   Prop., Stat.   Prop. 3. 18. 7; Stat.
Theb. 11. 670.

Iocose 'full of fun': 2. Term of praise.   Lit. High

(poetic).   Hor., Ov.   Hor. *Epod.* 3. 20; Ov. *Tr.* 1.
2. 80.

Iucunde, -a 'delightful': 4. Term of affection used by men to
valued male friends or objects.   Lit. High (poetic).
Catul., Ov., Mart.   Catul. 50. 16; Ov. *Pont.* 1. 8. 25.
Cf. *iucundior* (Catul. 64. 215).

Iucundissime, -us 'very delightful': 33. Term of affection
used by men to valued male friends. Adj.   Gen. Mid.
(Cic.), Catul., Plin. S., Mart., Suet., (Fro.), Gel.   Cic.
Fam. 9. 9. 3; Catul. 14. 2.

Iudex, -es 'judge, juror': 1,128. (1) In sing., rare (occurs twice)
address to someone in charge of judging something (not a
legal case); takes genitive. (2) In plural, standard address
from an orator to a jury. Normally unmodified but sometimes (not in Cic.) with *sanctissimi*.   (1) Lit. High
(poetic). (2) Gen. High–mid.   (1) Hor., Sil. (2) Cic.,
Sen. S., V. Max., Petr., Quint., Calp. F., [Quint.]   (1)
Hor. *Ep.* 1. 4. 1; Sil. 2. 456; (2) Cic. *Cael.* 1; Sen. *Con.* 1. 3. 5.

Iuste 'just': 3. Term of praise. Adj.   Lit. High (poetic).
Ov.   Ov. *Am.* 2. 12. 22, *Met.* 8. 704.

Iustissime, -a 'very just': 6. Term of praise, also used
sarcastically. Adj.   Lit. High (poetic).   Ov.,
Stat.   Ov. *Met.* 14. 245; Stat. *Theb.* 1. 250.

Iuvenis, -es 'young man': 148. Courteous, formal term for
young men and fairly young adult males, usually known to
the speaker. The speaker may be any age and gender and is
not infrequently divine. Plural very common, used as
singular but also to groups of adult men, especially
warriors.   Gen. High–mid.   Catul., Verg.,
Tib., Liv., Ov., Sen. S., Calp. S., Sen., *Laus Pis.*, Luc.,
Sil., Petr., Curt., Quint., Stat., Mart., V. Fl., Tac., Juv.,
Apul., Gel., [Quint.], inscr.   Verg. *A.* 12. 19; Liv. 3.
61. 7; Sil. 10. 366.

Iuventus 'youth': 5. Collective address for groups of young
adult males. Usually modified.   Lit. High (poetic).
Verg., Ov., Luc., Stat.   Verg. *A.* 8. 499; Ov. *Ars* 1.
459.

Labes 'disaster, disgrace': 3. Strong insult, often with genitive
of group afflicted.   Gen. Low?   Pl., Cic.
Pl. *Per.* 408; Cic. *Pis.* 56.

Larva 'devil': 2. Moderate rebuke.   ?   Pl.
Pl. *Mer.* 981, 983.

Lascive, -a, -i 'naughty, playful, lascivious': 9. Term for those
acting in a naughty, playful, or lascivious way; can range
from an affectionate comment to a nasty rebuke, depending
on context.   Lit. High–mid. (poetic).   Ov.,
Mart.   Ov. *Ep.* 16. 229; Mart. 6. 45. 1.

Latini, -ae 'Latins': 5. Term for Latins.   Gen. Var.?
Verg., V. Max.   Verg. *A.* 11. 108, 11. 302; V. Max. 3.
1. 2.

Latro 'bandit': 2. Angry address to people caught in some
misdeed.   Gen. Low.   Petr.   Petr. 98. 6,
107. 15.

Laudande 'to be praised': 2. Term of praise.   Lit. High
(poetic).   Hor., Sil.   Hor. *Carm.* 4. 2. 47; Sil. 5.
561.

Lecte, -a, -i 'chosen': 5. Complimentary address for a picked
group of warriors or for someone chosen in another sense, in
which case with modifiers identifying the chooser. Adj.
Lit. High (poetic).   Verg., Ov., Stat.   Verg. *A.*
10. 294; Ov. *Met.* 13. 640.   Cf. *lectissime* (Stat. *Silv.* 5.
1. 247); *delecta* (Verg. *A.* 8. 499).

Lector 'reader': 20. Used by the author of a literary work (or,
rarely, of an inscription) in his own voice to address the
unknown people who will read the work (not used for a
named dedicatee). May be modified by positive adjectives.
Lit. Mid.   Ov., Phaed., Mart., inscr.   Ov. *Tr.* 1.
11. 35; Mart. 1. 113. 4; *ILS* 6068.

Lena 'brothel-keeper (f.)': 2. Derogatory address for a woman
who runs a brothel or who urges infidelity on other women.
Lit.? Mid.?   Prop., Tib.   Prop. 4. 5. 1; Tib. 2. 6.
53.

Leno 'brothel-keeper (m.)': 33. Standard (and somewhat
derogatory) address for a pimp in comedy.   Gen.
Low.   Pl., Ter., Nov.   Pl. *Cur.* 455; Ter. *Ad.*
196.   Cf. *lenulle* (Pl. *Poen.* 471).

Lente, -a 'slow': 6.   Mild rebuke for sloth, usually to
lovers from women impatient at delay.   Lit. High
(poetic).   Ov., Prop., [Tib.]   Ov. *Ep.* 19. 70;
Prop. 2. 15. 8; [Tib.] 3. 6. 57.

Lepide, -a 'charming': 3. Term of praise and flattery. Gen.? Mid.? Pl. Pl. *Rud.* 419, *Cur.* 120.

Lepidissime 'very charming': 6. Term of praise or flattery, not for lovers. Adj. Gen. Mid. Pl., Ter. Pl. *Ps.* 323; Ter. *Ad.* 911.

Lepos, -es 'charm': 3. Term of endearment for lovers, can be used in plural for singular. Gen. Mid.? Pl., Catul. Pl. *Cas.* 235; Catul. 32. 2.

Lepus 'hare': 5. (1) Neutral address for a hare. (2) Term of endearment for lovers. ? (1) Mart. (2) Pl. (1) Mart. 1. 22. 1, 1. 48. 7; (2) Pl. *Cas.* 138.

Levamen 'solace': 2. With possessives, term of affection from parents to children. Lit. High (poetic). Prop., Sen. (trag.) Prop. 4. 11. 63; Sen. *Phoen.* 2.

Levis 'light, fleet, insubstantial, fickle': 3. Term for the fickle or insubstantial, often but not always a rebuke. Lit. High (poetic). Prop., Ov. Prop. 1. 18. 11; Ov. *Pont.* 4. 5. 1. Cf. *levior* (Pl. *Men.* 488).

Levissime 'most flighty': 2. Rebuke for those in some way inconsistent. Adj. Gen. Mid. [Cic.], [Sal.] [Cic.] *Sal.* 7; [Sal.] *Cic.* 7.

Libelle 'little book': 9. Neutral address from a poet to the book he has written. Lit. High–mid. (poetic). Pers., Mart. Pers. 1. 120; Mart. 3. 2. 1.

Liber 'book': 18. Neutral address from a poet to the book he has written. Lit. High–mid. (poetic). Hor., Ov., Mart. Ov. *Tr.* 1. 1. 15; Mart. 1. 3. 2.

Liberi 'children': 5. Term for the speaker's children, or for people in general as the offspring of someone (transferred). Lit. Var. Sen. (trag.), Calp. F., [Quint.] Sen. *Her. F.* 1227; [Quint.] *Decl.* 5. 12.

Liberte, -a, -i 'freedman, freedwoman': 5. Neutral term for nameless freedmen, or a way of emphasizing the changing status of a new (or future) freedman or freedwoman. Lit. Mid. Pl., Sen. S., Quint. Pl. *Per.* 789, *Rud.* 1266; Quint. *Decl.* 388. 35.

Lictor 'lictor': 10. Address used by magistrates giving orders to nameless lictors. Gen. Mid. Liv., Sen. S. Liv. 26. 16. 3; Sen. *Con.* 9. 2. 3.

Lingua 'tongue': 5. (1) Address to a tongue, the speaker's or someone else's. (2) Term of endearment for lovers.　　　? (1) Sen. S., Mart. (2) Pl.　　　(1) Sen. *Con.* 2. 3. 1; Mart. 7. 24. 2; (2) Pl. *Poen.* 388.

Livide 'jealous, spiteful': 3. Rebuke for those displaying jealousy or spite. Subst.　　　?　　　[Verg.], Mart. Mart. 1. 40. 2, 11. 20. 1.

Livor 'envy': 6. Term for envy or malice.　　　Lit. High–mid.?　　　Ov., Phaed., [Quint.]　　　Ov. *Am.* 1. 15. 1; Phaed. 4. 21. 1.

Lumen, -a 'light, eye': 4. (1) In singular, term of endearment for lovers. (2) In plural, address to speaker's eyes.　　　(1) Gen. Mid.? (2) Lit. High (poetic).　　　(1) Mart., Apul., graf. (2) Stat.　　　(1) Mart. 1. 68. 6; Apul. *Met.* 5. 13; (2) Stat. *Theb.* 11. 334.　　　Cf. Mart. 11. 29. 3.

Lupe, -a, -i 'wolf': 4. Neutral term for wolves, often in their absence.　　　Lit.? High–mid.?　　　Prop., Tib., Phaed. Prop. 4. 1. 55; Tib. 1. 1. 33.

Lusce 'blind in one eye': 2. Impolite but not seriously insulting term for a one-eyed man whose name is unknown. Gen. Low.　　　Pl., Pers.　　　Pl. *Cur.* 505; Pers. 1. 128. Cf. *unocule* (Pl. *Cur.* 392).

Lutum 'dirt': 3. Strong insult.　　　Gen. Low.　　　Pl., Cic.　　　Pl. *Per.* 414; Cic. *Pis.* 62.

Lux 'light': 23. Term of endearment or praise, often for lovers, normally with a possessive.　　　Gen. Var.　　　Pl., Enn., Cic., Verg., Prop., Tib., Ov., [Phaed.], Sil., Mart., Fro., graf.　　　Cic. *Fam.* 14. 2. 2; Verg. *A.* 2. 281; Prop. 2. 14. 29.

Machinator, -trix 'contriver': 2. Insult for famous plotters, with genitive of evil things contrived.　　　Lit. High (poetic).　　　Sen. (trag.)　　　Sen. *Tro.* 750, *Med.* 266.

Macte 'honoured, blessed': 20+. Term of praise, usually modified by an ablative or genitive of the reason for the honour, esp. *virtute*.　　　Lit. High.　　　Acc., Verg., Sil., Stat., Mart., V. Fl., Plin., Calp. F., and elsewhere in prayers or not as an address (though still in vocative case). Stat. *Silv.* 4. 8. 14; Mart. 12. 3. 7.

Magister, -i 'master, teacher, professor (m.)': 116. In singular: (1) Respectful term for a learned man in the imperial period.

(2) Neutral term for a teacher or master of something or someone (with genitive). (3) In plural, rare, to teachers in general.   (1) Gen. Mid. (2) Lit.? Mid. (3) Lit. Mid.? (1) Petr, Suet., (Fro.), Gel. (2) Sen. S., Mart., Juv. (3) Ov. (1) Petr. 55. 5; Fro. 28. 16; cf. Apul. *Apol.* 97; (2) Mart. 12. 48. 15; Juv. 2. 77; (3) Ov. *Fast.* 3. 829.

Magnanime, -i 'great-souled': 7. Term of praise for military heroes and those who can plausibly be flattered as such; used in both military and non-military contexts.   Lit. High (poetic).   Verg., Sen. (trag.), Stat.   Verg. *A.* 5. 17; Sen. *Oed.* 294; Stat. *Theb.* 7. 375.

Magne, -a, -um, -i 'great': 31 +. Term of great respect for gods, emperors, heroes, and important men. Adj.   Lit. High.   Enn., (Cic.), Verg., Hor., Prop., Ov., Sen. (trag.), Sil., Stat., Mart., V. Fl., [Quint.], and prayers. Verg. *A.* 6. 841; Stat. *Silv.* 4. 2. 15.

Maior, -us 'greater': 6. Intensifier used as part of larger address phrases, frequently but not necessarily positive. Lit. High–mid. (poetic).   Hor., Prop., Ov., V. Fl. Hor. *S.* 2. 3. 326; Ov. *Met.* 2. 429.

Male conciliate, -i 'badly bought' i.e. 'a bad bargain': 2. Strong insult for the speaker's slaves. Subst.   Gen.? Low.   Pl., Ter.   Pl. *Ps.* 133; Ter. *Eu.* 669. Cf. *male habiti* (Pl. *Ps.* 133).

Malus, -a, -um 'bad': 7. (1) Mild rebuke to a silly woman, used alone in feminine. (2) Usually neuter substantive, as part of a larger phrase rebuking someone or something that causes trouble.   (1) Gen. Low–mid. (2) Lit.? High– mid.   (1) Pl. (2) [Verg.], Ov., Sen. (prose), Curt., Mart.   (1) Pl. *Truc.* 132; (2) Ov. *Am.* 2. 5. 4.

Manes 'spirits': 5 +. Neutral address to specific dead people or to the dead in general.   Gen.? High–mid.? Prop., [Sen.] (trag.), Stat., Apul., Quint., and prayers. [Sen.] *Her. O.* 949; Apul. *Met.* 8. 14.

Manus 'hand, band': 11. (1) Address to the speaker's own hands. (2) With appropriate modifiers, term for a group of men, usually warriors, from their leader or another person. Positive or negative depending on modifiers.   Lit. High.   (1) Ov., Sen. (trag.), [Quint.] (2) Verg., Sen.

(trag.), Luc., Sil., V. Fl.   (1) Ov. *Met.* 9. 186; Sen.
Med. 809; (2) Verg. *A.* 10. 294; V. Fl. 4. 437.

Marite, -i 'husband': 26. (1) Address from wife to husband. (2)
In transferred sense to anyone's husband.   Lit.? Mid.
(1) Apul., Avit., [Quint.], inscr. (2) Catul., Verg., Sen. S.,
Mart., [Quint.]   (1) Apul. *Met.* 5. 6; [Quint.] *Decl.* 18.
17; *ILS* 8453; (2) Catul. 61. 184; Verg. *Ecl.* 8. 30.

Mastigia 'one who deserves a beating': 8. Strong insult
normally used to male slaves.   Gen. Low.   Pl.,
Ter.   Pl. *Mos.* 1; Ter. *Ad.* 781.

Mater, -es 'mother': 132 +. (1) Term used by sons or daugh-
ters to their mother. (2) With a genitive to anyone's mother.
(3) Alone in transferred sense to the mother of a person
under discussion. (4) Alone in extended usage as a respectful
and affectionate address to goddesses and older women.
Gen. (except 2). Var.   (1) Pl., Ter., Enn., Pac., Verg.,
Hor., Prop., Ov., Sen. S., Sen., Stat., Flor., [Quint.] (2)
Acc., Sen. (trag.), Juv., inscr. (3) Verg., Sen. S., Mart.,
Quint., [Quint.], inscr. (4) Pl., Verg., Sen. (trag.), Luc.,
Petr., Curt., Quint., Fron., V. Fl., Apul., [Quint.] Unclassifiable: Titin., Afran., com. frag. Also in prayers.   (1)
Pl. *As.* 535; Sen. *Dial.* 12. 1. 1; (2) [Sen.] *Her. O.* 1832; Juv.
6. 167; (3) Verg. *Ecl.* 8. 48; Quint. *Decl.* 388. 10; (4) Pl. *Rud.*
263; Petr. 7. 1.   Cf. *matercula* (Pl. *Cist.* 452); *mater
familias* (Apul. *Met.* 9. 7).

Matrona, -ae 'matron': 5. Term for married women.
Lit. Mid.   Ov., V. Max., Mart.   Ov. *Met.* 14.
833; V. Max. 1. 8. 4; Mart. 7. 35. 7.

Maxime, -a, -um, -i 'very great': 36 +. Term of very great
respect for gods, rulers, and heroes.   Gen. High.
Enn., Cic., Verg., Hor., Ov., Luc., Sil., Stat., Mart., V. Fl.,
Suet., Fro., and prayers.   Verg. *G.* 2. 170; Ov. *Met.* 14.
108.

Medice, -i 'doctor': 5. Address for nameless doctors.
Lit. Mid.   Pl., Juv., [Quint.]   Pl. *Men.* 946; Juv.
6. 46.

Mel 'honey': 12. Term of endearment, normally for lovers,
always with *meum*.   Gen. Low–mid.   Pl., Afran.
Pl. *Mos.* 325a, *Cur.* 164.   Cf. *melculum* (Pl. *Cas.* 836).

Melior 'better': 3. Term of praise, used as part of larger

address phrases.   Lit. High (poetic).   Enn.,
Prop., Sen. (trag.)   Enn. *trag.* 34; Sen. *Her. F.* 1067.

Mellilla 'little honey': 1. Term of endearment for lovers.
Gen. Low?   Pl.   Pl. *Cas.* 135.   Cf. Pl. *Cist.*
247.

Mellite 'honey-sweet': 2. Term of strong affection for lovers.
Gen. Mid.?   Catul., Apul.   Catul. 99. 1; Apul.
Met. 5. 6.   Cf. *mellitissime* (Fro. 63. 10); *mellitula*
(Apul. *Met.* 3. 22).

Memorande 'to be spoken of': 7. Term of praise used by the
author of a poem in his own voice.   Lit. High (poetic).
Verg., Ov., Sil., Mart., [Sen.]   Verg. *A.* 10. 793; Ov.
Tr. 1. 5. 1.

Mens 'mind': 3. Address to the speaker's own mind; normally
somewhat negative.   Lit. High (poetic).   Pac.,
Luc., Sil.   Sil. 12. 497; Luc. 7. 552.

Metuende, -a 'to be feared': 2 +. Mocking address used to
insult soldiers who do not inspire fear; also 'straight' use to
gods, submissive.   Lit. High (poetic).   Verg.,
Sil., and prayers.   Verg. *A.* 10. 557; Sil. 1. 390.

Mi, meus, mea, meum, mei, meae 'my': 871. Possessive
attached to vocatives (1) in letters, for positive politeness
(very common); elsewhere (2) to relatives and objects of
romantic love, usually to express affection, or (3) to express
positive politeness to people other than lovers or relatives.
Gen. Low–mid.   (1) Cic., (Plin.), Sen. (prose), Suet.,
Fro., Gel., epist., inscr. (2) Pl., Ter., Cic., Catul., Verg.,
Prop., Tib., Liv., Ov., Sen. S., *Ilias*, Sil., Stat., V. Fl., Stat.,
Mart., Apul., Gel., inscr., graf. (3) Pl., Ter., Var., Cic.,
Catul., [Verg.], Ov., Calp. S., SL, Sen. (prose), Petr., Pers.,
Stat., Mart., V. Fl., Apul., Gel., inscr., graf.   (1) Cic.
Att. 9. 6. 7; Plin. *Ep. Tra.* 10. 50; (2) Cic. *Div.* 1. 103; Catul.
5. 1; (3) Cic. *Brut.* 253; Petr. 90. 5; Pl. *Poen.* 1127.
Also in numerous dramatic fragments without sufficient
context to classify.

Miles, -tes 'soldier': 114. (1) In singular, neutral address for a
known or unknown soldier from anyone (alone in prose and
comedy, modified elsewhere). (2) In singular, neutral address for a group of soldiers, usually from their commander.
(3) In plural, neutral and standard address to an army or

smaller group of soldiers, usually from their commander. In all three senses is restricted to historical or invented settings; not used to mythological figures. Gen. Var. (1) Pl., Ter., [Caes.], Prop., Liv., Ov., Phaed., poet. frag., Luc., Curt., [Quint.] (2) Liv., Luc., Sil., V. Fl. (3) Cic., Caes., Sal., Liv., Curt., Fron. (1) Pl. *Poen.* 615; Luc. 8. 676; (2) Luc. 4. 213; Sil. 4. 68; (3) Cic. *Phil.* 14. 33; Caes. *Gal.* 6. 8. 4. Cf. Suet. *Jul.* 67. 2, 70, *Aug.* 25. 1; Liv. 45. 37. 14.

Minimi preti 'of least value, cheapest': 3. As genitive of value after a noun meaning 'man' *vel sim.*, a fairly strong insult. Gen. Low–mid. Pl. Pl. *Bac.* 444, *Men.* 489. Cf. *hau magni preti* (Pl. *Cas.* 98).

Minister, -ra 'servant': 4. Term for a servant, usually of the speaker or of something specified in the genitive; with modifiers. Lit. High (poetic). Catul., Prop., [Tib.], Ov. Catul. 27. 1; Prop. 4. 11. 52; [Tib.] 3. 6. 57.

Miselle, -a, -i 'poor little': 7. Term used to express pity and sympathy, scorn and contempt, or an intermediate emotion to an addressee who has or is claimed to have reason to be miserable, whether or not he or she is actually unhappy. Gen.? Mid.? Catul., Mart., Apul. Catul. 40. 1; Apul. *Met.* 6. 21.

Miser, -a, -i, -ae 'wretched': 79. Term used to express pity and sympathy, scorn and contempt, or an intermediate emotion to an addressee who has or is claimed to have reason to be miserable, whether or not he or she is actually unhappy. Gen. High–mid.? Cic., Catul., Verg., Hor., Ov., Sen. S., Sen., Luc., Sil., Curt., Pers., Quint., Stat., Mart., V. Fl., Juv., Apul., [Quint.] Cic. *Phil.* 13. 34; Verg. *A.* 3. 639; Stat. *Theb.* 12. 442; Mart. 10. 100. 2.

Miserande, -a 'pitiable': 35. Expression of deep sympathy, also (rarely) used for scorn. Lit. High? Verg., Ov., Sen. (trag.), Luc., Stat., V. Fl., Apul. Verg. *A.* 6. 882; Stat. *Theb.* 11. 678; V. Fl. 3. 290.

Miserrime, -a, -i 'very wretched': 17. Expression of pity and sympathy. Plural only in prose. Adj. Gen. Var. Verg., Ov., Sen. S., Quint., [Quint.] Verg. *A.* 2. 519; Sen. *Con.* 10. 5. 7.

Mitis 'mild': 3. Term of praise.   Lit. High (poetic).
Ov., Stat.   Ov. *Pont.* 4. 15. 32; Stat. *Theb.* 7. 547.

Mitissime, -a 'very mild': 12 +. Term of great respect for
gods, rulers, and important men being flattered.   Lit.?
High (poetic).   Ov., Stat., Mart.   Stat. *Theb.* 7.
355; Mart. 12. 9. 1.

Moderator 'director, guide (m.)': 2. Complimentary address
praising someone for his status as guiding or controlling
something. Does not imply subordination of speaker to
addressee.   Lit. High (poetic).   Ov., Mart.
Ov. *Met.* 8. 856; Mart. 2. 90. 1.

Moleste, -a 'annoying': 2. Expression of irritation or contempt.   Gen.?   Mid.?   *Priap.*,   Mart.
Priap. 17. 1; Mart. 1. 42. 6.

Monstrum, -a 'monster': 3. (1) Strong insult. (2) Neutral
address to monsters.   (1) Gen. Low. (2) Lit. High
(poetic).   (1) Ter., Cic. (2) Sen. (trag.)   (1) Ter.
Eu. 860; Cic. *Pis.* 31; (2) Sen. *Phaed.* 1204.

Moriture 'about to die': 4. Term for those whose projected
lifespan is short, either kindly or as a threat/insult.
Lit. High (poetic).   Verg., Hor., Luc.   Verg. *A.*
10. 811; Hor. *Carm.* 2. 3. 4.

Mors 'death': 7. Neutral term for Death.   Lit. High–
mid.   Prop., Tib., Sen. (trag.), Luc., [Quint.]
Prop. 2. 13. 50; Tib. 1. 3. 4.

Mortalis, -e, -es 'mortal': 11. Address to people in general
(either in plural or collective singular with *genus*) or to an
unknown or unspecified individual (singular).   Lit.
High?   Acc., Lucr., Prop., Ov., Sil., [Quint.], inscr.
Prop. 2. 27. 1; Ov. *Met.* 15. 139; Lucr. 3. 933; *ILS*
8173.

Mulier, -es 'woman': 115. Neutral term used for women (if
woman is known, speaker is always male), also used negatively by lovers or male relatives to signal displeasure. Plural
only in Pl. and Titin., used neutrally to any group of two or
more women, including relatives.   Gen. Var., but in
elevated poetry the address is more likely to be negative.
Andr., Pl., Caecil., Enn., Ter., Pac., Titin., Lucil., Acc.,
Cic., Hor., Prop., Tib., Sen. S., Quint., Gel., Calp. F.,

[Quint.]   Pl. *Cist.* 704, *Mer.* 528, *Rud.* 1209; Cic. *Cael.*
33; Prop. 3. 24. 1.

Mulsa 'honeyed': 2. Term of romantic affection for women.
Gen.? Low?   Pl.   Pl. *Cas.* 372, *St.* 755.

(G)nata, -ae 'born (f.), daughter': 46. (1) Address from a parent
to his or her daughter. (2) With genitive, ablative, or other
modifiers, used as a periphrastic patronymic or other indication of the addressee's origin. Usually polite. (3) Occasionally alone in extended sense to unrelated girls.   Gen.
Var. in early Latin; later Lit. High.   (1) Pl., Enn., Ter.,
Acc., [Verg.], Prop., Ov., Phaed., Sen. (trag.), Sil., Stat.,
V. Fl. (2) Hor., Prop., Ov., [Sen.] (trag.) (3) Sil., V. Fl.
(1) Pl. *Rud.* 1179; Ov. *Met.* 13. 521; (2) Hor. *Carm.* 3. 21. 1;
Prop. 1. 17. 25; [Sen.] *Oct.* 933; (3) Sil. 7. 479; V. Fl. 7. 229.
Cf. *prognata* (Enn. *Ann.* 36).

(G)nate, -i 'born (m.), son': 183. (1) Address from a parent to
his or her son. (2) With a genitive or ablative, used as a
periphrastic patronymic or other indication of the addressee's origin. Usually polite.   Gen. Var. in early
Latin; later Lit. High.   (1) Pl., Enn., Ter., Pac.,
Pompon., Nov., Catul., Cic. (poetry), Verg., Ov., Sen.
(trag.), Luc., Sil., Stat., V. Fl., inscr. (2) Pl., Catul., Verg.,
Hor., Liv., Ov., Sen. (trag.), Sil., Stat.   (1) Pl. *Trin.*
362; Verg. *A.* 2. 594; (2) Catul. 64. 22; Verg. *A.* 1. 615; Ov.
Met. 9. 12.

Nauta, -ae 'sailor': 7. Neutral term for nameless or unknown
sailors. Unmodified, usually plural.   Gen.? Var.
Pl., Acc., Hor., Prop., Ov., Luc.   Pl. *Mil.* 1335; Ov.
Met. 3. 632.

Navita 'sailor': 5. Term for a known sailor or sailors in
general.   Lit. High (poetic).   Prop., Ov., Sen.
(trag.)   Prop. 3. 11. 71; Ov. *Ep.* 6. 48.

Nefande, -a 'wicked': 7. Rebuke for wrongdoers. Subst.
Lit. High–mid.   Cic., [Sen.], Stat., [Quint.]
Cic. *Dom.* 133; Stat. *Theb.* 11. 341.   Cf. *nefandissime*
([Quint.] *Decl.* 18. 11).

Nepos 'grandson': 3 +. Affectionate address from a grandmother to her grandson (also once to a granddaughter); also
used with a genitive as a sort of periphrastic patronymic.

Lit. High (poetic).   Enn., Ov., [Sen.] (trag.), and prayers.   Ov. *Fast.* 1. 521; [Sen.] *Her. O.* 1428. Cf. *neptes* (Juv. 6. 265).

Nequissime, -a 'worthless': 6. Fairly strong insult. Adj. Gen. Low–mid.   Pl., Apul.   Pl. *Men.* 488; Apul. *Met.* 7. 27.

Nihili 'of nothing', i.e. 'worthless': 3. As genitive of value after *homo*, insult expressing contempt.   Gen. Low. Pl., Gel.   Pl. *Bac.* 1188; Gel. 10. 19. 2.

Nile 'Nile': 8. Neutral address for the river Nile.   Lit.? High (poetic).   Ov., Luc., Mart., V. Fl.   Ov. *Met.* 1. 728; Mart. 6. 80. 10.

Nocentissime 'most guilty': 2. Insult for an accused criminal. Adj.   ?   [Quint.]   [Quint.] *Decl.* 18. 4, 18. 9.   Cf. *nocentes* (Stat. *Silv.* 3. 3. 13).

Noster 'our': 26 +. Possessive attached to vocatives to express friendliness, usually between unrelated men.   Gen. Mid.   Andr., Pl., Enn., Ter., Var., Cic., and prayers. Ter. *Ad.* 883; Cic. *Leg.* 1. 1.

Noverca 'stepmother': 8. Address for the speaker's step-mother, or in transferred sense for the stepmother of a person under discussion. Implies that the addressee has the traditional vices of a stepmother.   Lit.? Mid.? Sen. S., Sen. (trag.), [Quint.]   Sen. *Con.* 9. 6. 1; [Sen.] *Her. O.* 1187.

Nugator 'joker': 5. Moderate insult, in Plautus to jokers of some sort, later more general and philosophical in character. Gen. Mid.   Pl., Lucil., Cic., Pers.   Pl. *Trin.* 972; Cic. *Sen.* 27.

Numen, -a 'divinity': 5 +. With modifiers, pos. or neg. address to divinities of all types.   Lit. High (poetic, cultic). Ov., Sil., Stat., and prayers.   Ov. *Met.* 2. 428; Stat. *Theb.* 11. 485.

Nupta, -ae 'married woman': 5. Polite term for brides and married women, from speakers who are not their husbands. Lit. Mid.?   Pl., Catul., Ov.   Catul. 61. 144; Ov. *Fast.* 2. 794.

Nurus 'daughter-in-law, young married woman': 3. Literary term for married women, occasionally used alone but more

often with the father-in-law in the genitive. Not used to
speaker's own daughter-in-law.   Lit. High (poetic).
Sen. (trag.), Mart.   [Sen.] *Oct.* 934; Mart. 14. 59. 2.

Nutrix 'nurse': 15. Affectionate term from a girl or woman to
her old nurse; also occasionally in transferred sense to someone else's nurse.   Gen. Var.   Pl., Ter., Afran.,
Sen. S., Verg., Ov., Sen. (trag.)   Pl. *Aul.* 691; Verg. *A.*
4. 634; Sen. *Con.* 9. 6. 13.   Cf. *nutricula* ([Verg.] *Ciris*
257, 277).

Nympha, -e, -ae 'nymph': 15 +. Neutral or mildly honorific
address to known or unknown nymphs.   Lit. High
(poetic).   Verg., Ov., Sil., Stat., Mart., V. Fl., and
prayers.   Verg. *A.* 12. 142; [Ov.] *Ep.* 15. 175; Stat.
Theb. 4. 684.

Oblite 'forgetful': 12. Fairly strong rebuke to those who forget
or fail to live up to something; with genitive of thing
forgotten. Subst.   Lit.? High?   Cic., Verg.,
Ov., Sen. (trag.), Luc., Sil., Stat.   Cic. *Pis.* 62; Ov.
Met. 8. 140.

Ocelle, -us 'little eye': 6. Term of endearment, normally for
lovers.   Gen. Mid.?   Pl., Catul.   Pl. *As.*
664; Catul. 50. 19.

Ocule, -us, -i 'eye': 13. (1) In singular, term of endearment,
normally for lovers, usually with *mi/meus.* (2) In plural,
address to a pair of eyes (often but not always the
speaker's).   (1) Gen. Low? (2) ?   (1) Pl. (2)
Sen. S., Sen. (trag.), Calp. F., [Quint.]   (1) Pl. *Mil.*
1330, *Mos.* 311; (2) Sen. *Con.* 2. 3. 1; Sen. *Phoen.* 233.
Cf. *oculissume* (Pl. *Cur.* 120a).

Odiose 'hateful': 2. Mild insult for people distanced from the
speaker. Adj.   Lit. High (poetic).   Ov.
Ov. *Ars* 2. 635, *Rem.* 471.   Cf. *odium* (Pl. *Poen.* 392).

Opportunitas 'opportunity': 2. Term of praise for useful
subordinates.   Lit.? Mid.?   Pl.   Pl. *Cur.*
305, *Men.* 137.

Optatissime, -a 'very desired': 3. Fairly strong term of
affection for relatives and close friends. Adj.   Gen.
Low–mid.   Cic., (Fro.)   Cic. *Q. fr.* 2. 7. 2; Fro.
13. 12.

Optime, -a, -i 'best': 122 +. Term of respect and affection, esp.

for family and social superiors. Gen. Var. Pl.,
Enn., Ter., Cic., Catul., Verg., Hor., Prop., Ov., Sen. S.,
Calp. S., Sen. (prose), *Ilias, Laus Pis.*, Sil., Quint., Stat.,
V. Fl., Tac., Plin., Fro., Apul., Gel., [Quint.], inscr., and
prayers. Cic. *Q. fr.* 3. 7. 9, *Sen.* 39; Plin. *Ep. Tra.* 10.
14. 1.

Parens, -es 'parent': 44 +. (1) In plural, affectionate address to
the speaker's parents. (2) In singular, affectionate? address to
the speaker's mother or father. (3) With a genitive, to the
(actual or metaphorical) mother or father of anything. (4)
Alone in transferred sense to the parent of a person under
discussion. (5) Alone in extended usage as a polite address to
gods or older men or women. (1, 5) Gen. Var. (2, 3)
Lit. High. (4) Lit. Mid. (1) Pl., Ter., Ov., Sen. (trag.),
inscr. (2) Verg., Ov., Sen. (trag.), *Ilias*, Sil., Stat.,V. Fl. (3)
Trag. frag., Stat., Mart. (4) Sen. (trag.), [Quint.] (5) Sil.,
Apul. (1) Pl. *Rud.* 1144; *ILS* 8129a; (2) Verg. *A.* 5. 80;
Sen. *Phoen.* 403; (3) Stat. *Silv.* 4. 3. 139; Mart. 9. 5. 1; (4)
Sen. *Med.* 1024, *Tro.* 785; (5) Sil. 17. 651; Apul. *Met.* 1. 21.
Cf. Apul. *Apol.* 97; *HA* 9. 4. 1.

Parricida 'murderer, traitor': 11. (1) Rebuke for men committing murder or treason. (2) Strong general insult. (1)
Lit.? High. (2) Gen. Low. Pl., Sen. S., Calp. F., Sen.
(trag.), Curt., [Quint.] Pl. *Ps.* 362; Sen. *Con.* 7. 2. 3;
Sen. *Oed.* 1002.

Pars 'part': 10. With partitive genitive, forms basis for expressions of praise, affection, or (less often) blame. Genitive is
most often *animae meae*. Lit. High (poetic).
Verg., Ov., Sen. (trag.), Luc., Stat. Verg. *G.* 2. 40;
Ov. *Met.* 8. 406; Luc. 3. 120; Stat. *Theb.* 4. 685.

Parve 'little': 14. Term for babies, boys, and small objects of
any type, often but not always conveying some pity. Adj.
? Verg., Ov., Luc., Stat., Mart., inscr. Verg.
Ecl. 4. 60; Ov. *Tr.* 1. 1. 1.

Passer 'sparrow': 5. (1) Address to a sparrow. (2) Term of
endearment for humans. (3) Once used to a human to
indicate sparrow-like frugality, mocking. Gen. Var.
(1) Catul. (2) Pl., Juv. (3) Quint. (1) Catul. 2. 1. (2) Pl.
Cas. 138; Juv. 9. 54; cf. Apul. *Met.* 10. 22. (3) Quint. *Inst.* 6.
3. 93. Cf. Pl. *As.* 666, 694.

Pastor 'shepherd': 2 +. Neutral address to unspecified shepherds or herdsmen. Lit. High (poetic). Verg., Ov. Verg. *G.* 3. 420; Ov. *Fast.* 4. 735.

Pater, -es 'father': 779 (incl. 354 plural). (1) Address from sons or daughters to their fathers. (2) With a genitive to anyone's real or metaphorical father. (3) Alone in transferred sense to the father of a person under discussion. (4) Alone in extended sense as an address for older men and as a respectful term for gods and for men of any age. (5) In plural, almost always with *conscripti* except in poetry, honorific address to senators used in speeches made to the Roman Senate by Romans or foreigners; also occasionally by extension in speeches to non-Roman senates. (1, 4) Gen. Var. (2) Lit. High (poetic). (3) Lit. Mid. (5) Gen. High. (1) Andr., Pl., Enn., Ter., Cic., Sal., Verg., Hor., Liv., Ov., Sen. S., V. Max., Sen. (trag.), Curt., Quint., Stat., Mart., V. Fl., Tac., Suet., Calp. F., [Quint.], epist., inscr. (2) Catul., Verg., Ov. (3) Catul., Verg., Sen. S., Sen. (trag.), Quint., Calp. F., [Quint.] (4) Pl., Enn., Verg., Hor., Liv., Ov., Sen. S., [Phaed.], Calp. S., Petr., Stat., V. Fl., Plin. (5) Cic., Sal., Liv., V. Max., Sen. (prose), Luc., Sil., Quint., Tac., Plin., Suet., Calp. F., [Quint.], inscr. (1) Cic. *Div.* 1. 103; Verg. *A.* 2. 707; (2) Verg. *A.* 1. 555; Ov. *Pont.* 3. 3. 88; (3) Sen. *Thy.* 442; Calp. *Decl.* 35; (4) Hor. *S.* 2. 1. 12; Petr. 100. 5; (5) Cic. *Catil.* 1. 4; Sal. *Jug.* 14. 1; Liv. 23. 12. 8.

Patria 'fatherland': 16. Affectionate address to the speaker's homeland. Gen. High–mid.? Pl., Enn., Cic., Catul., Ov., V. Max., Sil., Stat., V. Fl., Calp. F., [Quint.] Cic. *Sest.* 45; Catul. 63. 55.

Patrone, -i 'patron': 13. Deferential address from a client to his patron, or in Plautus by a slave or prostitute to a protector. Also used in comedy as a term of extreme flattery for slaves from their masters. Gen. Mid. Pl., (Cic.), Hor., Sen. S. Pl. *Men.* 1031, *Rud.* 1266; Cic. *Fam.* 7. 29. 2. Cf. *patrona virgo* (Catul. 1. 9).

Patrue 'paternal uncle': 18. Affectionate term for the speaker's father's brother or father's *frater patruelis*. Gen. Mid. Pl., Ter. Pl. *Poen.* 1076; Ter. *Ph.* 254. Cf. *patruissume* (Pl. *Poen.* 1197).

Pauper 'poor': 5. Term for those lacking in material prosperity; can express contempt or sympathy, or just identify a nameless addressee.   Lit. High.   Ov., [Verg.], [Quint.]   Ov. *Am.* 1. 8. 66; [Verg.] *Cat.* 8. 1.

Pax 'peace': 3. Term of praise for tranquil beings such as Sleep; with genitives or other modifiers.   Lit. High (poetic).   Ov., Sen. (trag.), Stat.   Ov. *Met.* 11. 624; Stat. *Theb.* 3. 296.

Pectus, -ora 'chests': 4. (1) Neutral address to the speaker's heart (sing. or pl.). (2) With appropriate modifiers, address to a group of people (pl. only).   (1) ? (2) Lit. High (poetic).   (1) Sen. S., Sen. (2) Verg., Ov.   (1) Sen. *Con.* 2. 3. 1; Sen. *Thy.* 920; (2) Verg. *A.* 2. 349; Ov. *Tr.* 4. 10. 92.

Peior 'worse': 2. Rebuke to those whose conduct is worse than that of some other wrongdoer; with ablative of comparison. Lit. High (poetic).   Sen. (trag.)   Sen. *Phaed.* 689, 1192.

Perdite, -a 'lost': 2. Term for those who are about to suffer a disaster, not hostile, sometimes a warning.   Lit. High (poetic).   Verg., V. Fl.   Verg. *A.* 4. 541; V. Fl. 4. 140.

Perditissime, -i 'most desperate': 2. Fairly strong insult. Adj. ?   Cic.   Cic. *Phil.* 11. 9, *Ver.* 3. 65; possibly also *Vat.* 26.

Perfide, -a 'treacherous, faithless': 40 +. Strong rebuke very often used to unfaithful lovers, and occasionally by extension to objects connected to a lover. Also to those faithless or treacherous in matters other than love, and occasionally as a general insult to those who cause suffering by a means other than treachery.   Lit. High (poetic).   Catul., Verg., Prop., [Tib.], Ov., Luc., Sil., Stat., Mart., Juv., and prayers.   Catul. 30. 3; Verg. *A.* 4. 305; Prop. 1. 16. 43; [Tib.] 3. 6. 56; Ov. *Met.* 2. 704; Mart. 2. 75. 9. Cf. *perfidiosae* ([Cic.] *Rhet. Her.* 4. 22).

Periture, -a 'about to perish': 4. Rebuke and threat for evildoers; also expression of sorrow.   Lit. High (poetic).   Ov., Luc., Stat.   Ov. *Met.* 3. 579; Luc. 8. 692; Stat. *Theb.* 10. 594.

Periure, -a 'perjured': 4. (1) Rebuke for faithless lovers etc.

(2) General strong insult.　　　(1) Gen.? High. (2) Gen.
Low.　　　Pl., Prop., Ov.　　　Pl. *Ps.* 363; Ov. *Fast.* 3.
473.　　　Cf. *peiiuri caput* (Pl. *Rud.* 1099); *fons . . . peiiuri*
(Pl. *Truc.* 612).

Periurissime 'very perjured': 3. Strong insult, usually applied
to those who have broken their word. Subst.　　　Gen.
Low.　　　Pl.　　　Pl. *Ps.* 351, *Rud.* 722.

Perverse, -i 'perverse': 2. Insult.　　　Lit. High (poetic)?
Verg.　　　Verg. *Ecl.* 3. 13, [Verg.] *Cat.* 11. 7.

Pessime, -a, -um, -i, -ae 'worst': 26. Moderate insult. Subst.
Gen. Var.　　　Naev., Pl., Ter., Turp., Catul., Sal., Verg.,
Hor., Ov., Phaed., Luc., Curt., Pers., Stat.　　　Pl. *Mos.*
897; Verg. *Ecl.* 3. 17.

Pestis 'plague': 2. Strong insult.　　　Gen.? Low?
Cic.　　　Cic. *Pis.* 56, *Dom.* 72.

Philosophe 'philosopher': 3. Term for nameless philosophers
and those acting like philosophers.　　　Lit. Low–mid.?
Pl., Quint., Gel.　　　Pl. *Rud.* 986; Gel. 19. 1. 8.

Pia, -i, -ae 'holy': 4. Term of praise.　　　Lit. High (poetic).
Ov., Stat., inscr.　　　Ov. *Am.* 2. 6. 3; Stat. *Silv.* 5. 3. 284.

Pietas 'piety, sense of duty': 9. (1) Address to a sense of duty,
whether that belonging to a specific individual or the abstract
virtue. (2) Term of praise and/or affection for humans.
Lit. High–mid.　　　(1) Ov., Sen. S., Sen. (trag.), Sil.,
[Quint.] (2) Pl., Enn.　　　(1) Ov. *Met.* 9. 679; Sen. *Con.* 1.
7. 5; (2) Pl. *Bac.* 1176; Enn. *Ann.* 4.

Piger 'sluggish': 2. Rebuke for inactivity.　　　Lit. High
(poetic).　　　Calp. S., Mart.　　　Calp. *Ecl.* 7. 4; Mart.
11. 36. 5.

Piissime, -i 'very dutiful': 2. Term of praise.　　　Gen.
Mid.?　　　Curt., [Quint.]　　　Curt. 9. 6. 17; [Quint.]
Decl. 10. 19.

Placidissime 'very kind, very tranquil': 6 +. Term of great
respect for gods, rulers, and important men being flattered.
Lit.? High (poetic).　　　Ov., Stat., and elsewhere in
prayers.　　　Stat. *Silv.* 3. 3. 167, 3. 3. 43.

Poene 'Carthaginian': 10. Possibly derogatory address for a
Carthaginian abroad, from non-Carthaginians. Subst.
Gen.? Var.?　　　Pl., Ov., Sil.　　　Pl. *Poen.* 1410; Sil. 1.
443.

Poeta, -ae 'poet': 14. Neutral address for any type of poet; often with positive or negative modifiers. Lit. Var. Enn., Catul., Verg., Prop., Ov., Sen. (prose), Mart. Prop. 1. 7. 24; Mart. 11. 94. 2.

Pontifex, -es 'pontiff': 31. Neutral address to members of the college of pontiffs, or (rarer and poetic) to priests in general. Usually plural; singular is probably purely literary. Gen. Mid. Cic., Liv., Ov., Pers. Cic. *Dom.* 1; Pers. 2. 69.

Popularis, -es 'fellow-citizen': 4. Positive term for fellow-citizens, invoking solidarity. Gen. Var. Pl., Ter., Sil. Pl. *Poen.* 1039; Ter. *Ad.* 155. Cf. *homo popularis* (Cic. *Dom.* 80).

Popule, -us, -i 'people': 8. Term for a community of people, Roman or otherwise. Lit.? Mid. [Cic.], Liv., Ov., Calp. S., Luc., Quint., [Quint.] Ov. *Fast.* 4. 731; Quint. *Decl.* 302. 5.

Potens, -es 'powerful': 5. Term of praise. Adj. Lit. High (poetic). Acc., Stat. Acc. *trag.* 196; Stat. *Silv.* 4. 1. 28.

Praeclare 'brilliant': 2. Sarcastic term of mock praise. Lit.? Mid.? Cic., Hor. Cic. *Pis.* 91; Hor. *S.* 1. 6. 110.

Praeco 'herald': 2. Neutral address used to give an order to the public herald. Gen.? Var.? Pl., Liv. Pl. *Poen.* 11; Liv. 24. 8. 20.

Praedo, -es 'brigand': 4. Fairly strong insult for those who can in some sense be considered brigands. Gen. Var. Pl., Cic., V. Fl., Mart. Cic. *Pis.* 57; V. Fl. 7. 50.

Praesidium, -a 'protection': 4. Term of praise for patrons and helpers, modified. Lit. High? Hor., Apul. Hor. *Carm.* 1. 1. 2; Apul. *Met.* 6. 28.

Praetor 'praetor': 4. Term for a praetor acting in an official capacity, esp. if unnamed. Gen. Mid. Lucil., Cic., Mart., Gel. Cic. *Ver.* 1. 142; Mart. 4. 67. 8.

Princeps, -es 'chief': 8. (1) In singular, with modifiers, very polite, elevated address to emperors and other very important men. (2) In plural, with genitive, used to groups of non-Roman dignitaries. (1) Lit. High. (2) Gen. Mid. (1) Ov., Stat., Mart. (2) Cic., Liv. (1) Ov. *Tr.* 2. 128;

Stat. *Theb.* 8. 367; cf. Hor. *Carm.* 4. 14. 6; (2) Cic. *Phil.* 8. 28; Liv. 32. 21. 1.

Proceres 'leaders': 5. Complimentary address, not from a subordinate, to a group of men, often the unspecified leaders of an army.　　　Lit. High (poetic).　　　Verg., Ov., Stat., Juv.　　　Verg. *A.* 3. 103; Stat. *Theb.* 6. 180.

Profani, -ae 'unclean': 4. Ritual term for those who should not participate in religious rites, warning them to depart. Gen. High (poetic, cultic).　　　Verg., Calp. S., Sil., Juv. Verg. *A.* 6. 258; Juv. 2. 89.

Progenies 'progeny': 11. Complimentary and highly literary address which is used with some type of possessive (usually a genitive) to form a periphrastic patronymic for men or women.　　　Lit. High (poetic).　　　Catul., Verg., Hor., Ov., Sen. (trag.), Stat., V. Fl.　　　Verg. *A.* 7. 97; Hor. *Carm.* 3. 29. 1.

Proles 'progeny': 17. Occasionally used by parents to their children, but normally used (with a genitive or adjective to show the parent) as a type of periphrastic patronymic for men, women, or groups. Complimentary.　　　Lit. High (poetic).　　　Verg., Ov., Sen. (trag.), Luc., Sil., Stat., V. Fl., Juv.　　　Verg. *A.* 6. 322; Ov. *Met.* 13. 45; Sen. *Med.* 945.

Propago 'progeny': 5. Complimentary address from a parent to his or her son, daughter, or children. Also used as a periphrastic patronymic with some type of possessive. Lit. High (poetic).　　　Ov., Sen. (trag.), Sil., Stat., V. Fl. Stat. *Theb.* 5. 278; V. Fl. 6. 547.　　　Cf. *propages* (Pac. *trag.* 20).

Propinque, -i 'relative': 3. Term for one's own relatives or (in transferred sense) for those of one's client.　　　Lit. Mid.? [Tib.], Sen. S., [Quint.]　　　[Tib.] 3. 14. 6; Sen. *Con.* 7. 8. 2.

Pudice, -a 'pure': 4. Term of praise.　　　Lit. High–mid. (poetic).　　　Catul., Ov., Mart., inscr.　　　Catul. 42. 24; Mart. 9. 5. 2.

Pudor 'modesty': 4. Address to Modesty as an abstraction. Lit. High (poetic).　　　Verg., Ov., Sen. (trag.), V. Fl. Verg. *A.* 4. 27; Ov. *Ars* 1. 608.

Puella, -ae 'girl': 72 +. Complimentary address to girls and young women; in plural to groups of girls or maidservants, or to girls in general.　　　Gen. Mid.?　　　Pl., Enn., Cic., Catul., [Verg.], Hor., Prop., Tib., Ov., Sen. S., Quint., Mart., Juv., Apul., Calp. F., graf., inscr.　　　Pl. *Rud.* 263; Cic. *Div.* 1. 104; Catul. 35. 16; Prop. 3. 20. 10; Ov. *Ep.* 20. 28, *Ars* 3. 417.

Puer, -e, -i 'boy': 207+. (1) Term for young males (from unborn babies to young men of military age) used by males and females, relatives and non-relatives, known and unknown, not necessarily older than the addressee. Usually friendly. (2) Term for unknown or nameless male slaves of any age, always used alone. (3) In plural, in addition to uses 1 and 2, can be addressed to a group of adult men by their leader.　　　Gen. Var.　　　(1) Pl., Ter., Afran., (Cic.), Verg., Hor., Prop., Tib., Ov., Sen. S., Calp. S., Sen. (trag.), *Buc. Eins.*, Luc., Sil., Pers., Quint., Stat., Mart., V. Fl., Juv., Apul., Calp. F., graf., inscr. (2) Pl., Ter., Caecil., Pompon., Afran., Cic., Catul., Verg., Hor., Prop., Tib., Ov., Pers., Stat., Mart., Apul. (3) Verg., Stat., Apul. Also used in prayers, esp. to Cupid.　　　(1) Cic. *Phil.* 13. 24; Verg. *A.* 8. 581; Ov. *Met.* 3. 454; Sil. 13. 758; Mart. 6. 3. 2; (2) Pl. *Mos.* 939; Cic. *De Orat.* 2. 247; (3) Verg. *A.* 5. 349; Apul. *Met.* 3. 5.

Pulcher 'beautiful': 3. Term of praise.　　　Lit. High–mid. Pl., Hor., Ov.　　　Pl. *Mil.* 1037; Ov. *Am.* 3. 9. 14. Cf. *pulchrior* (Hor. *Carm.* 1. 16. 1).

Pulcherrime, -a 'very beautiful': 17. General term of praise for attractive young men, women, boys, and gods; also term used by a woman to the object of her desire.　　　Lit.? Mid.?　　　Catul., Verg., Ov., Sil., Stat., Gel. Catul. 68. 105; Ov. *Met.* 14. 373.

Pullus 'chick': 1. Term of affection.　　　?　　　Pl. Pl. *Cas.* 138.　　　Cf. Hor. *S.* 1. 3. 45; Suet. *Cal.* 13.

Putide, -a, -um 'rotten': 8. Insult and expression of strong disgust.　　　Gen. Mid.?　　　Pl., Catul., [Verg.] Pl. *Bac.* 1163; Catul. 42. 11.

Quicumque/Quaecumque es 'whoever you are': 11. Neutral address for unknown, nameless, or hypothetical people. Lit. High (poetic).　　　Verg., Hor., Ov., Sen. (trag.),

Luc., Stat., V. Fl.   Ov. *Am.* 3. 5. 31; Stat. *Theb.* 5. 20;
V. Fl. 4. 191.

Quies 'repose': 2. Term of praise and/or affection.   Lit.
High (poetic).   Ov., Mart.   Ov. *Met.* 11. 623;
Mart. 11. 26. 1.

Quirites 'Roman citizens': 289. Honorific address used primarily in speeches to an assembly of the Roman people;
also sometimes to a subset of Romans, or to an assembly of
some other city.   Gen. High–mid.   Laber.,
Cic., Sal., Liv., Ov., V. Max., Luc., Pers., Quint., Juv.,
Plin., Gel., Apul.   Cic. *Man.* 1; Liv. 3. 17. 3; Apul.
Met. 2. 24.

Quisquis es 'whoever you are': 29+. Neutral address for
unknown, nameless, or hypothetical men or (rarely)
women.   Gen. Var.   Andr., Pl., Caecil., Verg.,
Prop., Tib., Ov., Sen. S., *Priap.*, Sen. (trag.), Sil., Curt.,
Pers., Stat., Mart., V. Fl., inscr.   Verg. *A.* 4. 577; Ov.
Met. 12. 80; Curt. 6. 10. 36; *ILS* 8178.

Rapax, -es 'rapacious': 2. Fairly strong insult. Subst.
Gen. Low.   Pl.   Pl. *Men.* 1015, *Per.* 410.

Raptor, -es 'robber, rapist': 4. Rebuke for those who commit
robbery or rape.   Lit. High?   Ov., Sen. S., Luc.
Ov. *Met.* 8. 438; Luc. 3. 125.

Rarissime, -a 'very rare': 4. Term of praise. Adj.   Gen.
Mid.   Stat., (Fro.)   Stat. *Silv.* 5. 1. 11; Fro. 34.
23.   Cf. *rara* (Prop. 4. 11. 52).

Rector 'ruler, guide (m.)': 17+. Complimentary address praising a god or important man for his status ruling or guiding
something or some group (very often specified in the
genitive). Does not imply subordination of speaker to addressee, though can be used by subordinates.   Lit.
High (poetic).   Hor., Ov., Sen. (trag.), Luc., Sil.,
Stat., Mart., V. Fl., and prayers.   Ov. *Met.* 12. 574;
Stat. *Ach.* 1. 350; Mart. 7. 7. 5.

Regia 'royal': 3+. Polite address for a queen or princess. Adj.
Lit. High (poetic).   Ov. and prayers.   Ov. *Met.*
13. 483, 523.

Regimen 'guidance': 2. Term of praise from the blind to those
who guide them; with genitive.   Lit. High (poetic).
Sen. (trag.), Stat.   Sen. *Phoen.* 1; Stat. *Theb.* 4. 536.

Regina 'queen, patroness': 21 +. (1) Complimentary address to a goddess or queen, often from someone not subject to her. (2) Highly respectful address used in requests to ordinary women in a position of power over the speaker.   Gen. Var.   (1) Acc., Catul., Verg., Ov., Sen. (trag.), Sil, Stat., and prayers. (2) Petr., Mart., V. Fl., graf.   (1) Catul. 66. 39; Verg. *A.* 2. 3; cf. Curt. 3. 12. 25; (2) Petr. 128. 2; Mart. 10. 64. 1; *CIL* iv. 2413h.

Regnator 'ruler (m.)': 3. Used with a genitive to characterize the addressee as ruling something; flattering, used to gods and emperors.   Lit. High (poetic).   Sen. (trag.), Stat.   Sen. *Phaed.* 945; Stat. *Silv.* 4. 2. 14.

Requies 'rest': 3. Term of praise; with genitive.   Lit. High (poetic).   Sen. (trag.), Stat.   Sen. *Her. F.* 1066; Stat. *Theb.* 3. 295.

Rex, -es 'king, patron': 49. (1) Complimentary address to a god or king, not necessarily (though usually) from his own subordinates; often with positive modifiers. (2) Respectful address from client to patron, coupled with *pater* or *domine*. (3) Plural, complimentary address to a group of important men.   (1) Gen. High–mid. (2) Gen. Low. (3) Lit. High (poetic).   (1) Enn., Acc., Cic., Sal., Verg., Liv., Ov., V. Max., *Ilias*, Sil., Curt., Stat., V. Fl., Apul., and prayers. (2) Not directly attested. (3) Sen. (trag.), Stat.   (1) Sal. *Jug.* 102. 5; Verg. *A.* 11. 294; Stat. *Theb.* 1. 448; (2) Cf. Hor. *Ep.* 1. 7. 37; Mart. 2. 68. 2; (3) Sen. *Ag.* 732; Stat. *Theb.* 7. 375.

Roma 'Rome': 52. Address from anyone to the city of Rome.   Gen. Var.   Enn., Cic., Hor., Prop., Liv., Ov., Sen. S., V. Max., Luc., Sil., Stat., Mart., graf.   Cic. *Fin.* 2. 106; Liv. 35. 21. 5; Ov. *Tr.* 4. 1. 106.

Romane, -a, -i 'Roman': 50. In singular, neutral address for the Roman people viewed collectively, or rarely from non-Romans to individual Romans; in plural, address from anyone to some group of Romans.   Sing.: Lit. Plural: Gen. Var.   Cic., Hor., Verg., Prop., Liv., Ov., V. Max., Luc., Sil.   Cic. *Sest.* 26; Hor. *Carm.* 3. 6. 2; Liv. 3. 2. 8; Luc. 10. 268.

Rosa 'rose': 2. Term of endearment for lovers, with *mea*.   Gen. Low?   Pl.   Pl. *Bac.* 83, *As.* 664.

Rustice, -a 'peasant, rustic': 11. Neutral address to an unnamed peasant *vel sim.*; also derogatory term for those lacking some element of urban skills, know-how, or graces. Gen.? Mid.? Hor., Ov., Phaed., Plin. S., Calp. S., Mart. Calp. *Ecl.* 7. 40; Mart. 10. 101. 4. Cf. Ov. *Ep.* 16. 287.

Rutuli 'Rutulians': 4. Address to Vergil's Rutulians. Lit. High (poetic). Verg. Verg. *A.* 9. 428, 12. 693.

Sacer, -a, -um 'sacred, accursed': 4. Term of praise, affection, or anger. Adj. Lit. High (poetic). [Verg.], Ov., Sen. (trag.), Stat. Ov. *Am.* 3. 9. 41; Sen. *Oed.* 931; Stat. *Theb.* 3. 295. Cf. *sacerrime* (Turp. *com.* 26); *sacrate* (Sen. *Oed.* 291); *sacratissime* (*ILS* 6870).

Sacerdos, -es 'priest, priestess': 7. Neutral address to a priest or priestess in a broad sense, named or not; often modified with complimentary adjectives. Lit.? High–mid. Verg., Ov., Quint., Stat., Apul. Verg. *A.* 6. 544; Quint. *Decl.* 304. 2.

Sacrilege, -a, -ae 'sacrilegious': 4. (1) Rebuke for those committing sacrilege. Subst. (2) Strong general insult. Subst. (1) Lit.? High–mid.? (2) Gen. Low. Pl., Ter., Ov., Sen. S. Pl. *Ps.* 363; Sen. *Con.* 8. 1.

Saeve, -a, -um, -i 'savage': 32 +. Rebuke for those causing suffering, normally the speaker's suffering. Often used to loved ones who die, depart, do not return the speaker's love, or cause strife; also to more distant trouble-causers and to gods and inanimate objects, esp. Cupid. Lit. High. Hor., Prop., Tib., Ov., Sen. (trag.), Luc., Stat., Mart., [Quint.], and prayers. Tib. 2. 4. 6; Ov. *Am.* 1. 1. 5; [Sen.] *Her. O.* 219; Luc. 5. 315; Stat. *Theb.* 10. 802.

Saevissime, -a 'very savage': 4 +. Rebuke for people doing something savage or cruel. Lit.? High–mid. Verg., Ov., Juv., [Quint.], and prayers. Verg. *A.* 10. 878; Juv. 6. 641.

Salus 'safety, salvation': 11. Term of praise and affection, always with a possessive. Gen. Var. Pl., Ov., V. Max., Sen. (trag.), Sil., Mart. Pl. *Bac.* 879; Ov. *Tr.* 2. 574; Sen. *Her. F.* 622.

Sancte, -a 'holy': 11 +. Term of great respect for gods, rulers, and important people, esp. if dead. Also used ironically.

Adj.   Lit. High (poetic).   Cic., Verg., Ov., Sil.,
V. Fl., and prayers.   Cic. *Ver.* 5. 49; Verg. *A.* 5. 80;
Ov. *Fast.* 2. 127; Sil. 7. 737.

Sanctissime, -a, -i 'very holy': 23. Term of respect for
rulers, the dead, ordinary friends, and (in plural) juries.
Adj.   Gen. High–mid.   Cic., Verg., Phaed.,
Petr., Mart., Plin., Fro., Apul., Calp. F., [Quint.], inscr.
Cic. *Rep.* 6. 15; Mart. 10. 37. 1; Plin. *Ep. Tra.* 10. 1. 1; Calp.
Decl. 13.

Sanguis 'blood': 4. With *meus* or another modifier, used like a
patronymic to individual men or (more often) groups of
men.   Lit. High (poetic).   Verg., Hor., Pers.,
Stat.   Verg. *A.* 6. 835; Hor. *Ars* 292.   Cf.
sanguen (Enn. *Ann.* 108).

Sata, -e 'offspring': 7. With an ablative, used as a periphrastic
patronymic. Polite.   Lit. High (poetic).   Verg.,
Sen. (trag.), Sil., Stat.   Verg. *A.* 7. 331; [Sen.] *Her. O.*
1648.

Sator 'progenitor (m.)': 5 +. Term for gods, esp. Jupiter, often
used by other gods, almost always with a genitive such as
divum. Very respectful.   Lit. High (poetic).
Sen. (trag.), Stat., V. Fl., and prayers.   Stat. *Theb.* 7.
155; V. Fl. 1. 505.

Savium 'kiss': 3. Term of endearment for lovers, with *meum.*
Gen. Low?   Pl., Ter.   Pl. *Poen.* 366; Ter. *Eu.*
456.   Cf. Pl. *Cist.* 247.

Scelerate 'guilty': 21. Moderate insult, not infrequently used
for relatives and (former) lovers. Subst.   Gen. Var.
Pl., Cic., Ov., Petr., *Ilias*, Quint., Mart., [Quint.]   Cic.
Phil. 13. 23; Petr. 137. 1; Ov. *Ep.* 10. 35.

Scelerum caput 'head of crimes': 4. Moderate insult, often
used by or to slaves.   Gen. Low.   Pl.   Pl.
Rud. 1098, *Cur.* 234. Cf. *scelerum cumulatissume* (Pl. *Aul.*
825); *scelerum . . . documentum* (Cic. *Dom.* 126).

Sceleste, -a, -i 'guilty': 28. Fairly strong insult, often used by
or to slaves. Subst.   Gen. Low.   Pl., Caecil.,
Ter., Catul., [Verg.], Phaed.   Pl. *As.* 424; Catul. 15.
15.   Cf. *scelestissume* (Pl. *Am.* 561).

Scelus 'crime': 23. Fairly strong insult, often used by or to
slaves of either gender. Can be followed by genitive *viri.*

Gen. Low.　　　Pl., Ter., Cic.　　　Pl. *Mil.* 841; Cic.
Pis. 56.

Scriptores 'writers': 2. With appropriate modifiers, used to
address some class of authors.　　　Lit. High (poetic).
Prop., Juv.　　　Prop. 2. 34b. 65; Juv. 7. 99.

Segnis, -es 'sluggish, lazy': 4. Rebuke for lack of exertion,
usually as a stimulus to action.　　　Lit. High (poetic).
Verg., Ov., Sen. (trag.), Stat.　　　Verg. *A.* 9. 787; Sen.
Ag. 108.

Senectus 'old age': 5. Neutral address to Age.　　　Lit.
Mid.?　　　Caecil., [Quint.]　　　[Quint.] *Decl.* 5. 12,
7. 13.

Senex, -es 'old man': 63. (1) Term for old men, normally
unrelated to the speaker, from men or women of any age.
Condescending if alone, positive or negative if modified. (2)
Neutral address for unknown old men, normally unmodi-
fied.　　　Gen. Var.　　　(1) Pl., trag. frag., Verg., Hor.,
Prop., Ov., Sen. S., Sen. (trag.), Luc., Stat., V. Fl., [Quint.]
(2) Pl., Ter.　　　(1) Pl. *Epid.* 488; Ov. *Met.* 8. 704; Sen.
Con. 10. 5. 7; (2) Pl. *Rud.* 782; Ter. *An.* 788.

Senior 'elder': 6. Term for old men, respectful or occasionally
condescending.　　　Lit. High (poetic).　　　Ov., Sen.
(trag.), Stat., Juv.　　　Ov. *Met.* 12. 540; Sen. *Her. F.*
1032; Stat. *Silv.* 3. 3. 43.

Serve, -us, -i 'slave (m.)': 7. (1) Singular, unmodified, insult-
ing address, usually for a slave.　　　(2) Plural, neutral
address for slaves (usually the speaker's own).　　　(1) Gen.
Low–mid. (2) Gen.? Mid.　　　(1) Pl., Hor. (2) Pl., Sen.
S., Mart.　　　(1) Pl. *Bac.* 775, *Ps.* 270; Hor. *S.* 2. 7. 70; (2)
Pl. *Cist.* 649; Mart. 14. 79. 1.

Severe, -i 'strict, stern': 2. Rebuke for people who are strict or
harsh.　　　Lit. High (poetic).　　　Ov., Mart.
Ov. *Am.* 2. 1. 3; Mart. 1 *pr.* 20.　　　Cf. *severissime*
([Quint.] *Decl.* 18. 15).

Sidus 'star': 2. Term of praise for social superiors; with
genitive.　　　Gen. High–mid.　　　Ov., [Sen.]
Ov. *Pont.* 3. 3. 2; [Sen.] *Oct.* 168.　　　Cf. Suet. *Cal.* 13.

Signifer 'standard-bearer': 3. Neutral address for orders to
nameless standard-bearers.　　　Gen.? Mid.　　　Liv.,
V. Max.　　　Liv. 5. 55. 2; V. Max. 1. 5. 1.

Silvae 'woods': 4. Neutral address for woods. Lit. High (poetic). Verg., Ov., Stat., V. Fl. Verg. *Ecl.* 8. 58; Stat. *Silv.* 2. 7. 13.

Socer 'father-in-law': 15. Term for the speaker's father-in-law, or father of his betrothed; or in transferred sense for someone else's father-in-law. Lit.? Var. Catul., [Verg.], Sen. S., Sen. (trag.), Sil., Quint., Stat. [Verg.] *Cat.* 6. 1; Sen. *Con.* 2. 3. 9; Sil. 5. 318; Stat. *Theb.* 11. 163.

Socia 'partner (f.)': 4 +. Used with a genitive to indicate the addressee's close association with the speaker or someone/something else. Lit. High (poetic). Sen. (trag.) Sen. *Ag.* 234, *Med.* 568.

Socii 'comrades, allies': 29. Used by a man to address a group of men (usually an army) of which he is the leader or (less often) a member; normally encouraging. Gen. Mid. Pac., Lucil., Nin., Verg., Hor., Prop., Liv., Ov., V. Max., Luc., Sil., Stat., V. Fl. Verg. *A.* 1. 198; V. Fl. 8. 183.

Sodalis, -es 'comrade': 8. Mildly affectionate address from a man to a male friend, or in plural to a group of male friends. Gen. Low–mid. Pl., Hor., Ov., graf. Pl. *Bac.* 489; Hor. *Carm.* 1. 27. 7; Ov. *Pont.* 1. 8. 25; *CIL* iv. 8908.

Solamen 'solace': 2. With genitive, used by women in laments for dead children. Lit. High (poetic). Sen. (trag.), Stat. Sen. *Med.* 946; Stat. *Theb.* 5. 609.

Soror, -es 'sister': 102 +. (1) Affectionate? address to the speaker's sister (or occasionally first cousin). (2) With a genitive to anyone's sister. (3) Alone in transferred sense to the sister of someone else. (4) Alone in extended usage as an affectionate address to a woman not far distant in age from the speaker (who in this sense is normally female). (1, 4) Gen. Var. (2) Lit. High (poetic). (3) Lit. Mid. (1) Pl., Enn., Acc., Pompon., Cic., Verg., Ov., Sen. S., Sen. (trag.), Sil., Stat., V. Fl., Apul. (2) Ov., Sen. (trag.) (3) [Verg.] (4) Verg., V. Fl., Apul., epist. Also in prayers. (1) Pl. *St.* 2; Cic. *Cael.* 36; Ov. *Met.* 1. 351; cf. Ov. *Met.* 9. 467; (2) Ov. *Fast.* 1. 463; [Sen.] *Oct.* 220; (3) [Verg.] *Aetna* 587; (4) Verg. *A.* 11. 823; Apul. *Met.* 1. 13. Cf. *sororcula* (Pl. *Cist.* 451).

Spectatores 'audience': 21. Address from a comic actor or other entertainer to his audience. Usually unmodified. Lit. Mid. Pl., Var. (poetry) Pl. *As.* 1, *Cist.* 678; Var. *Men.* 89.

Sperate 'longed-for': 3. Strong term of affection with sexual overtones. Gen. Mid.? Pl., Ov. Pl. *Poen.* 1268; Ov. *Ep.* 11. 123.

Spes 'hope': 18. Term of affection and praise for anyone but lovers, always with *mea* or another possessive. Gen. Var. Pl., Cic., Verg., Sen. (trag.), Luc., Sil., Stat., Mart. Pl. *Rud.* 247; Cic. *Fam.* 14. 4. 6; Verg. *A.* 2. 281.

Stolide 'stupid': 4. Insult. Subst. Gen.? Low. Pl., Enn., Caecil. Pl. *Am.* 1028, *Aul.* 415. Cf. *stolidissime* (Ov. *Met.* 13. 774).

Stulte, -a, -i 'stupid': 30. Fairly mild insult often used in rebukes to those acting foolishly. Subst. Gen. Var. Pl., Ter., Lucr., Prop., Ov., Sen. S., Phaed., Mart., Apul., Gel. Pl. *Per.* 830; Prop. 2. 21. 18.

Stultissime 'most stupid': 9. Moderately strong insult. Gen. Low–mid. Pl., Ter., Cic., Tib., Petr., Gel. Cic. *Phil.* 2. 29; Petr. 10. 1.

Suavis 'pleasant': 3. Term of affection, probably romantic. Gen.? Low–mid.? Pl., Phaed., graf. Pl. *St.* 736; Phaed. 3. 1. 5.

Suavissime, -a 'very pleasant': 12. Term of sincere affection for family and friends. Adj. Gen. Mid. Cic., Fro. Cic. *Q. fr.* 2. 6. 4, *Fam.* 14. 5. 2; Fro. 51. 6.

Suavitudo 'pleasantness': 2. Term of endearment. Lit.? Low–mid.? Pl. Pl. *Bac.* 18, *St.* 755. Cf. *suavitas* (Fro. 34. 15).

Subdole 'treacherous': 2. Fairly strong insult for those who have tricked the speaker. Gen. Low. Pl. Pl. *Aul.* 334, *Men.* 489.

Suboles 'offspring': 3. With genitive, forms periphrastic patronymic used in expressions of praise. Lit. High (poetic). Sen. (trag.), Mart. Sen. *Tro.* 463; Mart. 6. 25. 1.

Summe 'highest, supreme': 12 +. Term of praise and great respect for gods, emperors, and important men. Gen.

High.   Pl., Enn., Ov., *Ilias*, Sil., Stat., Mart., V. Fl.,
[Quint.], and prayers.   Ov. *Met.* 2. 280; Mart. 9. 5. 1;
[Quint.] *Decl.* 3. 1.

Superbe, -um 'proud': 10 +. Term for those displaying pride
or arrogance, normally but not always pejorative.   Lit.
Var.   Cic., [Verg.], Ov., Sen. (trag.), [Quint.], graf.,
and prayers.   Cic. *Luc.* 94; Sen. *Phaed.* 703.   Cf.
[Tib.] 3. 10. 2.

Taure, -i 'bull': 4. Neutral address for bulls, mostly absent
ones.   Lit. High (poetic).   [Verg.], Tib., Mart.,
V. Fl.   Mart. 2. 14. 18; V. Fl. 7. 547.

Tellus 'earth, land': 12. Address for a specific country, or for
Earth as an abstraction or a goddess. Often modified.
Lit. High (poetic).   Ov., Sen. (trag.), Luc., Stat.
Ov. *Met.* 1. 544; Luc. 7. 847.

Temerari, -a 'reckless': 5. Rebuke for rash people, may be
affectionate.   Lit. High (poetic).   Ov., Luc.,
Stat., [Quint.]   Ov. *Met.* 1. 514; Stat. *Theb.* 12. 366;
[Quint.] *Decl.* 17. 18.

Terra 'earth, land': 11. Address for a specific country or for
Earth as an abstraction or a goddess. Often modified.
Gen. High–mid.?   Enn., Verg., Ov., Sen. (trag.),
Fron., [Quint.]   Ov. *Ep.* 10. 100; Fron. *Str.* 1. 12. 2.

Teucri 'Trojans': 6. Neutral address to Trojans.   Lit.
High (poetic).   Verg.   Verg. *A.* 1. 562, 2. 48.

Thebane, -i 'Theban': 6. Neutral address to Thebans, in
singular only from non-Thebans.   Gen. Var.
Pl., Sen. (trag.), Stat.   Pl. *Am.* frag. 16; Stat. *Theb.* 6.
513.

Tibia 'pipe': 12. Neutral address to a musical instrument.
Lit. High (poetic).   Verg., Prop., Ov.   Verg. *Ecl.*
8. 21; Ov. *Ars* 3. 505.

Tibicen 'piper': 4. Neutral address for nameless or hypothetical pipers.   Gen.? Mid.?   Pl., Prop.
Pl. *St.* 715; Prop. 4. 4. 61.

Timide, -i 'timid': 2. Insult and expression of contempt for
warriors. Subst.   Lit. High (poetic).   Sen.
(trag.), Stat.   Sen. *Tro.* 302; Stat. *Theb.* 2. 668.

Timidissime 'very timid': 2. Expression of contempt for

warriors.   Lit. High (poetic).   Ov.   Ov.
Met. 5. 224, 13. 115.

Tribune, -i 'tribune': 16. Neutral address to tribunes, normally plural and unmodified except for the frequent addition of *plebis*.   Gen. Mid.   Cic., Liv., Calp. F. Cic. *Agr.* 1. 26; Liv. 38. 53. 2.

Trifurcifer 'triple *furcifer*': 2. Strong insult; strengthened form of *furcifer*.   Gen. Low.   Pl.   Pl. *Aul.* 326, *Rud.* 734.

Troia 'Troy': 6. Neutral address for the city of Troy. Lit. High (poetic).   Pl., Prop., Ov., Sen. (trag.), *Buc. Eins.*   Pl. *Bac.* 933; Sen. *Tro.* 4.

Troiane, -a, Tros, -es, Troades, Troice 'Trojan': 14. Neutral terms for Trojans; singular used only by people of other nations.   Lit. High (poetic).   Verg., Ov., Sen. (trag.)   Verg. *A.* 6. 52, 12. 359; Ov. *Met.* 13. 534.

Turba 'crowd': 9. Neutral address to a real or figurative group. Usually modified.   Lit. High (poetic).   Ov., Sen. (trag.), Sil., Stat., Mart.   Ov. *Tr.* 5. 3. 47; Sen. *Tro.* 409.

Tyranne 'tyrant': 4. Rebuke for people acting like tyrants. Lit.? Var.?   Pl., Enn., Sen. (trag.), [Quint.] Enn. *Ann.* 104; Sen. *Tro.* 303.

Umbra, -ae 'ghost': 6. Neutral address to ghosts or the dead. Usually modified.   Lit. High (poetic).   Ov., Sen. (trag.), Luc.   Ov. *Tr.* 4. 10. 87; Sen. *Ag.* 742.

Uxor 'wife': 51. (1) Address from husband to wife. (2) Occasionally with genitive to another's wife.   Gen. Mid.   (1) Pl., Ter., Cic., Ov., Sen. S., Quint., Stat., Mart., Apul., Scaev., [Quint.], inscr. (2) Cic., Hor., [Sen.] (1) Ter. *Hau.* 879; Cic. *Fam.* 14. 4. 6; Ov. *Tr.* 1. 6. 3; (2) Cic. *Inv.* 1. 51; Hor. *Carm.* 3. 15. 1; [Sen.] *Oct.* 934.   Cf. *uxorcula* (Pl. *Cas.* 844, 918).

Vates 'prophet, poet': 9. Honorific address to named men and women with any kind of divine or poetic inspiration, not infrequently spoken by deities.   Lit. High (poetic). Verg., Ov., Stat., Mart.   Verg. *A.* 6. 65; Ov. *Fast.* 1. 101.

Vecors 'mad': 2. Rebuke for those who act wrongly. Subst. Gen. High?   Cic., Sil.   Cic. *Pis.* 21; Sil. 12. 703.

Vector 'carrier': 3. Neutral address, with appropriate modifiers, for someone known in mythology for carrying someone (e.g. Nessus). Lit. High (poetic). [Sen.] (trag.), Luc., Mart. [Sen.] *Her. O.* 514; Mart. 2. 14. 17.

Venefice, -a 'poisoner': 5. Fairly strong insult. Gen. Low. Pl., Ter. Pl. *Per.* 278; Ter. *Eu.* 825. Cf. *tervenefice* (Pl. *Bac.* 813); *trivenefica* (Pl. *Aul.* 86).

Venerande 'venerable': 11 +. Respectful and distant address for gods, rulers, important men, and the dead. Lit. High (poetic, cultic). Verg., Ov., *Laus Pis.*, Sil., Stat., V. Fl., and prayers. Ov. *Fast.* 1. 646; Sil. 6. 424; Stat. *Theb.* 3. 546.

Venuste, -a 'attractive': 3. Term of praise for friends or places. Lit.? High (poetic). Catul., inscr. Catul. 13. 6, 31. 12.

Verbero 'one who deserves a beating': 25. Strong insult normally used to male slaves. Gen. Low. Pl., Ter., Gel. Pl. *Mil.* 500; Ter. *Ph.* 684; Gel. 1. 26. 8. Cf. *verberabilissume* (Pl. *Aul.* 633); *verbereum caput* (Pl. *Per.* 184).

Verende, -i 'to be revered': 2. Term of respect used by women pleading with more powerful males. Lit. High (poetic). Stat. Stat. *Theb.* 11. 709, 12. 569.

Verpe 'circumcised', 'erect penis': 4. Rude term, esp. for Jews. Gen.? Low. Mart., graf. Mart. 11. 94. 2; *CIL* iv. 1375.

Vervex 'wether': 2. Insult. Gen. Low. Pl., Petr. Pl. *Mer.* 567; Petr. 57. 2.

Vesane, -i 'mad': 7. Insult used in rebukes and warnings to people who are not doing the right thing, usually by someone with superior knowledge. Subst. Lit.? High. Prop., Luc., Stat., V. Fl., Apul. Prop. 3. 12. 7; Stat. *Theb.* 3. 627.

Vetule 'elderly' ('old chap'): 2. Term for friends who are not very close. Gen. Low–mid. Cic., Pers. Cic. *Fam.* 7. 16. 1; Pers. 1. 22.

Viator 'traveller': 30. Used by the author of an inscription for unknown readers. Lit. Mid. [Verg.], *Priap.*, [Ov.], Mart., inscr. [Verg.] *Priap.* 2. 2; Mart. 6. 28. 10; *ILLRP* 985.

Vicine, -i 'neighbour': 11. Neutral address to one's neighbours. Gen. Var.? Pl., Verg., Mart., graf. Pl. *Mer.* 793; Verg. *Ecl.* 3. 53; *CIL* iv. 7443.

Victor, -es 'conqueror (m.)': 8. Neutral address to a conqueror of someone or something (often expressed in genitive). Lit. Mid.–high. Verg., Prop., Ov., Sen. S., Sen. (trag.), Sil., Stat. Verg. *A.* 10. 740; Ov. *Ep.* 19. 181. Cf. *victrix* (*CIL* iv. 2212).

Vigil, -es 'sentry': 4. Neutral address to sentries, usually for giving orders. Lit.? High (poetic). Enn., Acc., Luc., Stat. Acc. *trag.* 579; Stat. *Theb.* 10. 492.

Vilice 'bailiff': 4. Neutral address to bailiffs from their equals or superiors. ? Pl., Hor., Ov., Sept. Pl. *Cas.* 98; Hor. *Ep.* 1. 14. 1.

Vilis 'cheap, worthless': 2. Expression of contempt or irritation. Adj. Lit. High (poetic). Hor., Prop. Hor. *Carm.* 3. 27. 57; Prop. 3. 7. 26. Cf. *vilissima* (Luc. 3. 120).

Violente, -a 'violent': 7. Strong rebuke for those behaving in an uncivilized manner. Subst. Lit. High (poetic). Tib., Ov., Sen. (trag.), *Ilias*, Stat. Ov. *Met.* 9. 121; Stat. *Theb.* 2. 466.

Vipera 'viper': 3. Insult for males or females. ? Afran., Juv., Flor. Juv. 6. 641; Flor. *Epit.* 2. 30 (4. 12. 38).

Vir, -i 'man': 117. (1) Singular, unmodified, used normally as a neutral address from a woman to her husband (usually with *mi*). (2) Singular, unmodified, occasionally used by anyone as a neutral term to a man to contrast with a word for 'woman' recently uttered. (3) Singular or plural, with a modifier, almost always a positive one, used as a polite address for known adult men or all-male groups. (4) Plural, normally without a modifier, used as a standard address (positive or neutral) for all-male groups of any size, normally warriors. (1) Gen. Mid.? (2) Lit. Var. (3) Gen. Var. (4) Lit. High (poetic). (1) Pl., Ter., Ov., V. Fl. (2) Pl., Tib., Ov. (3) Pl., Ter., Cic., Sal., Verg., Hor., Ov., Phaed., Sen. (prose), Stat., Mart., Tac., Plin., Suet., Gel., [Quint.], inscr. (4) Cic. (poetry), Verg., Prop., Ov., Luc., Sil., Stat., V. Fl., graf. Unclassifiable: trag. frag.

(1) Pl. *Cas.* 586; Ter. *Hec.* 235; (2) Tib. 2. 2. 2; Ov. *Rem.* 608; (3) Ter. *Eu.* 850; Cic. *Fam.* 11. 21. 3, *Agr.* 2. 50; Tac. *Dial.* 41. 5; (4) Verg. *A.* 4. 573; Sil. 15. 763.

Vires 'strength': 2. With possessives, term of praise from parents to children on whom they rely.   Lit. High (poetic).   Verg., Stat.   Verg. *A.* 1. 664; Stat. *Theb.* 4. 536.

Virgo, -es 'girl, virgin': 61 +. Polite, often respectful address from men or women to goddesses or human girls or virgins of any age, including the speaker's relatives. Probably used generally in early Latin and in religious language; aside from that, Lit. High.   Pl., Catul, Verg., Hor., Prop., Ov., Sen. S., Sen. (trag.), Sil., Stat., Mart., V. Fl., Apul., and prayers.   Pl. *Per.* 640; Verg. *A.* 6. 104; [Verg.] *Ciris* 372; Sen. *Phoen.* 50.

Vita 'life': 28. (1) Term of endearment, normally for lovers, often with *mea*. (2) Rarely as an address to Life.   (1) Gen. Mid. (2) Lit. Mid.?   (1) Pl., Cic., Catul., Maec., Prop., Ov., Apul. (poetry), graf. (2) Sen.   (1) Pl. *Cas.* 135; Cic. *Fam.* 14. 2. 3; Prop. 1. 2. 1; (2) Sen. *Dial.* 6. 20. 3, *Phaed.* 918.

Voluptas 'pleasure': 37 +. Term of endearment, normally for lovers, usually with *mea*.   Gen. Mid.   Pl., Verg., Ov., Stat., (Fro.), and prayers.   Pl. *Truc.* 426; Verg. *A.* 8. 581; Ov. *Ep.* 19. 17.   Cf. Petr. 139. 4 and Ov. *Met.* 7. 817.

Vorago, -es 'chasm': 2. With genitive, accusation of causing ruin to the thing in the genitive.   Lit.? Mid.?   Cic.   Cic. *Sest.* 111, *Pis.* 41.

USAGE TABLES

THESE tables are intended only as a rough guide to normal usage among educated Romans of the first century BC. They omit rare and poetic forms and simplify many complications. They will be of most use to those wishing to employ classical address forms in their own spoken or written Latin, and for the convenience of those wishing to use only Ciceronian Latin, Ciceronian addresses are marked with an asterisk. Post-classical terms are marked with [] and pre-classical ones with {}; such indications are given only if there is reason to believe that the term was not usable in the classical period, not if there is merely a lack of evidence. Where 'cognomen' is given as an address possibility, it is to be understood that addressees without a cognomen are addressed by gentilicium instead, and that those with unusual praenomina used like cognomina may be addressed by praenomen (see pp. 57, 64).

Table A. *Standard addresses*

Type of relationship	Addressee (and speaker if relevant)	Address normally used
Kinship	father	*pater** 'father', [*domine* 'master']
	mother	*mater* 'mother', [*domina* 'mistress']
	both parents	*parentes* 'parents'
	son	praenomen, cognomen*, *fili* 'son'
	daughter	*filia** 'daughter', nickname*
	brother	*frater** 'brother', praenomen, [*domine*]
	sister	*soror** 'sister', name
	uncle	*patrue* 'uncle'
	cousins, in-laws	addressed like friends
Romance	husband	cognomen, [*domine*], {*mi vir* 'my husband'}, endearments
	wife	*uxor** 'wife', name*, [*domina*], endearments*
	male lover	cognomen, *domine*, endearments
	female lover	name, *domina*, endearments
Power	[subject to emperor]	[*Caesar, Auguste, imperator* 'commander', *domine*, terms of praise, names]
	client to patron	name*, *rex* 'patron', *patrone* 'patron', [*domine*]
	slave to master	*ere* 'master', name
	slave to mistress	*era* 'mistress', name
	any superior to inferior	addressed like acquaintances
Friends and acquaintances	man, very formal context	praenomen + gentilicium + cognomen
	man, member of nobility, formal context	praenomen + cognomen*, praenomen + gentilicium, [gentilicium + cognomen], [cognomen + gentilicium]
	man, not a member of nobility, formal context	praenomen + gentilicium*, praenomen + cognomen, [gentilicium + cognomen], [cognomen + gentilicium]
	man, member of nobility, informal context	cognomen*, gentilicium
	man, not a member of nobility, informal context	gentilicium*, cognomen*

Type of relationship	Addressee (and speaker if relevant)	Address normally used
	boy	*puer* 'boy'
	young man	*puer*, *adulescens** 'young person', or as adult
	woman	*gentilicium**, [cognomen]
	young woman	*virgo* 'girl', or as adult
	slave	name
Strangers	woman	*mulier* 'woman'
	girl, young woman	*virgo*, *puella* 'girl'
	boy	*puer*
	young man	*adulescens*
	old man	*senex* 'old man'
	adult man	*hospes** 'visitor', *quisquis es* 'whoever you are', {*mi homo* 'my human being' (from women)}, {*adulescens*}
	male slave	*puer**, or as free man
Groups	senate	*patres conscripti** 'enrolled fathers'
	jurors	*iudices** 'jurors'
	Roman people	*Quirites** 'Roman citizens'
	non-Roman people	plural ethnic*
	army	*milites** 'soldiers', *commilitones* 'fellow-soldiers', *iuvenes* 'young men'
Non-humans	place	name*
	animal	species term*
	object or abstraction	generic term*

Table B. *Addresses expressing emotion*

Emotion	Address used
Affection	*dulcissime** 'very sweet', *iucundissime* 'very delightful' (between male friends), *optime** 'best', *suavissime** 'very pleasant', *spes** 'hope', use of *mi* with address*
Mild affection	*carissime** 'very dear'
Strong affection	two or more of the above terms*, *anima** 'soul', *anime* 'soul' (esp. for romance, speaker usu. female), *lux** 'light' (esp. for romance), *salus* 'salvation', *vita** 'life' (esp. for romance), *voluptas* 'pleasure' (esp. for romance)
Respect	*maxime* 'very great' (for rulers and heroes), *optime** 'best', *sanctissime* 'very holy', *summe* 'supreme' (for rulers)
Other praise	*decus* 'honour', [*domine* 'master'], [*domina* 'mistress'], *fidissime** 'very loyal' (for equals or subordinates), *fortissime** 'very strong' (for military heroes), *frater* 'brother', *mater* 'mother', *pater* 'father', *pulcherrime* 'very beautiful' (speaker usu. female), praenomen
Pity	*infelix** 'unhappy', *miser** 'wretched', *miserrime* 'very wretched'
Contempt	*infelix**, *miser**
Anger	*ignave* 'lazy, cowardly' (esp. in military contexts), *improbe* 'not good', *pessime* 'worst', *scelerate** 'guilty'
Mild anger	*inepte* 'foolish', *insane** 'crazy', *stulte* 'stupid'
Strong anger/ anger at slaves	*amentissime** 'very insane', *carnifex** 'executioner', *fur* 'thief', *furcifer** 'one punished with the *furca*', *impudens* 'shameless', *ingrate* 'ungrateful', *sceleste* 'guilty', *scelus** 'crime', *verbero* 'one who deserves a beating'

Note: The rules given here are for the expression of emotion towards friends and acquaintances; they do not always apply in other relationships. For example, parents are rarely addressed with insults, whatever the feelings of their children, and women close to the speaker can be addressed with *mulier* 'woman' as an expression of disapproval. In addition, addresses which would be standard in one relationship can be used in a different relationship for effect, as the flattering use of terms for rulers to men of lesser rank, or of terms for relatives to people unrelated to the speaker.

EDITIONS OF ANCIENT TEXTS

ABBREVIATIONS of authors' names follow the principles explained on p. 307; abbreviations of the titles of works and numerical references follow the system of the *Oxford Latin Dictionary* unless otherwise noted. Collections of fragments cited for several different authors are given their full references in the list of references. Series are indicated as follows: (OCT) = Oxford Classical Texts, (L) = Loeb Classical Library, (T) = Bibliotheca Scriptorum Graecorum et Romanorum Teubneriana, (B) = Collection des universités de France publiée sous le patronage de l'association Guillaume Budé. Only works to which specific references are given in the text or Glossary are included here; for abbreviations and editions of other works, see the *Oxford Latin Dictionary*.

Acc.	Accius, J. Dangel, Paris (B) 1995.
Andr.	Livius Andronicus (Blänsdorf 1995).
Apris.	Aprissius (Ribbeck 1897–8).
Apul.	Apuleius, R. Helm and C. Moreschini, Leipzig (T) 1959–91.
Avit.	Alfius Avitus (Courtney 1993).
Buc. Eins.	*Bucolica Einsidlensia*, D. Korzeniewski, *Hirtengedichte aus Neronischer Zeit*, Darmstadt 1971.
Caecil.	Caecilius Statius (Ribbeck 1897–8).
Caes.	Caesar, R. du Pontet, Oxford (OCT) 1900–1.
Calp. F.	Calpurnius Flaccus, L. Håkanson, Stuttgart (T) 1978.
Calp. S.	Calpurnius Siculus, D. Korzeniewski, *Hirtengedichte aus Neronischer Zeit*, Darmstadt 1971.
Cato	A. Mazzarino, Leipzig (T) 1962; fragments from H. Jordan, Leipzig (T) 1860.
Catul.	Catullus, R. A. B. Mynors, Oxford (OCT) 1958.
Cic.	Cicero. Speeches, letters, rhetorical works, and *De Finibus*: var. edd. and dates, Oxford (OCT); other philosophical works: var. edd. and dates, Leipzig (T); *frag. orat.*: J. Puccioni, 2nd edn. Milan 1972; *frag. phil.*: J. Garbarino, Milan 1984; poetic fragments: Blänsdorf 1995; [Cic.] *Oct.*: R. Lamacchia, Milan 1967; [Cic.] *Rhet. Her.*: G. Achard, Paris (B) 1989; [Cic.] *Sal.*: see Sallust.

Col.	Columella, V. Lundström *et al.*, Uppsala 1897–1968.
Corn. Sev.	Cornelius Severus (Courtney 1993).
Curt.	Q. Curtius, K. Müller, Utrecht 1954.
Dig.	*Digest* of Justinian, T. Mommsen and P. Krueger, Philadelphia 1985.
Dom. Mars.	Domitius Marsus (Courtney 1993).
Enn.	Ennius, O. Skutsch, Oxford 1985 for *Annales*; H. D. Jocelyn, Cambridge 1967 for tragedies; J. Vahlen, Leipzig (T) 1928 for other works.
Epist.	*Tab. Vindol. II, O. Claud., CEL*; see p. 307–8, 374–5.
Flor.	Florus, P. Jal, Paris (B) 1967.
Fro.	Fronto, M. P. J. van den Hout, Leipzig (T) 1988; references by page and line number of this edition.
Fron.	Frontinus, R. I. Ireland, Leipzig (T) 1990 for *Strategemata*; no vocatives in other works.
Gal.	Gallus (Courtney 1993).
Gel.	Aulus Gellius, P. K. Marshall, Oxford (OCT) 1990.
Germ.	Germanicus Iulius Caesar, A. Le Boeuffle, Paris (B) 1975.
Graf.	*CIL* iv; see pp. 307, 374.
Grat.	Grattus, C. Formicola, Bologna 1988.
HA	*Scriptores Historiae Augustae*, E. Hohl, Leipzig (T) 1965 (references follow Hohl's numbering).
Hadr.	Hadrian (Courtney 1993).
Hor.	Horace, H. W. Garrod, Oxford (OCT) 1901.
[Hyg.]	[Hyginus Gromaticus], M. Lenoir, Paris (B) 1979.
Ilias	*Ilias Latina,* M. Scaffai, Bologna 1982.
Inscr.	*ILLRP, ILS, EDH, CIL* (except iv); see pp. 308, 374.
Juv.	Juvenal, J. Willis, Stuttgart (T) 1997.
Laber.	Decimus Laberius (Ribbeck 1897–8).
Laev.	Laevius (Courtney 1993).
Laurea	M. Tullius Laurea (Courtney 1993).
Laus Pis.	*Laus Pisonis*, E. Baehrens, *Poetae Latini Minores*, Leipzig (T) 1879.
Liv.	Livy, R. M. Ogilvie *et al.*, Oxford (OCT) 1919–99 for books 1–40; J. Briscoe, Stuttgart (T) 1986 for 41–5.
Luc.	Lucan, A. E. Housman, Oxford 1926.
Lucil.	Lucilius, F. Charpin, Paris (B) 1978–9 (but using Marx's numbering system).
Lucr.	Lucretius, C. Bailey, Oxford (OCT) 2nd edn. 1922.
Maec.	C. Cilnius Maecenas (Courtney 1993).
Man.	Manilius (Courtney 1993).
Mart.	Martial, D. R. Shackleton Bailey, Stuttgart (T) 1990.

Nin.	Ninnius Crassus (Courtney 1993).
Ov.	Ovid, E. J. Kenney, Oxford (OCT) 1961 for *Amores*, *Medicamina*, *Ars*, and *Remedia*; W. S. Anderson, Stuttgart (T) 1991 for *Metamorphoses*; J. A. Richmond, Leipzig (T) 1990 for *Ex Ponto*; J. B. Hall, Stuttgart (T) 1995 for *Tristia*; A. H. Alton, D. E. W. Wormell, and E. Courtney, Stuttgart (T) 4th edn. 1997 for *Fasti*; H. Borneque, Paris (B) 1928 for *Heroides*; S. G. Owen, Oxford (OCT) 1915 for *Halieutica* and *Ibis*; J. Amat, Paris (B) 1997 for [Ov.] *Epic. Drusi*.
Pac.	Pacuvius (Ribbeck 1897–8).
Pers.	Persius, W. V. Clausen, Oxford (OCT) 1992.
Petr.	Petronius, K. Mueller, Stuttgart (T) 4th edn. 1995.
Phaed.	Phaedrus, J. P. Postgate, Oxford (OCT) 1919.
Pl.	Plautus, W. M. Lindsay, Oxford (OCT) 1904–5.
Plin.	Younger Pliny, R. A. B. Mynors, Oxford (OCT) 1963 for letters; M. Schuster and R. Hanslik, Leipzig (T) 3rd edn. 1958 for *Panegyric*.
Plin. S.	Elder Pliny, C. Mayhoff, Leipzig (T) 1892–1909.
Pompon.	L. Pomponius Bononiensis (Ribbeck 1897–8).
Priap.	*Priapea*, F. Buecheler and W. Heraeus, *Petronii Saturae et Liber Priapeorum*, Berlin 6th edn. 1922.
Prop.	Propertius, E. A. Barber, Oxford (OCT) 2nd edn. 1960.
Quint.	Quintilian, M. Winterbottom, Oxford (OCT) 1970 for *Institutio Oratoria*; M. Winterbottom, Berlin 1984 for *Declamationes Minores*.
[Quint.]	[Quintilian], *Declamationes Maiores*, L. Håkanson, Stuttgart (T) 1982.
Sal.	Sallust (including *Appendix Sallustiana*), L. D. Reynolds, Oxford (OCT) 1991.
Sen.	Younger Seneca, L. D. Reynolds, Oxford (OCT) 1965–77 for letters and dialogues; R. Roncali, Leipzig (T) 1990 for *Apocolocyntosis*; O. Zwierlein, Oxford (OCT) 1986 for tragedies; H. Hine, Leipzig (T) 1996 for *Naturales Quaestiones*; C. Hosius, Leipzig (T) 1914 for *De Beneficiis* and *De Clementia*; F. Haase, Leipzig (T) 1902 for fragments.
Sen. S.	Elder Seneca, M. Winterbottom, Cambridge Mass. (L) 1974.
Sept.	Septimius Serenus (Courtney 1993).
Sil.	Silius Italicus, J. Delz, Stuttgart (T) 1987.

SL   Scribonius Largus, G. Helmreich, Leipzig (T) 1887.
Stat.   Statius, A. Marastoni, A. Klotz, and T. C. Klinnert,
                Leipzig (T) 1970–4.
Suet.   Suetonius, M. Ihm, Leipzig (T) 1933 for imperial
                lives; R. A. Kaster, Oxford 1995 for grammarians
                and rhetoricians; A. Reifferscheid, Leipzig (T) 1860
                for other works.
Tac.   Tacitus, C. D. Fisher *et al.*, Oxford (OCT) 1906–75.
Ter.   Terence, R. Kauer and W. M. Lindsay, Oxford
                (OCT) 1958.
Tib.   Tibullus, J. P. Postgate, Oxford (OCT) 2nd edn. 1915.
Tic.   Ticida (Courtney 1993).
Trag. incert.
  auct.   unattributed tragic fragments (Ribbeck 1897–8).
Turp.   Sextus Turpilius, L. Rychlewska, Leipzig (T) 1971.
Val. Mes.   M. Valerius Messalla Corvinus, H. Malcovati, *Ora-
                torum Romanorum Fragmenta*, Turin 1953.
Var.   Varro, G. Goetz, Leipzig (T) 2nd edn. 1929 for *Res
                Rusticae*; R. Astbury, Leipzig (T) 1985 for *Saturae
                Menippeae*.
Verg.   Vergil (including *Appendix Vergiliana*), R. A. B.
                Mynors, Oxford (OCT) 1969 for genuine works;
                W. V. Clausen *et al.*, Oxford (OCT) 1966 for *Appen-
                dix*.
V. Fl.   Valerius Flaccus, W.-W. Ehlers, Stuttgart (T) 1980.
Vitr.   Vitruvius, F. Krohn, Leipzig (T) 1912.
V. Max.   Valerius Maximus, J. Briscoe, Stuttgart (T) 1998.
V. Sor.   Q. Valerius Soranus (Blänsdorf 1995).

ABBREVIATIONS FOR MODERN WORKS AND COLLECTIONS

Abbreviations for ancient authors are listed on pp. 370–3.

CEL	P. Cugusi (1992) (ed.), *Corpus Epistularum Latinarum* (Florence); references by letter number.
CIL	*Corpus Inscriptionum Latinarum* (Berlin); references by volume and inscription number.
EDH	G. Alföldy (ed.), *Epigraphische Datenbank Heidelberg*: http://www.uni-heidelberg.de/institute/sonst/adw/edh; references by inscription number.
GLK	H. Keil (1855–80) (ed.), *Grammatici Latini* (vols. ii–iii M. J. Hertz, Suppl. H. Hagen; Leipzig).
ILLRP	A. Degrassi (1963–5) (ed.), *Inscriptiones Latinae Liberae Rei Publicae*, 2nd edn. (Florence); references by inscription number.
ILS	H. Dessau (1892–1916) (ed.), *Inscriptiones Latinae Selectae* (Berlin); references by inscription number.
NP	H. Cancik and H. Schneider (1996–) (edd.), *Der Neue Pauly Enzyklopädie der Antike* (Stuttgart).
O. Claud.	Bingen 1992, 1997; references by tablet number.
OED	J. A. Simpson and E. S. C. Weiner (1989) (edd.), *The Oxford English Dictionary*, 2nd edn. (Oxford).
OLD	P. G. W. Glare (1982) (ed.), *Oxford Latin Dictionary* (Oxford).
Pap. Soc. Ital.	*Pubblicazioni della società italiana per la ricerca dei papiri greci e latini in Egitto: Papiri greci e latini* (Florence).
P. Mich. viii	H. C. Youtie and J. G. Winter (1951), *Papyri and Ostraca from Karanis*, 2nd series (Ann Arbor).
P. Oxy.	B. P. Grenfell, A. S. Hunt, *et al.* (1898–), *The Oxyrhynchus Papyri* (London).
P. Ryl. iv	C. H. Roberts and E. G. Turner (1952), *Catalogue of the Greek and Latin Papyri in the John Rylands Library, Manchester*, iv (Manchester).
RE	A. Pauly, G. Wissowa, and W. Kroll (1893–) (edd.), *Real-Encyclopädie der classischen Altertumswissenschaft* (Stuttgart).

Tab. Vindol. II A. K. Bowman and J. D. Thomas (1994), *The Vindolanda Writing-Tablets (Tabulae Vindolandenses II)* (London); references by tablet number.

TLL *Thesaurus Linguae Latinae* (Leipzig 1900–).

REFERENCES

ADAMS, J. N. (1972), 'Latin Words for "Woman" and "Wife"', *Glotta*, 50: 234–55.

——(1978), 'Conventions of Naming in Cicero', *Classical Quarterly*, NS 28: 145–66.

——(1982), 'Anatomical Terms Used *Pars pro Toto* in Latin', *Proceedings of the African Classical Associations*, 16: 37–45.

——(1983), 'Words for "Prostitute" in Latin', *Rheinisches Museum*, NS 126: 321–58.

——(1984), 'Female Speech in Latin Comedy', *Antichthon*, 18: 43–77.

——(1995), 'The Language of the Vindolanda Writing Tablets: An Interim Report', *Journal of Roman Studies*, 85: 86–134.

——(1999), 'The Poets of Bu Njem: Language, Culture and the Centurionate', *Journal of Roman Studies*, 89: 109–34.

AUSTIN, R. G. (1977), *P. Vergili Maronis Aeneidos Liber Sextus* (Oxford).

AXELSON, B. (1945), *Unpoetische Wörter: Ein Beitrag zur Kenntnis der lateinischen Dichtersprache* (Lund).

——(1948), 'Die Synonyme *Adulescens* und *Iuvenis*', in *Mélanges de philologie, de littérature et d'histoire anciennes offerts à J. Marouzeau* (Paris), 7–17.

AXTELL, H. R. (1915), 'Men's Names in the Writings of Cicero', *Classical Philology*, 10: 386–404.

BAILEY, C. (1947), *T. Lucreti Cari De Rerum Natura Libri Sex* (Oxford).

BAKOS, F. (1955), 'Contributions à l'étude des formules de politesse en ancien français I', *Acta Linguistica Academiae Scientiarum Hungaricae*, 5: 295–367.

BANG, M. (1921), Appendices to L. Friedlaender, *Darstellungen aus der Sittengeschichte Roms*, 9th–10th edn. ed. G. Wissowa (Leipzig), iv. 77–88.

BANNON, C. J. (1997), *The Brothers of Romulus: Fraternal Pietas in Roman Law, Literature, and Society* (Princeton).

BASLEZ, M.-F. (1996), 'La Première présence romaine à Délos (vers 250–vers 140)', in A. D. Rizakis (ed.), *Roman Onomastics in the Greek East: Social and Political Aspects* (Athens), 215–24.

BAŞOĞLU, S. (1987), *Anrede in Türkischer Gegenwartsliteratur: Eine sprachvergleichende Untersuchung türkischer Romane, Erzählungen und Filme und ihrer deutschen Übersetzungen* (Frankfurt am Main).

BATES, E., and BENIGNI, L. (1975), 'Rules of Address in Italy: A Sociological Survey', *Language in Society*, 4: 271–88.

BEAN, S. S. (1978), *Symbolic and Pragmatic Semantics: A Kannada System of Address* (Chicago).

BELL, A. (1984), 'Language Style as Audience Design', *Language in Society*, 13: 145–204.

BETTINI, M. (1979), 'Su alcuni modelli antropologici della Roma più arcaica: designazioni linguistiche e pratiche culturali (II)', *Materiali e discussioni per l'analisi dei testi classici*, 2: 9–41.

——(1986), *Antropologia e cultura romana: Parentela, tempo, immagini dell'anima* (Rome).

BIBER, D. (1994), 'An Analytical Framework for Register Studies', in Biber and Finegan (1994), 31–56.

——and FINEGAN, E. (1994) (edd.), *Sociolinguistic Perspectives on Register* (Oxford).

BICKEL, E. (1915), *Diatribe in Senecae Philosophi Fragmenta* (Leipzig).

BINGEN, J., et al. (1992), *Mons Claudianus: Ostraca Graeca et Latina I* (Cairo).

——(1997), *Mons Claudianus: Ostraca Graeca et Latina II* (Cairo).

BIRT, T. (1928), '*Macte esto* und zugehöriges', *Rheinisches Museum*, NS 77: 199–205.

BISHOP, J. H. (1954), 'Two Notes on Statius, *Silvae* iv. I', *Classical Review*, NS 4: 95–7.

BIVILLE, F. (1996a), 'La Voix signifiante', in J. Dangel and C. Moussy (edd.), *Les Structures de l'oralité en latin* (Paris), 147–54.

——(1996b), 'Niveaux de voix et relations spatiales: Énonciation, lexique et syntaxe', in A. Bammesberger and F. Heberlein (edd.), *Akten des VIII. internationale Kolloquiums zur lateinischen Linguistik* (Heidelberg), 125–37.

——(1996c), 'Ce que révèle la voix', *Bollettino di studi latini*, 1: 55–68.

BLÄNSDORF, J. (1995), *Fragmenta Poetarum Latinorum Epicorum et Lyricorum praeter Ennium et Lucilium* (Stuttgart).

BÖMER, F. (1957–8), *P. Ovidius Naso: Die Fasten* (Heidelberg).

——(1969–86), *P. Ovidius Naso: Metamorphosen* (Heidelberg).

BONFANTE, G. (1948), 'The Origin of the Latin Name-System', in *Mélanges de philologie, de littérature et d'histoire anciennes offerts à J. Marouzeau* (Paris).

BONNER, S. F. (1949), *Roman Declamation in the Late Republic and Early Empire* (Liverpool).

BOWMAN, A. K., and THOMAS, J. D. (1996), 'New Writing-Tablets from Vindolanda', *Britannia*, 27: 299–328.

BOWMAN, A. K., THOMAS, J. D., and ADAMS, J. N. (1990), 'Two Letters from Vindolanda', *Britannia*, 21: 33–52.

BOYANCÉ, P. (1956), 'La Connaissance du grec à Rome', *Revue des études latines*, 34: 111–31.

BOYCE, B. (1991), *The Language of the Freedmen in Petronius' Cena Trimalchionis* (Leiden).

BOYLE, A. J. (1985), 'In Nature's Bonds: A Study of Seneca's *Phaedra*', in W. Haase (ed.), *Aufstieg und Niedergang der Römischen Welt*, 2. 32. 2 (Berlin), 1284–1347.

BRADLEY, K. R. (1991), *Discovering the Roman Family: Studies in Roman Social History* (New York).

BRASSLOFF (1900), 'Conscripti', in *RE* iv. 891–6.

BRAUN, F. (1988), *Terms of Address: Problems of Patterns and Usage in Various Languages and Cultures* (Berlin).

—— KOHZ, A., and SCHUBERT, K. (1986), *Anredeforschung: Kommentierte Bibliographie zur Soziolinguistik der Anrede* (Tübingen).

BRÉHIER, L. (1906), 'L'Origine des titres impériaux à Byzance', *Byzantinische Zeitschrift*, 15: 161–78.

BREUER, H. (1983), 'Titel und Anreden bei Shakespeare und in der Shakespearezeit', *Anglia: Zeitschrift für englische Philologie*, 101: 49–77.

BRINK, C. O. (1971), *Horace on Poetry: The 'Ars Poetica'* (Cambridge).

BRISCOE, J. (1973), *A Commentary on Livy: Books XXXI–XXXIII* (Oxford).

BROWN, P., and LEVINSON, S. C. (1987), *Politeness: Some Universals in Language Usage* (London).

BROWN, R., and FORD, M. (1961), 'Address in American English', in Hymes (1964), 234–44.

—— and GILMAN, A. (1960), 'The Pronouns of Power and Solidarity', in T. A. Sebeok (ed.), *Style in Language* (London), 253–76.

—— —— (1989), 'Politeness Theory and Shakespeare's Four Major Tragedies', *Language in Society*, 18: 159–212.

BROWN, R. D. (1987), *Lucretius on Love and Sex* (Leiden).

BÜCHNER, K. (1984), *M. Tullius Cicero: De Re Publica* (Heidelberg).

BULHART, V. (1952), 'Meus', in *TLL* viii. 913–27.

BUTLER, H. E., CARY, M., and TOWNEND, G. B. (1982), *Suetonius: Divus Julius* (Bristol).

CHAO, Y. R. (1956), 'Chinese Terms of Address', *Language*, 32: 217–41.

CHARPIN, F. (1978–9), *Lucilius: Satires* (Paris).

CICHORIUS, C. (1922), *Römische Studien* (Leipzig).

CITRONI, M. (1975), *M. Valerii Martialis Epigrammaton Liber Primus* (Florence).

COLEMAN, K. M. (1988), *Statius, Silvae IV* (Oxford).

COLIN, J. (1955), 'Sobriquets de femmes dans la Rome Alexandrine (d'après Cicéron et Lucrèce)', *Revue Belge de philologie et d'histoire*, 33: 853–76.

CONANT, F. P. (1961), 'Jarawa Kin Systems of Reference and Address: A Componential Comparison', *Anthropological Linguistics*, 3/2: 19–33.

CONINGTON, J. (1883), *P. Vergili Maronis Opera*, 3rd edn. (London), iii.

CONSTANS, L.-A. (1940), *Cicéron: Correspondance* (Paris), i.

COPLEY, F. O. (1947), '*Servitium Amoris* in the Roman Elegists', *Transactions of the American Philological Association*, 78: 285–300.

COULMAS, F. (1979), 'On the Sociolinguistic Relevance of Routine Formulae', *Journal of Pragmatics*, 3: 239–66.

COURTNEY, E. (1993), *The Fragmentary Latin Poets* (Oxford).

——(1995), *Musa Lapidaria: A Selection of Latin Verse Inscriptions* (Atlanta).

CUGUSI, P. (1973), 'Le più antiche lettere papiracee latine', *Atti della accademia delle scienze di Torino*, 107: 641–92.

——(1983), *Evoluzione e forme dell'epistolografia latina nella tarda repubblica e nei primi due secoli dell'impero* (Rome).

——(1992), *Corpus Epistularum Latinarum* (Florence).

——(1996), *Aspetti letterari dei* Carmina Latina Epigraphica, 2nd edn. (Bologna).

DAVIAULT, A., LANCHA, J., and PALOMO, L. A. L. (1987), *Un mosaico con inscripciones* (Publications de la casa de Velazquez: Série études et documents, III, Madrid).

DEL RIO, P. (1939), 'Frater-Germanus', *Emerita*, 7: 1–5.

DICKEY, E. (1995), 'Forms of Address and Conversational Language in Aristophanes and Menander', *Mnemosyne*, 4th ser. 48: 257–71.

——(1996), *Greek Forms of Address: From Herodotus to Lucian* (Oxford).

——(1997a), '*Me autem Nomine Appellabat*—Avoidance of Cicero's Name in his Dialogues', *Classical Quarterly*, NS 47: 584–8.

——(1997b), 'Forms of Address and Terms of Reference', *Journal of Linguistics*, 33: 255–74.

——(2000), '*O Egregie Grammatice*: The Vocative Problems of Latin Words ending in -*ius*', *Classical Quarterly*, NS 50: 548–62.

——(2001), '*Κύριε, Δέσποτα, Domine*: Greek Politeness in the Roman Empire', *Journal of Hellenic Studies*, 121: 1–11.

——(forthcoming), '*O Dee Ree Pie*: The Vocative Problems of Latin Words ending in -*eus*', *Glotta*, 77.

DIERAUER, U. (1977), *Tier und Mensch im Denken der Antike: Studien zur Tierpsychologie, Anthropologie und Ethik* (Amsterdam).

DIXON, S. (1988), *The Roman Mother* (London).

——(1992), *The Roman Family* (Baltimore).

DOER, B. (1937), *Die römische Namengebung: Ein historischer Versuch* (Stuttgart).

DORIAN, N. C. (1994), 'Stylistic Variation in a Language Restricted to Private-Sphere Use', in Biber and Finegan (1994), 217–32.

DROWN, N. K. (1979), 'Racine's Use of "Tutoiement" and "Vouvoiement"', *Modern Languages*, 60: 142–56.

ECKHEL, J. (1798), *Doctrina Numorum Veterum* (Vienna).

ELLENDT, F. (1840), *M. Tulli Ciceronis De Oratore Libri Tres* (Königsberg).

ELLIS, R. (1889), *A Commentary on Catullus*, 2nd edn. (Oxford).

ENGELBRECHT, A. (1893), *Das Titelwesen bei den spätlateinischen Epistolographen* (Vienna).

ENK, P. J. (1932), *Plauti Mercator* (Leiden).

ERNOUT, A., and MEILLET, A. (1979), *Dictionnaire étymologique de la langue latine: Histoire des mots*, 4th edn. rev. J. André (Paris).

——and ROBIN, L. (1962), *Lucrèce: De Rerum Natura*, 2nd edn. (Paris).

ERVIN-TRIPP, S. M. (1969), 'Sociolinguistic Rules of Address', in Pride and Holmes (1972), 225–40.

EVANS, W. W. (1967), 'Dramatic Use of the Second-Person Singular Pronoun in *Sir Gawain and the Green Knight*', *Studia Neophilologica*, 39: 38–45.

FASCE, S. (1987), 'Nascor', *Enciclopedia Virgiliana* (Rome), 664–5.

FASOLD, R. W. (1990), *The Sociolinguistics of Language* (Oxford).

FERGER, G. (1889), *De Vocativi Usu Plautino Terentianoque*, Ph.D. thesis (Strasbourg).

FINKENSTAEDT, T. (1963), *You und Thou: Studien zur Anrede im Englischen, mit einem Exkurs über die Anrede im Deutschen* (Berlin).

FORDYCE, C. J. (1961), *Catullus* (Oxford).

——(1977), *P. Vergili Maronis Aeneidos Libri VII–VIII* (Oxford).

FRAENKEL, EDUARD (1957), *Horace* (Oxford).

——(1960), *Elementi Plautini in Plauto*, trans. F. Munari (Florence).

——(1965), 'Noch einmal Kolon und Satz', *Bayerische Akademie der Wissenschaften, philosophisch-historische Klasse: Sitzungsberichte*, 2 (Munich).

FRAENKEL, ERNST (1935), 'Namenwesen', in *RE* xvi. 1611–70.

FRÄNKEL, H. (1945), *Ovid: A Poet between Two Worlds* (Berkeley).

FRANK, F. H. W., and ANSHEN, F. (1983), *Language and the Sexes* (Albany).

FRIDBERG, G. (1912), *Die Schmeichelworte der antiken Literatur*, Ph.D. thesis (Rostock).

FRIEDLAENDER, L. (1913), *Roman Life and Manners under the Early Empire*, trans. A. B. Gough (London), iv.

——(1921–3), *Darstellungen aus der Sittengeschichte Roms*, 10th edn. (Leipzig).

FRIEDRICH, P. (1966), 'Structural Implications of Russian Pronominal Usage', in William Bright (ed.), *Sociolinguistics: Proceedings of the UCLA Sociolinguistics Conference, 1964* (The Hague), 214–59.

FRIEDRICH, W.-F. (1936), 'Erus', 'Era', in *TLL* v. ii. 848–50.

FRUYT, M. (1989), 'Étude sémantique des "diminutifs" latins: Les Suffixes *-ulus, -culus, -ellus, -illus* . . . Dé-substantivaux et dé-adjectivaux', in M. Lavency and D. Longrée (edd.), *Actes du Ve colloque de linguistique latine* (Cahiers de l'institut de linguistique de Louvain 15. 1–4; Louvain), 127–38.

GALLIVAN, P. (1992), 'The Nomenclature Patterns of the Roman Upper Class in the Early Empire: A Statistical Analysis', *Antichthon*, 26: 51–79.

GARBARINO, J. (1984), *M. Tulli Ciceronis Fragmenta ex Libris Philosophicis, ex Aliis Libris Deperditis, ex Scriptis Incertis* (Milan).

GARITTE, G. (1942), '*Morituri Te Salutant*: Note sur les formes allocutives', *Les Études classiques*, 11: 3–26.

GATES, H. P. (1971), *The Kinship Terminology of Homeric Greek* (Baltimore).

GIBSON, R. K. (1999), 'Aeneas as *Hospes* in Vergil, *Aeneid* 1 and 4', *Classical Quarterly*, NS 49: 184–202.

GIZEWSKI, C. (1997), 'Conscripti', in *NP* iii. 127.

GONDA, J. (1959), 'The Etymology of Latin *Mactus*', *Mnemosyne*, 4th ser. 12: 137–8.

GOOLD, G. P. (1965), 'Amatoria Critica', *Harvard Studies in Classical Philology*, 69: 1–107.

GOTOFF, H. C. (1993), *Cicero's Caesarian Speeches: A Stylistic Commentary* (Chapel Hill).

GRATWICK, A. S. (1973), Review of Krenkel (1970), *Journal of Roman Studies*, 63: 302–4.

——(1993), *Plautus: Menaechmi* (Cambridge).

GRENFELL, B. P. (1896), *An Alexandrian Erotic Fragment and Other Greek Papyri Chiefly Ptolemaic* (Oxford).

GRIFFIN, M. T. (1976), *Seneca: A Philosopher in Politics* (Oxford).

GRIMAUD, M. (1989), 'Tutoiement, titre et identité sociale: Le Système de l'adresse du *Cid* au *Théâtre en liberté*', *Poétique*, 77: 53–75.

GRÜNBART, M. (2000), *Die Anrede im byzantinischen Brief von Prokopios von Gaza bis Michael Choniates*, Ph.D. thesis (Vienna).

GUASTELLA, G. (1980), 'I Parentalia come testo antropologico: l'avunculato nel mondo celtico e nella famiglia di Ausonio', *Materiali e discussioni per l'analisi dei testi classici*, 4: 97–124.

GUDEMAN, A. (1914), *P. Cornelii Taciti Dialogus de Oratoribus* (Leipzig).

GUÐMUNDSSON, H. (1972), *The Pronominal Dual in Icelandic* (Reykjavík).

GUÉRAUD, O. (1942), 'Ostraca grecs et latins de l'Wâdi Fawâkhir', *Bulletin de l'institut français d'archéologie orientale du Caire*, 41: 141–96.

HAGEDORN, D., and WORP, K. A. (1980), 'Von κύριος zu δεσπότης: Eine Bemerkung zur Kaisertitulatur im 3./4. Jhdt.', *Zeitschrift für Papyrologie und Epigraphik*, 39: 165–77.

HAHN, E. A. (1957), 'A Linguistic Fallacy (Based on a Study of Vergil)' in E. Pulgram (ed.), *Studies Presented to Joshua Whatmough on his Sixtieth Birthday* (The Hague), 53–64.

HÅKANSON, L. (1969), *Statius' Silvae* (Lund).

HALLETT, J. P. (1984), *Fathers and Daughters in Roman Society: Women and the Elite Family* (Princeton).

HAMMER, S. (1906), 'Contumeliae, Quae in Ciceronis Invectivis et Epistulis Occurrunt, Quatenus Plautinum Redoleant Sermonem', *Rozprawy Akademii Umiejetności, Wydział Filolgiczny*, ser. 11, 26: 179–218.

HARDIE, P. (1994), *Virgil: Aeneid: Book IX* (Cambridge).

HARDY, E. G. (1889), *C. Plinii Caecilii Secundi Epistulae* (London).

HARRISON, S. J. (2000), *Apuleius: A Latin Sophist* (Oxford).

HARROD, S. G. (1909), *Latin Terms of Endearment and of Family Relationship*, Ph.D. thesis (Princeton).

HEAD, B. F. (1978), 'Respect Degrees in Pronominal Reference', in J. H. Greenberg (ed.), *Universals of Human Language* (Stanford, Calif.), iii. 151–211.

HELZLE, M. (1989), *Publii Ovidii Nasonis Epistularum ex Ponto Liber IV* (Hildesheim).

HILL, W. F., and ÖTTCHEN, C. J. (1991), *Shakespeare's Insults: Educating your Wit* (Cambridge).

HIRSCHFELD, O. (1901), 'Die Rangtitel der römischen Kaiserzeit', *Sitzungsberichte der königlich preussischen Akademie der Wissenschaften zu Berlin*, 1901: 579–610.

HOFFMANN, G. (1892), *Schimpfwörter der Griechen und Römer* (Wissenschaftliche Beilage zum Programm des Friedrichs-Realgymnasiums zu Berlin; Berlin).

HOFMANN, J. B. (1951), *Lateinische Umgangssprache*, 3rd edn. (Heidelberg).

——(1985), *La Lingua d'uso latina: Introduzione, traduzione italiana e note a cura di Licinia Ricottilli*, 2nd edn. (Bologna).

——and SZANTYR, A. (1965), *Lateinische Syntax und Stilistik* (Munich).

HOLMES, J. (1992), *An Introduction to Sociolinguistics* (London).

HOLMES, T. R. (1914), *C. Iuli Caesaris Commentarii* (Oxford).

HORSFALL, N. (1993), *La Villa sabina di Orazio: Il Galateo della gratitudine* (Venosa).

——(1995), *A Companion to the Study of Vergil* (Leiden).

——(2000), *Virgil, Aeneid 7: A Commentary* (Leiden).

HOUSMAN, A. E. (1930), 'The Latin for *Ass*', *Classical Quarterly*, 24: 11–13.

HOWELL, P. (1980), *A Commentary on Book One of the Epigrams of Martial* (London).

——(1995), *Martial: Epigrams V* (Warminster).

HOWELL, R. W. (1968), 'Linguistic Choice and Levels of Social Change', *American Anthropologist*, 70: 553–9.

HWANG, J.-R. (1975), 'Role of Sociolinguistics in Foreign Language Education with Reference to Korean and English Terms of Address and Levels of Deference', Ph.D. thesis (Austin, Tex.).

HYMES, D. H. (1964) (ed.), *Language in Culture and Society: A Reader in Linguistics and Anthropology* (London).

IAHN, O. (1843), *Auli Persii Flacci Satirarum Liber cum Scholiis Antiquis* (Leipzig).

IHNE, W. (1865), *Über die Patres Conscripti* (Leipzig).

JAWORSKI, A. (1982), 'A Note on the Types of Address Shifts', *Studia Anglica Posnaniensia*, 14: 259–66.

JOCELYN, H. D. (1973), 'Homo Sum: Humani Nil a me Alienum Puto (Terence, *Heauton Timoroumenos* 77)', *Antichthon*, 7: 14–46.

JONES, F. (1991), 'Naming in Pliny's Letters', *Symbolae Osloenses* 66: 147–70.

——(1996), *Nominum Ratio: Aspects of the Use of Personal Names in Greek and Latin* (Liverpool).

JONZ, J. G. (1975), 'Situated Address in the United States Marine Corps', *Anthropological Linguistics*, 17: 68–77.

JORDAN, H. (1860), *M. Catonis Praeter Librum De Re Rustica Quae Extant* (Leipzig).

JOSEPH, J. E. (1987), 'Subject Relevance and Deferential Address in the Indo-European Languages', *Lingua*, 73: 259–77.

KAIMIO, J. (1979), *The Romans and the Greek Language* (Helsinki).

KAJANTO, I. (1965), *The Latin Cognomina* (Helsinki).

——(1972), 'Women's Praenomina Reconsidered', *Arctos: Acta Philologica Fennica*, NS 7: 13–30.

KAJANTO, I. (1977a), 'On the Chronology of the Cognomen in the Republican Period', in *L'Onomastique latine*, 63–70.

——(1977b), 'On the Peculiarities of Women's Nomenclature', in *L'Onomastique latine*, 147–59.

KAPP, I. (1930), 'Dominus', 'Domina', in *TLL* v. i. 1907–41.

KAY, N. M. (1985), *Martial: Book XI: A Commentary* (London).

KELLER, R. (1990), *Sprachwandel: Von der unsichtbaren Hand in der Sprache* (Tübingen).

KEMPF, R. (1985), 'Pronouns and Terms of Address in *Neues Deutschland*', *Language in Society*, 14: 223–37.

KENNEY, E. J. (1990), *Apuleius: Cupid and Psyche* (Cambridge).

KEPARTOVÁ, J. (1986), '*Frater* in Militärinschriften: Bruder oder Freund?', *Listy filologické*, 109: 11–14.

KERTZER, D. I., and SALLER, R. P. (1991), *The Family in Italy: From Antiquity to the Present* (New Haven).

KEYES, C. W. (1935), 'The Greek Letter of Introduction', *American Journal of Philology*, 56: 28–44.

KIEŁKIEWICZ-JANOWIAK, A. (1992), *A Socio-Historical Study in Address: Polish and English* (Frankfurt).

KIESSLING, A., and HEINZE, R. (1961), *Q. Horatius Flaccus: Satiren*, 8th edn. (Berlin).

KISBYE, T. (1965), 'Zur pronominalen Anrede bei Aelfric', *Archiv für das Studium der neueren Sprachen und Literaturen*, 201: 432–5.

KNIGHT, G. (1990), *Honourable Insults: A Century of Political Invective* (London).

KNOCHE, U. (1956), 'Tibulls früheste Liebeselegie? (Tibull 3, 19)', in *Navicula Chiloniensis: Studia Philologa Felici Jacoby Professori Chiloniensi Emerito Octogenario Oblata* (Leiden), 173–90.

KOCH, C. (1960), *Religio: Studien zu Kult und Glauben der Römer* (Nuremberg).

KÖHM, J. (1905), *Altlateinische Forschungen* (Leipzig).

KRAUS, C. S. (1994), *Livy: Ab Urbe Condita: Book VI* (Cambridge).

KRENKEL, W. (1970), *Lucilius: Satiren* (Leiden).

KRETSCHMER, P. (1919), 'Lat. *Quirites* und *Quiritare*', *Glotta*, 10: 147–57.

——(1924), 'Σῦς und andere lautnachahmende Wörter', *Glotta*, 13: 132–8.

KRETZENBACHER, H. L., and SEGEBRECHT, W. (1991), *Vom Sie zum Du—mehr als eine neue Konvention?* (Hamburg).

KRIDALAKSANA, H. (1974), 'Second Participant in Indonesian Address', *Language Sciences*, 31: 17–20.

KROLL, W., and LUNELLI, A. (1980), *La Lingua poetica latina*, 2nd edn. (Bologna).

LAMBERT, W. E., and TUCKER, G. R. (1976), *Tu, Vous, Usted: A Social-Psychological Study of Address Patterns* (Rowley, Mass.).

LATTIMORE, R. (1942), *Themes in Greek and Latin Epitaphs* (Urbana).

LEARY, T. J. (1996), *Martial: Book XIV: The Apophoreta* (London).

LEEMAN, A. D., PINKSTER, H., et al. (1981–96), *M. Tullius Cicero: De Oratore Libri III* (Heidelberg).

LEPRE, M. Z. (1985), 'Interiezioni', in *Enciclopedia Virgiliana* (Rome), 993–6.

LEUMANN, M. (1977), *Lateinische Laut- und Formenlehre* (Munich).

LEWIS and SHORT (1879), *A Latin Dictionary* (Oxford).

LILJA, S. (1965*a*), *The Roman Elegists' Attitude to Women* (Annales Academiae Scientiarum Fennicae ser. B. cxxxv. i; Helsinki).

——(1965*b*), *Terms of Abuse in Roman Comedy* (Annales Academiae Scientiarum Fennicae ser. B. cxli. iii; Helsinki).

LINTOTT, A. (1999), *Violence in Republican Rome*, 2nd edn. (Oxford).

LIPSIUS, J. (1607), *C. Cornelii Taciti Opera Quae Exstant* (Antwerp).

LÖFSTEDT, E. (1956), *Syntactica: Studien und Beiträge zur historischen Syntax des Lateins*, 2nd edn. (Lund).

LYNE, R. O. A. M. (1978), *Ciris: A Poem Attributed to Vergil* (Cambridge).

——(1979), 'Servitium Amoris', *Classical Quarterly*, NS 29: 117–30.

LYONS, J. (1980), 'Pronouns of Address in *Anna Karenina*: The Stylistics of Bilingualism and the Impossibility of Translation', in S. Greenbaum, G. Leech, and J. Svartvik (edd.), *Studies in English Linguistics for Randolph Quirk* (London), 235–49.

McCARTHY, J. H. (1931), 'Octavianus Puer', *Classical Philology*, 26: 362–73.

McFAYDEN, D. (1920), *The History of the Title* Imperator *under the Roman Empire* (Chicago).

McKEOWN, J. C. (1987–), *Ovid: Amores* (Leeds).

MacMULLEN, R. (1984), 'The Legion as a Society', *Historia*, 33: 440–56.

MARTIN, R. H. (1976), *Terence: Adelphoe* (Cambridge).

MARX, F. (1904–5), *C. Lucilii Carminum Reliquiae* (Leipzig).

——(1959), *Plautus: Rudens: Text und Kommentar* (Amsterdam).

MASON, H. J. (1974), *Greek Terms for Roman Institutions: A Lexicon and Analysis* (Toronto).

MASON, P. E. (1990), 'The Pronouns of Address in Middle French', *Studia Neophilologica*, 62: 95–100.

MAURACH, G. (1988), *Der Poenulus des Plautus* (Heidelberg).

MAYOR, J. E. B. (1888–9), *Thirteen Satires of Juvenal*, 4th edn. (London).

MEHROTRA, R. R. (1977), 'Fluidity in Kinship Terms of Address in Hindi', *Anthropological Linguistics*, 19: 123–5.

——(1981), 'Non-Kin Forms of Address in Hindi', *International Journal of the Sociology of Language*, 32: 121–37.

MEISNER, C. (1752), *Sylloge Historico-Philologica Nominum Aliquot Contumeliosorum, Comicis Maxime Usurpatorum* (Dresden).

MEUSEL, H. (1886), 'Beiträge zur Kritik von Cäsars Kommentarien, besonders zur Handschriftenfrage', *Jahresberichte des philologischen Vereins zu Berlin*, 12: 262–93.

MEYER, G. (1929), 'Germanus', in *TLL* vi. 1914–20.

MINICONI, P.-J. (1958), 'Les Termes d'injure dans le théâtre comique', *Revue des études latines*, 36: 159–75.

MOMMSEN, T. (1864–79), *Römische Forschungen* (Berlin).

——(1887–8), *Römisches Staatsrecht*, 3rd edn. (Leipzig).

MOREAU, P. (1978), 'La Terminologie latine et indo-européenne de la parenté et le système de parenté et d'alliance à Rome: Questions de méthode', *Revue des études latines*, 56: 41–53.

MOREY, C. R., and FERRARI, G. (1959), *The Gold-Glass Collection of the Vatican Library* (Rome).

MORRIS, J. (1963), 'Changing Fashions in Roman Nomenclature in the Early Empire', *Listy Filologické*, 86: 34–46.

MORRISON, I. R. (1988), 'Remarques sur les pronoms allocutifs chez Rabelais', *Zeitschrift für romanische Philologie*, 104: 1–11.

MOSELEY, N. (1926), *Characters and Epithets: A Study in Vergil's Aeneid* (New Haven).

MÜHLHÄUSLER, P., and HARRÉ, R. (1990), *Pronouns and People: The Linguistic Construction of Social and Personal Identity* (Oxford).

MÜLLER, A. (1913a), 'Die Schimpfwörter in der griechischen Komödie', *Philologus*, 72: 321–37.

——(1913b), 'Die Schimpfwörter in der römischen Komödie', *Philologus*, 72: 492–502.

MUNRO, H. A. J. (1886–1928), *T. Lucreti Cari De Rerum Natura Libri Sex*, 4th edn. (Cambridge).

MURGATROYD, P. (1981), '*Servitium Amoris* and the Roman Elegists', *Latomus*, 40: 589–606.

NATHAN, N. (1959), 'Pronouns of Address in the "Canterbury Tales"', *Mediaeval Studies*, 21: 193–201.

NEHRING, A. (1933), 'Anruf, Ausruf und Anrede: Ein Beitrag zur Syntax des Einwortsatzes', in *Festschrift Theodor Siebs* (Breslau), 95–144.

NEUE, F., and WAGENER, C. (1892–1905), *Formenlehre der lateinischen Sprache*, 3rd edn. (Berlin).

NEUMANN, K. J., *et al.* (1903), 'Dominus', in *RE* v. 1305–11.

NICOLET, C. (1977), 'L'Onomastique des groupes dirigeants sous la République', *L'Onomastique latine*, 45–61.

NIELSEN, H. S. (1997), 'Interpreting Epithets in Roman Epitaphs', in Rawson and Weaver (1997), 169–204.

NISBET, R. G. M. (1961), *M. Tulli Ciceronis in L. Calpurnium Pisonem Oratio* (Oxford).

——(1967), Review of Opelt (1965), *Gnomon*, 39: 67–72.

——and HUBBARD, M. (1970), *A Commentary on Horace: Odes book I* (Oxford).

————(1978), *A Commentary on Horace: Odes book II* (Oxford).

NOCK, A. D. (1945), 'Asclepius: Introduction', in A. D. Nock and A.-J. Festugière (edd.), *Hermès Trismégiste* (Paris), ii. 259–95.

NORDEN, E. (1957), *P. Vergilius Maro: Aeneis Buch VI*, 4th edn. (Stuttgart).

OAKLEY, S. P. (1997–), *A Commentary on Livy: Books VI–X* (Oxford).

O'BRIEN, M. B. (1930), *Titles of Address in Christian Latin Epistolography to 543 AD*, Ph.D. thesis (Catholic University of America, Washington, DC).

OGILIVIE, R. M. (1965), *A Commentary on Livy: Books 1–5* (Oxford).

L'Onomastique latine (1977), Colloques internationaux du centre national de la recherche scientifique 564 (Paris).

OPELT, I. (1965), *Die lateinischen Schimpfwörter und verwandte sprachliche Erscheinungen: Eine Typologie* (Heidelberg).

PABÓN, J. M. (1939), 'El griego, lengua de la intimidad entre los romanos', *Emerita*, 7: 126–31.

PALMER, L. R. (1938), '*Macte, Mactare, Macula*', *Classical Quarterly*, 32: 57–62.

PAOLI, U. E. (1925), 'Uso ufficiale e familiare del *praenomen* romano', *Rivista di filologia e di istruzione classica*, NS 3: 542–50.

PARKINSON, D. B. (1985), *Constructing the Social Context of Communication: Terms of Address in Egyptian Arabic* (Berlin).

PEASE, A. S. (1973), *M. Tulli Ciceronis de Divinatione Libri Duo* (Darmstadt).

PERRET, D. (1968), 'Termes d'adresse et injures', *Cahiers de lexicologie*, 12: 3–14.

PETERSMANN, H. (1977), *Petrons urbane Prosa: Untersuchungen zu Sprache und Text (Syntax)* (Vienna).

PHILIPSEN, G., and HUSPEK, M. (1985), 'A Bibliography of Sociolinguistic Studies of Personal Address', *Anthropological Linguistics*, 27: 94–101.

PHILLIPPS, K. C. (1984), *Language and Class in Victorian England* (New York).

POWELL, J. G. F. (1984), 'A Note on the Use of the *Praenomen*', *Classical Quarterly*, NS 34: 238–9.

—— (1988), *Cicero: Cato Maior De Senectute* (Cambridge).

PRIDE, J. B., and HOLMES, J. (1972) (edd.), *Sociolinguistics: Selected Readings* (Harmondsworth).

RAWSON, B. (1991), *Marriage, Divorce, and Children in Ancient Rome* (Oxford).

—— and WEAVER, P. R. C. (1997) (edd.), *The Roman Family in Italy: Status, Sentiment, Space* (Oxford).

REIMERS, F. H. (1957), *Der plautinische Schimpfwörterkatalog*, Ph.D. thesis (Kiel).

REPLOGLE, C. (1973), 'Shakespeare's Salutations: A Study in Linguistic Etiquette', *Studies in Philology*, 70: 172–86.

RIBBECK, O. (1897–8), *Scenicae Romanorum Poesis Fragmenta* (Leipzig).

RICKFORD, J. R., and MCNAIR-KNOX, F. (1994), 'Addressee- and Topic-Influenced Style Shift: A Quantitative Sociolinguistic Study', in Biber and Finegan (1994), 235–76.

ROSS, D. O. (1969), *Style and Tradition in Catullus* (Cambridge, Mass.).

RUSSELL, D. A. (1974), 'Letters to Lucilius', in C. D. N. Costa (ed.), *Seneca* (London), 70–95.

SALLER, R. P. (1994), *Patriarchy, Property and Death in the Roman Family* (Cambridge).

—— (1997), 'Roman Kinship: Structure and Sentiment', in Rawson and Weaver (1997), 7–34.

SALMON, V. (1967), 'Elizabethan Colloquial English in the Falstaff Plays', *Leeds Studies in English*, NS 1: 37–70.

SALOMIES, O. (1987), *Die römischen Vornamen: Studien zur römischen Namengebung* (Helsinki).

SALWAY, B. (1994), 'What's in a Name? A Survey of Roman Onomastic Practice from c. 700 BC to AD 700', *Journal of Roman Studies*, 84: 124–45.

SANTORO L'HOIR, F. (1992), *The Rhetoric of Gender Terms* (Leiden).

SAVILLE-TROIKE, M. (1989), *The Ethnography of Communication: An Introduction*, 2nd edn. (Oxford).

SCHAPS, D. (1977), 'The Woman Least Mentioned: Etiquette and Women's Names', *Classical Quarterly*, NS 27: 323–30.

SCHIESARO, A. (1993), 'Il destinario discreto: Funzioni didascaliche e progetto culturale nelle Georgiche', *Materiali e discussioni per l'analisi dei testi classici*, 31: 129–47.

SCHOENER, C. (1881), *Über die Titulaturen der römischen Kaiser*, Ph.D. thesis (Erlangen).

SCHULZE, W. (1904), *Zur Geschichte lateinischer Eigennamen* (Abhandlungen der königlichen Gesellschaft der Wissenschaften zu Göttingen, philologisch-historische Klasse, NS 5/5; Berlin).

——(1918), 'Beiträge zur Wort- und Sittengeschichte', in *Kleine Schriften* (Göttingen 1934), 148–210; orig. pub. in *Sitzungsberichte der Preußischen Akademie der Wissenschaften*, 320–32, 481–511, 769–91.

SEDLEY, D. (1998), *Lucretius and the Transformation of Greek Wisdom* (Cambridge).

SEGAL, E. (1987), *Roman Laughter: The Comedy of Plautus*, 2nd edn. (Oxford).

SHACKLETON BAILEY, D. R. (1965–70), *Cicero's Letters to Atticus* (Cambridge).

——(1977), *Cicero: Epistulae ad Familiares* (Cambridge).

——(1986), 'Nobiles and Novi Reconsidered', *American Journal of Philology*, 107: 255–60.

——(1988), *Onomasticon to Cicero's Speeches*, 1st edn. (Stuttgart).

——(1992), *Onomasticon to Cicero's Speeches*, 2nd edn. (Stuttgart).

——(1993), *Martial: Epigrams* (Cambridge, Mass.).

——(1995), *Onomasticon to Cicero's Letters* (Stuttgart).

——(1996), *Onomasticon to Cicero's Treatises* (Stuttgart).

SHALEV, D. (1998), 'Vocatives in Responses: A Bridging Mechanism in Dialogue Exchange?', in B. García-Hernández (ed.), *Estudios de lingüística latina: Actas del IX coloquio internacional de lingüística latina* (Madrid), ii. 765–79.

SHERWIN-WHITE, A. N. (1966), *The Letters of Pliny: A Historical and Social Commentary* (Oxford).

SHIPP, G. B. (1953), 'Greek in Plautus', *Wiener Studien*, 66: 105–12.

SKUTSCH,O., and ROSE, H. J. (1938), '*Mactare—Macula?*', *Classical Quarterly*, 32: 220–3.

SOLIN, H. (1992), Review of Shackleton Bailey (1988), *Gnomon*, 64: 499–502.

SOMMERSTEIN, A. H. (1980), 'The Naming of Women in Greek and Roman Comedy', *Quaderni di storia*, 11: 393–409.

SONNENSCHEIN, E. A. (1907), *T. Macci Plauti Mostellaria* (Oxford).

SOUTHWORTH, F. C. (1974), 'Linguistic Masks for Power: Some Relationships between Semantic and Social Change', *Anthropological Linguistics*, 16: 177–91.

SPANHEIM, E. (1671), *Dissertationes de Praestantia et Usu Numismatum Antiquorum*, 2nd edn. (Amsterdam).

SVENNUNG, J. (1958), *Anredeformen: Vergleichende Forschungen zur indirekten Anrede in der dritten Person und zum Nominativ für den Vokativ* (Uppsala).

SYME, R. (1958), 'Imperator Caesar: A Study in Nomenclature', *Historia*, 7: 172–88.

SYNDIKUS, H. P. (1984–90), *Catull: Eine Interpretation* (Darmstadt).

SZELEST, H. (1996), '*Perge, O Libelle, Sirmium*: Zu Auson. Ep. X Prete', *Rheinisches Museum*, NS 139: 334–43.

TARRANT, R. J. (1976), *Seneca: Agamemnon* (Cambridge).

THOMSON, D. F. S. (1997), *Catullus* (Toronto).

THYLANDER, H. (1954), 'La Dénomination chez Cicéron dans les lettres à Atticus', *Opuscula Romana*, 1: 153–9.

TOWNEND, G. B. (1973), 'The Literary Substrata to Juvenal's Satires', *Journal of Roman Studies*, 63: 148–60.

TREGGIARI, S. (1991), *Roman Marriage* (Oxford).

TYRRELL, R. Y. (1927), *The Miles Gloriosus of T. Maccius Plautus* (London).

VAIREL, H. (1986), 'Le Problème du cas de *tu*: *Nominativus tantum, Vocativus tantum*, ou *Uterque?*', *Revue de philologie*, 60: 31–57.

VAN DEN HOUT, M. J. P. (1999), *A Commentary on the Letters of M. Cornelius Fronto* (Leiden).

VAN DER PAARDT, R. T. (1971), *L. Apuleius Madaurensis: The Metamorphoses* (Amsterdam).

VAN HOOK, L. R. (1949), 'On the Idiomatic Use of Κάρα, Κεφαλή, and *Caput*', in *Commemorative Studies in Honour of Theodore Leslie Shear* (*Hesperia* suppl. 8; Athens), 413–14.

VEYNE, P. (1983), *L'Élégie érotique romaine* (Paris).

VIDMAN, L. (1981), 'Die Namengebung bei Plinius dem Jüngeren', *Klio*, 63: 585–95.

VRETSKA, K. (1976), *C. Sallustius Crispus: De Catilinae Coniuratione* (Heidelberg).

WACKERNAGEL, J. (1908), 'Genetiv und Adjektiv', in *Mélanges de linguistique offerts à M. Ferdinand de Saussure* (Paris), 125–52.

——(1912), *Über einige antike Anredeformen* (Göttingen).

——(1926–8), *Vorlesungen über Syntax: mit besonderer Berücksichtigung von Griechisch, Lateinisch, und Deutsch* (Basle).

WALDE, A., and HOFMANN, J. B. (1938–54), *Lateinisches etymologisches Wörterbuch*, 3rd edn. (Heidelberg).

WALES, K. M. (1983), '*Thou* and *You* in Early Modern English: Brown and Gilman re-appraised', *Studia Linguistica*, 37: 107–25.

WARDHAUGH, R. (1992), *An Introduction to Sociolinguistics*, 2nd edn. (Oxford).

WARMINGTON, E. H. (1938), *Remains of Old Latin* (Cambridge, Mass.).

WATERHOUSE, R. (1982), 'Modes of Address in Aelfric's *Lives of the Saints* Homilies', *Studia Neophilologica*, 54: 3–24.

WATSON, P. (1983), 'Puella and Virgo', *Glotta*, 61: 119–43.

WEBER, F. (1941), 'Fórmulas de tratamiento en la lengua de Buenos Aires', *Revista de filología Hispánica*, 3: 105–39.

WELLESLEY, K. (1972), *Cornelius Tacitus: The Histories, Book III* (Sydney).

WHALEN, S. (1982), 'The Pronouns of Address in Dostoevskii's *Besy*: A Sociolinguistic Sketch', *Canadian Slavonic Papers*, 24: 67–72.

WHITE, P. (1978), '*Amicitia* and the Profession of Poetry in Early Imperial Rome', *Journal of Roman Studies*, 68: 74–92.

WIELAND, H. (1968), 'O', in *TLL* ix. ii. 1–13.

WIGTIL, D. N. (1984), 'Incorrect Apocalyptic: The Hermetic "Asclepius" as an Improvement on the Greek Original', in W. Haase (ed.), *Aufstieg und Niedergang der Römischen Welt*, 2. 17. 4 (Berlin), 2282–97.

WILKINS, A. S. (1892), *M. Tulli Ciceronis De Oratore Libri Tres* (Oxford).

——(1929), *The Epistles of Horace* (London).

WILLEMS, P. (1883), *Le Droit public romain, ou les institutions politiques de Rome*, 5th edn. (Louvain).

——(1885), *Le Sénat de la république romaine*, 2nd edn. (Paris).

WILLIAMS, R. D. (1960), *P. Vergili Maronis Aeneidos Liber Quintus* (Oxford).

WILLS, J. (1996), *Repetition in Latin Poetry: Figures of Allusion* (Oxford).

WINTERBOTTOM, M. (1984), *The Minor Declamations Ascribed to Quintilian* (Berlin).

WISEMAN, T. P. (1970), 'Pulcher Claudius', *Harvard Studies in Classical Philology*, 74: 207–21.

WOLFF, M. P. (1986), 'Premières recherches sur l'apparition du vouvoiement en latin médiéval', *Comptes rendus de l'académie des inscriptions & belles-lettres*, 370–83.

——(1988), 'Nouvelles recherches sur le vouvoiement: Quatre poèmes épiques, quatre formes d'adresses, quatre tempéraments nationaux?', *Comptes rendus de l'académie des inscriptions & belles-lettres*, 58–74.

WOYTEK, E. (1982), *T. Maccius Plautus: Persa* (Österreichische Akademie der Wissenschaften, philosophisch-historische Klasse: Sitzungsberichte 385; Vienna).

WÜNSCH, R. (1914), 'Anmerkungen zur lateinischen Syntax', *Rheinisches Museum*, NS 69: 123–38.

WYKE, M. (1989), 'Mistress and Metaphor in Augustan Elegy', *Helios*, 16: 25–47.

ZILLIACUS, H. (1949), *Untersuchungen zu den abstrakten Anredeformen und Höflichkeitstiteln im Griechischen* (Helsinki).

ZWICKY, A. M. (1974), 'Hey, Whatsyourname!', in M. W. La Galy, R. A. Fox, and A. Bruck (edd.), *Papers from the Tenth Regional Meeting of the Chicago Linguistic Society* (Chicago), 787–801.

INDEX OF WORDS DISCUSSED

This index is complete, listing every page on which the entries appear. The other two indices list only pages on which some information is given about the entries.

INDEX LOCORUM

Spurious works are listed under the name of the author to whom they are traditionally attributed.

INDEX OF TOPICS